William Shakespeare
Four Great Comedies

A Midsummer Night's Dream
Much Ado About Nothing
As You Like It
Twelfth Night

With Introductions by Judith Buchanan

D0096681

WORDSWORTH CLASSICS
OF WORLD LITERATURE

This edition published 1998 by Wordsworth Editions Limited
Cumberland House, Crib Street, Ware, Hertfordshire SG12 9ET

ISBN I 85326 784 8

Typeset by Antony Gray
Printed and bound in Great Britain by
Mackays of Chatham, Chatham, Kent

WORDSWORTH CLASSICS
OF WORLD LITERATURE

General Editor: Tom Griffith MA, MPhil

FOUR GREAT COMEDIES

CONTENTS

INTRODUCTION

The Name of the Rose, a novel by Umberto Eco and now also a film starring Sean Connery, is based upon the speculation that Aristotle wrote a second book of the *Poetics*, 'the book everyone . . . believed lost or never written'. Aristotle's first book of *Poetics* famously dealt with tragedy. Eco's fictional hypothesis about a lost sequel to this work, in line with scholarly debate on the subject, is that it would have considered comedy and the causes of laughter. Eco speculates that in this later book Aristotle would have revoked his disparaging asides about the debasing effects of comedy, and offered instead a more fully expounded vision of comedy that was life-affirming, showing how laughter may be both instructive and regenerative. But in *The Name of the Rose* the only copy of the hypothetical work is destroyed by a fire started by an elderly monk who believes laughter is a corrupting influence, and who fears the subversive effects of such a treatise. The world of Eco's story is thus left, as indeed our own has been, with no Aristotelian blue-print for what comedy is, or what social and psychological functions it fulfils.

In the absence of a developed Aristotelian pattern, Renaissance theorists produced their own. In particular, defences were offered to the specific charges thrown at comedy that it was an immoral influence on individuals and a destabilising influence on society; that it fostered a derisive cruelty and a social subversiveness. As comic theorists parried the blows struck by the moralists, definitions became skewed by the need to identify the form as actively fulfilling some social good. The point of greatest consistency across Renaissance defences of comedy, therefore, was an insistence upon its function as morally corrective of the ills of society. Sir Philip Sidney in his *Defence of Poetry* (*c.*1580), Ben Jonson in the prologue to *Every Man in His Humour* (1598), and Thomas Heywood in *An Apology for Actors* (1612), all made comedy's capacity to act as a model for instruction the bedrock of their argument: comedy, it was claimed, was improving. Sidney's argument is representative:

> Comedy is an imitation of the common errors of our life, which he [the comic writer] representeth in the most ridiculous and scornful sort that may be, so as it is impossible that any beholder can be content to be such a one . . . So . . . the right use of comedy will (I think) by nobody be blamed.

There were occasional forays into acknowledging some other role for comedy. Thomas Heywood, for example, allowed himself momentarily to outline a more frivolous function. The morally corrective lessons of comedy, he wrote, may be:

> mingled with sportful accidents . . . to refresh such weary spirits as are tired with labour or study, to moderate the cares and heaviness of the mind, that they may return to their trades and faculties with more zeal and earnestness, after some small soft and pleasant retirement.

In similar vein, Sidney suggested that a 'delightful laughter' might be possible which did not spring simply from mean-mindedness. Asserting the value of pleasant distraction in this way was not, however, the norm.

Renaissance defences of comedy sound nervous. They spring from the belief that comedy – a theatrical form either so frivolous as to be unworthy of serious critical attention, or so anarchic as to be worthy of the severest sort of moral censure – is the poor and disreputable relation of tragedy. It is to counter this cultural attitude that Renaissance defences of comedy are so over-insistent about its moral worth, and hence so misleading in their descriptions of what comic drama in reality is and does.

In the Induction to Shakespeare's comedy *The Taming of the Shrew*, a messenger is sent to inform Christopher Sly that the players are ready to perform 'a pleasant comedy'. He interrogates the messenger about the nature of the play: 'A Christmas gambol or a tumbling trick?' His suspicion is that comedies are either the frolics on offer during seasonal festivals ('A Christmas gambol') or a spectacle in clowning ('a tumbling trick'). The page gravely contradicts him. The promised play, he intimates, is neither of these things but rather something more weighty: 'a kind of history', a story with a design. Their bandying of definitions provides a useful starting point for a consideration of Shakespeare's comedies.

Christopher Sly's first guess, 'A Christmas gambol', highlights one significant facet of Shakespeare's comedies: their close association with the conventions of Elizabethan holiday festivals. When in *As You Like It* Rosalind says: 'Come, woo me, woo me; for now I am in a holiday humour and like enough to consent' (4.1.61–2), the implication is that being 'in a holiday humour' makes possible things that would not be so throughout the rest of the year. She may be inclined to consent to being wooed when 'in a holiday humour' although she might not have done when in her 'working-day world' (1.3.12). Shakespeare's festive comedies catch their characters in a moment of holiday humour, or they generate the circumstances to put them in one. Holiday festivals in Shakespeare create a sense of possibility and release. Such a sense is the driving force of all four of the comedies in this collection and springs directly from the high spirits of 'a holiday humour'. Typically, the plots of these plays offer a temporary escape from the usual run of life. Things which might not have been possible before suddenly become so in the new-found liberty of a festive moment.

The titles of the first and last plays in this volume – *A Midsummer Night's Dream* and *Twelfth Night* – are specifically derived from Elizabethan holiday festivals, and the celebration of both these festivals involved, to different degrees and with differing festive expressions, the joyous overturning of the norms of behaviour that usually regulated life. The holiday moment was known to be temporary, and with that limitation, it was accepted that liberties would be taken, hierarchies challenged, the usual ordering systems abandoned, and a taste for revelry indulged. All this was licensed on the understanding that life would be returned to its sober, ordered self the following day. Shakespeare's comedies trade upon this sense of a 'holiday humour' in order to explore what happens to characters when they are removed from their usual context, or released by some other means from the restrictions that normally govern their social interactions.

Thus the Athenian lovers in *A Midsummer Night's Dream* find themselves running around in a wood at night away from parents, home and the law of Athens. In *As You Like It* Rosalind disguises herself as a boy, Celia as a peasant girl, and the two friends go into temporary exile in the forest of Arden; here they enjoy their new identities in the freedom and unfamiliarity of a new context. In *Twelfth Night* Viola finds herself shipwrecked in an unknown land, disguises herself as a boy and tries out her new identity upon the inhabitants of the new land. Even in *Much Ado About Nothing*, in which no characters go away and some characters actually come home, there is nevertheless a sense that life has been jostled out of its ordinary routine into a moment of heightened festivity by the safe return of the men from the wars. Characters in Shakespeare's comedies therefore find themselves in a world that is less contained and regulated than the working-day world to which they are accustomed. In the liberty of the new context a playful inventiveness may be indulged, and discoveries made about how the world may be renewed.

The festive moment, the 'getting-away-from-it-all' experience, provides the opportunity for characters to experiment with alternative social forms from those which structure the rest of life. For example, the absolute nature of divisions of class, gender and sexuality may be challenged in the fluidity of the new context, and off-beat relationships may be formed with carefree abandon. Women may become men, men may consciously or otherwise woo men, women may woo women, a shepherdess may fall for a noble woman, a fairy queen sleep with an ass, a gentlewoman marry a knight, a beggar be convinced that he is a lord. These plays create the space in which such subversive attitudes to social organisation may be entertained. Their willingness to flirt with the notion that people and structures may be coaxed out of rigid positions into riskier ways of relating might quite reasonably be seen as threatening to any who had an interest in protecting the tight social hierarchies of the *status quo*. The moralist critics of comic form in the Renaissance, therefore, had a point: comedy *can* challenge the stability of things by suggesting that people may cross socially imposed boundaries. Its view of the world as adaptable and protean may even be frightening to those who wish to ensure that it remain anchored in a safely traditional place.

A fluid view of character may, however, be read more positively:

not as a threat, but as an expression of optimism about the world. In tragedy characters tend to be identifiable by consistent character traits and patterns of mind. Through the course of the action they are seen to live out something fundamental about themselves, and their refusal, or inability, to adjust leads them inexorably towards catastrophe. This is an uncompromising and brittle view of character. Comedy's more cheerful and pragmatic view, by contrast – that people can change, be transformed – means that a resolution to problems may be found. Potential catastrophes may be brought back from the brink. Whatever scrapes the world may get itself into, the optimistic implication of the comedies is that it will ultimately always be redeemable.

The page's assertion in *The Taming of the Shrew* that the 'pleasant comedy' to be played for Christopher Sly is to be 'a kind of history' intimates that it will be the unfolding of a story with form and design. It is not, that is, to be merely 'a tumbling trick', a spectacle of clowning. There may be some comic buffoonery within it, but this will be contained within a larger narrative framework with shape and purpose. This is the case for all of Shakespeare's comedies, and the particular narrative shape follows a similar general pattern across the comedies. Each plot emerges from a problem situation. In the course of each play, the opening problem is then intensified and complicated to a point of maximum confusion and potential upset. The liberation of being away from home, or in a moment set apart from the humdrum mainstream of life, then enables the component elements of the initial problem to come to rest in a different, and less problematic, configuration. In the closing stages of the play, the chaos is resolved, however improbably, into a general good-will, and a peaceful return to normal life is made possible. Typically, this resolution is defined and sealed by a spate of marriages, while any 'left-over' characters either offer benedictions upon the marriages, or comment ironically on proceedings, or are socially marginalised. The movement is therefore through chaos and pain, often via some process of displacement, to a point of marital union and the re-establishment of normal social conventions.

The most crucially defining feature of a comedy is its ending. The phrase 'comic ending' does not mean that it need be funny, but rather that the drama's problems and tensions are brought to a point of harmonious resolution in it. This may be achieved by the most improbable of circumstances and, in Shakespeare's comedies, it often is. The harmonious ending is part of the comic formula. It need not be realistic. In fact, there is often something ludicrously neat about the resolution achieved – far too neat to have much in common with real life. The comedies themselves are sometimes delightfully aware, even at the height of their confusion, of their ultimate comic narrative destination. In Act III of *A Midsummer Night's Dream*, for example, Puck offers a blithe prophecy about how all the muddles will end:

> Jack shall have Jill,
> Nought shall go ill;
> . . . and all shall be well.   (3.2.461–63)

His lack of concern for which particular Jack shall have which particular Jill acknowledges that the drama is adhering to a formula, that the neat pattern of the ending is ultimately more important than anything specific about characters:

> Yet but three? Come one more;
> Two of both kinds makes up four.   (3.2.437–38)

At the end of *As You Like It* Hymen feels a similar responsibility to count the lovers:

> Peace ho! I bar confusion.
> 'Tis I must make conclusion
> Of these most strange events.
> Here's eight that must take hands
> To join in Hymen's bands . . .

Where the nature of characters is important in the tragedies, in the comedies it is the overall narrative pattern they make that matters most. The neat choreography of a comic ending determines that as many 'Jacks' as are available marry as many 'Jills' as can be found.

This standard process of pairing off at the end of the comedies represents in part a formulaic abdication from the more daring or experimental issues explored earlier in each play. After a joyous flirtation with alternative forms of social interaction in the course of the play, a ringing endorsement of conservative structures is then offered in its closing moments. Yet even in the midst of this adherence to the comic convention, moments of self-parody may be found. In *As You Like It*, for example, the central characters are beset by a host of problems that need to be cleared away in order to make room for a comic ending. Some of these problems are solved organically by the unfolding action. Others, however, seem destined to haunt the ending with points of unresolved tension. These outstanding problems, however, are then dramatically solved by a sudden and extravagant explanation for which we are totally unprepared. Even in the context of a comedy, it seems excessive. In the final stages of the drama the wicked Duke Frederick is bearing down upon the central characters with an army in order to exact vengeance. Jaques de Boys narrates the story in all its delightful improbability:

> And to the skirts of this wild wood he came,
> Where, meeting with an old religious man,
> After some question with him, was converted
> Both from his enterprise and from the world,
> His crown bequeathing to his banish'd brother,
> And all their lands restor'd to them again
> That were with him exil'd.   (5.4.150–56)

No reason or excuse is offered in order to make this sudden conversion seem more probable. It arrives out of the blue and has no pretensions to psychological credibility. Its only logic is that it is a structural necessity to make possible the happy ending. It is offered as a self-conscious joke about the ludicrous neatness required for a comic ending. Shakespeare therefore provides the requisite tidy comic resolution while at the same time poking fun at the necessarily plastic nature of the resolution achieved. As the end of *As You Like It* powerfully illustrates, comic form is about finding a narrative patterning that may characterise a hearty optimism about life.

However, the four plays collected here do not all take an identical attitude to the comic resolution. Written between 1595 and 1602, and reproduced here in order of composition, they usefully demonstrate an evolution in Shakespeare's comic form. Most particularly, the development from *A Midsummer Night's Dream* to *Twelfth Night* testifies to an increasingly problematic view of comic endings. As Shakespeare was moving into his main tragic writing phase (1601–6), he seems to have become less convinced that any drama may be brought to a fully harmonious resolution. In this period he became increasingly interested in the elements in his dramas that militate *against* harmony. The more mature comedies do not, therefore, reach a point of absolute closure in the way the earlier ones did. The comic pattern is not as neat as it once was. In the later comedies, not every 'Jack' finds a compliant 'Jill', nor does every threatening Duke undergo a dramatic, eleventh hour conversion. *Twelfth Night*, the last play in this collection, marks a watershed in Shakespeare's comic writing: it exposes the fracture lines appearing in his vision of what comedy is and what it can do. It is an appreciably darker play than its predecessors and does not allow itself the consolation of banishing all problems in the encompassing warmth of a romantic haze. Instead, some key characters are painfully excluded from the final resolution and are left understandably embittered by the experience of watching others fall happily into couples.

In general, however, Shakespeare's comedies follow more the patterns of fantasy or wish-fulfilment than the uneven, and not entirely satisfying, patterns of real life. Typically, they present a world in which virtue is finally rewarded, wickedness either punished or converted, and love gloriously requited. With a few exceptions, they present a moral universal. Characters are taken where an audience's unconscious wish might want them taken. Whereas in *Romeo and Juliet* we might secretly will Juliet to wake up in time in order to avert catastrophe, or in *Othello* we might feel frustrated that Desdemona is unable to launch a more convincing defence and so save herself, in the comedies a characteristic response to the formulaic happy ending is a satisfied sigh. It is a sigh, however, made by a slightly distanced observing audience, not by one caught up crucially in an act of identification with any one of the protagonists. We are very rarely expected to feel *with* a character in the comedies. Laughter frequently operates as an alienating device, and more often than not we are able to enjoy the follies and the misunderstandings from a position of superior information. In this way we are spared the potential trauma of identification. Characters within the comedies themselves undergo traumas, but we are mostly held aloof from them. Our concentration, like Puck's, is more on the narrative pattern of events than on the mini-fates of individuals within it.

And then, just when we feel secure in our distance, and in our ability to laugh *at* the characters rather than feel *with* them, these plays have a tendency to pull the rug from under our feet and challenge the security of our distanced position. In *A Midsummer Night's Dream*, Puck attempts to persuade us that it is a very small leap from being 'an auditor' to being 'an actor' (3.1.70–71). We are manœuvred in stages into acknowledging our own agency, our own unwitting involvement in events. Puck concludes his argument with a flourish when, in the Epilogue, he persuades us that the whole action has emerged from *our* dream life, that whatever is capable of offending in it is the product of *our* fantasy world. In *As You Like It*, Rosalind is equally aware that the line between observation and participation may be a thin one. When asked if she would like to *see* a pageant, she replies, 'I'll prove a busy actor in their play' (3.4.55). The title of *As You Like It*, which denies us the luxury of believing ourselves unconnected with the action, perhaps suggests that we might even unconsciously be a 'busy actor' in hers: the play, that is, may be unfolding as *we* like it. In *Twelfth Night* we are made to feel keenly our responsibility in the gulling of Malvolio. The crucial role of an appreciative audience in the life of a joke is made explicit early in the play:

> unless you laugh and minister occasion to him, he is gagged.
>
> (1.5.80–81)

The joke played upon Malvolio becomes increasingly sadistic. Having found it funny in its early, tame stages, it is we, the audience, who have been 'laugh[ing] and minister[ing] occasion' to this particular joke, and so inadvertently driving it to the extremes that then make us feel uncomfortable. Shakespeare thus toys with audience sympathy, pulling us into a complicity with the mischief-makers in order then to make us feel guilty at the way our sympathy has tended. One of the features of Shakespeare's comedies, therefore, is the complex play of alienation and disconcerting involvement that they typically encourage in their audience. In amongst the delight afforded by seeing these plays in performance, an audience can also intermittently be disorientated as its spectating position is pulled around by the sophisticated wiles of the play.

The four Shakespeare comedies in this volume incorporate

elements of all three definitions offered by Christopher Sly and the page: 'a Christmas gambol' (a festive piece of holiday entertainment), 'a tumbling trick' (a spectacle in clowning) and a 'kind of history' (a shaped and meaningful narrative). The plays are irreducibly individual in character and frustrate efforts to produce any one definition that might apply equally to them all. Nevertheless, some general characteristics apply. They are all, for example, playfully self-conscious about their own theatricality and wise to their manipulations of audience involvement. The comedies, more, perhaps, than any other generic group of Shakespeare plays, pay repeated and conscious tribute to the role of an audience in imaginatively colluding to bring the theatrical event to life.

The collective triumph of these plays lies in mingling delightfully humorous stage business and dexterous word-play with a more serious consideration of issues of identity, gender, dreaming, the meaning of love and of the theatre itself. Phrases from them have infiltrated our language and culture ('All the world's a stage', 'The course of true love never did run smooth', 'Lord, what fools these mortals be!', 'If music be the food of love, play on', 'O mistress mine, where are you roaming?', 'I will be horribly in love with her', 'I was adored once too') and several of their characters – Bottom, Dogberry, Jaques, Malvolio, Sir Toby Belch – have passed into our communal affection. A small percentage of the humour is dependent on knowing something of the time in which they were written. Much of it, however, is timeless, dependent only on an awareness of the persistent idiosyncracies and cycles of human folly, aspiration and desire.

JUDITH BUCHANAN
Worcester College, Oxford

NOTE ON THE TEXT

None of Shakespeare's plays exists in an original manuscript. Ever since the earliest sixteenth- and seventeenth-century editions, therefore, the plays have been shaped, in small but significant ways, by publication. There is no 'original' – except a printed one – to revert to. Different editors see their role in different ways, but most modern editions try to balance authenticity with accessibility. Thus, most modern editions, like this one, have modernised spelling and punctuation, *dramatis personae*, and additional stage directions. Where two early texts of a play exist, the editor must adjudicate between their competing claims in order to draw up his or her own text.

This edition is derived from the New Shakespeare series produced under the general editorship of Sir Arthur Quiller-Couch and John Dover Wilson. In it the following typographical conventions have been adopted to indicate editorial intervention:

Original stage directions are indicated between two single quotation marks; all other stage directions are editorial.

Where two differing versions of the play exist, passages which are not found in both are enclosed in square brackets.

Readers who would like to find out more about the early texts of Shakespeare's plays and the issues involved in editing are referred to Stanley Wells and Gary Taylor, *William Shakespeare: A Textual Companion* (Oxford, 1987).

A MIDSUMMER NIGHT'S DREAM

INTRODUCTION

When Bottom the Weaver awakes in Act 4 of *A Midsummer Night's Dream*, he is awed and bemused at the half-recollection of the dream he has had:

> I have had a most rare vision. I have had a dream, past the wit of man to say what dream it was. Man is but an ass if he go about to expound this dream.

Bottom thinks that he would sound silly if he tried to explain his dream. Despite his fear of sounding like an ass, however, he then does make efforts to describe it. He has a compelling sense of the importance of what he has experienced. He cannot, however, tease that feeling into words: his stumbling efforts to do so are comically inadequate. His instinct to fight shy of expounding is thus proved sound: it is easy to slip into idiotic commentary in attempting to make sense of a dream that, by definition, defies the logic of the waking world.

As the play's Epilogue suggests, *A Midsummer Night's Dream* itself, like Bottom's 'most rare vision' within it, has a dream-like quality that resists rational analysis. Like Bottom's experience of *his* dream, the experience of watching or reading the play leaves one both with a sense of having been exposed to something profound and with a sense of frustration as one recognises the tantalisingly elusive character of that something. Those intending 'to expound this dream' should therefore be alert to Bottom's warning. Nevertheless, significantly more may be ventured by way of analysis of the play than Bottom is prepared to risk in relation to his private dream.

History

Written *c*.1595, *A Midsummer Night's Dream* lacks a single literary source. Instead it draws loosely upon a wide range of earlier poems and plays, both classical and English, including works by Ovid, Apuleius, Seneca, Plutarch, Chaucer, Lyly and Spenser. These partial literary debts are woven together with a few subtly encoded topical references and a healthy dose of fantasy to produce a play genuinely from Shakespeare's own imagination. Although there is no conclusive proof, there is a certain amount of evidence within the play itself to suggest that it was first performed as part of a noble couple's wedding celebration. The entire movement of the play is given direction by the preparations for Duke Theseus' marriage to Hippolyta, and the fairies' formal marriage blessings at the end are succeeded by an entirely gratuitous blessing upon the owner of 'this palace'. The play may well have been first performed in a private house, whose owner is therefore being formally recompensed for his hospitality by a brief tribute in the closing moments of the play.

The occasion which is most likely to have been its inspiration was Elizabeth Carey's marriage to Thomas, son of Henry Lord Berkeley, on 19 February 1596 at the Carey family mansion, property of Sir George Carey, in Blackfriars. Queen Elizabeth I herself may well have been present at these celebrations and so could have been in the audience for the first performance of the play, to receive in person the tributes paid to her in it. This performance context is even parodied within the play itself: some honest workmen earnestly desire to produce a play, as part of a marriage celebration, that will please their ruler and be performed in his presence. Thus the play-within-the-play represents a comically exaggerated burlesque of the project of *A Midsummer Night's Dream* as a whole. Queen Elizabeth I made a public and political virtue of her virginity, and in Elizabethan England an artistic trend evolved in which the virgin queen was respectfully represented in various allegorical ways. Because the Roman goddess Diana was goddess of both chastity and the moon, these two things came to be associated with each other. Thus it was that the cult of Elizabeth often courteously chose to represent her as a lunar presence, casting her chaste and benevolent beams upon the world. The prevalence of references to the moon and moonshine in the play may be read as part of this culture in which the influence of the chaste monarch is universally felt. Oberon's description of a 'fair vestal' and, more particularly, an 'imperial votaress' (2.1.158,163), entirely superfluous to the plot, are also among the play's passing tributes to Elizabeth. The play, however, opens on a more problematic note in relation to the moon. Theseus is complaining about the amount of time that must elapse before he may marry Hippolyta, and he does so by reference to the cycles of the moon:

> . . . but O, methinks, how slow
> This old moon wanes! She lingers my desires . . . (1.1.3–4)

Performed in the mid-1590s, quite possibly in the presence of a chaste and elderly queen who was often represented by lunar imagery and who showed little sign of dying, this complaint against the 'old moon' for refusing to wane is, perhaps, an opening of no little daring.

If A *Midsummer Night's Dream* started life as part of a private festivity, as seems probable, it would have been transferred to the public playhouses soon afterwards. There is no record of it in the Stationer's Register as a publicly performed play until 7 September 1598, but it was almost certainly performed on the public stage considerably earlier than that.

Plot summary

Set in ancient Athens, the play refers to Greek mythology for some of its characters and action. We discover at its opening that Duke Theseus has first forcibly subdued, and then wooed, the Amazon Hippolyta, whom he is now preparing to marry. Egeus bursts in upon these preparations with a serious matter for Theseus' consideration. Hermia, Egeus' daughter, will not consent to marry Demetrius, her father's choice of husband for her, and instead stubbornly asserts her love for Lysander. Theseus pronounces judgment by invoking the ancient law of Athens. The disobedient daughter in such a case has three options: she must either consent to her father's wishes, or live out the rest of her life as a virgin in a closed convent, or be put to death. In response to this ultimatum, Lysander and Hermia resolve to flee together that night through the wood to Lysander's aunt, some seven leagues away, where they may then safely be married. This plan they confide to Helena, Hermia's long-time friend. Helena is herself desperately in love with Demetrius and perversely decides that she may find some favour with him by telling him that the woman he loves, Hermia, will be fleeing the town under cover of darkness. Demetrius resolves to follow Hermia, and in turn Helena resolves to follow Demetrius. Meanwhile Theseus has commissioned the people of Athens to prepare entertainments for his forthcoming wedding celebrations. In response to this commission, some simple-minded working men, later referred to as 'rude mechanicals', are rehearsing a version of 'Pyramus and Thisbe' under the direction of Peter Quince, in the hope of being chosen to perform for the royal nuptials. Bottom the Weaver, a particular enthusiast for the play, is cast in the role of Pyramus. These mechanicals arrange to reconvene later in the wood outside the town, where they will be able to rehearse in greater privacy.

The play's action then removes to the less civilised, and less regulated, environment of the same wood near Athens which, we discover, is inhabited by fairies and ruled over by Oberon, the Fairy King. Here, three different plot threads are pursued – the mechanicals' play rehearsals, the amorous tangles of the fleeing (and chasing) lovers, and the events in fairy world. It quickly transpires that the fairy world is in turmoil. Their Queen, Titania, is in fierce dispute with her lover, Oberon. Tremors are being felt in the natural world as a result. Out of spite towards Titania, Oberon instructs a mischievous spirit, Puck, to go in search of a 'little Western flower', the juice of which, when administered to a sleeper's eyes, magically makes that sleeper fall in love with whatever s/he sees first upon awakening. Puck fetches the flower and Oberon drops the juice into the eyes of the sleeping Titania.

Meanwhile, for his own amusement, Puck disrupts the mechanicals' play rehearsal by magically converting Bottom's head into the head of an ass. To Puck's intense satisfaction, the rest of the acting troupe all flee in terror at the sight of their friend thus transformed. As it happens, it is Bottom's ass's head that Titania then sees first upon awakening. She duly falls in love with the hybrid monster, offering him fairy hospitality that is both gracious and amorously demanding. The Fairy Queen and the man-turned-ass fall asleep in each other's arms. Partly mistaking Oberon's instructions, Puck drops the same magical juice into the eyes of first Lysander and then Demetrius, each of whom sees Helena upon awakening. As a consequence, each forswears his previous love for Hermia and vehemently asserts his undying love for Helena. Helena herself is convinced that the men are cruelly mocking her by their sudden and excessive declarations of love, and that Hermia must be complicit in this mockery. Hermia, by contrast, becomes convinced that Lysander's sudden and inexplicable rejection of her is part of some dreadful scheme of Helena's making. The four become embroiled in hot dispute, but through Puck's intervention lose each other in a frantic chase through the wood before any real harm can be done. Exhausted, each of the four lovers then falls asleep and Puck drops the magical antidote into Lysander's eyes so that his former affection for Hermia will be restored to him when he awakes.

Meanwhile Oberon has similarly undone the effects of the juice on Titania, with whom he is then immediately reconciled, and Puck has returned the still sleeping Bottom to his human form. Theseus and Hippolyta, out on a dawn hunt, are surprised to discover the sleeping bodies of the four lovers in the wood. The sound of the hunting horn awakens the young people who, in some bemusement, try to account for their dream-like experiences of the night just passed. Theseus, seeing that they have now resolved themselves into two happy couples, overrules Egeus' wishes, and decrees instead that they shall all four be married as part of the same ceremony which will solemnise his own union with Hippolyta. Bottom awakes to find himself alone but with an odd memory of an extraordinary dream. He decides he shall ask Peter Quince to compose a ballad about this momentous dream and that it shall be called Bottom's Dream 'because it hath no bottom'.

The action shifts back to Athens where Theseus chooses 'Pyramus and Thisbe' as the entertainment for the collective nuptial celebrations. It is performed with charming ineptitude in front of the royal party, and the performance is punctuated throughout by ludicrous reassurances from the actors that their play is not real and by sarcastic comments from the floor. The newly wedded lovers go to bed and the fairies appear in the Duke's palace to bestow blessings upon the three marriages. Puck delivers the epilogue in which he reasserts the dream quality of the whole performance.

The wood near Athens

A temporary displacement from a familiar urban setting to an
unfamiliar rural one is the structuring principle of several Shakespeare comedies. The intensity of a problem encountered in the
town provides the momentum for a hasty removal to the country.
In the apparent freedom of this new setting, the conventions and
constraints that governed the old life naturally fall away. This
liberation provides the space and opportunity for the component
elements of the initial problem to be cast into the air and so to
come to rest in a different, and less problematic, configuration. A
peaceful return to the town is thus made possible. Through the
temporary disruption of being away from home, therefore, characters gain not only a refreshed vision but, crucially, a material
improvement in their circumstances. By the end of each play, the
town has ceased to function as the oppressive citadel from which
one must escape, and has been reconfigured as the centre of
civilised courtesy and familial belonging to which one may gladly
return.

This pattern of escape from a (problem-ridden) urban to a
(problem-solving) rural environment implies a starkly value-laden
contrast between the two settings. It is easy to imagine the urban
setting as a place of overbearing authority and cramping regulations
pitted against a pastoral ideal or Arcadian retreat, a place of
innocence, virtue and wholesome simplicity. Although this notion
of the rural retreat is helpful in relation to that on offer in a play
such as *As You Like It*, it is not at all appropriate in *A Midsummer
Night's Dream*. Romantics in the nineteenth century consistently
found a delicate beauty and poetic sweetness in the wood near
Athens, and in the action of the play as a whole. The play was read
most frequently as a celebration of the redemptive power of the
imagination. Without denying the beauty and delicacy of the
poetry, it is also appropriate, however, to attend to those elements
in the wood, and in the play more generally, that are far from sweet
and that testify not only to the redemptive power of imagination
but also, on occasion, to its murky depths.

The wood in which the majority of the play's action takes place
is, the text tells us, 'A wood *near* Athens' (2.1 – my italics). Its
proximity to everything that is familiar to the Athenians is repeatedly emphasised. As Lysander reminds Hermia, it is but 'a league

without the town' (1.1.165) and Peter Quince is similarly insistent, locating it only 'a mile without the town' (1.2.93). Lysander
remembers meeting Hermia and Helena there once to do observance to a May morning, and Hermia reminds Helena of the many
times they have lain out upon banks of primroses in that wood
and shared confidences. Because it is both local and apparently
familiar, there is no expectation that this wood should be out of
the ordinary. As things turn out, however, it proves to be thoroughly disconcerting. It is its seeming familiarity that makes this
enchanted wood constantly bemusing for the mortals, since it
stubbornly refuses to be what they expect of it. Athens was threatening and oppressive for Hermia and Lysander, but the hostility
encountered there was a known quantity. The strangenesses and
hostilities encountered in the wood are both unexpected and
incomprehensible. The mortals are therefore constantly discon-
certed by the wood's refusal either to be the comfortable and
knowable place they would like to believe it, or to be an honest
and identifiable enemy. It feels as if it *should* be familiar because it
is close to home, but it proves very far from homely.

The hasty escape from the barbaric and patriarchal law of Athens does not, therefore, lead *A Midsummer Night's Dream*'s
characters into a soothing pastoral ideal. The lullaby with which
Titania's fairy retinue sings her to sleep implicitly acknowledges
that any moment of peace in the wood, even for the Fairy Queen
herself, has to be earned by the active suppression of some of the
opposing forces at large:

> You spotted snakes with double tongue,
> Thorny hedgehogs, be not seen;
> Newts and blind-worms, do no wrong,
> Come not near our fairy queen.   (2.2.9–12)

Hermia's sleep at the end of the same scene is troubled by just
such a snake as has been banished by the fairies from Titania's
sleeping presence. In Hermia's dream, a 'crawling serpent'
(2.2.154) appears on her breast and eats her heart away while
Lysander sits smiling at this predatory act done upon his lover.
Clearly there is some point to the fairies' lullaby of banishment:
women sleeping in this wood *are* vulnerable to predatory snakes,
real or imaginary. Seeking the comfort of the waking world,

Hermia awakes in panic from the nightmare of seeing her lover condoning the violence being done to her. However, she discovers very little comfort in the waking world. Lysander has disappeared leaving her alone in the wood, and when she finally does find him, he treats her with summary disdain. The waking world does not precisely duplicate the dreamworld with which she has to contend, but it imitates its tone. In both she feels frighteningly alone in a world of predators.

Helena too encounters a potential aggressor in the wood. Demetrius is anxious to shake her off to enable him to pursue Hermia the more easily. His contempt for her leads him at one point to threaten that if she does not return to Athens, he may 'do [her] mischief in the wood' (2.1.237). The specifically sexual nature of the threatened 'mischief' he has already made clear to her:

> You do impeach your modesty too much
> To leave the city and commit yourself
> Into the hands of one that loves you not,
> To trust the opportunity of night
> And the ill counsel of a desert place
> With the rich worth of your virginity.   (2.1.214–19)

Rather than being fearful for her virginity, however, Helena has in fact already implored him to abuse her in some fashion:

> I am your spaniel; and, Demetrius,
> The more you beat me, I will fawn on you.
> Use me but as your spaniel, spurn me, strike me,
> Neglect me, lose me; only give me leave,
> Unworthy as I am, to follow you.
> What worser place can I beg in your love –
> And yet a place of high respect with me –
> Than to be used as you use your dog?   (2.1.203–10)

Thus Demetrius' sexual threat, if not exactly what Helena might have wished, is arguably the logical extension of the exploitative treatment she has explicitly sought. Helena, accustomed to habitual neglect, seems to have developed a fantasy life that has taken a disturbing, and specifically masochistic, turn. The less controlled environment of the wood removes the constraints that have prevented these otherwise civilised Athenians from revealing their more primitive and instinctive selves. In the frightening absence of civilised checks and balances, both Helena and Demetrius find themselves exposing their basest impulses. He, it seems, would rape her as an act of contempt. She, it seems, would almost have him do so.

Titania's fantasies also become disturbing – she lusts after an ass – but in her case this happens directly through Oberon's magical intervention. Once in possession of the magical flower, he exults in the destructive power he wields over her:

> And with the juice of this I'll streak her eyes,
> And make her full of hateful fantasies.   (2.1.257–58)

His particular choice of the word 'streak', rather than some more innocuous verb (dab, sprinkle, anoint, wet, treat), suggests an act of violence upon the tenderness and fragility of an eyeball, as if something is to be scraped across its vulnerable surface. As a result of this physical interference, he looks forward too to warping her inner life. No fairy lullaby of banishment can, it seems, rescue Titania from Oberon's venomous influence. Like the complicitly smiling Lysander in Hermia's nightmare, Oberon will take pleasure in observing his lover become a prey to 'hateful fantasies'. When in the next act Hermia calls Demetrius 'thou serpent' (3.2.73), the implied elision between predatory, sexually intrusive serpents and predatory, sexually aggressive men finally becomes explicit.

Although most of the acts, or threatened acts, of aggression in the play are committed by men on women (Theseus' wooing of Hippolyta with his sword, Egeus' insistent call for the death of his own daughter, Oberon's desire to exact physical and psychological revenge on Titania, Demetrius' rape threat to Helena), there is one occasion when an aggressive female sexuality impresses itself insistently upon a man – or a man of sorts at least. When Bottom-turned-ass is entertained by Titania and her retinue, he initially expresses his keen desire to find his way out of the wood. The Queen of the Fairies replies:

> Out of this wood do not desire to go:
> Thou shalt remain here, whether thou wilt or no.
> (3.1.138–9)

Since he has been forbidden to leave, Bottom nobly makes small talk instead with four of Titania's fairies. Titania then imperiously instructs these same fairies about the exact nature of the hospitality their guest-prisoner is to receive:

> Come, wait upon him; lead him to my bower.
> The moon, methinks, looks with a watery eye,
> And when she weeps, weeps every little flower,
> Lamenting some enforced chastity.
> Tie up my love's tongue, bring him silently.   (3.1.182–6)

Bottom is to be gagged and led to her bower, whether he will or not. Titania's momentary digression about the weeping moon and the corresponding weeping of 'every little flower' is scarcely a digression at all. It will be recalled that the moon was associated with chastity through the figure of the goddess Diana. Besides contributing to the play's tapestry of allusions to the chastity of Elizabeth I, Titania's lines also reveal her own plans in relation to Bottom. 'Enforced' has changed its meaning over time. Here it means not 'insisted upon' but rather 'forced' or 'violated'. The moon, and with her the flowers, are therefore weeping in sorrow for the forcing of someone's virginity. 'Tie up my love's tongue, bring him silently', Titania says immediately afterwards. He is led like a lamb to the slaughter. Little wonder the moon and the flowers are weeping.

There is a pervasive brutality and a violent sexuality in the play that simmers below the surface of many of its interactions. This violent potential is just about contained for much of the action, but it erupts intermittently as an indicator of the ugly depths only partially disguised by the shimmeringly poetic surfaces. Puck intimates at one point that the mechanicals are shedding their clothes in the wood:

> For briars and thorns at their apparel snatch;   (3.2.29)

There is a sense in which the wood reduces all characters to the most naked and basic version of themselves. Just as literally it strips the mechanicals of their clothes, so emotionally it pares away decorum and the veneer of civilisation and exposes the raw, unrefined essence of *all* the characters caught within its spell. Their threats, desires, fantasies, fears and dreams are frequently

found to be of a troubling character. The removed context of
Oberon's enchanted wood therefore acts as a catalyst, bringing to
the surface those darker human impulses which might well have
remained more decorously suppressed in a more civilised environment. Being in a context of unchecked psychological and
sexual expression, the play suggests, may bring to light some
truths about humanity which are far from pretty. The wood's
'musk-rose bud' may look beautiful at a first glance, but, as its
flower is opened up, it is found to be inhabited by 'cankers',
destructive worms eating it from within (2.2.3). The unmasking
of hidden ugliness is, it seems, integral to the processes of the
wood.

The ending

Having confronted the depths of human ugliness, however, the
play then negotiates a dramatic change of tone in its ending.
Everything that has tended towards violence, brutality or a dark
sexuality is wilfully fought down, and Puck's blithe prophecy is
fulfilled:

> Jack shall have Jill,
> Nought shall go ill;
> . . . and all shall be well.   (3.2.461–63)

The Athenians emerge from a dark night of exploring the
confused and confusing world of their own inner selves into the
literal and moral light of the morning where more wholesome
truths may be, and perhaps need to be, asserted. Hermia and
Lysander are restored to each other, she wisely deciding to forget
her fantasy fears about him and he his aggression to her.
Demetrius, still under the influence of Oberon's magical juice,
now reciprocates Helena's love for him, each of them choosing
not to remember the dangerous sexual edge of their conversation
of the night before. Oberon abandons his campaign to brutalise
and humiliate Titania, and she stares in horror at the ass with
whom she has spent the night. The resulting reconciliation
between the Fairy King and Queen restores the cycle of the
seasons and the balance of the natural world, both of which had
been disturbed by the ferocity of the earlier dissension between
them. Theseus' relationship with Hippolyta is no longer to be

dictated by his sword, but rather he is to wed her, as he promised, 'in another key' (1.1.18). The harmony of the end is therefore won by the active overcoming of some of the dominant forces of confusion and perversion that have held sway in the play.

In Act 1 Lysander had lamented how swiftly 'quick bright things' may 'come to confusion' (1.1.149). The end of the play reverses this process, showing the equally swift rescue of these particular 'quick bright things' from the confusion into which they had indeed speedily tumbled. The pervasive 'hateful fantasies' are diffused, transformed into a harmonious resolution through the agency of magic and, more schematically, through the exigencies of comic form. Puck's formulation that 'Jack shall have Jill' suggests that the lovers' individual identities are not crucially relevant. They vehemently insist upon their distinction from each other and upon the specific appeal of one over another. Puck, however, mistakes one Athenian youth for another, Helena claims that she and Hermia are 'like to a double cherry' (3.2.209), and we tend to find all four of them more generically definable than individually knowable. They are young, headstrong, humourless, hyperbolic lovers, and as such they are types far more than personalities. As Puck's lack of concern for their specific names indicates, they are more interesting for the entertaining patterns they form as affiliations between them are made, broken, exchanged, broken and remade than for anything inherent in them as individuals. Puck's hearty confidence that 'all shall be well' is finally justified, but which specific Jack has which specific Jill has been fairly arbitrarily determined simply to ensure a satisfying pattern at the end.

One of the slightly barbed jokes of the play is, therefore, to point out how highly specific lovers feel to each other and how simultaneously interchangeable they can seem to an onlooker. For a play which may well have been first performed as part of the celebrations for a real marriage, it is peculiarly cynical both about the processes of falling in love and about the nature and reliability of the bonds that then hold couples together. Puck's scathing 'Lord, what fools these mortals be!' (3.2.115) is entirely apt in the terms of the play, but might well have had a slightly odd resonance in the context of a real wedding.

The mechanicals and humour

What, ironically, might have been *more* appropriate for the festivities of a wedding celebration would have been the energetic good humour generated by the scenes that do not feature lovers directly at all – the mechanicals' scenes. Henri Bergson's theory of laughter suggests that humour is often derived from a sense of 'le méchanique plaqué sur le vivant', the automated superimposed upon the living. In other words, it is from the encounter between an entirely consistent, unchanging thing and a world of living fluctuation that comedy emerges. The world of *A Midsummer Night's Dream* is dramatically in flux. Not only do lovers fall in and out of love with each other and a fairy princess dote upon and then abhor an ass, but nature is in drastic upheaval, the seasons are in disorder, and all things are feeling the concomitant tremors. In the midst of all this, the mechanicals are a point of astonishing consistency. Surprisingly for players (who might have been expected to be more versatile in their identities), they are the most fixed characters in the play, and are most obviously themselves no matter where they are, what they are wearing or what role they are endeavouring to fulfil. Despite their fixity, they are touchingly concerned lest the quality of their performances dupe their audience into believing the presentation to be real. Their fear is that the audience will fail to discriminate between the dramatic fiction of 'Pyramus and Thisbe' on the one hand and actuality on the other, and so become convinced that the tragic and disturbing events in the play are *really* taking place. Such is their anxiety on the matter that they incorporate into their presentation over-insistent disclaimers about the reality of the event, as a means of reassuring their audience that no harm is really being done and that, for example, no real lion is about to savage them:

> Fair ladies . . . I would entreat you, not to fear, not to tremble: my life for yours! If you think I come hither as a lion, it were pity of my life. No, I am no such thing; I am a man, as other men are. (3.1.34–38)

This naive belief in the transcendent power of their own illusions is all the funnier since it is abundantly clear (most obviously, of course, in their literal embodiments of Wall and Moonshine) that their illusions are crude and *un*convincing. While firmly believing themselves to be protean, then, these artisan players are remarkably unchanging and personally uncompromised through an impressive range of encounters – with fairies, with royalty and with the possibilities of stage production.

Of all the mechanicals, Bottom is the most dramatic illustration of Bergson's notion of the comic clash between consistency and change. Even as an ass, Bottom remains gloriously himself, an entirely consistent 'mechanical' point in a world of vacillation. Confronted with a fairy, and one, moreover, 'of no common rate', Bottom is polite with his usual robust good humour, but he is not overawed. Told that she loves him, he says she can have little reason for that, but then again, he continues, reason and love do not always go together, so perhaps she does after all. Even with long hairy ears and calling for 'good dry oats' (4.1.32), he is still entirely recognisable as a good-hearted, literal-minded, enthusiastic artisan with a slight tendency to smugness about his own (pedestrian) wit: he is, that is, unchanged from the Bottom to whom we were introduced at the mechanicals' first rehearsal in Athens. In the flurry of other restorations at the end of the play, therefore, Bottom does not fundamentally need to be restored to a self he has lost – for he never lost it. In fact, it is Bottom's fate not to be able to lose himself or to transform himself into something else, even when, for dramatic purposes, he might need to. Thus, when trying to play Pyramus, he keeps breaking in as himself, Bottom the Weaver, to answer comments from the floor about how the action is proceeding. It is the combination of the mechanicals' inflexibility with their contrary conviction that they will be believed to have become everything they play, that makes them such endearing figures of fun, both for us and for their on-stage audience.

The most vigorous humour of the play, then, is provided by the mechanicals. But other areas of the action are funny as well. The murky depths and troubling undertones of the lovers' and the fairies' stories do not disable the comic humour which can, despite simmering darknesses around and beneath and within it, be genuinely hilarious. The unnerving nature of some aspects of the play may even make the relief at being able to laugh at it the greater. Discussing the comedies in over-sombre terms, as if they were tracts rather than pieces of dramatic entertainment, is a critical tendency that misrepresents what the plays are. They undeniably deal with subjects of some seriousness, but they do not do so in a sombre way: they are funny plays. There is, for example, both a poetic lightness of touch and a highly energetic comic will in *A Midsummer Night's Dream* that ensures that the seriousness, and the poignancy, of some of its material is contained within a wider framework of delight.

Offending shadows

Interpretations of *A Midsummer Night's Dream*, on both page and stage, have undergone a shift over this century. The play has moved from being a delicate ballet of tripping fairies and momentarily wayward lovers frolicking entertainingly in an Arcadian retreat to being a more tonally mixed exploration of the power of the imagination. Imagination as explored in the play is now understood to have the power not only to liberate but also to ensnare, as the brutality and perversity of its own darkest repressions surface. It may redeem, but it may also degrade. Productions have become darker. Accordingly, an understanding of the significance of the play's ending has also shifted. No longer may it be considered merely the natural outworking of the action that precedes it. Rather the comic ending has to be earned, to be won by the active suppression of those powerful forces and influences that tend away from harmony and away from comedy. In the early stages of the play Helena, musing on the processes of love, has offered an optimistic assessment of its transforming power:

> Things base and vile, holding no quantity,
> Love can transpose to form and dignity.   (1.1.232–33)

In *A Midsummer Night's Dream* those emotions and impulses which are 'base and vile' *are* finally 'transpose[d] to form and dignity' in the graceful pairings of the noble lovers. It is not 'Love', however, as Helena had supposed, which effects this transposition. Love had merely enhanced the agony and the confusion. Rather it is the play's internal dramatist, the destiny-deciding figure of Oberon, who intervenes to right the situational and emotional muddles of the night. Demetrius is, necessarily,

still under the influence of the magical aphrodisiac at the end of
the play. That this is integral to the harmony of the ending serves
to illustrate the constructed nature of the resolution achieved.
The solution found is not organic, but imposed.

In the Epilogue, Puck delivers a conventional, and tongue-in-
cheek, apology on behalf of the actors for any offence that may
have been caused by the performance:

> If we shadows have offended,
> Think but this and all is mended,
> That you have but slumber'd here
> While these visions did appear.
> And this weak and idle theme,
> No more yielding but a dream . . .   (5.1.407–12)

His courteous plea is that, if anything controversial be found in it,
the play should be dismissed as a dream. This seemingly converts
it into a thing of nought, something ephemeral and insubstantial.
Yet it has another effect too. Redefining the play as something
that has emerged from the audience's dream offloads the responsibility for it onto us, the audience, since we are asked to believe
that we have conjured the details of the drama from our *own*
dreamworld imaginations. If the dream has moments of nightmare about it, claims the Epilogue, it is *our* designing fantasy that
is leading it into those dark realms.

Earlier, when Puck stumbled upon the rehearsals for the play-
within-the-play, he had become excited at the prospective role
he saw for himself:

> What a play towards? I'll be an auditor;
> An actor too perhaps, if I see cause.   (3.1.70–71)

Now, in the Epilogue, Puck implicitly encourages his audience
to realise that not he alone, but *all* 'auditors' are 'actor[s] too
perhaps'. The implication of depicting the play as the audience's
dream is that the audience is involved in making it happen, that
the movement of the drama needs to be seen as following the
dictates of some communal imaginative will. We are not merely
'auditors', with the luxury of remaining at a neutral, observing
distance from the action, but 'actor[s] too perhaps', with an
active, determining involvement in it. The audience's own

agency, or active involvement, is hinted at again, and more disturbingly, in the last few lines of the Epilogue:

> Now to 'scape the serpent's tongue,
> We will make amends ere long;
> Else the Puck a liar call.
> So, goodnight unto you all.
> Give me your hands, if we be friends,
> And Robin shall restore amends.   (5.1.417–22)

In seeking to 'scape the serpent's tongue' Puck is, literally, hoping that the performance will be applauded by the audience rather than hissed. The mention of a serpent cannot, however, fail to trigger other associations in the context of a play that has been crawling with serpents of one sort or another. The recurring serpent imagery thoughout the play makes this cumulative association inevitable. The snake and blind-worms in the fairies' lullaby are banished from Titania's sleeping presence lest they disrupt her peace. Lysander's persistently expressed desire to sleep with Hermia is quickly followed by a predatory and aggressive serpent invading her dreamlife and eating her heart away. The canker-worms inside the musk-rose bud are destroying its beauty from within. Hermia wonders if a worm or an adder might have killed her love while he slept, and then accuses Demetrius of being himself a serpent. The serpent is a pervasive image of threat in the play. It represents the tug downwards of the imagination, the tug away from harmony and health towards the perverse and the destructive. In the play's final moments, we the audience are then asked to refrain from using *our* 'serpent's tongue'. The play's cumulative serpent imagery thus comes to rest by casually casting its audience in the association-laden role of the serpent.

A Midsummer Night's Dream, like many Shakespeare comedies, denies its audience the space to sit back and enjoy the spectacle from a consistently detached perspective. And, like Titania's double-edged entertainment of Bottom, it makes its demands with disarming delicacy and charm. We are manœuvred into acknowledging that we are somehow implicated in the drama unfolding before us, as we discover that we are being held accountable for having ourselves dreamt it. If we see perversity and brutality in the wood, and identify it as emerging from the ugly depths of liberated imaginations, we are asked to consider whether those troubling imaginations might not in fact be our own. In the very act of expressing the hope that the play has not offended, therefore, the Epilogue is potentially, although very gracefully, the moment of greatest offence in the play. We are courteously asked to acknowledge our own capacity to be the destructive, hissing serpent of the dream, and, yet more fundamentally, to recognise that anything we find offensive in *The Dream* may have emerged from our own murky fantasy world.

Scene: Athens, and a wood hard by

CHARACTERS IN THE PLAY

THESEUS, *Duke of Athens*
HIPPOLYTA, *Queen of the Amazons, betrothed to Theseus*
EGEUS, *an old man, father to Hermia*
LYSANDER ⎫
DEMETRIUS ⎭ *young gentlemen, in love with Hermia*
PHILOSTRATE, *master of the revels to Theseus*
HERMIA *(short and dark), daughter to Egeus, in love with*
    Lysander
HELENA *(tall and fair), in love with Demetrius*

PETER QUINCE, *a carpenter*
NICK BOTTOM, *a weaver*
FRANCIS FLUTE, *a bellows-mender*
TOM SNOUT, *a tinker*
ROBIN STARVELING, *a tailor*
SNUG, *a joiner*

OBERON, *King of the Fairies*
TITANIA, *Queen of the Fairies*
ROBIN GOODFELLOW, THE PUCK
PEASEBLOSSOM ⎫
COBWEB ⎪
MOTH ⎬ *fairies*
MUSTARDSEED ⎭

Other fairies attending their King and Queen

Attendants on Theseus and Hippolyta

ACT I SCENE I

The hall in the palace of Duke Theseus. On one side a small platform with two chairs of state; on the other side a hearth; at the back doors to right and left, the wall between them opening out into a lobby

THESEUS *and* HIPPOLYTA *enter and take their seats, followed by* PHILOSTRATE *and attendants*

THESEUS   Now, fair Hippolyta, our nuptial hour
Draws on apace: four happy days bring in
Another moon: but O, methinks how slow
This old moon wanes! She lingers my desires,
Like to a step-dame, or a dowager,
Long withering out a young man's revenue.

HIPPOLYTA Four days will quickly steep themselves in night:
Four nights will quickly dream away the time:
And then the moon, like to a silver bow
New-bent in heaven, shall behold the night   10
Of our solemnities.

THESEUS   Go, Philostrate,
Stir up the Athenian youth to merriments,
Awake the pert and nimble spirit of mirth,
Turn melancholy forth to funerals:
The pale companion is not for our pomp.
                    [Philostrate bows and departs
Hippolyta, I wooed thee with my sword,
And won thy love doing thee injuries:
But I will wed thee in another key,
With pomp, with triumph, and with revelling.

EGEUS *enters, haling along his daughter* HERMIA *by the arm, followed by* LYSANDER *and* DEMETRIUS

EGEUS   [*bows*] Happy be Theseus, our renownéd duke   20
THESEUS Thanks, good Egeus. What's the news with thee?
EGEUS   Full of vexation come I, with complaint
Against my child, my daughter Hermia.

Stand forth, Demetrius. My noble lord,
This man hath my consent to marry her.
Stand forth, Lysander. And, my gracious duke,
This man hath witched the bosom of my child.
Thou, thou, Lysander, thou hast given her rhymes,
And interchanged love-tokens with my child:
Thou hast by moonlight at her window sung,   30
With feigning voice, verses of feigning love:
And stol'n the impression of her fantasy
With bracelets of thy hair, rings, gauds, conceits,
Knacks, trifles, nosegays, sweetmeats – messengers
Of strong prevailment in unhardened youth.
With cunning hast thou filched my daughter's heart,
Turned her obedience, which is due to me,
To stubborn harshness. And, my gracious duke,
Be it so she will not here before your grace
Consent to marry with Demetrius,   40
I beg the ancient privilege of Athens:
As she is mine, I may dispose of her:
Which shall be either to this gentleman,
Or to her death; according to our law
Immediately provided in that case.

THESEUS   What say you, Hermia? Be advised, fair maid.
To you your father should be as a god;
One that composed your beauties; yea and one
To whom you are but as a form in wax
By him imprinted, and within his power   50
To leave the figure or disfigure it.
Demetrius is a worthy gentleman.

HERMIA   So is Lysander.

THESEUS   In himself he is:
But in this kind, wanting your father's voice,
The other must be held the worthier.

HERMIA   I would my father looked but with my eyes.

THESEUS   Rather your eyes must with his judgment look.

HERMIA   I do entreat your grace to pardon me.
I know not by what power I am made bold;
Nor how it may concern my modesty   60
In such a presence here to plead my thoughts:

But I beseech your grace that I may know
The worst that may befall me in this case
If I refuse to wed Demetrius.

THESEUS   Either to die the death, or to abjure
For ever the society of men.
Therefore, fair Hermia, question your desires,
Know of your youth, examine well your blood,
Whether, if you yield not to your father's choice,
You can endure the livery of a nun,   70
For aye to be in shady cloister mewed,
To live a barren sister all your life,
Chanting faint hymns to the cold fruitless moon.
Thrice blessèd they that master so their blood,
To undergo such maiden pilgrimage:
But earthlier happy is the rose distilled,
Than that which withering on the virgin thorn
Grows, lives and dies in single blessedness.

HERMIA   So will I grow, so live, so die, my lord,
Ere I will yield my virgin patent up   80
Unto his lordship, whose unwishèd yoke
My soul consents not to give sovereignty.

THESEUS   Take time to pause, and by the next new moon –
The sealing-day betwixt my love and me
For everlasting bond of fellowship –
Upon that day either prepare to die
For disobedience to your father's will,
Or else to wed Demetrius as he would,
Or on Diana's altar to protest
For aye austerity and single life.   90

DEMETR.   Relent, sweet Hermia – and, Lysander, yield
Thy crazèd title to my certain right.

LYSANDER   You have her father's love, Demetrius;
Let me have Hermia's: do you marry him.

EGEUS   Scornful Lysander! True, he hath my love;
And what is mine my love shall render him.
And she is mine, and all my right of her
I do estate unto Demetrius.

LYSANDER   I am, my lord, as well derived as he,
As well possessed: my love is more than his   100

My fortunes every way as fairly ranked –
If not with vantage – as Demetrius':
And, which is more than all these boasts can be,
I am beloved of beauteous Hermia.
Why should not I then prosecute my right?
Demetrius, I'll avouch it to his head,
Made love to Nedar's daughter, Helena,
And won her soul; and she, sweet lady, dotes,
Devoutly dotes, dotes in idolatry,
Upon this spotted and inconstant man.   110

THESEUS   I must confess that I have heard so much:
And with Demetrius thought to have spoke thereof;
But, being over-full of self-affairs,
My mind did lose it. [*he rises*] But Demetrius come,
And come Egeus, you shall go with me:
I have some private schooling for you both.
For you, fair Hermia, look you arm yourself
To fit your fancies to your father's will;
Or else the law of Athens yields you up
(Which by no means we may extenuate)   120
To death, or to a vow of single life.
Come, my Hippolyta: what cheer, my love?
Demetrius and Egeus, go along:
I must employ you in some business
Against our nuptial, and confer with you
Of something nearly that concerns yourselves.

EGEUS   With duty and desire we follow you.
                          [*all depart save Hermia and Lysander*

LYSANDER   How now, my love? Why is your cheek so pale?
             How chance the roses there do fade so fast?

HERMIA   Belike for want of rain, which I could well   130
             Beteem them from the tempest of my eyes.

LYSANDER   Ay me! [*he comforts her*]
                        For aught that I could ever read,
             Could ever hear by tale or history,
             The course of true love never did run smooth;
             But, either it was different in blood –

HERMIA   O cross! Too high to be enthralled to low.

LYSANDER   Or else misgraffèd in respect of years –

HERMIA	O spite! Too old to be engaged to young.
LYSANDER	Or else it stood upon the choice of friends –
HERMIA	O hell! To choose love by another's eyes!

140

LYSANDER	Or, if there were a sympathy in choice,

War, death, or sickness did lay siege to it –
Making it momentany as a sound,
Swift as a shadow, short as any dream,
Brief as the lightning in the collied night
That, in a spleen, unfolds both heaven and earth;
And ere a man hath power to say 'Behold!'
The jaws of darkness do devour it up:
So quick bright things come to confusion.

HERMIA   If then true lovers have been ever crossed,

150

It stands as an edict in destiny:
Then let us teach our trial patience,
Because it is a customary cross,
As due to love as thoughts and dreams and sighs,
Wishes and tears, poor Fancy's followers.

LYSANDER   A good persuasion: therefore hear me, Hermia:
I have a widow aunt, a dowager
Of great revénue, and she hath no child:
From Athens is her house remote seven leagues:
And she respects me as her only son.

160

There, gentle Hermia, may I marry thee:
And to that place the sharp Athenian law
Cannot pursue us. If thou lovest me then,
Steal forth thy father's house tomorrow night;
And in the wood, a league without the town,
Where I did meet thee once with Helena,
To do observance to a morn of May,
There will I stay for thee.

HERMIA   My good Lysander,
I swear to thee by Cupid's strongest bow,
By his best arrow with the golden head,

170

By the simplicity of Venus' doves,
By that which knitteth souls and prospers loves,
And by that fire which burned the Carthage queen,
When the false Troyan under sail was seen,
By all the vows that ever men have broke –

In number more than ever women spoke –
In that same place thou hast appointed me,
Tomorrow truly will I meet with thee.

LYSANDER Keep promise, love. Look, here comes Helena.

HELENA is seen passing through the lobby

HERMIA   God speed, fair Helena: whither away?   180

HELENA   [*coming forward into the hall*]
Call you me fair? That 'fair' again unsay.
Demetrius loves your fair: O happy fair!
Your eyes are lode-stars, and your tongue's sweet air
More tuneable than lark to shepherd's ear,
When wheat is green, when hawthorn buds appear.
Sickness is catching: O, were favour so,
Yours would I catch, fair Hermia, ere I go!
My ear should catch your voice, my eye your eye,
My tongue should catch your tongue's sweet melody.
Were the world mine, Demetrius being bated,   190
The rest I'ld give to be to you translated.
O, teach me how you look, and with what art
You sway the motion of Demetrius' heart.

HERMIA   I frown upon him; yet he loves me still.

HELENA   O that your frowns would teach my smiles such skill.

HERMIA   I give him curses; yet he gives me love.

HELENA   O that my prayers could such affection move.

HERMIA   The more I hate, the more he follows me.

HELENA   The more I love, the more he hateth me.

HERMIA   His folly, Helena, is no fault of mine.   200

HELENA   None, but your beauty; would that fault were mine.

HERMIA   Take comfort: he no more shall see my face:
Lysander and myself will fly this place.
Before the time I did Lysander see,
Seemed Athens as a paradise to me:
O then, what graces in my love do dwell,
That he hath turned a heaven unto a hell!

LYSANDER Helen, to you our minds we will unfold:
Tomorrow night, when Phoebe doth behold
Her silver visage in the wat'ry glass,   210
Decking with liquid pearl the bladed grass –
A time that lovers' flights doth still conceal –

	Through Athens' gates have we devised to steal.
HERMIA	And in the wood, where often you and I

Through Athens' gates have we devised to steal.

HERMIA   And in the wood, where often you and I
Upon faint primrose beds were wont to lie,
Emptying our bosoms of their counsel sweet,
There my Lysander and myself shall meet,
And thence from Athens turn away our eyes,
To seek new friends and stranger companies.
Farewell, sweet playfellow: pray thou for us   220
And good luck grant thee thy Demetrius!
Keep word, Lysander: we must starve our sight
From lovers' food till morrow deep midnight. [*she goes*

LYSANDER   I will, my Hermia. Helena, adieu:
As you on him, Demetrius dote on you!   [*he goes*

HELENA   How happy some o'er other some can be!
Through Athens I am thought as fair as she,
But what of that? Demetrius thinks not so:
He will not know what all but he do know.
And as he errs, doting on Hermia's eyes,   230
So I, admiring of his qualities.
Things base and vile, holding no quantity,
Love can transpose to form and dignity.
Love looks not with the eyes, but with the mind:
And therefore is winged Cupid painted blind.
Nor hath Love's mind of any judgment taste:
Wings and no eyes figure unheedy haste.
And therefore is Love said to be a child,
Because in choice he is so oft beguiled.
As waggish boys in game themselves forswear,   240
So the boy Love is perjured every where.
For ere Demetrius looked on Hermia's eyne,
He hailed down oaths that he was only mine.
And when this hail some heat from Hermia felt,
So he dissolved, and show'rs of oaths did melt.
I will go tell him of fair Hermia's flight:
Then to the wood will he tomorrow night
Pursue her: and for this intelligence
If I have thanks, it is a dear expense:
But herein mean I to enrich my pain,   250
To have his sight thither and back again.   [*she goes*

SCENE 2

A room in the cottage of Peter Quince

QUINCE, BOTTOM, SNUG, FLUTE, SNOUT, *and* STARVELING

QUINCE   Is all our company here?

BOTTOM   You were best to call them generally, man by man, according to the scrip.

QUINCE   Here is the scroll of every man's name, which is thought fit, through all Athens, to play in our interlude before the duke and the duchess, on his wedding-day at night.

BOTTOM   First, good Peter Quince, say what the play treats on: then read the names of the actors: and so grow to a point.   10

QUINCE   Marry, our play is 'The most lamentable comedy, and most cruel death, of Pyramus and Thisby.'

BOTTOM   A very good piece of work, I assure you, and a merry. Now, good Peter Quince, call forth your actors by the scroll. Masters, spread yourselves.

QUINCE   Answer, as I call you. Nick Bottom, the weaver.

BOTTOM   Ready: name what part I am for, and proceed.

QUINCE   You, Nick Bottom, are set down for Pyramus.

BOTTOM   What is Pyramus? A lover, or a tyrant?

QUINCE   A lover that kills himself, most gallant for love.   20

BOTTOM   That will ask some tears in the true performing of it. If I do it, let the audience look to their eyes: I will move storms: I will condole in some measure. To the rest — yet my chief humour is for a tyrant. I could play Ercles rarely, or a part to tear a cat in, to make all split.

                         'The raging rocks
                          And shivering shocks
                          Shall break the locks
                             Of prison-gates,
                          And Phibbus' car   30
                          Shall shine from far
                          And make and mar
                             The foolish Fates.'

This was lofty. Now name the rest of the players. This

	is Ercles' vein, a tyrant's vein: a lover is more condoling.
QUINCE	Francis Flute, the bellows-mender.
FLUTE	Here, Peter Quince.
QUINCE	Flute, you must take Thisby on you.
FLUTE	What is Thisby? A wand'ring knight?
QUINCE	It is the lady that Pyramus must love.

QUINCE   It is the lady that Pyramus must love.   40

FLUTE   Nay, faith: let not me play a woman: I have a beard
         coming.

quince   That's all one: you shall play it in a mask: and you may
         speak as small as you will.

BOTTOM   An I may hide my face, let me play Thisby too: I'll
         speak in a monstrous little voice. 'Thisne? Thisne?' –
         'Ah, Pyramus, my lover dear, thy Thisby dear, and
         lady dear.'

QUINCE   No, no, you must play Pyramus: and Flute, you
         Thisby.   50

BOTTOM   Well, proceed.

QUINCE   Robin Starveling, the tailor.

STARV'LING Here, Peter Quince.

QUINCE   Robin Starveling, you must play Thisby's mother. Tom
         Snout, the tinker.

SNOUT   Here, Peter Quince.

QUINCE   You, Pyramus' father; myself, Thisby's father; Snug,
         the joiner, you the lion's part: and I hope here is a play
         fitted.

SNUG   Have you the lion's part written? pray you, if it be,   60
         give it me: for I am slow of study.

QUINCE   You may do it extempore: for it is nothing but roar-
         ing.

BOTTOM   Let me play the lion too. I will roar that I will do any
         man's heart good to hear me. I will roar that I will
         make the duke say, 'Let him roar again: let him roar
         again.'

QUINCE   An you should do it too terribly, you would fright the
         duchess and the ladies, that they would shriek: and that
         were enough to hang us all.   70

ALL   That would hang us, every mother's son.

BOTTOM   I grant you, friends, if you should fright the ladies out
         of their wits, they would have no more discretion but

	to hang us: but I will aggravate my voice so, that I will roar you as gently as any sucking dove: I will roar you an 'twere any nightingale.
QUINCE	You can play no part but Pyramus: for Pyramus is a sweet-faced man; a proper man as one shall see in a summer's day; a most lovely, gentleman-like man: therefore you must needs play Pyramus.
BOTTOM	Well, I will undertake it. What beard were I best to play it in?
QUINCE	Why, what you will.
BOTTOM	I will discharge it in either your straw-colour beard, your orange-tawny beard, your purple-in-grain beard, or your French-crown-colour beard, your perfect yellow.
QUINCE	Some of your French crowns have no hair at all; and then you will play barefaced. [*he distributes strips of paper among them*] But, masters, here are your parts, and I am to entreat you, request you, and desire you, to con them by tomorrow night: and meet me in the palace wood, a mile without the town, by moon-light; there will we rehearse: for if we meet in the city, we shall be dogged with company, and our devices known. In the meantime, I will draw a bill of properties, such as our play wants. I pray you, fail me not.
BOTTOM	We will meet, and there we may rehease most obscenely and courageously. Take pains, be perfect: adieu.
QUINCE	At the duke's oak we meet.
BOTTOM	Enough: hold, or cut bow-strings. [*they go*

80

90

100

ACT 2 SCENE I

The palace wood, a league from Athens. A mossy stretch
of broken ground, cleared of trees by wood-cutters and
surrounded by thickets. Moonlight.

PUCK *and a* FAIRY, *meeting*

PUCK	How now, spirit! Whither wander you?
FAIRY	Over hill, over dale,
	Thorough bush, thorough briar,
	Over park, over pale,
	Thorough flood, thorough fire,
	I do wander everywhere,
	Swifter than the moonës sphere:
	And I serve the Fairy Queen,
	To dew her orbs upon the green.

The cowslips tall her pensioners be,   10
In their gold coats spots you see:
Those be rubies, fairy favours:
In those freckles live their savours.
I must go seek some dewdrops here,
And hang a pearl in every cowslip's ear.
Farewell, thou lob of spirits: I'll be gone –
Our queen and all her elves come here anon.

PUCK   The king doth keep his revels here tonight.
Take heed the queen come not within his sight.
For Oberon is passing fell and wrath,   20
Because that she as her attendant hath
A lovely boy, stol'n from an Indian king:
She never had so sweet a changeling.
And jealous Oberon would have the child
Knight of his train, to trace the forests wild.
But she, perforce, withholds the lovéd boy,
Crowns him with flowers, and makes him all her joy.
And now they never meet in grove, or green,
By fountain clear, or spangled starlight sheen,
But they do square – that all their elves, for fear,   30

Creep into acorn cups and hide them there.

FAIRY Either I mistake your shape and making quite,
Or else you are that shrewd and knavish sprite
Called Robin Goodfellow. Are not you he
That frights the maidens of the villagery,
Skim milk, and sometimes labour in the quern,
And bootless make the breathless housewife churn,
And sometime make the drink to bear no barm,
Mislead night-wanderers, laughing at their harm?
Those that Hobgoblin call you and sweet Puck,   40
You do their work, and they shall have good luck
Are not you he?

PUCK   Thou speak'st aright;
I am that merry wanderer of the night.
I jest to Oberon, and make him smile
When I a fat and bean-fed horse beguile,
Neighing in likeness of a filly foal;
And sometime lurk I in a gossip's bowl,
In very likeness of a roasted crab,
And, when she drinks, against her lips I bob,
And on her withered dewlap pour the ale.   50
The wisest aunt, telling the saddest tale,
Sometime for three-foot stool mistaketh me:
Then slip I from her bum, down topples she,
And 'tailor' cries, and falls into a cough:
And then the whole choir hold their hips and laugh,
And waxen in their mirth, and neeze, and swear
A merrier hour was never wasted there.
But room, faëry: here comes Oberon.

FAIRY And here my mistress. Would that he were gone.

The clearing is suddenly thronged with fairies:
OBERON *and* TITANIA *confront each other*

OBERON Ill met by moonlight, proud Titania.   60
TITANIA What, jealous Oberon! Fairies, skip hence –
I have forsworn his bed and company.
OBERON Tarry, rash wanton. Am not I thy lord?
TITANIA Then I must be thy lady: but I know
When thou hast stol'n away from fairy land,

And in the shape of Corin sat all day,
Playing on pipes of corn, and versing love,
To amorous Phillida. Why art thou here,
Come from the farthest steep of India?
But that, forsooth, the bouncing Amazon,   70
Your buskined mistress and your warrior love,
To Theseus must be wedded; and you come
To give their bed joy and prosperity.

OBERON   How canst thou thus for shame, Titania,
Glance at my credit with Hippolyta,
Knowing I know thy love to Theseus?
Didst thou not lead him through the glimmering night
From Perigouna, whom he ravishéd?
And make him with fair Aegles break his faith,
With Ariadne, and Antiopa?   80

TITANIA   These are the forgeries of jealousy:
And never, since the middle summer's spring,
Met we on hill, in dale, forest, or mead,
By pavéd fountain, or by rushy brook,
Or in the beachéd margent of the sea,
To dance our ringlets to the whistling wind,
But with thy brawls thou hast disturbed our sport.
Therefore the winds, piping to us in vain,
As in revenge, have sucked up from the sea
Contagious fogs: which falling in the land,   90
Hath every pelting river made so proud
That they have overborne their continents.
The ox hath therefore stretched his yoke in vain,
The ploughman lost his sweat, and the green corn
Hath rotted ere his youth attained a beard;
The fold stands empty in the drownéd field,
And crows are fatted with the murrion flock;
The nine men's morris is filled up with mud,
And the quaint mazes in the wanton green
For lack of tread are indistinguishable.   100
The human mortals want their winter cheer;
No night is now with hymn or carol blest;
Therefore the moon, the governess of floods,

Pale in her anger, washes all the air,
That rheumatic diseases do abound.
And thorough this distemperature we see
The seasons alter: hoary-headed frosts
Fall in the fresh lap of the crimson rose,
And on old Hiems' thin and icy crown
An odorous chaplet of sweet summer buds   110
Is, as in mockery, set. The spring, the summer,
The childing autumn, angry winter, change
Their wonted liveries; and the mazéd world,
By their increase, now knows not which is which.
And this same progeny of evils comes
From our debate, from our dissension:
We are their parents and original.

OBERON   Do you amend it then: it lies in you.
Why should Titania cross her Oberon?
I do but beg a little changeling boy,   120
To be my henchman.

TITANIA   Set your heart at rest,
The fairy land buys not the child of me.
His mother was a vot'ress of my order;
And in the spicéd Indian air, by night,
Full often hath she gossiped by my side;
And sat with me on Neptune's yellow sands,
Màrking th' embarkéd traders on the flood;
When we have laughed to see the sails conceive
And grow big-bellied with the wanton wind;
Which she, with pretty and with swimming gait   130
Following – her womb then rich with my young
                                        squire –
Would imitate, and sail upon the land,
To fetch me trifles, and return again,
As from a voyage, rich with merchandise.
But she, being mortal, of that boy did die;
And for her sake do I rear up her boy;
And for her sake I will not part with him.

OBERON   How long within this wood intend you stay?
TITANIA   Perchance till after Theseus' wedding-day.

	If you will patiently dance in our round,	140
	And see our moonlight revels, go with us:	
	If not, shun me, and I will spare your haunts.	
OBERON	Give me that boy, and I will go with thee.	
TITANIA	Not for thy fairy kingdom. Fairies, away!	
	We shall chide downright, if I longer stay.	

[Titania departs in anger with her train

OBERON Well, go thy way. Thou shalt not from this grove,
Till I torment thee for this injury.
My gentle Puck, come hither. Thou rememb'rest
Since once I sat upon a promontory,
And heard a mermaid, on a dolphin's back,   150
Uttering such dulcet and harmonious breath
That the rude sea grew civil at her song,
And certain stars shot madly from their spheres
To hear the sea-maid's music.
PUCK   I remember.
OBERON That very time I saw – but thou couldst not –
Flying between the cold moon and the earth,
Cupid all armed: a certain aim he took
At a fair Vestal, thronéd by the west,
And loosed his love-shaft smartly from his bow,
As it should pierce a hundred thousand hearts   160
But I might see young Cupid's fiery shaft
Quenched in the chaste beams of the wat'ry moon:
And the imperial Vot'ress passéd on,
In maiden meditation, fancy-free.
Yet marked I where the bolt of Cupid fell.
It fell upon a little western flower;
Before, milk-white; now purple with love's wound –
And maidens call it Love-in-idleness.
Fetch me that flower, the herb I showed thee once.
The juice of it, on sleeping eyelids laid,   170
Will make or man or woman madly dote
Upon the next live creature that it sees.
Fetch me this herb, and be thou here again
Ere the leviathan can swim a league.
PUCK I'll put a girdle round about the earth

In forty minutes.   *[he vanishes*

OBERON   Having once this juice,
I'll watch Titania when she is asleep,
And drop the liquor of it in her eyes:
The next thing then she waking looks upon —
Be it on lion, bear, or wolf, or bull,   180
On meddling monkey, or on busy ape —
She shall pursue it with the soul of love.
And ere I take this charm from off her sight —
As I can take it with another herb —
I'll make her render up her page to me.
But who comes here? I am invisible,
And I will overhear their conference.

DEMETRIUS *enters the clearing,* 'HELENA *following him'*

DEMETR.   I love thee not. Therefore pursue me not.
Where is Lysander and fair Hermia?
The one I'll slay. The other slayeth me.   190
Thou told'st me they were stol'n unto this wood:
And here am I, and wood within this wood,
Because I cannot meet my Hermia:
Hence, get thee gone, and follow me no more.

HELENA   You draw me, you hard-hearted adamant;
But yet you draw not iron, for my heart
Is true as steel. Leave you your power to draw,
And I shall have no power to follow you.

DEMETR.   Do I entice you? Do I speak you fair?
Or rather do I not in plainest truth   200
Tell you I do not nor I cannot love you?

HELENA   And even for that do I love you the more:
I am your spaniel; and, Demetrius,
The more you beat me, I will fawn on you.
Use me but as your spaniel: spurn me, strike me,
Neglect me, lose me: only give me leave,
Unworthy as I am, to follow you.
What worser place can I beg in your love —
And yet a place of high respect with me —
Than to be uséd as you use your dog?   210

DEMETR.   Tempt not too much the hatred of my spirit,
For I am sick when I do look on thee.

HELENA	And I am sick when I look not on you.
DEMETR.	You do impeach your modesty too much
	To leave the city and commit yourself
	Into the hands of one that loves you not,
	To trust the opportunity of night
	And the ill counsel of a desert place
	With the rich worth of your virginity.
HELENA	Your virtue is my privilege for that 220
	It is not night when I do see your face,
	Therefore I think I am not in the night –
	Nor doth this wood lack worlds of company,
	For you in my respect are all the world.
	Then how can it be said I am alone
	When all the world is here to look on me?
DEMETR.	I'll run from thee and hide me in the brakes,
	And leave thee to the mercy of wild beasts.
HELENA	The wildest hath not such a heart as you.
	Run when you will; the story shall be changed. 230
	Apollo flies, and Daphne holds the chase;
	The dove pursues the griffin; the mild hind
	Makes speed to catch the tiger. Bootless speed,
	When cowardice pursues and valour flies.
DEMETR.	I will not stay thy questions – let me go:
	Or, if thou follow me, do not believe
	But I shall do thee mischief in the wood.
HELENA	Ay, in the temple, in the town, the field,
	You do me mischief. Fie, Demetrius!
	Your wrongs do set a scandal on my sex 240
	We cannot fight for love, as men may do;
	We should be wooed and were not made to woo.

                 [*he goes*

    I'll follow thee and make a heaven of hell,
    To die upon the hand I love so well. [*she follows after*

OBERON	Fare thee well, nymph. Ere he do leave this grove,
	Thou shalt fly him, and he shall seek thy love.

        PUCK *reappears*

    Welcome, wanderer. Hast thou the flower there?

PUCK	Ay, there it is.
OBERON	I pray thee, give it me.

I know a bank where the wild thyme blows,
Where oxlips and the nodding violet grows,   250
Quite over-canopied with luscious woodbine,
With sweet musk-roses, and with eglantine:
There sleeps Titania sometime of the night,
Lulled in these flowers with dances and delight;
And there the snake throws her enamelled skin,
Weed wide enough to wrap a fairy in.
And with the juice of this I'll streak her eyes,
And make her full of hateful fantasies.
Take thou some of it, and seek through this grove:
A sweet Athenian lady is in love   260
With a disdainful youth; anoint his eyes –
But do it when the next thing he espies
May be the lady. Thou shalt know the man
By the Athenian garments he hath on.
Effect it with some care, that he may prove
More fond on her than she upon her love.
And look thou meet me ere the first cock crow.

PUCK   Fear not, my lord: your servant shall do so.

                                        [*they depart*

SCENE 2

Another part of the wood. A grassy plot before a great oak-tree,
behind the tree a high bank overhung with creepers, and at one
side a thorn-bush. The air is heavy with the scent of blossom

TITANIA *lies couched in her bower beneath the bank;*
her fairies attending her

TITANIA   Come now, a roundel and a fairy song:
Then, for the third part of a minute, hence –
Some to kill cankers in the musk-rose buds,
Some war with rere-mice for their leathern wings,
To make my small elves coats, and some keep back
The clamorous owl that nightly hoots and wonders
At our quaint spirits. Sing me now asleep;
Then to your offices, and let me rest.

'Fairies sing'

You spotted snakes, with double tongue,
   Thorny hedgehogs, be not seen;   10
Newts and blind-worms do no wrong,
   Come not near our Fairy Queen.

   Philomele, with melody,
   Sing in our sweet lullaby,
      Lulla, lulla, lullaby,
      Lulla, lulla, lullaby,
    Never harm,
    Nor spell, nor charm,
   Come our lovely lady nigh.
   So good night, with lullaby.   20

1 FAIRY   Weaving spiders come not here:
   Hence you long-legged spinners, hence:
Beetles black approach not near:
   Worm nor snail do no offence.

   Philomele, with melody,
   Sing in our sweet lullaby,
      Lulla, lulla, lullaby,
      Lulla, lulla, lullaby,
    Never harm,
    Nor spell, nor charm   30
   Come our lovely lady nigh.
   So good night, with lullaby.   *[Titania sleeps*

2 FAIRY   Hence, away: now all is well:
   One aloof stand sentinel.   *[the fairies steal away*

   OBERON *appears, hovering above the bank; he alights and*
   anoints the eyes of Titania with the juice of the flower

OBERON   What thou see'st when thou dost wake,
   Do it for thy true-love take;
   Love and languish for his sake.
   Be it ounce, or cat, or bear,
   Pard, or boar with bristled hair,
   In thy eye that shall appear   40
   When thou wak'st, it is thy dear:
   Wake when some vile thing is near.   *[he vanishes*

LYSANDER approaches with HERMIA leaning upon his arm

LYSANDER   Fair love, you faint with wand'ring in the wood;
           And to speak troth I have forgot our way.
           We'll rest us, Hermia, if you think it good,
           And tarry for the comfort of the day.

HERMIA   Be't so, Lysander: find you out a bed:
           For I upon this bank will rest my head.

LYSANDER   One turf shall serve as pillow for us both,
           One heart, one bed, two bosoms, and one troth.   50

HERMIA   Nay, good Lysander: for my sake, my dear,
           Lie further off yet; do not lie so near.

LYSANDER   O take the sense, sweet, of my innocence!
           Love takes the meaning in love's conference.
           I mean that my heart unto yours is knit,
           So that but one heart we can make of it:
           Two bosoms interchainéd with an oath,
           So then two bosoms and a single troth.
           Then by your side no bed-room me deny,
           For lying so, Hermia, I do not lie.   60

HERMIA   Lysander riddles very prettily.
           Now much beshrew my manners and my pride,
           If Hermia meant to say Lysander lied.
           But, gentle friend, for love and courtesy
           Lie further off – in human modesty:
           Such separation as may well be said
           Becomes a virtuous bachelor and a maid.
           So far be distant – and good night, sweet friend:
           Thy love ne'er alter till thy sweet life end!

LYSANDER   Amen, amen, to that fair prayer, say I –   70
           And then end life when I end loyalty!
           Here is my bed: sleep give thee all his rest.

HERMIA   With half that wish the wisher's eyes be pressed.

                                        ['*they sleep*'

                    PUCK *appears*

PUCK   Through the forest have I gone,
              But Athenian found I none
              On whose eyes I might approve
              This flower's force in stirring love.

Night and silence – who is here?
Weeds of Athens he doth wear:
This is he, my master said,   80
Despiséd the Athenian maid:
And here the maiden, sleeping sound,
On the dank and dirty ground.
Pretty soul, she durst not lie
Near this lack-love, this kill-courtesy.
                    [*he anoints the eyelids of Lysander*
Churl, upon thy eyes I throw
All the power this charm doth owe:
When thou wak'st, let love forbid
Sleep his seat on thy eyelid.
So awake when I am gone;   90
For I must now to Oberon.   [*he vanishes*

'*Enter* DEMETRIUS *and* HELENA, *running*'

HELENA   Stay; though thou kill me, sweet Demetrius.
DEMETR.   I charge thee, hence, and do not haunt me thus.
HELENA   O, wilt thou darkling leave me? Do not so.
DEMETR.   Stay, on thy peril; I alone will go.
                [*he breaks from her and disappears into the wood*
HELENA   O, I am out of breath in this fond chase!
          The more my prayer, the lesser is my grace.
          Happy is Hermia, wheresoe'er she lies;
          For she hath blesséd and attractive eyes.
          How came her eyes so bright? Not with salt tears –   100
          If so, my eyes are oft'ner washed than hers.
          No, no: I am as ugly as a bear,
          For beasts that meet me run away for fear.
          Therefore no marvel though Demetrius
          Do, as a monster, fly my presence thus.
          What wicked and dissembling glass of mine
          Made me compare with Hermia's sphery eyne?
          But who is here? Lysander! On the ground!
          Dead? Or asleep? I see no blood, no wound.
          Lysander, if you live, good sir, awake.   110
LYSANDER [*leaps up*]
          And run through fire I will, for thy sweet sake.
          Transparent Helena! Nature shows her art,

That through thy bosom makes me see thy heart.
Where is Demetrius? O, how fit a word
Is that vile name to perish on my sword!

HELENA   Do not say so, Lysander, say not so.
What though he love your Hermia? Lord! what
                             though?
Yet Hermia still loves you: then be content.

LYSANDER Content with Hermia? No: I do repent
The tedious minutes I with her have spent.   120
Not Hermia, but Helena I love –
Who will not change a raven for a dove?
The will of man is by his reason swayed;
And reason says you are the worthier maid.
Things growing are not ripe until their season:
So I, being young, till now ripe not to reason –
And touching now the point of human skill,
Reason becomes the marshal to my will,
And leads me to your eyes; where I o'erlook
Love's stories, written in Love's richest book.   130

HELENA   Wherefore was I to this keen mockery born?
When at your hands did I deserve this scorn?
Is't not enough, is't not enough, young man,
That I did never, no, nor never can,
Deserve a sweet look from Demetrius' eye,
But you must flout my insufficiency?
Good troth, you do me wrong, good sooth, you do,
In such disdainful manner me to woo.
But fare you well: perforce I must confess
I thought you lord of more true gentleness.   140
O, that a lady, of one man refused,
Should of another therefore be abused!   [she goes

LYSANDER She sees not Hermia. Hermia, sleep thou there,
And never mayst thou come Lysander near.
For, as a surfeit of the sweetest things
The deepest loathing to the stomach brings,
Or as the heresies that men do leave
Are hated most of those they did deceive,
So thou, my surfeit and my heresy,
Of all be hated, but the most of me!   150

And all my powers, address your love and might
To honour Helen, and to be her knight.

[he follows Helena

HERMIA   [*awaking*] Help me, Lysander, help me; do thy best
To pluck this crawling serpent from my breast.
Ay me, for pity! What a dream was here?
Lysander, look how I do quake with fear.
Methought a serpent eat my heart away,
And you sat smiling at his cruel prey.
Lysander! What, removed? Lysander! Lord!
What, out of hearing gone? No sound, no word?   160
Alack, where are you? Speak, an if you hear;
Speak, of all loves! I swoon almost with fear.
No? Then I will perceive you are not nigh.
Either death or you I'll find immediately.   *[she goes*

ACT 3 SCENE 1

QUINCE *(carrying a bag)*, SNUG, BOTTOM, FLUTE,
SNOUT, *and* STARVELING *come up severally or in pairs
and gather beneath the oak-tree*

BOTTOM	Are we all met?
QUINCE	Pat, pat: and here's a marvellous convenient place for our rehearsal. This green plot shall be our stage, this hawthorn-brake our tiring-house – and we will do it in action as we will do it before the duke.
BOTTOM	Peter Quince!
QUINCE	What say'st thou, bully Bottom?
BOTTOM	There are things in this comedy of Pyramus and Thisby that will never please. First, Pyramus must draw a sword to kill himself; which the ladies cannot abide. 10 How answer you that?
SNOUT	By'r lakin, a parlous fear.
STARV'LING	I believe we must leave the killing out, when all is done.
BOTTOM	Not a whit: I have a device to make all well. Write me a prologue, and let the prologue seem to say we will do no harm with our swords, and that Pyramus is not killed indeed: and, for the more better assurance, tell them that I, Pyramus, am not Pyramus but Bottom the weaver: this will put them out of fear.
QUINCE	Well, we will have such a prologue, and it shall be 20 written in eight and six.
BOTTOM	No, make it two more: let it be written in eight and eight.
SNOUT	Will not the ladies be afeard of the lion?
STARV'LING	I fear it, I promise you.
BOTTOM	Masters, you ought to consider with yourselves – to bring in (God shield us!) a lion among ladies is a most dreadful thing. For there is not a more fearful wild-fowl than your lion living; and we ought to look to't.
SNOUT	Therefore, another prologue must tell he is not a lion. 30
BOTTOM	Nay, you must name his name, and half his face must be

seen through the lion's neck, and he himself must speak
through, saying thus, or to the same defect: 'Ladies', or
'Fair ladies – I would wish you', or 'I would request
you', or 'I would entreat you, not to fear, not to tremble: my life for yours. If you think I come hither as a
lion, it were pity of my life. No: I am no such thing: I
am a man as other men are.' And there indeed let him
name his name, and tell them plainly he is Snug the
joiner.   40

QUINCE   Well, it shall be so. But there is two hard things: that is,
to bring the moonlight into a chamber: for you know,
Pyramus and Thisby meet by moonlight.

SNOUT   Doth the moon shine that night we play our play?

BOTTOM   A calendar, a calendar! Look in the almanac; find out
moonshine, find out moonshine.

QUINCE *takes an almanac from his bag and searches therein*

QUINCE   Yes, it doth shine that night.

BOTTOM   Why, then may you leave a casement of the great
chamber window, where we play, open; and the
moon may shine in at the casement.   50

QUINCE   Ay, or else one must come in with a bush of thorns and
a lantern, and say he comes to disfigure or to present
the person of Moonshine. Then, there is another thing:
we must have a wall in the great chamber; for Pyramus
and Thisby, says the story, did talk through the chink
of a wall.

SNOUT   You can never bring in a wall. What say you, Bottom?

BOTTOM   Some man or other must present wall; and let him have
some plaster, or some loam, or some rough-cast about
him, to signify wall; and let him hold his fingers thus 60
[*he stretches out his fingers*], and through that cranny shall
Pyramus and Thisby whisper.

QUINCE   If that may be, then all is well. [*takes out a book and
opens it*] Come, sit down, every mother's son, and
rehearse your parts. Pyramus, you begin: when you
have spoken your speech, enter into that brake – and so
every one according to his cue.

PUCK *appears behind the oak*

PUCK   What hempen home-spuns have we swagg'ring here,
            So near the cradle of the Fairy Queen?
            What, a play toward? I'll be an auditor,   70
            An actor too perhaps, if I see cause.
QUINCE   Speak, Pyramus. Thisby, stand forth.
BOTTOM   'Thisby, the flowers ha' odious savours sweet' —
QUINCE   [*prompts*] 'Odious' — odorous!
BOTTOM   — 'odours savours sweet,
            So hath thy breath, my dearest Thisby dear.
            But hark, a voice! Stay thou but here awhile,
            And by and by I will to thee appear.' [*exit into the brake*
PUCK   A stranger Pyramus than e'er played here!
                                        [*he follows Bottom*
FLUTE   Must I speak now?   80
QUINCE   Ay, marry, must you. For you must understand he
            goes but to see a noise that he heard, and is to come
            again.
FLUTE   'Most radiant Pyramus, most lily-white of hue,
            Of colour like the red rose on triumphant briar,
            Most brisky juvenal, and eke most lovely Jew,
            As true as truest horse that yet would never tire,
            I'll meet thee, Pyramus, at Ninny's tomb.'
QUINCE   'Ninus' tomb', man! Why, you must not speak that yet!
            That you answer to Pyramus. You speak all your part 90
            at once, cues and all. Pyramus enter; your cue is past; it
            is, 'never tire'.
FLUTE   O — 'As true as truest horse that yet would never tire.'

            Enter from the brake BOTTOM *with an ass's head;* PUCK *following*

BOTTOM   'If I were fair, Thisby, I were only thine.'
QUINCE   O monstrous! O strange! We are haunted.
            Pray, masters! Fly, masters! Help!
                            [*they all run away and hide them in the bushes*
PUCK   I'll follow you: I'll lead you about a round,
            Through bog, through bush, through brake, through
                                                        briar;
            Sometime a horse I'll be, sometime a hound,
            A hog, a headless bear, sometime a fire,   100
            And neigh, and bark, and grunt, and roar, and burn,

Like horse, hound, hog, bear, fire, at every turn.

[he pursues them

BOTTOM   Why do they run away? This is a knavery of them to
make me afeard.

SNOUT *peers from behind a bush*

SNOUT   O Bottom, thou art changed! What do I see on thee?

BOTTOM   What do you see? You see an ass-head of your own, do
you?   *[Snout disappears*

QUINCE *stealthily returns*

QUINCE   Bless thee Bottom, bless thee! Thou art translated.

[he turns and flees

BOTTOM   I see their knavery. This is to make an ass of me, to
fright me if they could: but I will not stir from this   110
place, do what they can. I will walk up and down here,
and will sing that they shall hear I am not afraid.

[he sings through his nose, braying at whiles

The ousel cock, so black of hue,
With orange-tawny bill,
The throstle with his note so true,
The wren with little quill . . .

TITANIA   *[comes from the bower]*
What angel wakes me from my flow'ry bed?

BOTTOM   The finch, the sparrow, and the lark,
The plain-song cuckoo gray,
Whose note full many a man doth mark,   120
And dares not answer, nay . . .
For indeed, who would set his wit to so foolish a bird?
Who would give a bird the lie, though he cry 'cuckoo'
never so?

TITANIA   I pray thee, gentle mortal, sing again!
Mine ear is much enamoured of thy note;
So is mine eye enthrallèd to thy shape,
And thy fair virtue's force – perforce – doth move me,
On the first view, to say, to swear, I love thee.

BOTTOM   Methinks, mistress, you should have little reason for   130
that. And yet, to say the truth, reason and love keep
little company together now-a-days. The more the
pity, that some honest neighbours will not make them

	friends. Nay, I can gleek upon occasion.
TITANIA	Thou art as wise as thou art beautiful.
BOTTOM	Not so, neither: but if I had wit enough to get out of this wood, I have enough to serve mine own turn.
TITANIA	Out of this wood do not desire to go:

Thou shalt remain here, whether thou wilt or no.
I am a spirit of no common rate: 140
The summer still doth tend upon my state,
And I do love thee: therefore go with me.
I'll give thee fairies to attend on thee:
And they shall fetch thee jewels from the deep,
And sing, while thou on presséd flowers dost sleep:
And I will purge thy mortal grossness so,
That thou shalt like an airy spirit go.   [*she calls*
Peaseblossom, Cobweb, Moth, and Mustardseed!
                        [*as she utters each name a fairy*
                          alights before her and replies

PEASE.	Ready!
COBWEB	And I –
MOTH	And I –
MUSTARD.	And I –
ALL	[*bowing*] Where shall we go?
TITANIA	Be kind and courteous to this gentleman; 150

Hop in his walks and gambol in his eyes,
Feed him with apricocks and dewberries,
With purple grapes, green figs, and mulberries;
The honey-bags steal from the humble-bees,
And for night-tapers crop their waxen thighs,
And light them at the fiery glow-worm's eyes,
To have my love to bed and to arise;
And pluck the wings from painted butterflies,
To fan the moonbeams from his sleeping eyes.
Nod to him, elves, and do him courtesies.   160

PEASE.	Hail, mortal!
COBWEB	Hail!
MOTH	Hail!
MUSTARD.	Hail!
BOTTOM	I cry your worships mercy, heartily. I beseech your worship's name.

COBWEB   [*bows*] Cobweb.

BOTTOM   I shall desire you of more acquaintance, good Master
Cobweb: if I cut my finger, I shall make bold with
you. Your name, honest gentleman?   170

PEASE.   [*bows*] Peaseblossom.

BOTTOM   I pray you, commend me to Mistress Squash, your
mother, and to Master Peascod, your father. Good Master Peaseblossom, I shall desire you of more acquaintance
too. Your name, I beseech you sir?

MUSTARD. [*bows*] Mustardseed.

BOTTOM   Good Master Mustardseed, I know your patience well.
That same cowardly, giant-like, Oxbeef hath devoured
many a gentleman of your house. I promise you your
kindred hath made my eyes water ere now. I desire   180
you of more acquaintance, good Master Mustardseed.

TITANIA Come, wait upon him; lead him to my bower.
The moon, methinks, looks with a wat'ry eye:
And when she weeps, weeps every little flower,
Lamenting some enforcéd chastity.
Tie up my love's tongue, bring him silently.

[*they move towards the bower*

SCENE 2

The clearing with the mossy slopes

OBERON *appears*

OBERON   I wonder if Titania be awaked;
Then, what it was that next came in her eye,
Which she must dote on in extremity.

PUCK *enters the clearing*

Here comes my messenger. How now, mad spirit?
What night-rule now about this haunted grove?

PUCK   My mistress with a monster is in love.
Near to her close and consecrated bower,
While she was in her dull and sleeping hour,
A crew of patches, rude mechanicals
That work for bread upon Athenian stalls,   10

Were met together to rehearse a play
Intended for great Theseus' nuptial-day.
The shallowest thick-skin of that barren sort,
Who Pyramus presented, in their sport
Forsook his scene and ent'red in a brake;
When I did him at this advantage take,
An ass's noll I fixéd on his head.
Anon his Thisbe must be answeréd,
And forth my mimic comes. When they him spy,
As wild geese that the creeping fowler eye,   20
Or russet-pated choughs, many in sort,
Rising and cawing at the gun's report,
Sever themselves and madly sweep the sky,
So, at his sight, away his fellows fly;
And at a stump here o'er and o'er one falls –
He 'murder' cries, and help from Athens calls.
Their sense thus weak, lost with their fears thus strong,
Made senseless things begin to do them wrong.
For briars and thorns at their apparel snatch:
Some sleeves, some hats; from yielders all things catch.   30
I led them on in this distracted fear,
And left sweet Pyramus translated there:
When in that moment (so it came to pass)
Titania waked and straightway loved an ass.

OBERON	This falls out better than I could devise.
	But hast thou yet latched the Athenian's eyes
	With the love-juice, as I did bid thee do?
PUCK	I took him sleeping – that is finished too –
	And the Athenian woman by his side;
	That, when he waked, of force she must be eyed. 40

DEMETRIUS and HERMIA approach

OBERON	Stand close; this is the same Athenian.
PUCK	This is the woman: but not this the man.
DEMETR.	O, why rebuke you him that loves you so?
	Lay breath so bitter on your bitter foe.
HERMIA	Now I but chide: but I should use thee worse,
	For thou, I fear, hast given me cause to curse.
	If thou hast slain Lysander in his sleep,

Being o'er-shoes in blood, plunge in the deep,
And kill me too.
The sun was not so true unto the day   50
As he to me. Would he have stolen away
From sleeping Hermia? I'll believe as soon
This whole earth may be bored, and that the moon
May through the centre creep and so displease
Her brother's noontide with th' Antipodes.
It cannot be but thou hast murd'red him –
So should a murderer look; so dead, so grim.

DEMETR.   So should the murdered look, and so should I,
Pierced through the heart with your stern cruelty.
Yet you, the murderer, look as bright, as clear,   60
As yonder Venus in her glimmering sphere.

HERMIA   What's this to my Lysander? Where is he?
Ah, good Demetrius, wilt thou give him me?

DEMETR.   I had rather give his carcase to my hounds.

HERMIA   Out, dog! Out, cur! Thou driv'st me past the bounds
Of maiden's patience. Hast thou slain him then?
Henceforth be never numb'red among men!
O, once tell true: tell true, even for my sake:
Durst thou have looked upon him being awake?
And hast thou killed him, sleeping? O brave touch!   70
Could not a worm, an adder, do so much?
An adder did it; for with doubler tongue
Than thine, thou serpent, never adder stung.

DEMETR.   You spend your passion on a misprised mood:
I am not guilty of Lysander's blood;
Nor is he dead, for aught that I can tell.

HERMIA   I pray thee, tell me then that he is well.

DEMETR.   An if I could, what should I get therefore?

HERMIA   A privilege never to see me more,
And from thy hated presence part I so   80
See me no more, whether he be dead or no.
                                        [she hurries away

DEMETR.   There is no following her in this fierce vein.
Here therefore for a while I will remain.
So sorrow's heaviness doth heavier grow
For debt that bankrupt sleep doth sorrow owe;

Which now in some slight measure it will pay,
If for his tender here I make some stay. [*he lies down*

OBERON What hast thou done? Thou hast mistaken quite,
And laid the love-juice on some true-love's sight.
Of thy misprision must perforce ensue   90
Some true love turned, and not a false turned true.

PUCK Then fate o'er-rules, that, one man holding troth,
A million fail, confounding oath on oath.

OBERON About the wood go swifter than the wind,
And Helena of Athens look thou find.
All fancy-sick she is, and pale of cheer
With sighs of love that costs the fresh blood dear.
By some illusion see thou bring her here:
I'll charm his eyes against she do appear.

PUCK I go, I go – look how I go –   100
Swifter than arrow from the Tartar's bow. [*he vanishes*

OBERON bends over the sleeping DEMETRIUS

OBERON   Flower of this purple dye,
            Hit with Cupid's archery,
            Sink in apple of his eye.
            When his love he doth espy,
            Let her shine as gloriously
            As the Venus of the sky.
            When thou wak'st, if she be by,
            Beg of her for remedy.

PUCK reappears

PUCK   Captain of our fairy band,   110
            Helena is here at hand,
            And the youth, mistook by me,
            Pleading for a lover's fee.
            Shall we their fond pageant see?
            Lord, what fools these mortals be!

OBERON   Stand aside. The noise they make
            Will cause Demetrius to awake.

PUCK   Then will two at once woo one;
            That must needs be sport alone.
            And those things do best please me   120
            That befall prepost'rously. [*they stand aside*

HELENA *comes up, followed by* LYSANDER

LYSANDER Why should you think that I should woo in scorn?
Scorn and derision never come in tears.
Look when I vow, I weep; and vows so born
In their nativity all truth appears.
How can these things in me seem scorn to you,
Bearing the badge of faith to prove them true?

HELENA You do advance your cunning more and more.
When truth kills truth, O devilish-holy fray!
These vows are Hermia's – will you give her o'er?   130
Weigh oath with oath, and you will nothing weigh:
Your vows, to her and me, put in two scales,
Will even weigh; and both as light as tales.

LYSANDER I had no judgment when to her I swore.

HELENA Nor none, in my mind, now you give her o'er.

LYSANDER Demetrius loves her: and he loves not you.

DEMETR. [*awaking*] O Helen, goddess, nymph, perfect, divine!
To what, my love, shall I compare thine eyne?
Crystal is muddy. O, how ripe in show
Thy lips, those kissing cherries, tempting grow!   140
That pure congealéd white, high Taurus' snow,
Fanned with the eastern wind, turns to a crow,
When thou hold'st up thy hand. O let me kiss
This princess of pure white, this seal of bliss!

HELENA O spite! O hell! I see you all are bent
To set against me for your merriment.
If you were civil and knew courtesy,
You would not do me thus much injury.
Can you not hate me, as I know you do,
But you must join in souls to mock me too?   150
If you were men, as men you are in show,
You would not use a gentle lady so:
To vow, and swear, and superpraise my parts,
When I am sure you hate me with your hearts.
You both are rivals, and love Hermia;
And now both rivals, to mock Helena.
A trim exploit, a manly enterprise,
To conjure tears up in a poor maid's eyes
With your derision! None of noble sort

| | Would so offend a virgin, and extort | 160 |

Would so offend a virgin, and extort   160
A poor soul's patience, all to make you sport.

LYSANDER   You are unkind, Demetrius; be not so –
For you love Hermia; this you know I know;
And here, with all good will, with all my heart,
In Hermia's love I yield you up my part:
And yours of Helena to me bequeath,
Whom I do love, and will do till my death.

HELENA   Never did mockers waste more idle breath.

DEMETR.   Lysander, keep thy Hermia: I will none.
If e'er I loved her, all that love is gone.   170
My heart to her but as guest-wise sojourned,
And now to Helen is it home returned,
There to remain.

LYSANDER   Helen, it is not so.

DEMETR.   Disparage not the faith thou dost not know,
Lest to thy peril thou aby it dear.

HERMIA is seen approaching

Look where thy love comes: yonder is thy dear.

HERMIA spies LYSANDER and runs towards him

HERMIA   Dark night, that from the eye his function takes,
The ear more quick of apprehension makes.
Wherein it doth impair the seeing sense,
It pays the hearing double recompense.   180
Thou art not by mine eye, Lysander, found;
Mine ear, I thank it, brought me to thy sound.
But why unkindly didst thou leave me so?

LYSANDER   [*turning away*]
Why should he stay whom love doth press to go?

HERMIA   What love could press Lysander from my side?

LYSANDER   Lysander's love, that would not let him bide –
Fair Helena! Who more engilds the night
Than all yon fiery oes and eyes of light.
Why seek'st thou me? Could not this make thee know
The hate I bear thee made me leave thee so?   190

HERMIA   You speak not as you think: it cannot be.

HELENA   Lo! She is one of this confederacy.
Now I perceive they have conjoined all three

To fashion this false sport in spite of me.
Injurious Hermia, most ungrateful maid,
Have you conspired, have you with these contrived,
To bait me with this foul derision?
Is all the counsel that we two have shared,
The sisters' vows, the hours that we have spent,
When we have chid the hasty-footed time   200
For parting us – O! Is all forgot?
All school-days' friendship, childhood innocence?
We, Hermia, like two artificial gods,
Have with our needles created both one flower,
Both on one sampler, sitting on one cushion,
Both warbling of one song, both in one key;
As if our hands, our sides, voices, and minds,
Had been incorporate. So we grew together,
Like to a double cherry, seeming parted,
But yet an union in partition,   210
Two lovely berries moulded on one stem:
So, with two seeming bodies, but one heart,
Two of the first, like coats in heraldry,
Due but to one, and crownéd with one crest.
And will you rend our ancient love asunder,
To join with men in scorning your poor friend?
It is not friendly, 'tis not maidenly –
Our sex, as well as I, may chide you for it;
Though I alone do feel the injury.

HERMIA   Helen, I am amazéd at your words.   220
I scorn you not – it seems that you scorn me.

HELENA   Have you not set Lysander, as in scorn,
To follow me and praise my eyes and face?
And made your other love, Demetrius
(Who even but now did spurn me with his foot!)
To call me goddess, nymph, divine and rare
Precious, celestial? Wherefore speaks he this
To her he hates? And wherefore doth Lysander
Deny your love (so rich within his soul)
And tender me (forsooth!) affection,   230
But by your setting on, by your consent?
What though I be not so in grace as you,

	So hung upon with love, so fortunate,
	But miserable most, to love unloved?
	This you should pity rather than despise.
HERMIA	I understand not what you mean by this.
HELENA	Ay, do! Perséver, counterfeit sad looks,
	Make mouths upon me when I turn my back,
	Wink at each other, hold the sweet jest up.
	This sport, well carried, shall be chronicled.

HERMIA I understand not what you mean by this.

HELENA Ay, do! Perséver, counterfeit sad looks,
Make mouths upon me when I turn my back,
Wink at each other, hold the sweet jest up.
This sport, well carried, shall be chronicled.   240
If you have any pity, grace, or manners,
You would not make me such an argument.
But, fare ye well: 'tis partly my own fault:
Which death or absence soon shall remedy.

LYSANDER Stay, gentle Helena; hear my excuse,
My love, my life, my soul, fair Helena!

HELENA O excellent!

HERMIA   Sweet, do not scorn her so.

DEMETR. If she cannot entreat, I can compel.

LYSANDER Thou canst compel no more than she entreat.
Thy threats have no more strength than her weak
                                        prayers.   250
Helen, I love thee – by my life I do;
I swear by that which I will lose for thee,
To prove him false that says I love thee not.

DEMETR. I say I love thee more than he can do.

LYSANDER If thou say so, withdraw, and prove it too.

DEMETR. Quick, come –

HERMIA [*staying him*]   Lysander, whereto tends all this?

LYSANDER Away, you Ethiop!

HERMIA   No, no!

DEMETR. [*scoffs*]   Ye will
Seem to break loose! Take on as you would follow!
But yet come not. You are a tame man, go!

LYSANDER Hang off, thou cat, thou burr! Vile thing, let loose;   260
Or I will shake thee from me like a serpent.

HERMIA Why are you grown so rude? What change is this,
Sweet love?   [*she keeps her hold upon him*

LYSANDER   Thy love! out, tawny Tartar, out!
Out, loathéd med'cine! O hated potion, hence!

HERMIA Do you not jest?

HELENA   Yes, sooth: and so do you.

LYSANDER Demetrius, I will keep my word with thee.

DEMETR.   I would I had your bond, for I perceive
          A weak bond holds you. I'll not trust your word.

LYSANDER What? Should I hurt her, strike her, kill her dead?
          Although I hate her, I'll not harm her so.   270

HERMIA   What? Can you do me greater harm than hate?
          Hate me! Wherefore? O me, what news, my love!
          Am not I Hermia? Are not you Lysander?
          I am as fair now as I was erewhile.
          Since night you loved me; yet since night you left me.
          Why then, you left me – O, the gods forbid! –
          In earnest, shall I say?

LYSANDER   Ay, by my life!
          And never did desire to see thee more.
          Therefore be out of hope, of question or doubt:
          Be certain: nothing truer: 'tis no jest   280
          That I do hate thee and love Helena.

HERMIA   [to Helena] O me, you juggler, you canker-blossom.
          You thief of love! What! Have you come by night
          And stol'n my love's heart from him?

HELENA   Fine, i'faith!
          Have you no modesty, no maiden shame,
          No touch of bashfulness? What! Will you tear
          Impatient answers from my gentle tongue?
          Fie, fie, you counterfeit, you puppet you!

HERMIA   'Puppet?' Why, so – ay, that way goes the game!
          Now I perceive that she hath made compare   290
          Between our statures; she hath urged her height;
          And with her personage, her tall personage,
          Her height, forsooth, she hath prevailed with him.
          And are you grown so high in his esteem
          Because I am so dwarfish and so low?
          How low am I, thou painted maypole? Speak;
          How low am I? I am not yet so low,
          But that my nails can reach unto thine eyes.
                              [she makes towards her

HELENA   I pray you, though you mock me, gentlemen,
          Let her not hurt me. I was never curst   300

I have no gift at all in shrewishness:
I am a right maid for my cowardice:
Let her not strike me. You perhaps may think,
Because she is something lower than myself,
That I can match her.

HERMIA   Lower! Hark, again.

HELENA Good Hermia, do not be so bitter with me.
I evermore did love you, Hermia,
Did ever keep your counsels, never wronged you;
Save that, in love unto Demetrius,
I told him of your stealth unto this wood.   310
He followed you; for love I followed him.
But he hath chid me hence, and threat'ned me
To strike me, spurn me; nay, to kill me too.
And now, so you will let me quiet go,
To Athens will I bear my folly back,
And follow you no further. Let me go.
You see how simple and how fond I am.

HERMIA Why, get you gone. Who is't that hinders you?

HELENA A foolish heart that I leave here behind.

HERMIA What! With Lysander?

HELENA   With Demetrius.   320

LYSANDER Be not afraid: she shall not harm thee, Helena.

DEMETR. No, sir; she shall not, though you take her part.

HELENA When she is angry, she is keen and shrewd.
She was a vixen when she went to school;
And though she be but little, she is fierce.

HERMIA 'Little' again? Nothing but 'low' and 'little'!
Why will you suffer her to flout me thus?
Let me come to her.

LYSANDER   Get you gone, you dwarf;
You minimus, of hind'ring knot-grass made;
You bead, you acorn.

DEMETR.   You are too officious   330
In her behalf that scorns your services.
Let her alone; speak not of Helena;
Take not her part; [*he draws his sword*]
                    for if thou dost intend
Never so little show of love to her,

Thou shalt aby it.

LYSANDER [*also draws*]   Now she holds me not;
Now follow, if thou dar'st, to try whose right,
Of thine or mine, is most in Helena.

[*he turns into the wood*

DEMETR. Follow! Nay, I'll go with thee, cheek by jowl.

[*he hastens after*

HERMIA You, mistress, all this coil is 'long of you:
Nay: go not back.

HELENA   I will not trust you, I,   340
Nor longer stay in your curst company.
Your hands than mine are quicker for a fray;
My legs are longer though to run away.   [*she runs off*

HERMIA I am amazed, and know not what to say.

[*she follows slowly*

OBERON [*to Puck*] This is thy negligence. Still thou mistak'st,
Or else commit'st thy knaveries wilfully.

PUCK Believe me, king of shadows, I mistook.
Did not you tell me I should know the man
By the Athenian garments he had on?
And so far blameless proves my enterprise   350
That I have 'nointed an Athenian's eyes:
And so far am I glad it so did sort,
As this their jangling I esteem a sport.

OBERON Thou see'st these lovers seek a place to fight:
Hie therefore, Robin, overcast the night,
The starry welkin cover thou anon
With drooping fog as black as Acheron,
And lead these testy rivals so astray,
As one come not within another's way.
Like to Lysander sometime frame thy tongue;   360
Then stir Demetrius up with bitter wrong;
And sometime rail thou like Demetrius:
And from each other look thou lead them thus;
Till o'er their brows death-counterfeiting sleep
With leaden legs and batty wings doth creep:
Then crush this herb into Lysander's eye;
Whose liquor hath this virtuous property,
To take from thence all error with his might,

And make his eyeballs roll with wonted sight.
When they next wake, all this derision   370
Shall seem a dream and fruitless vision,
And back to Athens shall the lovers wend
With league whose date till death shall never end.
Whiles I in this affair do thee employ,
I'll to my queen and beg her Indian boy;
And then I will her charméd eye release
From monster's view, and all things shall be peace.

PUCK   My fairy lord, this must be done with haste,
For night's swift dragons cut the clouds full fast;
And yonder shines Aurora's harbinger,   380
At whose approach ghosts wand'ring here and there,
Troop home to churchyards. Damnéd spirits all,
That in crossways and floods have burial,
Already to their wormy beds are gone;
For fear lest day should look their shames upon,
They wilfully themselves exile from light,
And must for aye consort with black-browed night.

OBERON   But we are spirits of another sort.
I with the morning's love have oft made sport,
And like a forester the groves may tread,   390
Even till the eastern gate, all fiery-red,
Opening on Neptune with fair blesséd beams,
Turns into yellow gold his salt green streams.
But, notwithstanding, haste – make no delay:
We may effect this business yet ere day.   [he goes

                    A fog descends

PUCK   Up and down, up and down,
              I will lead them up and down.
              I am feared in field and town.
              Goblin, lead them up and down.
              Here comes one.   [he vanishes 400

          LYSANDER *returns, groping in the dark*

LYSANDER Where art thou, proud Demetrius? Speak thou now.
PUCK   Here, villain! Drawn and ready. Where art thou?
LYSANDER I will be with thee straight.
PUCK   Follow me then

To plainer ground.   [*Lysander follows the voice*
               DEMETRIUS *approaches, groping likewise*

DEMETR.   Lysander! Speak again.
           Thou runaway, thou coward, art thou fled?
           Speak! In some bush? Where dost thou hide thy head?
PUCK   Thou coward, art thou bragging to the stars,
           Telling the bushes that thou look'st for wars,
           And wilt not come? Come recreant, come thou child,
           I'll whip thee with a rod. He is defiled   410
           That draws a sword on thee.
DEMETR.   Yea, art thou there?
PUCK   Follow my voice: we'll try no manhood here.
                        [*Demetrius follows the voice*
                    LYSANDER *returns*

LYSANDER   He goes before me and still dares me on:
           When I come where he calls, then he is gone.
           The villain is much lighter-heeled than I:
           I followed fast; but faster he did fly;
           That fallen am I in dark uneven way,
           And here will rest me.   [*he lies down upon a bank*]
                        Come, thou gentle day,
           For if but once thou show me thy grey light,
           I'll find Demetrius and revenge this spite.   [*he sleeps* 420
                    DEMETRIUS *returns, running*

PUCK   Ho, ho, ho! Coward, why com'st thou not?
DEMETR.   Abide me if thou dar'st, for well I wot
           Thou runn'st before me, shifting every place,
           And dar'st not stand, nor look me in the face.
           Where art thou now?
PUCK   Come hither; I am here.
DEMETR.   Nay, then thou mock'st me. Thou shalt buy this dear,
           If ever I thy face by daylight see.
           Now, go thy way. Faintness constraineth me
           To measure out my length on this cold bed.
           By day's approach look to be visited.   430
                   [*he lies down upon another bank and sleeps*

HELENA *enters the clearing*

HELENA O weary night, O long and tedious night,
          Abate thy hours! Shine comforts from the east,
        That I may back to Athens by daylight,
          From these that my poor company detest.
        And sleep, that sometimes shuts up sorrow's eye,
        Steal me awhile from mine own company.

                    [*she gropes her way to the bank where
                    Demetrius lies and falls asleep thereon*

PUCK *reappears*

PUCK   Yet but three? Come one more.
        Two of both kinds makes up four.
        Here she comes, curst and sad.
        Cupid is a knavish lad,   440
        Thus to make poor females mad.

HERMIA *returns, dejected*

HERMIA Never so weary, never so in woe;
          Bedabbled with the dew and torn with briars;
        I can no further crawl, no further go;
          My legs can keep no pace with my desires.
        Here will I rest me till the break of day.
        Heavens shield Lysander, if they mean a fray!

                    [*she gropes her way to the bank on
                    which Lysander lies and falls asleep*

PUCK   On the ground
                 Sleep sound:
                 I'll apply   450
                 To your eye,
              Gentle lover, remedy.

                    [*he anoints Lysander's eyes with the love-juice*
                 When thou wak'st,
                 Thou tak'st
                 True delight
                 In the sight
              Of thy former lady's eye:
              And the country proverb known,
              That every man should take his own,

In your waking shall be shown.　　　
Jack shall have Jill;
Nought shall go ill;
The man shall have his mare again, and all shall be well.
[he vanishes; the fog disperses

ACT 4 SCENE I

TITANIA *approaches with* BOTTOM, *his ass's head garlanded with flowers; fairies follow in their train;* OBERON *behind all, unseen*

TITANIA   Come, sit thee down upon this flow'ry bed,
    While I thy amiable cheeks do coy,
And stick musk-roses in thy sleek smooth head,
    And kiss thy fair large ears, my gentle joy.
                                    [*they sit; she embraces him*

BOTTOM   Where's Peaseblossom?

PEASE.   Ready.

BOTTOM   Scratch my head, Peaseblossom. Where's Monsieur Cobweb?

COBWEB   Ready.

BOTTOM   Monsieur Cobweb, good monsieur, get you your weap- 10
ons in your hand and kill me a red-hipped humble-bee
on the top of a thistle; and, good monsieur, bring me
the honey-bag. Do not fret yourself too much in the
action, monsieur; and, good monsieur, have a care the
honey-bag break not – I would be loath to have you
overflown with a honey bag, signior. Where's Monsieur
Mustardseed?

MUSTARD.   Ready.

BOTTOM   Give me your neaf, Monsieur Mustardseed. Pray you,
leave your curtsy, good monsieur.   20

MUSTARD.   What's your will?

BOTTOM   Nothing, good monsieur, but to help Cavalery Cobweb to scratch. I must to the barber's, monsieur; for
methinks I am marvellous hairy about the face – and I
am such a tender ass, if my hair do but tickle me I must
scratch.

TITANIA   What, wilt thou hear some music, my sweet love?

BOTTOM   I have a reasonable good ear in music. Let's have the
tongs and the bones.

TITANIA   Or say, sweet love, what thou desir'st to eat.   30

BOTTOM   Truly, a peck of provender. I could munch your good
dry oats. Methinks I have a great desire to a bottle of

hay. Good hay, sweet hay, hath no fellow.

TITANIA I have a venturous fairy, that shall seek
　　　　　The squirrel's hoard, and fetch thee thence new nuts.

BOTTOM I had rather have a handful or two of dried peas. But, I
　　　　　pray you, let none of your people stir me; I have an
　　　　　exposition of sleep come upon me.

TITANIA Sleep thou, and I will wind thee in my arms.
　　　　　Fairies, be gone, and be all ways away.　　　　　　　40

　　　　　　　　　　　　　　[the fairies leave them

　　　　　So doth the woodbine the sweet honeysuckle
　　　　　Gently entwist: the female ivy so
　　　　　Enrings the barky fingers of the elm.
　　　　　O, how I love thee! How I dote on thee!　　*[they sleep*

　　　OBERON *draws nigh and looks upon them;* PUCK *appears*

OBERON Welcome, good Robin. See'st thou this sweet sight?
　　　　　Her dotage now I do begin to pity.
　　　　　For meeting her of late behind the wood,
　　　　　Seeking sweet favours for this hateful fool,
　　　　　I did upbraid her and fall out with her.
　　　　　For she his hairy temples then had rounded　　　　50
　　　　　With coronet of fresh and fragrant flowers;
　　　　　And that same dew which sometime on the buds
　　　　　Was wont to swell like round and orient pearls
　　　　　Stood now within the pretty flowerets' eyes
　　　　　Like tears that did their own disgrace bewail.
　　　　　When I had at my pleasure taunted her,
　　　　　And she in mild terms begged my patience,
　　　　　I then did ask of her her changeling child;
　　　　　Which straight she gave me, and her fairy sent
　　　　　To bear him to my bower in Fairyland.　　　　　　60
　　　　　And now I have the boy, I will undo
　　　　　This hateful imperfection of her eyes.
　　　　　And, gentle Puck, take this transforméd scalp
　　　　　From off the head of this Athenian swain;
　　　　　That he, awaking when the other do,
　　　　　May all to Athens back again repair,
　　　　　And think no more of this night's accidents
　　　　　But as the fierce vexation of a dream.

But first I will release the Fairy Queen.
    Be as thou wast wont to be: [*he anoints her eyes* 70
    See as thou wast wont to see.
    Dian's bud o'er Cupid's flower
    Hath such force and blessèd power.
Now, my Titania! Wake you, my sweet queen.

TITANIA   My Oberon! What visions have I seen!
Methought I was enamoured of an ass.

OBERON   There lies your love.

TITANIA   How came these things to pass?
O, how mine eyes do loathe his visage now!

OBERON   Silence, awhile. Robin, take off this head.
Titania, music call; and strike more dead   80
Than common sleep of all these five the sense.

TITANIA   Music, ho! Music! Such as charmeth sleep.   [*soft music*

PUCK   Now, when thou wak'st, with thine own fool's
                       eyes peep.
             [*he plucks the ass's head from him*

OBERON   Sound, music. [*the music waxes loud*]
           Come, my queen, take hands with me,
And rock the ground whereon these sleepers be.
                    [*they dance*

Now thou and I are new in amity,
And will tomorrow midnight solemnly
Dance in Duke Theseus' house triumphantly,
And bless it to all fair prosperity.
There shall the pairs of faithful lovers be   90
Wedded, with Theseus, all in jollity.

PUCK   Fairy King, attend, and mark:
I do hear the morning lark.

OBERON   Then, my queen, in silence sad,
Trip we after the night's shade:
We the globe can compass soon,
Swifter than the wand'ring moon.

TITANIA   Come my lord, and in our flight,
Tell me how it came this night
That I sleeping here was found   100
With these mortals on the ground.   [*they vanish*

There is a sound of horns; THESEUS, HIPPOLYTA, EGEUS
and others are seen approaching, arrayed for the hunt

THESEUS   Go, one of you, find out the forester;
For now our observation is performed,
And since we have the vaward of the day,
My love shall hear the music of my hounds.
Uncouple in the western valley, let them go:
Dispatch, I say, and find the forester.
                          [*a servant bows and departs*
We will, fair queen, up to the mountain's top,
And mark the musical confusion
Of hounds and echo in conjunction.   110

HIPPOLYTA I was with Hercules and Cadmus once,
When in a wood of Crete they bayed the bear
With hounds of Sparta: never did I hear
Such gallant chiding; for, besides the groves,
The skies, the fountains, every region near
Seemed all one mutual cry. I never heard
So musical a discord, such sweet thunder.

THESEUS   My hounds are bred out of the Spartan kind:
So flewed, so sanded; and their heads are hung
With ears that sweep away the morning dew –   120
Crook-kneed, and dewlapped like Thessalian bulls;
Slow in pursuit; but matched in mouth like bells,
Each under each. A cry more tuneable
Was never hollaed to, nor cheered with horn,
In Crete, in Sparta, nor in Thessaly.
Judge when you hear. But, soft, what nymphs are these?

EGEUS   My lord, this is my daughter here asleep –
And this Lysander – this Demetrius is –
This Helena, old Nedar's Helena.
I wonder of their being here together.   130

THESEUS   No doubt they rose up early to observe
The rite of May; and, hearing our intent,
Came here in grace of our solemnity.
But, speak, Egeus; is not this the day
That Hermia should give answer of her choice?

EGEUS   It is, my lord.

THESEUS   Go, bid the huntsmen wake them with their horns.

[horns, and a shout; the lovers awake and 'start up'

Good morrow, friends. Saint Valentine is past;
Begin these wood-birds but to couple now?

LYSANDER Pardon, my lord.   *[they kneel to Theseus*

THESEUS   I pray you all, stand up.   14

I know you two are rival enemies:
How comes this gentle concord in the world,
That hatred is so far from jealousy
To sleep by hate, and fear no enmity?

LYSANDER My lord, I shall reply amazedly,
Half sleep, half waking. But as yet, I swear,
I cannot truly say how I came here.
But, as I think – for truly would I speak,
And now I do bethink me, so it is –
I came with Hermia hither. Our intent   15
Was to be gone from Athens, where we might,
Without the peril of the Athenian law –

EGEUS Enough, enough, my lord; you have enough.
I beg the law, the law, upon his head.
They would have stol'n away, they would, Demetrius,
Thereby to have defeated you and me:
You of your wife, and me of my consent –
Of my consent that she should be your wife.

DEMETR. My lord, fair Helen told me of their stealth,
Of this their purpose hither to this wood,   16
And I in fury hither followed them;
Fair Helena in fancy following me.
But, my good lord, I wot not by what power –
But by some power it is – my love to Hermia,
Melted as melts the snow, seems to me now
As the remembrance of an idle gaud
Which in my childhood I did dote upon:
And all the faith, the virtue of my heart,
The object and the pleasure of mine eye,
Is only Helena. To her, my lord,   17
Was I betrothed ere I saw Hermia:
But, like in sickness did I loathe this food,
So, as in health, come to my natural taste,
Now I do wish it, love it, long for it,

And will for evermore be true to it.

THESEUS   Fair lovers, you are fortunately met.
Of this discourse we more will hear anon.
Egeus, I will overbear your will;
For in the temple, by and by, with us,
These couples shall eternally be knit.   180
And, for the morning now is something worn,
Our purposed hunting shall be set aside.
Away with us, to Athens! Three and three,
We'll hold a feast in great solemnity.
Come, Hippolyta.

           [*Theseus, Hippolyta, Egeus and their train depart*

DEMETR.   These things seem small and undistinguishable,
Like far-off mountains turnéd into clouds.

HERMIA   Methinks I see these things with parted eye,
When everything seems double.

HELENA   So methinks:
And I have found Demetrius like a jewel,   190
Mine own, and not mine own.

DEMETR.   Are you sure
That we are well awake? It seems to me,
That yet we sleep, we dream. Do not you think
The duke was here, and bid us follow him?

HERMIA   Yea, and my father.

HELENA   And Hippolyta.

LYSANDER   And he did bid us follow to the temple.

DEMETR.   Why then, we are awake; let's follow him;
And by the way let us recount our dreams.

           [*they follow* THESEUS

BOTTOM   [*awaking*] When my cue comes, call me, and I will
answer. My next is, 'Most fair Pyramus'. Heigh-ho!   200
[*he yawns, and looks about him*] Peter Quince! Flute, the
bellows-mender! Snout, the tinker! Starveling! God's
my life! Stol'n hence, and left me asleep! I have had a
most rare vision. I have had a dream – past the wit of
man to say what dream it was. Man is but an ass, if he
go about to expound this dream. [*he rises*] Methought I
was – there is no man can tell what . . . [*he passes his
hand across his head, touching his ears*] Methought I was,

and methought I had . . . but man is but a patched fool,
if he will offer to say what methought I had. The eye 21
of man hath not heard, the ear of man hath not seen,
man's hand is not able to taste, his tongue to conceive,
nor his heart to report, what my dream was. I will get
Peter Quince to write a ballad of this dream: it shall be
called Bottom's Dream, because it hath no bottom: and
I will sing it in the latter end of our play, before the
duke. Peradventure, to make it the more gracious, I
shall sing it at her death.   [*he goes*

SCENE 2

The room in Peter Quince's cottage

QUINCE, FLUTE, SNOUT *and* STARVELING

QUINCE   Have you sent to Bottom's house? Is he come home yet?
STARV'LING   He cannot be heard of. Out of doubt he is transported.
FLUTE   If he come not, then the play is marred. It goes not
             forward, doth it?
QUINCE   It is not possible. You have not a man in all Athens able
             to discharge Pyramus but he.
FLUTE   No, he hath simply the best wit of any handicraft man
             in Athens.
QUINCE   Yea, and the best person too – and he is a very paramour
             for a sweet voice.   10
FLUTE   You must say 'paragon'. A paramour is, God bless us, a
             thing of naught.

SNUG *enters*

SNUG   Masters, the duke is coming from the temple, and there
             is two or three lords and ladies more married – if our
             sport had gone forward, we had all been made men.
FLUTE   O sweet bully Bottom! Thus hath he lost sixpence a
             day during his life: he could not have 'scaped sixpence
             a day. An the duke had not given him sixpence a day
             for playing Pyramus, I'll be hanged. He would have
             deserved it: sixpence a day in Pyramus, or nothing.   20

BOTTOM *enters*

BOTTOM   Where are these lads? Where are these hearts?

QUINCE   Bottom! O most courageous day! O most happy hour!
                              [*they all crowd about him*

BOTTOM   Masters, I am to discourse wonders: but ask me not
          what; for if I tell you, I am not true Athenian. I will
          tell you everything, right as it fell out.

QUINCE   Let us hear, sweet Bottom.

BOTTOM   Not a word of me. All that I will tell you is, that the
          duke hath dined. Get your apparel together – good
          strings to your beards, new ribbons to your pumps –
          meet presently at the palace, every man look o'er his   30
          part; for the short and the long is, our play is preferred.
          In any case, let Thisby have clean linen; and let not him
          that plays the lion pare his nails; for they shall hang out
          for the lion's claws. And, most dear actors, eat no on-
          ions nor garlic; for we are to utter sweet breath; and I
          do not doubt but to hear them say, it is a sweet comedy.
          No more words. Away, go away!
                                        [*they hurry forth*

ACT 5 SCENE I

The hall in the palace of Duke Theseus. A curtain
conceals the entrance to the lobby at the back. A fire
burns upon the hearth. Lights and torches

THESEUS *and* HIPPOLYTA *enter, followed by* PHILOSTRATE,
lords and attendants. The Duke and Duchess take their seats

HIPPOLYTA 'Tis strange, my Theseus, that these lovers speak of.
THESEUS   More strange than true. I never may believe
            These antic fables, nor these fairy toys.
            Lovers and madmen have such seething brains,
            Such shaping fantasies, that apprehend
            More than cool reason ever comprehends.
            The lunatic, the lover, and the poet,
            Are of imagination all compact.
            One sees more devils than vast hell can hold;
            That is, the madman. The lover, all as frantic,   10
            Sees Helen's beauty in a brow of Egypt.
            The poet's eye, in a fine frenzy rolling,
            Doth glance from heaven to earth, from earth to heaven;
            And as imagination bodies forth
            The forms of things unknown, the poet's pen
            Turns them to shapes, and gives to airy nothing
            A local habitation and a name.
            Such tricks hath strong imagination
            That, if it would but apprehend some joy,
            It comprehends some bringer of that joy;   20
            Or in the night, imagining some fear,
            How easy is a bush supposed a bear!
HIPPOLYTA But all the story of the night told over,
            And all their minds transfigured so together,
            More witnesseth than fancy's images,
            And grows to something of great constancy –
            But howsoever strange and admirable.
THESEUS   Here come the lovers, full of joy and mirth.

LYSANDER *and* HERMIA, DEMETRIUS *and* HELENA *enter,*
laughing and talking together

       Joy, gentle friends! Joy and fresh days of love
       Accompany your hearts!

LYSANDER   More than to us   30
       Wait in your royal walks, your board, your bed!

THESEUS   Come now; what masques, what dances shall we have,
       To wear away this long age of three hours
       Between our after-supper and bed-time?
       Where is our usual manager of mirth?
       What revels are in hand? Is there no play
       To ease the anguish of a torturing hour?
       Call Philostrate.

PHILOSTR.   Here, mighty Theseus.

THESEUS   Say, what abridgment have you for this evening?
       What masque? What music? How shall we beguile   40
       The lazy time, if not with some delight?

PHILOSTR. There is a brief how many sports are ripe;
       Make choice of which your highness will see first.
                           [he presents a paper

THESEUS   'The battle with the Centaurs, to be sung
       By an Athenian eunuch to the harp.'
       We'll none of that: that have I told my love,
       In glory of my kinsman Hercules.
       'The riot of the tipsy Bacchanals,
       Tearing the Thracian singer in their rage.'
       That is an old device; and it was played   50
       When I from Thebes came last a conqueror.
       'The thrice three Muses mourning for the death
       Of Learning, late deceased in beggary.'
       That is some satire, keen and critical,
       Not sorting with a nuptial ceremony.
       'A tedious brief scene of young Pyramus
       And his love Thisby; very tragical mirth.'
       Merry and tragical! Tedious and brief!
       That is hot ice and wondrous strange snow.
       How shall we find the concord of this discord?   60

PHILOSTR. A play there is, my lord, some ten words long;
       Which is as brief as I have known a play;

But by ten words, my lord, it is too long;
Which makes it tedious: for in all the play
There is not one word apt, one player fitted.
And tragical, my noble lord, it is;
For Pyramus therein doth kill himself.
Which when I saw rehearsed, I must confess,
Made mine eyes water; but more merry tears
The passion of loud laughter never shed.   70

THESEUS   What are they that do play it?
PHILOSTR. Hard-handed men that work in Athens here,
Which never laboured in their minds till now;
And now have toiled their unbreathed memories
With this same play against your nuptial.

THESEUS   And we will hear it.
PHILOSTR.   No, my noble lord,
It is not for you: I have heard it over,
And it is nothing, nothing in the world;
Unless you can find sport in their intents,
Extremely stretched and conned with cruel pain,   80
To do you service.

THESEUS   I will hear that play:
For never anything can be amiss,
When simpleness and duty tender it.
Go bring them in; and take your places, ladies.

                    [Philostrate departs; the rest of the court
                        make ready to hear the play

HIPPOLYTA I love not to see wretchedness o'ercharged,
And duty in his service perishing.

THESEUS   Why, gentle sweet, you shall see no such thing.
HIPPOLYTA He says they can do nothing in this kind.
THESEUS   The kinder we, to give them thanks for nothing.
Our sport shall be to take what they mistake   90
And what poor duty cannot do, noble respect
Takes it in might not merit.
Where I have come, great clerks have purposéd
To greet me with premeditated welcomes;
Where I have seen them shiver and look pale,
Make periods in the midst of sentences,
Throttle their practised accent in their fears,

And in conclusion dumbly have broke off,
Not paying me a welcome. Trust me, sweet,
Out of this silence yet I picked a welcome;   100
And in the modesty of fearful duty
I read as much as from the rattling tongue
Of saucy and audacious eloquence.
Love, therefore, and tongue-tied simplicity
In least speak most, to my capacity.

             PHILOSTRATE *returns*

PHILOSTR. So please your grace, the Prologue is addressed.
THESEUS   Let him approach.

     Enter before the curtain QUINCE *for the Prologue*

QUINCE   If we offend, it is with our good will.
       That you should think, we come not to offend,
    But with good will. To show our simple skill,   110
       That is the true beginning of our end.
    Consider then, we come but in despite.
       We do not come, as minding to content you,
    Our true intent is. All for your delight
       We are not here. That you should here repent you,
    The actors are at hand: and, by their show,
       You shall know all, that you are like to know,
                  [*he whips behind the curtains*

THESEUS   This fellow doth not stand upon points.
LYSANDER He hath rid his prologue like a rough colt: he knows
    not the stop. A good moral, my lord – it is not enough 120
    to speak; but to speak true.
HIPPOLYTA Indeed he hath played on his prologue like a child on a
    recorder – a sound, but not in government.
THESEUS   His speech was like a tangled chain; nothing impaired,
    but all disordered. Who is next?

   Enter before the curtain PYRAMUS *and* THISBY, WALL, MOONSHINE,
      and LION, *as in dumb-show, with* QUINCE *for the Presenter*

QUINCE   Gentles, perchance you wonder at this show,
       But wonder on, till truth make all things plain.
    This man is Pyramus, if you would know:
       This beauteous lady Thisby is certain.

This man, with lime and rough-cast, doth present   130
    Wall, that vile Wall which did these lovers sunder:
And through Wall's chink, poor souls, they are content
    To whisper. At the which let no man wonder.
This man, with lantern, dog, and bush of thorn,
    Presenteth Moonshine. For, if you will know,
By moonshine did these lovers think no scorn
    To meet at Ninus' tomb, there, there to woo:
This grisly beast (which Lion hight by name)
The trusty Thisby, coming first by night,
Did scare away, or rather did affright   140
And, as she fled, her mantle she did fall:
    Which Lion vile with bloody mouth did stain.
Anon comes Pyramus, sweet youth, and tall,
    And finds his trusty Thisby's mantle slain:
Whereat, with blade, with bloody blameful blade,
    He bravely broached his boiling bloody breast.
And Thisby, tarrying in mulberry shade,
    His dagger drew, and died. For all the rest,
Let Lion, Moonshine, Wall, and lovers twain
At large discourse, while here they do remain.   150

THESEUS   I wonder if the lion be to speak.
DEMETR.   No wonder, my lord:
One lion may, when many asses do.
                    [exeunt all save Wall and Pyramus

                WALL *steps forward*

WALL   In this same interlude it doth befall
That I, one Snout by name, present a wall:
And such a wall, as I would have you think,
That had in it a crannied hole or chink:
Through which the lovers, Pyramus and Thisby,
Did whisper often very secretly.
This loam, this rough-cast, and this stone, doth show   160
That I am that same wall; the truth is so.
And this the cranny is, right and sinister,
                    [he stretches forth his fingers
Through which the fearful lovers are to whisper.

THESEUS   Would you desire lime and hair to speak better?

DEMETR.　It is the wittiest partition that ever I heard discourse, my lord.

PYRAMUS *steps forward*

THESEUS　Pyramus draws near the wall: silence!

PYRAMUS　O grim-looked night! O night with hue so black!
　　　　　　O night, which ever art when day is not
　　　　　　O night, O night, alack, alack, alack,　　　　　　170
　　　　　　　　I fear my Thisby's promise is forgot!
　　　　　　And thou, O wall! O sweet, O lovely wall!
　　　　　　　That stand'st between her father's ground and mine,
　　　　　　Thou wall, O wall! O sweet and lovely wall!
　　　　　　　Show me thy chink to blink through with mine eyne.
　　　　　　　　　　　　　　　　　　　　　[*Wall obeys*
　　　　　　Thanks, courteous wall. Jove shield thee well for this!
　　　　　　　But what see I? No Thisby do I see.
　　　　　　O wicked wall, through whom I see no bliss,
　　　　　　　Cursed be thy stones for thus deceiving me!

THESEUS　The wall, methinks, being sensible, should curse again.　180

PYRAMUS　No, in truth, sir, he should not. 'Deceiving me' is Thisby's cue: she is to enter now, and I am to spy her through the wall. You shall see, it will fall pat as I told you. Yonder she comes.

Enter THISBY

THISBY　O wall! Full often hast thou heard my moans,
　　　　　　For parting my fair Pyramus and me.
　　　　　My cherry lips have often kissed thy stones;
　　　　　　Thy stones with lime and hair knit up in thee.

PYRAMUS　I see a voice: now will I to the chink
　　　　　To spy an I can hear my Thisby's face.　　　　　　190
　　　　　Thisby!

THISBY　　　　　　My love! thou art my love, I think.

PYRAMUS　Think what thou wilt, I am thy lover's grace;
　　　　　And, like Limander, am I trusty still.

THISBY　And I like Helen, till the Fates me kill.

PYRAMUS　Not Shafalus to Procrus was so true.

THISBY　As Shafalus to Procrus, I to you.

PYRAMUS　O! Kiss me through the hole of this vile wall.

THISBY　I kiss the wall's hole, not your lips at all.

PYRAMUS	Wilt thou at Ninny's tomb meet me straightway?
THISBY	'Tide life, 'tide death, I come without delay.

[exeunt Pyramus and Thisby 200

WALL	Thus have I, Wall, my part dischargéd so;
	And being done, thus Wall away doth go. *[exit Wall*
THESEUS	Now is the mural down between the two neighbours.
DEMETR.	No remedy, my lord, when walls are so wilful to hear without warning.
HIPPOLYTA	This is the silliest stuff that ever I heard.
THESEUS	The best in this kind are but shadows: and the worst are no worse, if imagination amend them.
HIPPOLYTA	It must be your imagination then; and not theirs.
THESEUS	If we imagine no worse of them than they of them- selves, they may pass for excellent men. Here come two noble beasts, in a moon and a lion.

Enter LION *and* MOONSHINE

LION	You ladies, you, whose gentle hearts do fear
	The smallest monstrous mouse that creeps on floor,
	May now perchance both quake and tremble here,
	When lion rough in wildest rage doth roar.
	Then know that I as Snug the joiner am
	A lion fell, nor else no lion's dam.
	For if I should as lion come in strife
	Into this place, 'twere pity on my life.
THESEUS	A very gentle beast, and of a good conscience.
DEMETR.	The very best at a beast, my lord, that e'er I saw.
LYSANDER	This lion is a very fox for his valour.
THESEUS	True: and a goose for his discretion.
DEMETR.	Not so, my lord, for his valour cannot carry his dis- cretion; and the fox carries the goose.
THESEUS	His discretion, I am sure, cannot carry his valour, for the goose carries not the fox. It is well: leave it to his discretion, and let us listen to the moon.
MOON.	This lanthorn doth the hornéd moon present –
DEMETR.	He should have worn the horns on his head.
THESEUS	He is no crescent, and his horns are invisible within the circumference.
MOON.	This lanthorn doth the hornéd moon present,

210

220

230

             Myself the man i'th' moon do seem to be.

THESEUS   This is the greatest error of all the rest: the man should
             be put into the lantern. How is it else the man i'th'
             moon?

DEMETR.   He dares not come there for the candle – for, you see,
             it is already in snuff.   240

HIPPOLYTA I am aweary of this moon. Would he would change!

THESEUS   It appears, by his small light of discretion, that he is in
             the wane: but yet, in courtesy, in all reason, we must
             stay the time.

LYSANDER Proceed, Moon.

MOON.   All that I have to say, is to tell you that the lanthorn is
             the moon, I the man i'th' moon, this thorn-bush my
             thorn-bush, and this dog my dog.

DEMETR.   Why, all these should be in the lantern; for all these are
             in the moon. But, silence; here comes Thisby.   250

Enter THISBY; LION *and* MOONSHINE *draw back the curtain before the
lobby, discovering a placard within inscribed* NINUS' TOMB

THISBY   This is old Ninny's tomb. Where is my love?

LION   [*roars*] Oh –
                   [*Thisby casts her mantle from her and runs away*

DEMETR.   Well roared, Lion.

THESEUS   Well run, Thisby.

HIPPOLYTA Well shone, Moon. Truly, the moon shines with a
             good grace.   [*Lion paws Thisby's mantle*

THESEUS   Well moused, Lion.

DEMETR.   And then came Pyramus.

Enter PYRAMUS; *exit* LION

LYSANDER And so the lion vanished.

PYRAMUS Sweet moon, I thank thee for thy sunny beams.
             I thank thee, moon, for shining now so bright.   260
             For, by thy gracious, golden, glittering gleams,
               I trust to take of truest Thisby sight.
                   But stay. O spite!
                   But mark, poor knight,
              What dreadful dole is here!
                Eyes, do you see?
                How can it be?

        O dainty duck, O dear!
           Thy mantle good,
           What, stained with blood?   270
        Approach, ye Furies fell!
           O Fates, come, come,
           Cut thread and thrum,
        Quail, crush, conclude, and quell!

THESEUS This passion – and the death of a dear friend – would
go near to make a man look sad.

HIPPOLYTA Beshrew my heart, but I pity the man.

PYRAMUS O wherefore, Nature, didst thou lions frame?
        Since lion vile hath here deflowered my dear.
    Which is – no, no – which was the fairest dame   280
        That lived, that loved, that liked, that looked
                        with cheer.
           Come, tears, confound;
           Out, sword, and wound
        The pap of Pyramus:
           Ay, that left pap,
           Where heart doth hop.   *[he stabs himself*
        Thus die I, thus, thus, thus.
                [he drops the sword and staggers across
                    the floor to fall within the tomb
           Now am I dead,
           Now am I fled,
         My soul is in the sky.   290
           Tongue, lose thy light!
           Moon, take thy flight!   *[exit Moonshine*
        Now die, die, die, die, die.'   *[he muffles his face*

DEMETR. No die, but an ace, for him – for he is but one.

LYSANDER Less than an ace, man – for he is dead, he is nothing.

THESEUS With the help of a surgeon, he might yet recover, and
prove an ass.

HIPPOLYTA How chance Moonshine is gone before Thisby comes
back and finds her lover?

THESEUS She will find him by starlight. Here she comes, and her 300
passion ends the play.

                  Enter THISBY

HIPPOLYTA Methinks she should not use a long one for such a
            Pyramus: I hope she will be brief.
DEMETR.   A mote will turn the balance, which Pyramus, which
            Thisby, is the better: he for a man, God warr'nt us; she
            for a woman, God bless us.
LYSANDER She hath spied him already with those sweet eyes.
                              [THISBY *discovers* PYRAMUS *in the tomb*
DEMETR.   And thus she moans, videlicet –
THISBY   Asleep, my love?
                    What, dead, my dove?   310
                O Pyramus, arise,
                    Speak, speak. Quite dumb?
                                      [*she uncovers his face*
                    Dead, dead? A tomb
                Must cover thy sweet eyes.
                    These lily lips,
                    This cherry nose,
                These yellow cowslip cheeks,
                    Are gone, are gone:
                    Lovers, make moan:
                His eyes were green as leeks.   320
                    O Sisters Three,
                    Come, come to me,
                With hands as pale as milk;
                    Lay them in gore,
                    Since you have shore
                With shears his thread of silk.
                    Tongue, not a word:
                    Come, trusty sword,
                Come, blade, my breast imbrue.
                    [*she searches Pyramus for the sword and not finding
                        it stabs herself perforce with the scabbard*
                    And farewell, friends: 330
                    Thus Thisby ends:
                Adieu, adieu, adieu.
                            [*she falls heavily across the body*
        Enter LION, MOONSHINE *and* WALL; *they close the curtain
                    before "Ninny's tomb"*

THESEUS   Moonshine and Lion are left to bury the dead.

DEMETR.   Ay and Wall too.

LION   No, I assure you, the wall is down that parted their
fathers. [*he plucks a paper from his bosom*] Will it please
you to see the Epilogue, or to hear a Bergomask dance
between two of our company?

THESEUS   No Epilogue, I pray you — for your play needs no
excuse. Never excuse; for when the players are all   34
dead, there need none to be blamed. Marry, if he that
writ it had played Pyramus and hanged himself in
Thisby's garter, it would have been a fine tragedy: and
so it is truly, and very notably discharged. But come,
your Bergomask: let your Epilogue alone.

         MOONSHINE *and* WALL *dance the Bergomask*
            and go out; THESEUS *rises*

The iron tongue of midnight hath told twelve!
Lovers, to bed — 'tis almost fairy time.
I fear we shall out-sleep the coming morn,
As much as we this night have overwatched.
This palpable-gross play hath well beguiled   35
The heavy gait of night. Sweet friends, to bed.
A fortnight hold we this solemnity,
In nightly revels, and new jollity.

   The Duke leads HIPPOLYTA *forth, followed by the lovers, hand
in hand, and the rest of the court; the lights are extinguished and
all is dark, save for the dying embers on the hearth*

           PUCK *appears broom in hand*

PUCK   Now the hungry lion roars,
     And the wolf behowls the moon;
Whilst the heavy ploughman snores,
     All with weary task fordone.
Now the wasted brands do glow,
     Whilst the screech-owl, screeching loud,
Puts the wretch that lies in woe   36
     In remembrance of a shroud.
Now it is the time of night,
     That the graves, all gaping wide,

Every one lets forth his sprite,
   In the church-way paths to glide.
And we fairies, that do run
   By the triple Hecate's team
From the presence of the sun,
   Following darkness like a dream,
Now are frolic. Not a mouse   370
Shall disturb this hallowed house.
I am sent with broom before,
To sweep the dust behind the door.

Of a sudden OBERON, TITANIA *and the fairy-host stream
into the hall, with rounds of waxen tapers on their heads,
which they swiftly kindle at the hearth as they pass it by,
until the great chamber is full of light*

OBERON   Through the house give glimmering light,
   By the dead and drowsy fire;
Every elf and fairy sprite
   Hop as light as bird from briar;
And this ditty after me
Sing, and dance it trippingly.

TITANIA   [*to Oberon*]
   First rehearse your song by rote,   380
To each word a warbling note;
Hand in hand, with fairy grace,
Will we sing and bless this place.

OBERON *leads and all the fairies sing in chorus; as they sing,
they take hands and dance about the hall*

Now, until the break of day,
Through this house each fairy stray.
To the best bride-bed will we,
Which by us shall blessèd be:
And the issue there create
Ever shall be fortunate:
So shall all the couples three   390
Ever true in loving be:
And the blots of Nature's hand
Shall not in their issue stand.
Never mole, hare-lip, nor scar,

Nor mark prodigious, such as are
Despiséd in nativity,
Shall upon their children be.
With this field–dew consecrate,
Every fairy take his gait,
And each several chamber bless,   400
Through this palace, with sweet peace;
And the owner of it blest
Ever shall in safety rest.
        Trip away:
        Make no stay
Meet me all by break of day.

They pass out: the hall is dark and silent once again

Epilogue
spoken by PUCK

If we shadows have offended,
Think but this, and all is mended,
That you have but slumb'red here
While these visions did appear.   410
And this weak and idle theme,
No more yielding but a dream,
Gentles, do not reprehend.
If you pardon, we will mend.
And, as I am an honest Puck,
If we have unearnéd luck
Now to 'scape the serpent's tongue,
We will make amends, ere long:
Else the Puck a liar call.
So, good night unto you all.   420
Give me your hands, if we be friends:
And Robin shall restore amends.   [*he vanishes*

MUCH ADO ABOUT NOTHING

INTRODUCTION

Much Ado About Nothing, like both *Othello* and *The Winter's Tale*, is a drama about a woman wrongfully accused of sexual infidelity. In all three plays, the wronged woman dies, or is thought to have died, under the weight of the accusations thrown at her. In the tragedy of Othello the heroine's death is irreversible. In both *Much Ado* and *The Winter's Tale*, however, a way out of the pain may be found: the slandered heroine may be resurrected and a comic ending by some means secured.

Much Ado flirts with the forms of tragedy – Hero, the slandered woman, undergoes a mock death that she may be lamented and pitied. The audience, however, knows at every stage that the death is counterfeited. 'One Hero died defil'd, but I do live . . . ' (5.2.63) she says once her reputation has been cleared. It is in no sense a play which makes light of the existence of pain in the world but, being a comedy, it optimistically chooses to believe that pain may nevertheless be dissipated, problems overcome and characters rescued even from the edge of catastrophe.

In this, Shakespeare differs from his principal sources in which the material is not treated as a comedy. The story of a lover believing a false report of the sexual infidelity of his beloved is derived from several variants of a fifth century bc Greek romance by Chariton. The two most significant sixteenth century versions of this are to be found in the fifth canto of Ariosto's *Orlando Furioso* (1516), and the twenty second story of Bandello's *La Prima Parte de le Novelle* (1554). From Ariosto Shakespeare borrows several key plot details – including the villain's exploitation of the maid's innocent impersonation of her mistress to convince the lover of his beloved's unfaithfulness. From Bandello Shakespeare takes the Messina setting, the names of Leonato and Don Pedro, and several more plot details – including the heroine's swoon, mock death, and subsequent restoration to her lover in disguise. The other main plot strand – following the fates of two disdainful antagonists to romance – equally springs from several sources, the most significant of which in relation to *Much Ado* is Castiglione's *Il Cortegiano* (1528).

It seems probable that the play was written in late 1598. In this period, the comic actor in Shakespeare's company, The Lord Chamberlain's Men, was Will Kemp. In the 1600 Quarto edition of the play (probably prepared for publication from Shakespeare's own manuscript), Kemp's name (variously spelt) appears in place of Dogberry's in some speech-headings. Shakespeare evidently wrote the part of Dogberry with Kemp fully in mind – so much so that he used Dogberry's and Kemp's name interchangeably in his writing. Kemp, however, was no longer in the employ of The Lord Chamberlain's Men by early 1599, so no Shakespearean part could have been written for him after that date. Since *Much Ado* does not appear in the entry in the Stationer's Register for 7 September 1598, it is therefore possible to place its composition with some confidence to late 1598.

Plot summary

A triumphant company of men, led by Don Pedro, returns to Messina from the wars. They are welcomed into the home of Leonato, the governor of Messina, where they determine to stay 'at least a month' (1.1.129–30). Hero, Leonato's only daughter, finds favour with Count Claudio, one of Don Pedro's company, and after a slight misunderstanding, it is arranged that they shall marry. Hero's cousin Beatrice resumes her 'merry war' (1.1.52) with Claudio's friend Signior Benedick, each vehemently protesting a complete antipathy to marriage. Don Pedro, Claudio and Hero resolve to trick these two cynics into falling in love with each other. By holding staged conversations within earshot of first Benedick and then Beatrice, they succeed in convincing each that s/he is dearly loved by the other. Beatrice and Benedick determine to reciprocate the love they each now believe the other secretly holds.

Meanwhile Don John, Don Pedro's misanthropic and villainous brother, schemes to disrupt the harmony of the community. With the aid of his mercenary friend Borachio, he manages to spoil Claudio's happiness by convincing him that Hero is unchaste. Borachio is then overheard by the night watch bragging to his companion Conrade about his part in the plot to discredit Hero. Despite the watch's astonishing ineptitude, they manage to arrest both Borachio and Conrade and take them away for questioning.

Claudio appears at the wedding in order to shame Hero publicly. He accuses her of being 'an approved wanton' (4.1.41) and Don Pedro accuses her of being 'a common stale' (4.1.62). Even her father, Leonato, becomes convinced that his daughter has behaved immodestly. Horrified at these accusations, Hero swoons. The Friar contrives a plan: it should be put about that Hero has in fact died, in the hope that 'slander' may change to 'remorse' (4.1.208). Beatrice is so incensed at the unfair treatment her cousin has received that she persuades Benedick to challenge Claudio to a duel.

Borachio and Conrade are cross-examined by Dogberry, the master constable. During the course of this chaotic interrogation, it emerges that Borachio has received a thousand ducats from Don John for his part in the conspiracy, that Don John has now fled, and that the slandered Hero is entirely innocent. Informed of all this, Leonato presents the news both of Hero's 'death' and of her established innocence to Claudio, who asks what he may do to make amends. He is told to mourn for Hero and then to be ready the next day to marry her (unnamed) cousin who happens to resemble her closely.

The next day Hero is presented to Claudio in disguise and he agrees to marry her in accordance with Leonato's will. Hero reveals her true identity and is greeted as one returned from the dead. The double marriage of Hero and Claudio and Beatrice and Benedick is delayed only by an all-inclusive dance and by the news that Don John has been taken in flight and so will be punished.

Soldiers and Lovers

Much Ado focuses on a military community in an off-duty moment. In the leisured calm after the wars, soldiers become lovers. Claudio says that before he went to war, he 'had a rougher task in hand':

> But now I am return'd, and that war-thoughts
> Have left their places vacant. In their rooms
> Come thronging soft and delicate desires . . .   (1.1.264–66)

As 'soft and delicate desires' displace 'war-thoughts', the soldiers' established allegiances to each other are tested by their newly emerging allegiances to women. In the terms of the play, the life of a soldier is characterised by a shared pride in jocular camaraderie, masculine courage and a sense of honour. The life of a lover, by contrast, is the stuff of jokes – peace-loving, domestic, tame, emasculating.   On one level there is a desire to trade in the military drum and fife for the recreational and romantic tabor and pipe (2.3.13–14). On another, however, there is a fear of the vulnerability acquired in the exchange. The prevalence of witticisms throughout the male community about cuckoldry and horns betrays a deep-seated anxiety. Once in thrall to women, men fear they may never again feel peace of mind. Thus, although they good-humouredly tease each other about becoming sexual 'double-dealers', their good-humour in this respect does *not* extend to any prospective 'double-dealing' on the part of women. In fact, their words and actions reveal an acute anxiety about female sexuality. When the suggestion arises that one of the women, the innocent Hero, may herself have been less than chaste, there is an immediate reaffirmation of the bonds of male friendship in collective contempt for, and unbridled aggression towards, the woman.

The degree of male aggression that Hero's supposed crime unleashes is shocking. Claudio and Don Pedro are ready, with troubling haste, to devise a plan for shaming Hero, before they have even been offered any proof of her infidelity:

> If I see anything tonight why I should not marry her, tomorrow, in the congregation, where I should wed, there will I shame her.

says Claudio, and Don Pedro replies:

> And as I wooed for thee to obtain her, I will join thee to disgrace her.   (3.2.109–10)

Even Leonato, Hero's father, is ready to believe his daughter a

wanton merely on the report of others. In common with many
possessive Shakespearean fathers, he seems more obsessed with his
own grief, loss and shame than he is with the pain suffered by
Hero. When she swoons, he wishes her dead:

> Do not live, Hero, do not ope thine eyes;
> For did I think thou wouldst not quickly die,
> Thought I thy spirits were stronger than thy shames
> Myself would on the rearward of reproaches
> Strike at thy life.   (4.1.120–24)

There is a male assumption that female sexuality is a commodity
that belongs to them. Even after the slanderous nature of the
accusations is known, Leonato's brother says to him: 'Make those
that so offend you suffer too' (5.1.40), as if the offence committed
had been primarily against him, not Hero. Men, it seems, can
only conceive of crimes against men.

Beatrice, on the other hand, feels keenly the injustice that has
been done to her cousin. In the early stages of the play she had
poured scorn on Benedick's military prowess:

> I pray you, how many hath he killed and eaten in these wars?
> But how many hath he killed? For indeed I promised to eat all
> of his killing.   (1.1.36–38)

Now, however, aware of her powerlessness in the face of an
accumulation of male aggression, she decides to use Benedick's
masculinity to strike back at the male perpetrators of the injustice
done to Hero. In her instruction to Benedick that he should 'Kill
Claudio' she re-directs male violence to act on behalf of women
rather than against them. In doing so she breaks in on the male
bonds of the regiment and challenges Benedick to assess where
his primary allegiance now lies.

Balthasar's song in Act 2 blithely recommends that the best
thing for women to do in life is, simply, to 'convert . . . all your
sounds of woe' into a far merrier 'Hey nonny, nonny' (2.3.66–
67). The violence and extremity of the male responses to Hero's
'guilt' ensures that there will indeed need to be some drastic
'converting' before the women can feel comfortable voicing anything as frolicsome as 'Hey nonny, nonny'. That the play does
finally find such a carefree tone, making possible an untroubled

comic ending, does not make light of the genuine 'sounds of woe' that have preceded it. Rather, it testifies to the transforming power of comic form, which insists that characters need not be fixed for ever in folly, but may instead be redeemed even from the depth of their own foolishness.

Unredeemable Villainy

Thus Claudio, Don Pedro and Leonato are all offered dignified routes out of their mistake in believing ill of Hero too quickly, and in acting on that belief too viciously. Don John, however, is not susceptible to such gentle realignment. Unlike *As You Like It*, in which both villains undergo dramatic conversions to lives of generosity and holiness in order to secure the comic ending, *Much Ado* boasts a villain whose wickedness proves to be beyond redemption.

> [I]t must not be denied but that I am a plain-speaking villain.
> (1.3.25–26)

says Don John, and the only definitive explanation for his acknow-ledged villainy seems to be a misanthropic distaste for the world.

> Will it serve for any model to build mischief on?   (1.3.38–39)

he asks when told of Claudio's forthcoming marriage. He is committed to poisoning others' delight and constantly seeks 'food to [his] displeasure' (1.3.53–54). As a distant forerunner to Iago (the pernicious influence in *Othello*), Don John seems to derive his villainous momentum, in Coleridge's famous phrase, from a 'motiveless malignity'. Lacking a clear motive that might be divertible to some better purpose or accessible to redemption, Don John cannot, then, be converted and absorbed into the warmth and good humour of the Messina community for the final dance. Leonato had made a point of welcoming him specifically by name when the company first arrived in Messina, but, having abused that welcome, Don John must be excluded from the community. His attempt to exclude himself by fleeing is inadequate in the moral scheme of the play. He must be apprehended and brought back, that those who were so easily duped by him may themselves have the luxury of proclaiming his exclusion.

Don John is a moral convenience in the world of Messina: the blame for the near-catastrophe of the broken nuptials may be neatly placed on him. Castigating him implicitly exonerates all the other characters. Yet Don John's poisonous presence in Messina acts as a catalyst, exposing much that is ugly or morally suspect in other characters too. In their willingness to believe the worst of Hero, their violence of language and action towards her, and their apparent callous indifference to the news of her death, neither Don Pedro nor Claudio emerges unstained. Equally, Leonato publicly abhors his daughter's 'foul-tainted flesh' (4.1.140) before he has heard a single word from her. Don John's spite therefore uncovers a latent vein of misogyny in the world of Messina. Had he not provided so obvious an excuse for it, this tendency may well have found minimal opportunity for expression. Although he releases it, he certainly cannot be held responsible for generating it: the effectiveness of his villainous scheme is dependent upon an inherently prejudiced attitude in a patriarchal and military society. The last word we hear before the pipers are instructed to 'strike up' for the final dance is that 'brave punishments' (5.4.124–25) will be devised for Don John. Messina's morality requires that innocence is finally vindicated and self-proclaimed villainy punished. The presence of such an obvious scapegoat for all the evils in Messina, however, ensures that its pervasive misogynist values remain unchallenged.

Much Ado About Nothing
Much Ado has been very popular throughout its stage history. A large measure of the delight to be found in the play derives from the energetic, biting and flirtatious banter that crackles between Beatrice and Benedick. Each claims to be immune to the ravishes of love. Benedick laughs at the 'shallow follies' of lovers (2.3.10). Beatrice says she will not take a husband 'till God make men of some other metal than earth' (2.1.51–52). The comedy lies in watching them swallow their pride and grudgingly admit to loving each other. In their antagonism to romantic cliché and sentiment, and in their taste for unsparing exchanges of wit, they are well suited to each other. Their function in the play is to provide some relief from the seriousness of the Claudio-Hero plot. Dogberry's inability to select the appropriate word and his blundering effectiveness in apprehending and cross-examining

villains constitutes the other centre of humour in the play. Unlike Beatrice, who claims she was 'born to speak all mirth and no matter' (2.1.292), *Much Ado About Nothing* offers a sophisticated mingling of mirth and matter. The genuineness of its mirth is not compromised by the seriousness of its matter; its 'sighs of woe' are not invalidated by the resounding 'Hey nonny, nonny' of its close. In its real engagement with pain and its refusal to let that pain ultimately obscure a life optimism, it points the way to the later tragi-comedies.

The scene: Messina

CHARACTERS IN THE PLAY

DON PEDRO, *Prince of Arragon*

DON JOHN, *his bastard brother*

CLAUDIO, *a young lord of Florence*

BENEDICK, *a young lord of Padua*

LEONATO, *governor of Messina*

ANTONIO, *an old man, his brother*

BALTHAZAR, *a singer in the service of Don Pedro*

BORACHIO
CONRADE } *followers of Don John*

A Messenger

FRIAR FRANCIS

DOGBERRY, *a constable*

VERGES, *a headborough*

First Watchman

Second Watchman

A Sexton

A Boy

A Lord

HERO, *daughter to Leonato*

BEATRICE, *niece to Leonato*

MARGARET
URSULA } *waiting-gentlewomen to Hero*

Antonio's son, musicians, watchmen, attendants, etc.

MUCH ADO ABOUT NOTHING

ACT I SCENE I

An orchard, adjoining the house of Leonato; at one side a covered alley of thick-pleached fruit-trees; at the back an arbour overgrown with honeysuckle

'LEONATO, *governor of Messina,* HERO *his daughter, and* BEATRICE *his niece, with a messenger*'

LEONATO I learn in this letter that Don Pedro of Arragon comes this night to Messina.

MESSENG'R He is very near by this. He was not three leagues off when I left him.

LEONATO How many gentlemen have you lost in this action?

MESSENG'R But few of any sort, and none of name.

LEONATO A victory is twice itself when the achiever brings home full numbers. I find here that Don Pedro hath bestowed much honour on a young Florentine called Claudio.   10

MESSENG'R Much deserved on his part, and equally remembered by Don Pedro. He hath borne himself beyond the promise of his age, doing in the figure of a lamb the feats of a lion. He hath indeed better bettered expectation than you must expect of me to tell you how.

LEONATO He hath an uncle here in Messina will be very much glad of it.

MESSENG'R I have already delivered him letters, and there appears much joy in him – even so much, that joy could not show itself modest enough without a badge of bitterness. 20

LEONATO Did he break out into tears?

MESSENG'R In great measure.

LEONATO A kind overflow of kindness. There are no faces truer than those that are so washed. How much better is it to weep at joy than to joy at weeping!

BEATRICE I pray you, is Signior Mountanto returned from the wars or no?

MESSENG'R I know none of that name, lady. There was none such in the army of any sort.

| LEONATO | What is he that you ask for, niece? | 30 |

LEONATO   What is he that you ask for, niece?   30
HERO   My cousin means Signior Benedick of Padua.
MESSENG'R   O, he's returned, and as pleasant as ever he was.
BEATRICE   He set up his bills here in Messina and challenged
            Cupid at the flight, and my uncle's fool reading the
            challenge subscribed for Cupid, and challenged him at
            the birdbolt. I pray you, how many hath he killed and
            eaten in these wars? But how many hath he killed? For
            indeed I promised to eat all of his killing.
LEONATO   Faith, niece, you tax Signior Benedick too much – but
            he'll be meet with you, I doubt it not.   40
MESSENG'R   He hath done good service, lady, in these wars.
BEATRICE   You had musty victual, and he hath holp to eat it. He
            is a very valiant trencher-man, he hath an excellent
            stomach.
MESSENG'R   And a good soldier too, lady.
BEATRICE   And a good soldier to a lady, but what is he to a lord?
MESSENG'R   A lord to a lord, a man to a man – stuffed with all
            honourable virtues.
BEATRICE   It is so, indeed. He is no less than a stuffed man, but for
            the stuffing – well, we are all mortal.   50
LEONATO   You must not, sir, mistake my niece. There is a kind of
            merry war betwixt Signior Benedick and her. They
            never meet but there's a skirmish of wit between them.
BEATRICE   Alas, he gets nothing by that. In our last conflict, four
            of his five wits went halting off, and now is the whole
            man governed with one – so that if he have wit enough
            to keep himself warm, let him bear it for a difference
            between himself and his horse, for it is all the wealth
            that he hath left to be known a reasonable creature.   60
            Who is his companion now? He hath every month a
            new sworn brother.
MESSENG'R   Is't possible?
BEATRICE   Very easily possible. He wears his faith but as the
            fashion of his hat, it ever changes with the next block.
MESSENG'R   I see, lady, the gentleman is not in your books.
BEATRICE   No, an he were, I would burn my study. But I pray you
            who is his companion? Is there no young squarer now
            that will make a voyage with him to the devil?

MESSENG'R He is most in the company of the right noble Claudio. 70

BEATRICE O Lord, he will hang upon him like a disease – he is
sooner caught than the pestilence, and the taker runs
presently mad. God help the noble Claudio. If he have
caught the Benedict, it will cost him a thousand pound
ere a' be cured.

MESSENG'R I will hold friends with you, lady.

BEATRICE Do, good friend.

LEONATO You will never run mad, niece.

BEATRICE No, not till a hot January.

MESSENG'R Don Pedro is approached. 80

> 'DON PEDRO, CLAUDIO, BENEDICK, BALTHAZAR and
> JOHN the Bastard' enter the orchard

D. PEDRO Good Signior Leonato, are you come to meet your
trouble? The fashion of the world is to avoid cost, and
you encounter it.

LEONATO Never came trouble to my house in the likeness of
your grace. For trouble being gone, comfort should
remain: but when you depart from me, sorrow abides
and happiness takes his leave.

D. PEDRO You embrace your charge too willingly. I think this is
your daughter.

LEONATO Her mother hath many times told me so. 90

BENEDICK Were you in doubt, sir, that you asked her?

LEONATO Signior Benedick, no – for then were you a child.

D. PEDRO You have it full, Benedick – we may guess by this what
you are, being a man. Truly the lady fathers herself. Be
happy, lady, for you are like an honourable father.

> [he talks apart with Hero and Leonato

BENEDICK If Signior Leonato be her father, she would not have
his head on her shoulders for all Messina, as like him as
she is.

BEATRICE I wonder that you will still be talking, Signior Bene- 100
dick – nobody marks you.

BENEDICK What, my dear Lady Disdain! Are you yet living?

BEATRICE Is it possible Disdain should die, while she hath such
meet food to feed it as Signior Benedick? Courtesy
itself must convert to disdain, if you come in her
presence.

BENEDICK   Then is courtesy a turn-coat. But it is certain I am
loved of all ladies, only you excepted: and I would I
could find in my heart that I had not a hard heart, for
truly I love none.   110

BEATRICE   A dear happiness to women – they would else have
been troubled with a pernicious suitor. I thank God
and my cold blood, I am of your humour for that. I
had rather hear my dog bark at a crow than a man
swear he loves me.

BENEDICK   God keep your ladyship still in that mind, so some
gentleman or other shall 'scape a predestinate scratched
face.

BEATRICE   Scratching could not make it worse, an 'twere such a
face as yours were.   120

BENEDICK   Well, you are a rare parrot-teacher.

BEATRICE   A bird of my tongue is better than a beast of yours.

BENEDICK   I would my horse had the speed of your tongue, and so
good a continuer. But keep your way a God's name – I
have done.

BEATRICE   You always end with a jade's trick. I know you of old.

D. PEDRO   That is the sum of all, Leonato. [he turns] Signior
Claudio and Signior Benedick, my dear friend Leonato
hath invited you all. I tell him we shall stay here at the
least a month, and he heartily prays some occasion may   130
detain us longer. I dare swear he is no hypocrite, but
prays from his heart.

LEONATO   If you swear, my lord, you shall not be forsworn. [to
DON JOHN] Let me bid you welcome, my lord – being
reconciled to the prince your brother. [bows] I owe you
all duty.

DON JOHN   I thank you. I am not of many words, but I thank you.

LEONATO   Please it your grace lead on?

D PEDRO   Your hand, Leonato – we will go together.
                        [all depart save Benedick and Claudio

CLAUDIO   Benedick, didst thou note the daughter of Signior   140
Leonato?

BENEDICK   I noted her not, but I looked on her.

CLAUDIO   Is she not a modest young lady?

BENEDICK   Do you question me as an honest man should do, for

my simple true judgement? Or would you have me
speak after my custom, as being a professed tyrant to
their sex?

CLAUDIO   No, I pray thee speak in sober judgement.

BENEDICK   Why, i'faith, methinks she's too low for a high praise,
too brown for a fair praise, and too little for a great   150
praise – only this commendation I can afford her, that
were she other than she is, she were unhandsome, and
being no other but as she is, I do not like her.

CLAUDIO   Thou thinkest I am in sport. I pray thee tell me truly
how thou lik'st her.

BENEDICK   Would you buy her, that you inquire after her?

CLAUDIO   Can the world buy such a jewel?

BENEDICK   Yea, and a case to put it into. But speak you this with a
sad brow? Or do you play the flouting Jack, to tell us
Cupid is a good hare-finder, and Vulcan a rare carpenter?   160
Come, in what key shall a man take you to go in the
song?

CLAUDIO   In mine eye, she is the sweetest lady that ever I looked
on.

BENEDICK   I can see yet without spectacles, and I see no such
matter: there's her cousin, an she were not possessed
with a fury, exceeds her as much in beauty as the first
of May doth the last of December. But I hope you
have no intent to turn husband, have you?

CLAUDIO   I would scarce trust myself, though I had sworn the   170
contrary, if Hero would be my wife.

BENEDICK   Is't come to this? In faith hath not the world one man
but he will wear his cap with suspicion? Shall I never
see a bachelor of threescore again? Go to i'faith, an
thou wilt needs thrust thy neck into a yoke, wear the
print of it, and sigh away Sundays.

           DON PEDRO *re-enters the orchard*

           Look, Don Pedro is returned to seek you.

D. PEDRO   What secret hath held you here, that you followed not
to Leonato's?

BENEDICK   I would your grace would constrain me to tell.   180

D. PEDRO   I charge thee on thy allegiance.

BENEDICK   You hear, Count Claudio. I can be secret as a dumb

man, I would have you think so – but on my allegiance,
mark you this, on my allegiance! He is in love – with
who? Now that is your grace's part. Mark, how short
his answer is – with Hero, Leonato's short daughter.

CLAUDIO   If this were so, so were it uttered.

BENEDICK   Like the old tale, my lord – 'it is not so, nor 'twas not
so: but indeed, God forbid it should be so.'

CLAUDIO   If my passion change not shortly, God forbid it should 190
be otherwise.

D. PEDRO   Amen, if you love her – for the lady is very well
worthy.

CLAUDIO   You speak this to fetch me in, my lord.

D. PEDRO   By my troth, I speak my thought.

CLAUDIO   And in faith, my lord, I spoke mine.

BENEDICK   And by my two faiths and troths, my lord, I spoke
mine.

CLAUDIO   That I love her, I feel.

D. PEDRO   That she is worthy, I know. 200

BENEDICK   That I neither feel how she should be loved, nor know
how she should be worthy, is the opinion that fire
cannot melt out of me – I will die in it at the stake.

D. PEDRO   Thou wast ever an obstinate heretic in the despite of
beauty.

CLAUDIO   And never could maintain his part but in the force of
his will.

BENEDICK   That a woman conceived me, I thank her: that she
brought me up, I likewise give her most humble
thanks: but that I will have a recheat winded in my 210
forehead, or hang my bugle in an invisible baldric, all
women shall pardon me. Because I will not do them
the wrong to mistrust any, I will do myself the right to
trust none: and the fine is – for the which I may go the
finer – I will live a bachelor.

D. PEDRO   I shall see thee, ere I die, look pale with love.

BENEDICK   With anger, with sickness, or with hunger, my lord –
not with love: prove that ever I lose more blood with
love than I will get again with drinking, pick out mine
eyes with a ballad-maker's pen, and hang me up at the 220
door of a brothel-house for the sign of blind Cupid.

D. PEDRO Well, if ever thou dost fall from this faith, thou wilt prove a notable argument.

BENEDICK If I do, hang me in a bottle like a cat and shoot at me, and he that hits me, let him be clapped on the shoulder and called Adam.

D. PEDRO Well, as time shall try:
    'In time the savage bull doth bear the yoke.'

BENEDICK The savage bull may – but if ever the sensible Benedick bear it, pluck off the bull's horns and set them in my 230 forehead. And let me be vilely painted – and in such great letters as they write, 'Here is good horse to hire,' let them signify under my sign, 'Here you may see Benedick the married man.'

CLAUDIO If this should ever happen, thou wouldst be horn-mad.

D. PEDRO Nay, if Cupid have not spent all his quiver in Venice, thou wilt quake for this shortly.

BENEDICK I look for an earthquake too then.

D. PEDRO Well, you will temporize with the hours. In the mean-time, good Signior Benedick, repair to Leonato's, 240 commend me to him, and tell him I will not fail him at supper – for indeed he hath made great preparation.

BENEDICK I have almost matter enough in me for such an embassage, and so I commit you –

CLAUDIO To the tuition of God: from my house if I had it –

D. PEDRO The sixth of July: your loving friend, Benedick.

BENEDICK Nay, mock not, mock not. The body of your discourse is sometime guarded with fragments, and the guards are but slightly basted on neither. Ere you flout old ends any further, examine your conscience – and so I 250 leave you.   [he goes

CLAUDIO My liege, your highness now may do me good.

D. PEDRO My love is thine to teach. Teach it but how,
    And thou shalt see how apt it is to learn
    Any hard lesson that may do thee good.

CLAUDIO Hath Leonato any son, my lord?

D. PEDRO No child but Hero, she's his only heir:
    Dost thou affect her, Claudio

CLAUDIO   O my lord,
    When you went onward on this ended action,   260

I looked upon her with a soldier's eye,
That liked, but had a rougher task in hand
Than to drive liking to the name of love:
But now I am returned, and that war-thoughts
Have left their places vacant. In their rooms
Come thronging soft and delicate desires,
All prompting me how fair young Hero is,
Saying I liked her ere I went to wars.

D. PEDRO   Thou wilt be like a lover presently,
And tire the hearer with a book of words.   270
If thou dost love fair Hero, cherish it,
And I will break with her, and with her father,
And thou shalt have her. Was't not to this end
That thou began'st to twist so fine a story?

CLAUDIO   How sweetly you do minister to love,
That know love's grief by his complexion!
But lest my liking might too sudden seem,
I would have salved it with a longer treatise.

D. PEDRO   What need the bridge much broader than the flood?
The fairest grant is the necessity: 280
Look, what will serve is fit: 'tis once, thou lovest,
And I will fit thee with the remedy.
I know we shall have revelling tonight –
I will assume thy part in some disguise,
And tell fair Hero I am Claudio,
And in her bosom I'll unclasp my heart,
And take her hearing prisoner with the force
And strong encounter of my amorous tale:
Then after to her father will I break –
And the conclusion is, she shall be thine.   290
In practice let us put it presently.

                       [they leave the orchard

SCENE 2

The hall of Leonato's house; three doors, one in the centre leading
to the great chamber; above it a gallery with doors at the back.
Servants preparing the room for a dance; ANTONIO *directing them*

LEONATO *enters in haste*

LEONATO   How now brother, where is my cousin your son? Hath
he provided this music?

ANTONIO   He is very busy about it. But brother, I can tell you
strange news that you yet dreamt not of.

LEONATO   Are they good?

ANTONIO   As the event stamps them, but they have a good cover.
They show well outward. The prince and Count
Claudio, walking in a thick-pleached alley in mine
orchard, were thus much overheard by a man of mine:
the prince discovered to Claudio that he loved my   10
niece your daughter, and meant to acknowledge it this
night in a dance – and if he found her accordant, he
meant to take the present time by the top and instantly
break with you of it.

LEONATO   Hath the fellow any wit that told you this?

ANTONIO   A good sharp fellow. I will send for him, and question
him yourself.

LEONATO   No, no, we will hold it as a dream till it appear itself:
but I will acquaint my daughter withal, that she may
be the better prepared for an answer, if peradventure   20
this be true. Go you and tell her of it. [ANTONIO *goes*
out at one door; his son enters at another, followed by a
musician] Cousin, you know what you have to do –
[*seeing the musician*] O, I cry you mercy friend, go you
with me and I will use your skill. Good cousin, have a
care this busy time.

> [*he goes out with the musician; after a brief space*
> *Antonio's son and the servants depart likewise*

SCENE 3

A door opens in the gallery: DON JOHN *and* CONRADE *come forth*

CONRADE   What the good-year, my lord! why are you thus out of
measure sad?

DON JOHN   There is no measure in the occasion that breeds, therefore the sadness is without limit.

CONRADE   You should hear reason.

DON JOHN   And when I have heard it, what blessing brings it?

CONRADE   If not a present remedy, at least a patient sufferance.

DON JOHN   I wonder that thou – being as thou say'st thou art born
under Saturn – goest about to apply a moral medicine to
a mortifying mischief. I cannot hide what I am: I must be   10
sad when I have cause, and smile at no man's jests; eat
when I have stomach, and wait for no man's leisure; sleep
when I am drowsy, and tend on no man's business; laugh
when I am merry, and claw no man in his humour.

CONRADE   Yea, but you must not make the full show of this till
you may do it without controlment. You have of late
stood out against your brother, and he hath ta'en you
newly into his grace, where it is impossible you should
take true root but by the fair weather that you make
yourself. It is needful that you frame the season for   20
your own harvest.

DON JOHN   I had rather be a canker in a hedge than a rose in his
grace, and it better fits my blood to be disdained of all
than to fashion a carriage to rob love from any: in this,
though I cannot be said to be a flattering honest man, it
must not be denied but I am a plain-dealing villain. I
am trusted with a muzzle and enfranchised with a clog –
therefore I have decreed not to sing in my cage. If I had
my mouth, I would bite: if I had my liberty, I would do
my liking: in the meantime, let me be that I am, and   30
seek not to alter me.

CONRADE   Can you make no use of your discontent?

DON JOHN   I make all use of it, for I use it only. Who comes here?

BORACHIO *enters the gallery*

What news, Borachio?

BORACHIO I came yonder from a great supper. The prince your
brother is royally entertained by Leonato, and I can
give you intelligence of an intended marriage.

DON JOHN Will it serve for any model to build mischief on? What
is he for a fool that betroths himself to unquietness?

BORACHIO Marry, it is your brother's right hand.   40

DON JOHN Who, the most exquisite Claudio?

BORACHIO Even he.

DON JOHN A proper squire! And who, and who, which way looks
he?

BORACHIO Marry, on Hero the daughter and heir of Leonato.

DON JOHN A very forward March-chick! How came you to this?

BORACHIO Being entertained for a perfumer, as I was smoking a
musty room, comes me the prince and Claudio, hand
in hand in sad conference: I whipt me behind the
arras, and there heard it agreed upon that the prince   50
should woo Hero for himself, and having obtained
her, give her to Count Claudio.

DON JOHN Come, come, let us thither – this may prove food to my
displeasure. That young start-up hath all the glory of
my overthrow: if I can cross him any way, I bless myself
every way. You are both sure, and will assist me?

CONRADE To the death, my lord.

DON JOHN Let us to the great supper – their cheer is the greater
that I am subdued. Would the cook were o' my mind.
Shall we go prove what's to be done?   60

BORACHIO We'll wait upon your lordship.

                              [*they leave the gallery*

ACT 2 SCENE 1

The door of the great chamber opens; LEONATO, ANTONIO,
HERO, BEATRICE, MARGARET, URSULA, *and others of*
Leonato's household come forth

LEONATO   Was not Count John here at supper?

ANTONIO   I saw him not.

BEATRICE   How tartly that gentleman looks. I never can see him
but I am heart-burned an hour after.

HERO   He is of a very melancholy disposition.

BEATRICE   He were an excellent man that were made just in the
mid-way between him and Benedick. The one is too
like an image and says nothing, and the other too like
my lady's eldest son, evermore tattling.

LEONATO   Then half Signior Benedick's tongue in Count John's   10
mouth, and half Count John's melancholy in Signior
Benedick's face –

BEATRICE   With a good leg and a good foot, uncle, and money
enough in his purse, such a man would win any
woman in the world if a' could get her good will.

LEONATO   By my troth, niece, thou wilt never get thee a husband, if thou be so shrewd of thy tongue.

ANTONIO   In faith, she's too curst.

BEATRICE   Too curst is more than curst. I shall lessen God's
sending that way, for it is said, 'God sends a curst cow   20
short horns' – but to a cow too curst he sends none.

LEONATO   So by being too curst, God will send you no horns?

BEATRICE   Just, if he send me no husband – for the which blessing
I am at him upon my knees every morning and
evening. Lord! I could not endure a husband with a
beard on his face – I had rather lie in the woollen!

LEONATO   You may light on a husband that hath no beard.

BEATRICE   What should I do with him? Dress him in my apparel
and make him my waiting-gentlewoman? He that hath
a beard is more than a youth; and he that hath no   30
beard is less than a man: and he that is more than a
youth is not for me, and he that is less than a man I am
not for him. Therefore I will even take sixpence in

earnest of the bear'ard and lead his apes into hell.

LEONATO   Well then, go you into hell?

BEATRICE   No – but to the gate, and there will the devil meet me
like an old cuckold with horns on his head, and say,
'Get you to heaven, Beatrice, get you to heaven –
here's no place for you maids.' So deliver I up my
apes, and away to Saint Peter: for the heavens, he   40
shows me where the bachelors sit, and there live we as
merry as the day is long.

ANTONIO   [to HERO] Well niece, I trust you will be ruled by your
father.

BEATRICE   Yes faith, it is my cousin's duty to make curtsy, and say,
'Father, as it please you'. But yet for all that, cousin, let
him be a handsome fellow, or else make another curtsy,
and say, 'Father, as it please me.'

LEONATO   Well, niece, I hope to see you one day fitted with a
husband.   50

BEATRICE   Not till God make men of some other mettle than
earth. Would it not grieve a woman to be over-mas-
tered with a piece of valiant dust? To make an account
of her life to a clod of wayward marl? No, uncle, I'll
none: Adam's sons are my brethren, and truly I hold it
a sin to match in my kindred.

LEONATO   Daughter, remember what I told you. If the prince do
solicit you in that kind, you know your answer.

BEATRICE   The fault will be in the music, cousin, if you be not
wooed in good time: if the prince be too important,   60
tell him there is measure in every thing, and so dance
out the answer. For hear me, Hero – wooing, wedding, and repenting, is as a Scotch jig, a measure, and a
cinque-pace: the first suit is hot and hasty like a Scotch
jig, and full as fantastical; the wedding mannerly-mod-
est, as a measure, full of state and ancientry; and then
comes Repentance, and with his bad legs falls into the
cinque-pace faster and faster, till he sink into his grave.

LEONATO   Cousin, you apprehend passing shrewdly.

BEATRICE   I have a good eye, uncle – I can see a church by daylight.   70

LEONATO   The revellers are ent'ring, brother. Make good room.

[ANTONIO gives orders to the servants and goes out

DON PEDRO, CLAUDIO, BENEDICK, DON JOHN, BORACHIO *and*
others of Don Pedro's party enter masked, with a drummer before them;
ANTONIO *returns later, also masked. Musicians enter the gallery and*
prepare to play; the couples take their places for a round dance

D. PEDRO   [*leading* HERO *forth*] Lady, will you walk a bout with
your friend?

HERO   So you walk softly and look sweetly and say nothing, I
am yours for the walk – and especially when I walk
away.

D. PEDRO   With me in your company?

HERO   I may say so when I please.

D. PEDRO   And when please you to say so?

HERO   When I like your favour, for God defend the lute
should be like the case!   80

D. PEDRO   My visor is Philemon's roof – within the house is Jove.

HERO   Why, then your visor should be thatched.

D. PEDRO   Speak low if you speak love.
[*they pass on round the room*

BORACHIO   Well, I would you did like me.

MARGARET   So would not I for your own sake, for I have many ill
qualities.

BORACHIO   Which is one?

MARGARET   I say my prayers aloud.

BORACHIO   I love you the better, the hearers may cry Amen.

MARGARET   God match me with a good dancer.   90

BORACHIO   Amen.

MARGARET   And God keep him out of my sight when the dance is
done: answer, clerk.

BORACHIO   No more words – the clerk is answered.
[*they pass on round the room*

URSULA   I know you well enough – you are Signior Antonio.

ANTONIO   At a word, I am not.

URSULA   I know you by the waggling of your head.

ANTONIO   To tell you true, I counterfeit him.

URSULA   You could never do him so ill-well, unless you were
the very man: here's his dry hand up and down – you   100
are he, you are he.

ANTONIO   At a word, I am not.

URSULA   Come, come, do you think I do not know you by your

excellent wit? Can virtue hide itself? Go to, mum, you are he. Graces will appear, and there's an end.

[*they pass on round the room*

BEATRICE Will you not tell me who told you so?

BENEDICK No, you shall pardon me.

BEATRICE Nor will you not tell me who you are?

BENEDICK Not now.

BEATRICE That I was disdainful, and that I had my good wit out 110 of the 'Hundred Merry Tales'. Well, this was Signior Benedick that said so.

BENEDICK What's he?

BEATRICE I am sure you know him well enough.

BENEDICK Not I, believe me.

BEATRICE Did he never make you laugh?

BENEDICK I pray you, what is he?

BEATRICE Why, he is the prince's jester, a very dull fool – only his gift is in devising impossible slanders. None but libertines delight in him, and the commendation is not in 120 his wit but in his villainy, for he both pleases men and angers them, and then they laugh at him and beat him. [*surveying the company*] I am sure he is in the fleet – I would he had boarded me.

BENEDICK When I know the gentleman, I'll tell him what you say.

BEATRICE Do, do. He'll but break a comparison or two on me, which peradventure, not marked or not laughed at, strikes him into melancholy – and then there's a partridge wing saved, for the fool will eat no supper that 130 night. We must follow the leaders.

BENEDICK In every good thing.

BEATRICE Nay, if they lead to any ill, I will leave them at the next turning.

The musicians strike up, and the couples break into a lively dance; at the end thereof DON PEDRO *beckons to* LEONATO *and they go forth together. The door of the great chamber is thrown open;* HERO *leads the couples to the banquet,* DON JOHN, BORACHIO *and* CLAUDIO *remaining behind*

DON JOHN [*aloud*] Sure my brother is amorous on Hero, and hath withdrawn her father to break with him about it. The ladies follow her, and but one visor remains.

BORACHIO And that is Claudio. I know him by his bearing.

DON JOHN Are not you Signior Benedick?

CLAUDIO You know me well – I am he.   140

DON JOHN Signior, you are very near my brother in his love. He
is enamoured on Hero. I pray you, dissuade him from
her, she is no equal for his birth. You may do the part
of an honest man in it.

CLAUDIO How know you he loves her?

DON JOHN I heard him swear his affection.

BORACHIO So did I too, and he swore he would marry her tonight.

DON JOHN Come, let us to the banquet.

                    [*he goes within, followed by Borachio*

CLAUDIO Thus answer I in name of Benedick,
But hear these ill news with the ears of Claudio.   150
'Tis certain so – the prince wooes for himself.
Friendship is constant in all other things
Save in the office and affairs of love:
Therefore all hearts in love use their own tongues.
Let every eye negotiate for itself,
And trust no agent: for beauty is a witch
Against whose charms faith melteth into blood:
This is an accident of hourly proof,
Which I mistrusted not. Farewell, therefore, Hero.

    BENEDICK, *unmasked, comes from the great chamber*
                  to seek for CLAUDIO

BENEDICK Count Claudio?   160

CLAUDIO Yea, the same.

BENEDICK Come, will you go with me?

CLAUDIO Whither?

BENEDICK Even to the next willow, about your own business,
county. What fashion will you wear the garland of?
About your neck, like an usurer's chain? Or under
your arm, like a lieutenant's scarf? You must wear it one
way, for the prince hath got your Hero.

CLAUDIO I wish him joy of her.

BENEDICK Why, that's spoken like an honest drover – so they sell 170
bullocks: but did you think the prince would have
served you thus?

CLAUDIO   I pray you, leave me.

BENEDICK   Ho, now you strike like the blind man. 'Twas the boy
           that stole your meat, and you'll beat the post.

CLAUDIO   If it will not be, I'll leave you.   [*he goes out*

BENEDICK   Alas, poor hurt fowl – now will he creep into sedges.
           But, that my Lady Beatrice should know me, and not
           know me. The prince's fool! Ha, it may be I go under
           that title because I am merry: yea, but so I am apt to do   180
           myself wrong: I am not so reputed – it is the base, the
           bitter disposition of Beatrice that puts the world into her
           person, and so gives me out. Well, I'll be revenged as I
           may.

               DON PEDRO *returns with* LEONATO *and* HERO;
                    LEONATO *and* HERO *talk apart*

D. PEDRO   Now, signior, where's the count? Did you see him?

BENEDICK   Troth, my lord, I have played the part of Lady Fame. I
           found him here as melancholy as a lodge in a warren. I
           told him, and I think I told him true, that your grace
           had got the good will of this young lady – and I off'red
           him my company to a willow tree, either to make him   190
           a garland, as being forsaken, or to bind him up a rod,
           as being worthy to be whipped.

D. PEDRO   To be whipped! What's his fault?

BENEDICK   The flat transgression of a school-boy, who, being
           overjoyed with finding a bird's-nest, shows it his com-
           panion, and he steals it.

D. PEDRO   Wilt thou make a trust a transgression? The transgression
           is in the stealer.

BENEDICK   Yet it had not been amiss the rod had been made, and
           the garland too – for the garland he might have worn   200
           himself, and the rod he might have bestowed on you,
           who, as I take it, have stolen his bird's-nest.

D. PEDRO   I will but teach them to sing, and restore them to the
           owner.

BENEDICK   If their singing answer your saying, by my faith you say
           honestly.

D. PEDRO   The Lady Beatrice hath a quarrel to you. The gentle-
           man that danced with her told her she is much

wronged by you.

BENEDICK   O, she misused me past the endurance of a block: an oak   210
but with one green leaf on it would have answered her:
my very visor began to assume life and scold with her.
She told me, not thinking I had been myself, that I was
the prince's jester, that I was duller than a great thaw –
huddling jest upon jest with such impossible conveyance
upon me, that I stood like a man at a mark, with a whole
army shooting at me. She speaks poniards, and every
word stabs: if her breath were as terrible as her termin-
ations, there were no living near her, she would infect to
the north star. I would not marry her, though she were   220
endowed with all that Adam had left him before he trans-
gressed. She would have made Hercules have turned spit,
yea, and have cleft his club to make the fire too. Come,
talk not of her. You shall find her the infernal Ate in good
apparel – I would to God some scholar would conjure
her, for certainly, while she is here, a man may live as
quiet in hell as in a sanctuary – and people sin upon
purpose because they would go thither, so indeed all
disquiet, horror, and perturbation follow her.

CLAUDIO *and* BEATRICE *enter, talking together*

D. PEDRO   Look, here she comes.   230

BENEDICK   Will your grace command me any service to the
world's end? I will go on the slightest errand now to
the Antipodes that you can devise to send me on: I
will fetch you a tooth-picker now from the furthest
inch of Asia: bring you the length of Prester John's
foot: fetch you a hair off the great Cham's beard: do
you any embassage to the Pigmies – rather than hold
three words' conference with this harpy. You have no
employment for me?

D. PEDRO   None, but to desire your good company.   240

BENEDICK   O God, sir, here's a dish I love not – I cannot endure
my Lady Tongue.   [*he goes within*

D. PEDRO   Come, lady, come, you have lost the heart of Signior
Benedick.

BEATRICE   [*comes forward*] Indeed my lord, he lent it me awhile,
and I gave him use for it – a double heart for his single

	one. Marry, once before he won it of me with false
	dice, therefore your grace may well say I have lost it.
D. PEDRO	You have put him down, lady, you have put him
	down. 250
BEATRICE	So I would not he should do me, my lord, lest I should
	prove the mother of fools. I have brought Count
	Claudio, whom you sent me to seek.
D. PEDRO	Why, how now count, wherefore are you sad?
CLAUDIO	Not sad, my lord.
D. PEDRO	How then? Sick?
CLAUDIO	Neither, my lord.
BEATRICE	The count is neither sad, nor sick, nor merry, nor well:
	but civil count – civil as an orange, and something of
	that jealous complexion. 260
D. PEDRO	I'faith lady, I think your blazon to be true, though I'll be
	sworn, if he be so, his conceit is false. Here, Claudio, I
	have wooed in thy name and fair Hero is won, I have
	broke with her father and his good will obtained. Name
	the day of marriage, and God give thee joy.
LEONATO	[*leads* HERO *forward*] Count, take of me my daughter,
	and with her my fortunes: his grace hath made the
	match, and all grace say Amen to it.
BEATRICE	Speak, count, 'tis your cue.
CLAUDIO	Silence is the perfectest herald of joy – I were but little 270
	happy, if I could say how much! Lady, as you are
	mine, I am yours. I give away myself for you and dote
	upon the exchange.
BEATRICE	Speak cousin, or, if you cannot, stop his mouth with a
	kiss, and let not him speak neither.
D. PEDRO	In faith, lady, you have a merry heart.
BEATRICE	Yea, my lord, I thank it – poor fool, it keeps on the
	windy side of care. My cousin tells him in his ear that
	he is in her heart.
CLAUDIO	And so she doth, cousin. 280
BEATRICE	Good Lord, for alliance! Thus goes every one to the
	world but I, and I am sun-burnt. I may sit in a corner
	and cry 'heigh-ho for a husband'.
D. PEDRO	Lady Beatrice, I will get you one.
BEATRICE	I would rather have one of your father's getting: hath

your grace ne'er a brother like you? Your father got
excellent husbands if a maid could come by them.

D. PEDRO   Will you have me, lady?

BEATRICE   No my lord, unless I might have another for working-
days – your grace is too costly to wear every day. But I 2?
beseech your grace pardon me, I was born to speak all
mirth and no matter.

D. PEDRO   Your silence most offends me, and to be merry best
becomes you, for out o' question you were born in a
merry hour.

BEATRICE   No, sure, my lord, my mother cried – but then there
was a star danced, and under that was I born. Cousins,
God give you joy!

LEONATO   Niece, will you look to those things I told you of?

BEATRICE   I cry you mercy, uncle. By your grace's pardon.   3?

[she bows and goes out

D. PEDRO   By my troth, a pleasant-spirited lady.

LEONATO   There's little of the melancholy element in her, my
lord. She is never sad but when she sleeps, and not
ever sad then: for I have heard my daughter say, she
hath often dreamt of unhappiness and waked herself
with laughing.

D. PEDRO   She cannot endure to hear tell of a husband.

LEONATO   O by no means – she mocks all her wooers out of suit.

D. PEDRO   She were an excellent wife for Benedick.

LEONATO   O Lord, my lord, if they were but a week married, 31
they would talk themselves mad.

D. PEDRO   Count Claudio, when mean you to go to church?

CLAUDIO   Tomorrow, my lord. Time goes on crutches till love
have all his rites.

LEONATO   Not till Monday, my dear son, which is hence a just
seven-night – and a time too brief too, to have all
things answer my mind.

D. PEDRO   Come, you shake the head at so long a breathing – but
I warrant thee, Claudio, the time shal not go dully by
us. I will in the interim undertake one of Hercules' 32
labours, which is, to bring Signior Benedick and the
Lady Beatrice into a mountain of affection th'one with
th'other. I would fain have it a match – and I doubt

not but to fashion it, if you three will but minister such
assistance as I shall give you direction.

LEONATO   My lord, I am for you, though it cost me ten nights'
watchings.

CLAUDIO   And I, my lord.

D. PEDRO   And you too, gentle Hero?

HERO   I will do any modest office, my lord, to help my cousin   330
to a good husband.

D. PEDRO   And Benedick is not the unhopefullest husband that I
know: thus far can I praise him − he is of a noble
strain, of approved valour, and confirmed honesty. [*to
Hero*] I will teach you how to humour your cousin,
that she shall fall in love with Benedick. [*to Leonato and
Claudio*] And I, with your two helps, will so practise on
Benedick that, in despite of his quick wit and his
queasy stomach, he shall fall in love with Beatrice. If
we can do this, Cupid is no longer an archer, his glory   340
shall be ours − for we are the only love-gods. Go in
with me, and I will tell you my drift.

        [*they go within, Hero on the arm of Claudio*

SCENE 2

*DON JOHN and BORACHIO, coming from the banquet,
meet them in the door*

DON JOHN   It is so − the Count Claudio shall marry the daughter
of Leonato.

BORACHIO   Yea my lord, but I can cross it.

DON JOHN   Any bar, any cross, any impediment will be medicinable
to me. I am sick in displeasure to him, and whatsoever
comes athwart his affection ranges evenly with mine.
How canst thou cross this marriage?

BORACHIO   Not honestly, my lord − but so covertly that no
dishonesty shall appear in me.

DON JOHN   Show me briefly how.   10

BORACHIO   I think I told your lordship, a year since, how much I
am in the favour of Margaret, the waiting gentlewoman
to Hero.

DON JOHN I remember.

BORACHIO I can, at any unseasonable instant of the night, appoint
her to look out at her lady's chamber-window.

DON JOHN What life is in that to be the death of this marriage?

BORACHIO The poison of that lies in you to temper. Go you to
the prince your brother, spare not to tell him that he
hath wronged his honour in marrying the renowned 20
Claudio – whose estimation do you mightily hold up –
to a contaminated stale, such a one as Hero.

DON JOHN What proof shall I make of that?

BORACHIO Proof enough to misuse the prince, to vex Claudio, to
undo Hero, and kill Leonato. Look you for any other
issue?

DON JOHN Only to despite them, I will endeavour any thing.

BORACHIO Go then, find me a meet hour to draw Don Pedro and
the Count Claudio alone, tell them that you know
that Hero loves me, intend a kind of zeal both to the 30
prince and Claudio, as in love of your brother's honour, who hath made this match, and his friend's
reputation, who is thus like to be cozened with the
semblance of a maid. That you have discovered this
they will scarcely believe without trial: offer them
instances, which shall bear no less likelihood than to
see me at her chamber-window, hear me call Margaret
Hero, hear Margaret term me Claudio – and bring
them to see this the very night before the intended
wedding. For in the meantime I will so fashion the 40
matter that Hero shall be absent, and there shall appear
such seeming truth of Hero's disloyalty, that jealousy
shall be called assurance, and all the preparation overthrown.

DON JOHN Grow this to what adverse issue it can, I will put it in
practice. Be cunning in the working this, and thy fee is
a thousand ducats.

BORACHIO Be you constant in the accusation, and my cunning shall
not shame me.

DON JOHN I will presently go learn their day of marriage. [*they go*

SCENE 3

The orchard adjoining the house of Leonato

BENEDICK *enters the orchard, musing; he yawns*

BENEDICK [*calls*] Boy!   [*a boy runs up*
BOY   Signior.
BENEDICK In my chamber-window lies a book, bring it hither to
          me in the orchard.
BOY   I am here already, sir.
BENEDICK I know that – but I would have thee hence, and here
          again. [*the boy departs;* BENEDICK *sits*] I do much wonder,
          that one man seeing how much another man is a fool
          when he dedicates his behaviours to love, will after he
          hath laughed at such shallow follies in others, become   10
          the. argument of his own scorn by falling in love. And
          such a man is Claudio. I have known when there was no
          music with him but the drum and the fife, and now had
          he rather hear the tabor and the pipe: I have known
          when he would have walked ten mile afoot, to see a
          good armour, and now will he lie ten nights awake
          carving the fashion of a new doublet: he was wont to
          speak plain, and to the purpose (like an honest man and a
          soldier) and now is he turned orthography – his words
          are a very fantastical banquet, just somany strange dishes.   20
          May I be so converted, and see with these eyes? I cannot
          tell – I think not: I will not be sworn but love may
          transform me to an oyster, but I'll take my oath on it, till
          he have made an oyster of me, he shall never make me
          such a fool. One woman is fair, yet I am well: another is
          wise, yet I am well: another virtuous, yet I am well: but
          till all graces be in one woman, one woman shall not
          come in my grace. Rich she shall be, that's certain: wise,
          or I'll none: virtuous, or I'll never cheapen her: fair, or
          I'll never look on her: mild, or come not near me: noble,   30
          or not I for an angel: of good discourse, an excellent
          musician, and her hair shall be of what colour it please
          God. [*voices heard*] Ha! The prince and Monsieur Love! I
          will hide me in the arbour.   [*he does so*

DON PEDRO, LEONATO, *and* CLAUDIO *approach, followed by*
BALTHAZAR *with a lute;* CLAUDIO *stands beside the arbour*
and peeps through the honeysuckle

D. PEDRO   Come, shall we hear this music?

CLAUDIO   Yea, my good lord. How still the evening is,
          As hushed on purpose to grace harmony!

D. PEDRO   See you where Benedick hath hid himself?

CLAUDIO   O very well, my lord: the music ended,
          We'll fit the hid-fox with a pennyworth.   40

D. PEDRO   Come Balthazar, we'll hear that song again.

BALTH'R   O good my lord, tax not so bad a voice
          To slander music any more than once.

D. PEDRO   It is the witness still of excellency,
          To put a strange face on his own perfection.
          I pray thee sing, and let me woo no more.

BALTH'R   Because you talk of wooing, I will sing –
          Since many a wooer doth commence his suit
          To her he thinks not worthy, yet he wooes,
          Yet will he swear he loves.

D. PEDRO   Nay, pray thee come,   50
          Or if thou wilt hold longer argument,
          Do it in notes.

BALTH'R   Note this before my notes –
          There's not a note of mine that's worth the noting.

D. PEDRO   Why these are very crotchets that he speaks –
          Note notes, forsooth, and nothing!

                                [*Balthazar begins to play*

BENEDICK   Now, divine air! now is his soul ravished. Is it not
          strange that sheeps' guts should hale souls out of men's
          bodies Well, a horn for my money, when all's done.

                       Balthazar sings

      Sigh no more, ladies, sigh no more,   60
          Men were deceivers ever,
      One foot in sea, and one on shore,
          To one thing constant never.
          Then sigh not so, but let them go,
            And be you blithe and bonny,
          Converting all your sounds of woe
           Into Hey nonny, nonny.

> Sing no more ditties, sing no moe
> > Of dumps so dull and heavy,
> The fraud of men was ever so,   70
> > Since summer first was leavy.
> > > Then sigh not so, but let them go,
> > > And be you blithe and bonny,
> > > Converting all your sounds of woe
> > > Into Hey nonny, nonny.

D. PEDRO   By my troth, a good song.

BALTH'R   And an ill singer, my lord.

D. PEDRO   Ha, no, no, faith – thou sing'st well enough for a shift.

> *[he talks apart with Claudio and Leonato*

BENEDICK   An he had been a dog that should have howled thus,
they would have hanged him. And I pray God his bad 80
voice bode no mischief – I had as lief have heard the
night-raven, come what plague could have come after it.

D. PEDRO   Yea, marry. *[turns]* Dost thou hear, Balthazar? I pray
thee get us some excellent music: for tomorrow night
we would have it at the Lady Hero's chamber-window.

BALTH'R   The best I can, my lord.

D. PEDRO   Do so, farewell.   *[Balthazar goes*
Come hither, Leonato. What was it you told me of to-
day? That your niece Beatrice was in love with Signior
Benedick?   90

> BENEDICK *crouches close to the side of the arbour*
> *that he may hear the better*

CLAUDIO   *[peeping]* O ay, stalk on, stalk on – the fowl sits. *[aloud]*
I did never think that lady would have loved any
man.

LEONATO   No, nor I neither – but most wonderful that she
should so dote on Signior Benedick, whom she hath in
all outward behaviours seemed ever to abhor.

BENEDICK   Is't possible? Sits the wind in that corner?

LEONATO   By my troth, my lord, I cannot tell what to think of it,
but that she loves him with an enraged affection. It is
past the infinite of thought.   100

D. PEDRO   May be she doth but counterfeit.

CLAUDIO   Faith, like enough.

LEONATO   O God! Counterfeit? There was never counterfeit of
          passion came so near the life of passion as she dis-
          covers it.

D. PEDRO Why, what effects of passion shows she?

CLAUDIO   [*peeps again*] Bait the hook well – this fish will bite.

LEONATO   What effects, my lord! She will sit you – [*to Claudio*]
          You heard my daughter tell you how.

CLAUDIO   She did, indeed.   110

D. PEDRO How, how, I pray you! You amaze me. I would have
          thought her spirit had been invincible against all assaults
          of affection.

LEONATO   I would have sworn it had, my lord – especially against
          Benedick.

BENEDICK I should think this a gull, but that the white-bearded
          fellow speaks it: knavery cannot, sure, hide himself in
          such reverence.

CLAUDIO   He hath ta'en th'infection – hold it up.

D. PEDRO Hath she made her affection known to Benedick?   120

LEONATO   No, and swears she never will. That's her torment.

CLAUDIO   'Tis true indeed, so your daughter says: 'Shall I,' says
          she, 'that have so oft encountered him with scorn, write
          to him that I love him?'

LEONATO   This says she now when she is beginning to write to
          him, for she'll be up twenty times a night, and there
          will she sit in her smock till she have writ a sheet of
          paper: my daughter tells us all.

CLAUDIO   Now you talk of a sheet of paper, I remember a pretty
          jest your daughter told us of.   130

LEONATO   O, when she had writ it, and was reading it over, she
          found 'Benedick' and 'Beatrice' between the sheet?

CLAUDIO   That.

LEONATO   O, she tore the letter into a thousand half-pence, railed
          at herself that she should be so immodest to write to
          one that she knew would flout her. 'I measure him,'
          says she, 'by my own spirit, for I should flout him if he
          writ to me – yea, though I love him, I should.'

CLAUDIO   Then down upon her knees she falls, weeps, sobs, beats
          her heart, tears her hair, prays, curses – 'O sweet   140
          Benedick! God give me patience!'

LEONATO	She doth indeed – my daughter says so. And the ecstasy hath so much overborne her, that my daughter is some-time afeard she will do a desperate outrage to herself. It is very true.
D. PEDRO	It were good that Benedick knew of it by some other, if she will not discover it.
CLAUDIO	To what end? He would make but a sport of it, and torment the poor lady worse.
D. PEDRO	An he should, it were an alms to hang him. She's an 150 excellent sweet lady, and – out of all suspicion – she is virtuous.
CLAUDIO	And she is exceeding wise.
D. PEDRO	In every thing but in loving Benedick.
LEONATO	O my lord, wisdom and blood combating in so tender a body, we have ten proofs to one that blood hath the victory. I am sorry for her, as I have just cause, being her uncle and her guardian.
D. PEDRO	I would she had bestowed this dotage on me. I would have daffed all other respects, and made her half my- 160 self. I pray you tell Benedick of it, and hear what 'a will say.
LEONATO	Were it good, think you?
CLAUDIO	Hero thinks surely she will die – for she says she will die if he love her not, and she will die ere she make her love known, and she will die if he woo her rather than she will bate one breath of her accustomed crossness.
D. PEDRO	She doth well. If she should make tender of her love, 'tis very possible he'll scorn it – for the man, as you know all, hath a contemptible spirit. 170
CLAUDIO	He is a very proper man.
D. PEDRO	He hath indeed a good outward happiness.
CLAUDIO	Before God, and in my mind, very wise.
D. PEDRO	He doth indeed show some sparks that are like wit.
CLAUDIO	And I take him to be valiant.
D. PEDRO	As Hector, I assure you. And in the managing of quarrels you may say he is wise, for either he avoids them with great discretion, or undertakes them with a most Christian-like fear.
LEONATO	If he do fear God, 'a must necessarily keep peace. If he 180

break the peace, he ought to enter into a quarrel with fear and trembling.

D. PEDRO   And so will he do – for the man doth fear God, how-soever it seems not in him by some large jests he will make . . . Well, I am sorry for your niece. Shall we go seek Benedick, and tell him of her love?

CLAUDIO   Never tell him, my lord. Let her wear it out with good counsel.

LEONATO   Nay, that's impossible – she may wear her heart out first.   190

D. PEDRO   Well, we will hear further of it by your daughter. Let it cool the while. I love Benedick well, and I could wish he would modestly examine himself, to see how much he is unworthy so good a lady.

LEONATO   My lord, will you walk? Dinner is ready.

[they draw away from the arbour

CLAUDIO   If he do not dote on her upon this, I will never trust my expectation.

D. PEDRO   Let there be the same net spread for her – and that must your daughter and her gentlewomen carry. The sport will be, when they hold one an opinion of another's 200 dotage, and no such matter. That's the scene that I would see, which will be merely a dumb-show. Let us send her to call him in to dinner.

They depart; BENEDICK *comes from the arbour*

BENEDICK   This can be no trick. The conference was sadly borne. They have the truth of this from Hero. They seem to pity the lady. It seems her affections have their full bent. Love me! Why, it must be requited. I hear how I am censured – they say I will bear myself proudly, if I perceive the love come from her: they say too that she will rather die than give any sign of affection. I did 210 never think to marry. I must not seem proud. Happy are they that hear their detractions, and can put them to mending. They say the lady is fair – 'tis a truth, I can bear them witness: and virtuous – 'tis so, I cannot reprove it: and wise, but for loving me – by my troth, it is no addition to her wit, nor no great argument of

her folly, for I will be horribly in love with her. I may
chance have some odd quirks and remnants of wit
broken on me, because I have railed so long against
marriage: but doth not the appetite alter? A man loves 220
the meat in his youth that he cannot endure in his age.
Shall quips and sentences and these paper bullets of the
brain awe a man from the career of his humour? No –
the world must be peopled. When I said I would die a
bachelor, I did not think I should live till I were
married.

                    BEATRICE *approaches*

Here comes Beatrice. By this day, she's a fair lady. I do
spy some marks of love in her.

BEATRICE   Against my will I am sent to bid you come in to
dinner.   230

BENEDICK   Fair Beatrice, I thank you for your pains.

BEATRICE   I took no more pains for those thanks than you take
pains to thank me. If it had been painful, I would not
have come.

BENEDICK   You take pleasure then in the message.

BEATRICE   Yea, just so much as you may take upon a knife's point,
and choke a daw withal. You have no stomach, signior
– fare you well.   [*she goes*

BENEDICK   Ha! 'Against my will I am sent to bid you come in to
dinner': there's a double meaning in that. 'I took no   240
more pains for those thanks than you took pains to
thank me' – that's as much as to say, Any pains that I
take for you is as easy as thanks. If I do not take pity of
her, I am a villain. If I do not love her, I am a Jew. I
will go get her picture.   [*he departs in haste*

                    A day passes

ACT 3 SCENE I

The orchard; HERO, MARGARET, *and* URSULA *enter the alley of fruit-trees*

HERO   Good Margaret, run thee to the parlour,
              There shalt thou find my cousin Beatrice
              Proposing with the prince and Claudio.
              Whisper her ear, and tell her I and Ursley
              Walk in the orchard, and our whole discourse
              Is all of her. Say that thou overheard'st us,
              And bid her steal into the pleachéd bower,
              Where honeysuckles, ripened by the sun,
              Forbid the sun to enter, like favourites,
              Made proud by princes, that advance their pride   10
              Against that power that bred it. There will she hide her,
              To listen our propose. This is thy office –
              Bear thee well in it and leave us alone.
MARGARET I'll make her come, I warrant you, presently.
                                                    [*she leaves them*
HERO   Now, Ursula, when Beatrice doth come,
              As we do trace this alley up and down,
              Our talk must only be of Benedick.
              When I do name him, let it be thy part
              To praise him more than ever man did merit.
              My talk to thee must be how Benedick   20
              Is sick in love with Beatrice: of this matter
              Is little Cupid's crafty arrow made,
              That only wounds by hearsay.

          BEATRICE *approaches, and stealing behind the walls of the alley, enters the arbour*

                                        Now begin,
              For look where Beatrice like a lapwing runs
              Close by the ground, to hear our conference.
URSULA   The pleasant'st angling is to see the fish
              Cut with her golden oars the silver stream,
              And greedily devour the treacherous bait:
              So angle we for Beatrice, who even now

Is couchéd in the woodbine coverture.   30
Fear you not my part of the dialogue.

HERO   Then go we near her, that her ear lose nothing
Of the false sweet bait that we lay for it.

                              [*they draw nigh the arbour*

No, truly, Ursula, she is too disdainful –
I know her spirits are as coy and wild
As haggards of the rock.

URSULA   But are you sure
That Benedick loves Beatrice so entirely?

HERO   So says the prince, and my new-trothéd lord.

URSULA   And did they bid you tell her of it, madam?

HERO   They did entreat me to acquaint her of it.   40
But I persuaded them, if they loved Benedick,
To wish him wrestle with affection,
And never to let Beatrice know of it.

URSULA   Why did you so? Doth not the gentleman
Deserve at full as fortunate a bed
As ever Beatrice shall couch upon?

HERO   O god of love! I know he doth deserve
As much as may be yielded to a man:
But nature never framed a woman's heart
Of prouder stuff than that of Beatrice   50
Disdain and scorn ride sparkling in her eyes,
Misprizing what they look on, and her wit
Values itself so highly, that to her
All matter else seems weak: she cannot love,
Nor take no shape nor project of affection,
She is so self-endeared.

URSULA   Sure, I think so.
And therefore certainly it were not good
She knew his love, lest she'll make sport at it.

HERO   Why, you speak truth. I never yet saw man,
How wise, how noble, young, how rarely featured,   60
But she would spell him backward: if fair-faced,
She would swear the gentleman should be her sister;
If black, why nature, drawing of an antic,
Made a foul blot: if tall, a lance ill-headed;
If low, an agate very vilely cut:

If speaking, why a vane blown with all winds;
If silent, why a block movéd with none.
So turns she every man the wrong side out,
And never gives to truth and virtue that
Which simpleness and merit purchaseth.   70

URSULA Sure, sure, such carping is not commendable.

HERO   No, nor to be so odd and from all fashions,
As Beatrice is, cannot be commendable.
But who dare tell her so? If I should speak,
She would mock me into air – O, she would laugh me
Out of myself, press me to death with wit.
Therefore let Benedick, like covered fire,
Consume away in sighs, waste inwardly:
It were a better death than die with mocks,
Which is as bad as die with tickling.   80

URSULA Yet tell her of it, hear what she will say.

HERO   No rather I will go to Benedick,
And counsel him to fight against his passion.
And, truly, I'll devise some honest slanders
To stain my cousin with. One doth not know,
How much an ill word may empoison liking.

URSULA O do not do your cousin such a wrong.
She cannot be so much without true judgment –
Having so swift and excellent a wit,
As she is prized to have – as to refuse   90
So rare a gentleman as Signior Benedick.

HERO   He is the only man of Italy,
Always excepted my dear Claudio.

URSULA I pray you be not angry with me, madam,
Speaking my fancy: Signior Benedick,
For shape, for bearing, argument, and valour,
Goes foremost in report through Italy.

HERO   Indeed, he hath an excellent good name.

URSULA His excellence did earn it, ere he had it.
When are you married, madam?   100

HERO   Why, every day tomorrow! Come, go in.
I'll show thee some attires, and have thy counsel
Which is the best to furnish me tomorrow.

URSULA   She's limed, I warrant you – we have caught her,
                                                    madam.

HERO   If it prove so, then loving goes by haps,
            Some Cupid kills with arrows, some with traps.

                                                    [*they go*

              BEATRICE *comes from the arbour*

BEATRICE   What fire is in mine ears? Can this be true?
            Stand I condemned for pride and scorn so much?
            Contempt, farewell! And maiden pride, adieu!
            No glory lives behind the back of such.   110
            And, Benedick, love on, I will requite thee,
            Taming my wild heart to thy loving hand:
            If thou dost love, my kindness shall incite thee
            To bind our loves up in a holy band:
            For others say thou dost deserve, and I
            Believe it better than reportingly.   [*she goes*

                        SCENE 2

              The parlour in Leonato's house

      DON PEDRO, CLAUDIO, BENEDICK (*very spruce*), and LEONATO

D. PEDRO   I do but stay till your marriage be consummate, and
            then go I toward Arragon.

CLAUDIO   I'll bring you thither, my lord, if you'll vouchsafe me.

D. PEDRO   Nay, that would be as great a soil in the new gloss of
            your marriage, as to show a child his new coat and
            forbid him to wear it. I will only be bold with
            Benedick for his company – for, from the crown of his
            head to the sole of his foot, he is all mirth. He hath
            twice or thrice cut Cupid's bowstring, and the little
            hangman dare not shoot at him. He hath a heart as   10
            sound as a bell, and his tongue is the clapper – for what
            his heart thinks his tongue speaks.

BENEDICK   Gallants, I am not as I have been.

LEONATO   So say I. Methinks you are sadder.

CLAUDIO   I hope he be in love.

D. PEDRO   Hang him, truant! There's no true drop of blood in him to be truly touched with love. If he be sad, he wants money.

BENEDICK I have the toothache.

D. PEDRO Draw it.

BENEDICK Hang it!

CLAUDIO You must hang it first, and draw it afterwards.

D. PEDRO What! Sigh for the toothache?

LEONATO Where is but a humour or a worm?

BENEDICK Well, every one can master a grief but he that has it.

CLAUDIO Yet say I, he is in love.

D. PEDRO There is no appearance of fancy in him, unless it be a fancy that he hath to strange disguises – as, to be a Dutchman today, a Frenchman tomorrow, or in the shape of two countries at once, as a German from the waist downward, all slops, and a Spaniard from the hip upward, no doublet. Unless he have a fancy to this foolery, as it appears he hath, he is no fool for fancy, as you would have it appear he is.

CLAUDIO If he be not in love with some woman, there is no believing old signs. A' brushes his hat a mornings – what should that bode?

D. PEDRO Hath any man seen him at the barber's?

CLAUDIO No, but the barber's man hath been seen with him, and the old ornament of his cheek hath already stuffed tennis-balls.

LEONATO Indeed, he looks younger than he did, by the loss of a beard.

D. PEDRO Nay, a' rubs himself with civet – can you smell him out by that?

CLAUDIO That's as much as to say the sweet youth's in love.

D. PEDRO The greatest note of it is his melancholy.

CLAUDIO And when was he wont to wash his face?

D. PEDRO Yea, or to paint himself? For the which, I hear what they say of him.

CLAUDIO Nay, but his jesting spirit, which is new-crept into a lute-string and now governed by stops.

D. PEDRO Indeed, that tells a heavy tale for him. Conclude, conclude, he is in love.

CLAUDIO Nay, but I know who loves him.

D. PEDRO	That would I know too. I warrant, one that knows him not.
CLAUDIO	Yes, and his ill conditions – and in despite of all, dies for him.
D. PEDRO	She shall be buried with her face upwards. 60
BENEDICK	Yet is this no charm for the toothache. Old signior, walk aside with me. I have studied eight or nine wise words to speak to you, which these hobby-horses must not hear. [*Benedick and Leonato go out*
D. PEDRO	For my life, to break with him about Beatrice.
CLAUDIO	'Tis even so. Hero and Margaret have by this played their parts with Beatrice, and then the two bears will not bite one another when they meet.

DON JOHN *enters*

DON JOHN	My lord and brother, God save you.
D. PEDRO	Good-den, brother. 70
DON JOHN	If your leisure served, I would speak with you.
D. PEDRO	In private?
DON JOHN	If it please you – yet Count Claudio may hear, for what I would speak of concerns him.
CLAUDIO	What's the matter?
DON JOHN	Means your lordship to be married tomorrow?
D. PEDRO	You know he does.
DON JOHN	I know not that, when he knows what I know.
CLAUDIO	If there be any impediment, I pray you discover it.
DON JOHN	You may think I love you not – let that appear here- 80 after, and aim better at me by that I now will manifest. For my brother, I think he holds you well, and in dearness of heart hath holp to effect your ensuing marriage: surely, suit ill spent, and labour ill bestowed.
D. PEDRO	Why, what's the matter?
DON JOHN	I came hither to tell you, and, circumstances shortened – for she has been too long a talking of – the lady is disloyal.
CLAUDIO	Who, Hero?
DON JOHN	Even she – Leonato's Hero, your Hero, every man's 90 Hero.
CLAUDIO	Disloyal?

DON JOHN The word is too good to paint out her wickedness. I
could say she were worse. Think you of a worse title, and
I will fit her to it. Wonder not till further warrant: go but
with me tonight, you shall see her chamber-window
entered, even the night before her wedding-day. If you
love her then, tomorrow wed her. But it would better fit
your honour to change your mind.

CLAUDIO May this be so?   100

D. PEDRO I will not think it.

DON JOHN If you dare not trust that you see, confess not that you
know: if you will follow me, I will show you enough,
and when you have seen more and heard more,
proceed accordingly.

CLAUDIO If I see any thing tonight why I should not marry her,
tomorrow, in the congregation, where I should wed,
there will I shame her.

D. PEDRO And as I wooed for thee to obtain her, I will join with
thee to disgrace her.   110

DON JOHN I will disparage her no farther till you are my witnesses. Bear it coldly but till midnight, and let the issue
show itself.

D. PEDRO O day untowardly turned!

CLAUDIO O mischief strangely thwarting!

DON JOHN O plague right well prevented! So will you say, when
you have seen the sequel.   [*they go*

SCENE 3

*A street in Messina: on one side the door of Leonato's house, in the
centre the porch of a church, having a bench within it: midnight; rain
and wind*

*The Watch, armed with bills, stand a-row before the porch; Master
Constable* DOGBERRY, *bearing a lantern, and* VERGES, *the
Headborough, survey them*

DOGBERRY Are you good men and true?

VERGES Yea, or else it were pity but they should suffer salvation,
body and soul.

DOGBERRY Nay, that were a punishment too good for them, if

they should have any allegiance in them, being chosen
for the prince's watch.

VERGES   Well, give them their charge, neighbour Dogberry.

DOGBERRY First, who think you the most desertless man to be
constable?

1 WATCH. Hugh Oatcake, sir, or George Seacoal, for they can   10
write and read.

DOGBERRY Come hither, neighbour Seacoal. God hath blessed you
with a good name: to be a well-favoured man is the gift
of fortune, but to write and read comes by nature.

2 WATCH. Both which, Master Constable –

DOGBERRY You have: I knew it would be your answer. Well, for
your favour, sir, why give God thanks, and make no
boast of it – and for your writing and reading, let that
appear when there is no need of such vanity. You are
thought here to be the most senseless and fit man for   20
the constable of the watch: therefore bear you the
lantern [*he gives it to him*]. This is your charge – you
shall comprehend all vagrom men, you are to bid any
man stand, in the prince's name.

2 WATCH. How if 'a will not stand?

DOGBERRY Why then take no note of him, but let him go, and
presently call the rest of the watch together, and thank
God you are rid of a knave.

VERGES   If he will not stand when he is bidden, he is none of
the prince's subjects.   30

DOGBERRY True, and they are to meddle with none but the
prince's subjects. You shall also make no noise in the
streets: for, for the watch to babble and to talk, is most
tolerable and not to be endured.

2 WATCH. We will rather sleep than talk – we know what belongs to a watch.

DOGBERRY Why, you speak like an ancient and most quiet watchman, for I cannot see how sleeping should offend: only
have a care that your bills be not stolen. Well, you are
to call at all the ale-houses, and bid those that are   40
drunk get them to bed.

2 WATCH. How if they will not?

DOGBERRY Why then, let them alone till they are sober. If they
          make you not then the better answer, you may say
          they are not the men you took them for.

2 WATCH. Well, sir.

DOGBERRY If you meet a thief, you may suspect him, by virtue of
          your office, to be no true man: and, for such kind of
          men, the less you meddle or make with them, why the
          more is for your honesty.   50

2 WATCH. If we know him to be a thief, shall we not lay hands
          on him?

DOGBERRY Truly by your office you may, but I think they that
          touch pitch will be defiled: the most peaceable way for
          you, if you do take a thief, is to let him show himself
          what he is, and steal out of your company.

VERGES   You have been always called a merciful man, partner.

DOGBERRY Truly, I would not hang a dog by my will, much more
          a man who hath any honesty in him.

VERGES   If you hear a child cry in the night, you must call to 60
          the nurse and bid her still it.

2 WATCH. How if the nurse be asleep and will not hear us?

DOGBERRY Why then, depart in peace, and let the child wake her
          with crying – for the ewe that will not hear her lamb
          when it baes, will never answer a calf when he bleats.

VERGES   'Tis very true.

DOGBERRY This is the end of the charge. You, constable, are to
          present the prince's own person – if you meet the
          prince in the night, you may stay him.

VERGES   Nay, by'r lady, that I think 'a cannot.   70

DOGBERRY Five shillings to one on't with any man that knows the
          statutes, he may stay him – marry, not without the
          prince be willing, for indeed the watch ought to of-
          fend no man, and it is an offence to stay a man against
          his will.

VERGES   By'r lady, I think it be so.

DOGBERRY Ha, ah, ha! Well, masters, good night. An there be any
          matter of weight chances, call up me. Keep your fel-
          lows' counsels and your own, and good night. Come,
          neighbour.   [*they walk away* 80

2 WATCH. Well, masters, we hear our charge. Let us go sit here
            upon the church-bench till two, and then all to bed.

                        [*they all enter the porch and prepare to sleep*

DOGBERRY [*turns*] One word more, honest neighbours. I pray you,
            watch about Signior Leonato's door, for the wedding
            being there tomorrow, there is a great coil tonight.
            Adieu, be vigitant, I beseech you.

                            [*Dogberry and Verges go*

The door of Leonato's house opens and BORACHIO *staggers forth,*
       followed after a short space by CONRADE

BORACHIO [*stops*] What, Conrade!

2 WATCH. Peace, stir not.

BORACHIO Conrade, I say!   90

CONRADE Here, man, I am at thy elbow.

BORACHIO Mass, and my elbow itched – I thought there would a
            scab follow.

CONRADE I will owe thee an answer for that, and now forward
            with thy tale.

BORACHIO Stand thee close then under this pent-house, for it
            drizzles rain, and I will, like a true drunkard, utter all
            to thee.   [*they stand beneath the eaves of the porch*

2 WATCH. Some treason, masters – yet stand close.

BORACHIO Therefore know, I have earned of Don John a thousand   100
            ducats.

CONRADE Is it possible that any villainy should be so dear?

BORACHIO Thou shouldst rather ask if it were possible any villainy
            should be so rich, for when rich villains have need of
            poor ones, poor ones may make what price they will.

CONRADE I wonder at it.

BORACHIO That shows thou art unconfirmed. Thou knowest that
            the fashion of a doublet, or a hat, or a cloak, is nothing
            to a man.

CONRADE Yes it is apparel.   110

BORACHIO I mean the fashion.

CONRADE Yes, the fashion is the fashion.

BORACHIO Tush, I may as well say the fool's the fool. But seest
            thou not what a deformed thief this fashion is?

2 WATCH. I know that Deformed, 'a has been a vile thief this

seven year, 'a goes up and down like a gentleman: I
remember his name.

BORACHIO Didst thou not hear somebody?

CONRADE No, 'twas the vane on the house.

BORACHIO Seest thou not, I say, what a deformed thief this fashion 120
is? How giddily 'a turns about all the hot-bloods
between fourteen and five-and-thirty? Sometimes
fashioning them like Pharaoh's soldiers in the reechy
painting, sometime like god Bel's priests in the old
church window, sometime like the shaven Hercules
in the smirched worm-eaten tapestry, where his cod-
piece seems as massy as his club?

CONRADE All this I see, and I see that the fashion wears out more
apparel than the man. But art not thou thyself giddy
with the fashion too, that thou hast shifted out of thy 130
tale into telling me of the fashion?

BORACHIO Not so neither. But know that I have tonight wooed
Margaret, the Lady Hero's gentlewoman, by the name
of Hero. She leans me out at her mistress' chamber-
window, bids me a thousand times good night. I tell
this tale vilely – I should first tell thee how the prince,
Claudio, and my master, planted and placed and possessed by my master Don John, saw afar off in the
orchard this amiable encounter.

CONRADE And thought they Margaret was Hero?   140

BORACHIO Two of them did, the prince and Claudio. But the
devil, my master, knew she was Margaret – and partly
by his oaths, which first possessed them, partly by the
dark night, which did deceive them, but chiefly by my
villainy, which did confirm any slander that Don John
had made, away went Claudio enraged, swore he
would meet her as he was appointed next morning at
the temple, and there, before the whole congregation,
shame her with what he saw o'er-night, and send her
home again without a husband. [*the watchmen sally forth* 150

2 WATCH. We charge you in the prince's name, stand.

1 WATCH. Call up the right Master Constable. We have here recovered the most dangerous piece of lechery that ever
was known in the commonwealth.

2 WATCH. And one Deformed is one of them – I know him, 'a
          wears a lock.

CONRADE   Masters, masters.

2 WATCH. You'll be made bring Deformed forth, I warrant you.

CONRADE   Masters –

1 WATCH. Never speak, we charge you. Let us obey you to go   160
          with us.

BORACHIO We are like to prove a goodly commodity, being taken
          up of these men's bills.

CONRADE   A commodity in question, I warrant you. Come, we'll
          obey you.   [*the watchmen hale them away*

SCENE 4

A room opening into Hero's bed-chamber

HERO, *before a mirror,* MARGARET, *and* URSULA

HERO   Good Ursula, wake my cousin Beatrice, and desire her
          to rise.

URSULA   I will, lady.

HERO   And bid her come hither.

URSULA   Well.   [*she goes out*

MARGARET Troth, I think your other rebato were better.

HERO   No, pray thee good Meg, I'll wear this.

MARGARET By my troth's not so good, and I warrant your cousin
          will say so.

HERO   My cousin's a fool, and thou art another. I'll wear none   10
          but this.

MARGARET I like the new tire within excellently, if the hair were a
          thought browner: and your gown's a most rare fashion
          i'faith. I saw the Duchess of Milan's gown that they
          praise so –

HERO   O, that exceeds, they say.

MARGARET By my troth's but a night-gown in respect of yours –
          cloth o' gold and cuts, and laced with silver, set with
          pearls down sleeves, side-sleeves, and skirts, round
          underborne with a bluish tinsel – but for a fine quaint   20
          graceful and excellent fashion, yours is worth ten on't.

HERO   God give me joy to wear it, for my heart is exceeding
                heavy.

MARGARET   'Twill be heavier soon by the weight of a man.

HERO   Fie upon thee, art not ashamed?

MARGARET   Of what, lady? Of speaking honourably? Is not marriage
                honourable in a beggar? Is not your lord honourable
                without marriage? I think you would have me say,
                'saving your reverence, a husband': an bad thinking do
                not wrest true speaking – I'll offend nobody – is there   30
                any harm in 'the heavier for a husband'? None I think,
                an it be the right husband, and the right wife, otherwise
                'tis light and not heavy – ask my Lady Beatrice else,
                here she comes.

BEATRICE *enters*

HERO   Good morrow, coz.

BEATRICE   Good morrow, sweet Hero.

HERO   Why how now? Do you speak in the sick tune?

BEATRICE   I am out of all other tune, methinks.

MARGARET   Clap's into 'Light o' love' – that goes without a burden
                – do you sing it, and I'll dance it.   40

BEATRICE   Yea, light o' love with your heels – then if your husband
                have stables enough you'll see he shall lack no barns.

MARGARET   O illegitimate construction! I scorn that with my heels.

BEATRICE   'Tis almost five o'clock cousin, 'tis time you were
                ready. By my troth I am exceeding ill. Heigh-ho!

MARGARET   For a hawk, a horse, or a husband?

BEATRICE   For the letter that begins them all, H.

MARGARET   Well, an you be not turned Turk, there's no more
                sailing by the star.

BEATRICE   What means the fool, trow?   50

MARGARET   Nothing I – but God send every one their heart's desire.

HERO   These gloves the count sent me, they are an excellent
                perfume.

BEATRICE   I am stuffed, cousin, I cannot smell.

MARGARET   A maid and stuffed! There's goodly catching of cold.

BEATRICE   O God help me, God help me, how long have you
                professed apprehension?

MARGARET   Ever since you left it. Doth not my wit become me
                rarely?

BEATRICE   It is not seen enough, you should wear it in your cap. 60
            By my troth I am sick.

MARGARET   Get you some of this distilled Carduus Benedictus, and
            lay it to your heart – it is the only thing for a qualm.

HERO   There thou prick'st her with a thistle.

BEATRICE   Benedictus, why Benedictus? You have some moral in
            this Benedictus.

MARGARET   Moral? No, by my troth, I have no moral meaning – I
            meant plain holy-thistle. You may think perchance that
            I think you are in love – nay by'r lady I am not such a
            fool to think what I list, nor I list not to think what I 70
            can, nor indeed I cannot think, if I would think my
            heart out of thinking, that you are in love, or that you
            will be in love, or that you can be in love: yet Benedick
            was such another and now is he become a man. He
            swore he would never marry, and yet now in despite of
            his heart he eats his meat without grudging – and how
            you may be converted I know not, but methinks you
            look with your eyes as other women do.

BEATRICE   What pace is this that thy tongue keeps?

MARGARET   Not a false gallop.   80

                    URSULA *returns in haste*

URSULA   Madam, withdraw. The prince, the count, Signior
            Benedick, Don John, and all the gallants of the town
            are come to fetch you to church.

HERO   Help to dress me, good coz, good Meg, good Ursula.
                                [*they hasten to the bed-chamber*

                          SCENE 5

                The hall in Leonato's house

                LEONATO, DOGBERRY *and* VERGES

LEONATO   What would you with me, honest neighbour?

DOGBERRY   Marry, sir, I would have some confidence with you,
            that decerns you nearly.

LEONATO   Brief I pray you, for you see it is a busy time with me.

DOGBERRY   Marry, this it is, sir.

VERGES   Yes, in truth it is, sir.

LEONATO   What is it, my good friends?

DOGBERRY   Goodman Verges, sir, speaks a little off the matter – an
            old man, sir, and his wits are not so blunt, as God help
            I would desire they were, but in faith honest, as the   10
            skin between his brows.

VERGES   Yes, I thank God, I am as honest as any man living,
            that is an old man, and no honester than I.

DOGBERRY   Comparisons are odorous – palabras, neighbour Verges.

LEONATO   Neighbours, you are tedious.

DOGBERRY   It pleases your worship to say so, but we are the poor
            duke's officers. But truly for mine own part if I were as
            tedious as a king I could find in my heart to bestow it
            all of your worship.

LEONATO   All thy tediousness on me, ah?   20

DOGBERRY   Yea, an 'twere a thousand pound more than 'tis, for I
            hear as good exclamation on your worship as of any
            man in the city, and though I be but a poor man, I am
            glad to hear it.

VERGES   And so am I.

LEONATO   I would fain know what you have to say.

VERGES   Marry sir, our watch tonight, excepting your worship's
            presence, ha' ta'en a couple of as arrant knaves as any in
            Messina.

DOGBERRY   A good old man, sir, he will be talking – as they say,   30
            'when the age is in, the wit is out.' God help us, it is
            a world to see. Well said, i'faith, neighbour Verges.
            Well, God's a good man – an two men ride of a horse,
            one must ride behind. An honest soul i'faith, sir, by
            my troth he is, as ever broke bread, but – God is to be
            worshipped – all men are not alike, alas, good
            neighbour.

LEONATO   Indeed, neighbour, he comes too short of you.

DOGBERRY   Gifts that God gives.

LEONATO   I must leave you.   40

DOGBERRY   One word, sir – our watch, sir, have indeed compre-
            hended two aspicious persons, and we would have
            them this morning examined before your worship.

LEONATO   Take their examination yourself, and bring it me, I am now in great haste, as it may appear unto you.

DOGBERRY It shall be suffigance.

LEONATO Drink some wine ere you go: fare you well.

[*he meets a messenger at the door*

MESSENG'R My lord, they stay for you to give your daughter to
her husband.

LEONATO I'll wait upon them – I am ready.   50

[*Leonato and the messenger go out*

DOGBERRY Go good partner, go get you to Francis Seacoal, bid
him bring his pen and inkhorn to the gaol: we are now
to examination these men.

VERGES And we must do it wisely.

DOGBERRY We will spare for no wit, I warrant you: here's that
[*touches his forehead*] shall drive some of them to a 'non-
come'. Only get the learned writer to set down our
excommunication, and meet me at the gaol.

[*they depart*

ACT 4 SCENE 1

Before the altar of a church

DON PEDRO, DON JOHN, LEONATO, FRIAR FRANCIS, CLAUDIO,
BENEDICK, HERO, BEATRICE, *etc.*

LEONATO Come Friar Francis, be brief – only to the plain form of
marriage, and you shall recount their particular duties
afterwards.

FRIAR You come hither, my lord, to marry this lady?

CLAUDIO No.

LEONATO To be married to her: friar, you come to marry her.

FRIAR Lady, you come hither to be married to this count?

HERO I do.

FRIAR If either of you know any inward impediment why
you should not be conjoined, I charge you on your 10
souls to utter it.

CLAUDIO Know you any, Hero?

HERO None my lord.

FRIAR Know you any, count?

LEONATO I dare make his answer, 'none'.

CLAUDIO O, what men dare do! What men may do! What men
daily do, not knowing what they do!

BENEDICK How now! Interjections? Why then, some be of laughing, as 'ah! ha! he!'

CLAUDIO Stand thee by, friar. Father, by your leave – 20
Will you with free and unconstrainéd soul
Give me this maid your daughter?

LEONATO As freely, son, as God did give her me.

CLAUDIO And what have I to give you back whose worth
May counterpoise this rich and precious gift?

D. PEDRO Nothing, unless you render her again.

CLAUDIO Sweet prince, you learn me noble thankfulness.
There Leonato, take her back again,
Give not this rotten orange to your friend,
She's but the sign and semblance of her honour. 30
Behold how like a maid she blushes here!
O, what authority and show of truth
Can cunning sin cover itself withal!

	Comes not that blood, as modest evidence,	
	To witness simple virtue? Would you not swear,	
	All you that see her, that she were a maid,	
	By these exterior shows? But she is none:	
	She knows the heat of a luxurious bed	
	Her blush is guiltiness, not modesty.	
LEONATO	What do you mean my lord?	
CLAUDIO	Not to be married,	40
	Not to knit my soul to an approvéd wanton.	
LEONATO	Dear my lord, if you in your own proof	
	Have vanquished the resistance of her youth,	
	And made defeat of her virginity –	
CLAUDIO	I know what you would say: if I have known her,	
	You will say she did embrace me as a husband,	
	And so extenuate the 'forehand sin:	
	No Leonato,	
	I never tempted her with word too large,	
	But as a brother to his sister showed	50
	Bashful sincerity, and comely love.	
HERO	And seemed I ever otherwise to you?	
CLAUDIO	Out on the seeming, I will write against it.	
	You seem to me as Dian in her orb,	
	As chaste as is the bud ere it be blown:	
	But you are more intemperate in your blood	
	Than Venus, or those pamp'red animals	
	That rage in savage sensuality.	
HERO	Is my lord well that he doth speak so wide?	
LEONATO	Sweet prince, why speak not you?	
D. PEDRO	What should I speak?	60
	I stand dishonoured that have gone about	
	To link my dear friend to a common stale.	
LEONATO	Are these things spoken, or do I but dream?	
DON JOHN	Sir, they are spoken, and these things are true.	
BENEDICK	This looks not like a nuptial.	
HERO	'True,' O God!	
CLAUDIO	Leonato, stand I here?	
	Is this the prince? Is this the prince's brother?	
	Is this face Hero's? Are our eyes our own?	
LEONATO	All this is so, but what of this my lord?	

CLAUDIO	Let me but move one question to your daughter,	70
	And by that fatherly and kindly power	
	That you have in her, bid her answer truly.	
LEONATO	I charge thee do so, as thou art my child.	
HERO	O God defend me how am I beset!	
	What kind of catechizing call you this?	
CLAUDIO	To make you answer truly to your name.	
HERO	Is it not Hero? Who can blot that name	
	With any just reproach?	

CLAUDIO   Marry, that can Hero –
Hero itself can blot out Hero's virtue.
What man was he talked with you yesternight,   80
Out at your window betwixt twelve and one?
Now if you are a maid, answer to this.

HERO   I talked with no man at that hour my lord.

D. PEDRO Why then are you no maiden. Leonato,
I am sorry you must hear: upon mine honour,
Myself, my brother, and this grievéd count,
Did see her, hear her, at that hour last night,
Talk with a ruffian at her chamber-window –
Who hath indeed, most like a liberal villain,
Confessed the vile encounters they have had   90
A thousand times in secret.

DON JOHN Fie, fie! They are not to be named, my lord,
Not to be spoke of.
There is not chastity enough in language,
Without offence, to utter them. Thus, pretty lady,
I am sorry for thy much misgovernment.

CLAUDIO O Hero! What a Hero hadst thou been,
If half thy outward graces had been placed
About the thoughts and counsels of thy heart!
But, fare thee well, most foul, most fair – farewell,   100
Thou pure impiety, and impious purity.
For thee I'll lock up all the gates of love,
And on my eyelids shall conjecture hang,
To turn all beauty into thoughts of harm,
And never shall it more be gracious.

LEONATO Hath no man's dagger here a point for me?

                                        [*Hero swoons*

BEATRICE   Why, how now cousin, wherefore sink you down?
DON JOHN   Come let us go: these things, come thus to light,
           Smother her spirits up.   [*Don Pedro, Don John,*
                              and Claudio leave the church
BENEDICK   How doth the lady?
BEATRICE   Dead I think – help, uncle –   110
           Hero – why Hero – uncle – Signior Benedick – Friar!
LEONATO   O Fate! Take not away thy heavy hand.
           Death is the fairest cover for her shame
           That may be wished for.
BEATRICE   How now cousin Hero?
FRIAR   Have comfort lady.
LEONATO   Dost thou look up?
FRIAR   Yea, wherefore should she not?
LEONATO   Wherefore? Why, doth not every earthly thing
           Cry shame upon her? Could she here deny
           The story that is printed in her blood?
           Do not live Hero, do not ope thine eyes: 120
           For did I think thou wouldst not quickly die,
           Thought I thy spirits were stronger than thy shames,
           Myself would on the rearward of reproaches
           Strike at thy life. Grieved I, I had but one?
           Chid I for that at frugal nature's frame?
           O, one too much by thee. Why had I one?
           Why ever wast thou lovely in my eyes?
           Why had I not with charitable hand
           Took up a beggar's issue at my gates,
           Who smirchéd thus, and mired with infamy,   130
           I might have said, 'No part of it is mine,
           This shame derives itself from unknown loins'?
           But mine, and mine I loved, and mine I praised,
           And mine that I was proud on, mine so much
           That I myself was to myself not mine,
           Valuing of her – why she, O she is fall'n
           Into a pit of ink, that the wide sea
           Hath drops too few to wash her clean again,
           And salt too little which may season give
           To her foul tainted flesh.   140

BENEDICK   Sir, sir, be patient. For my part, I am so
           Attired in wonder, I know not what to say.
BEATRICE   O, on my soul, my cousin is belied!
BENEDICK   Lady, were you her bedfellow last night?
BEATRICE   No, truly, not – although, until last night,
           I have this twelvemonth been her bedfellow.
LEONATO   Confirmed, confirmed – O, that is stronger made,
           Which was before barred up with ribs of iron.
           Would the two princes lie? And Claudio lie,
           Who loved her so, that, speaking of her foulness,   150
           Washed it with tears! Hence from her, let her die.
FRIAR   Hear me a little –
           [For I have only been silent so long,
           And given way unto this course of fortune,]
           By noting of the lady, I have marked
           A thousand blushing apparitions
           To start into her face, a thousand innocent shames
           In angel whiteness beat away those blushes,
           And in her eye there hath appeared a fire,
           To burn the errors that these princes hold   160
           Against her maiden truth. Call me a fool,
           Trust not my reading, nor my observations,
           Which with experimental seal doth warrant
           The tenour of my book: trust not my age,
           My reverence, calling, nor divinity,
           If this sweet lady lie not guiltless here
           Under some biting error.
LEONATO   Friar, it cannot be.
           Thou seest that all the grace that she hath left
           Is that she will not add to her damnation
           A sin of perjury – she not denies it: 170
           Why seek'st thou then to cover with excuse
           That which appears in proper nakedness?
FRIAR   Lady, what man is he you are accused of?
HERO   They know that do accuse me, I know none.
           If I know more of any man alive
           Than that which maiden modesty doth warrant,
           Let all my sins lack mercy. O my father,
           Prove you that any man with me conversed

	At hours unmeet, or that I yesternight	
	Maintained the change of words with any creature –	180
	Refuse me, hate me, torture me to death.	
FRIAR	There is some strange misprision in the princes.	
BENEDICK	Two of them have the very bent of honour.	
	And if their wisdoms be misled in this,	
	The practice of it lives in John the bastard,	
	Whose spirits toil in frame of villainies.	
LEONATO	I know not. If they speak but truth of her,	
	These hands shall tear her – if they wrong her	
	honour,	
	The proudest of them shall well hear of it.	
	Time hath not yet so dried this blood of mine,	190
	Nor age so eat up my invention,	
	Nor fortune made such havoc of my means,	
	Nor my bad life reft me so much of friends,	
	But they shall find, awaked in such a kind,	
	Both strength of limb, and policy of mind,	
	Ability in means, and choice of friends,	
	To quit me of them throughly.	
FRIAR	Pause awhile,	
	And let my counsel sway you in this case.	
	Your daughter here the princes left for dead.	
	Let her awhile be secretly kept in,	200
	And publish it that she is dead indeed.	
	Maintain a mourning ostentation,	
	And on your family's old monument	
	Hang mournful epitaphs, and do all rites	
	That appertain unto a burial.	
LEONATO	What shall become of this? What will this do?	
FRIAR	Marry, this well carried, shall on her behalf	
	Change slander to remorse – that is some good.	
	But not for that dream I on this strange course,	
	But on this travail look for greater birth:	210
	She dying, as it must be so maintained,	
	Upon the instant that she was accused,	
	Shall be lamented, pitied, and excused	
	Of every hearer: for it so falls out	
	That what we have we prize not to the worth,	

    Whiles we enjoy it, but being lacked and lost,
    Why then we rack the value, then we find
    The virtue that possession would not show us
    Whiles it was ours – so will it fare with Claudio:
    When he shall hear she died upon his words,   220
    Th'idea of her life shall sweetly creep
    Into his study of imagination,
    And every lovely organ of her life
    Shall come apparelled in more precious habit,
    More moving-delicate and full of life,
    Into the eye and prospect of his soul,
    Than when she lived indeed: then shall he mourn –
    If ever love had interest in his liver –
    And wish he had not so accuséd her:
    No, though he thought his accusation true.   230
    Let this be so, and doubt not but success
    Will fashion the event in better shape
    Than I can lay it down in likelihood.
    But if all aim but this be levelled false,
    The supposition of the lady's death
    Will quench the wonder of her infamy.
    And if it sort not well, you may conceal her –
    As best befits her wounded reputation –
    In some reclusive and religious life,
    Out of all eyes, tongues, minds, and injuries.   240

BENEDICK Signior Leonato, let the friar advise you,
    And though you know my inwardness and love
    Is very much unto the prince and Claudio,
    Yet, by mine honour, I will deal in this
    As secretly and justly as your soul
    Should with your body.

LEONATO   Being that I flow in grief,
    The smallest twine may lead me.

FRIAR 'Tis well consented – presently away –
    For to strange sores strangely they strain the cure.
    Come lady, die to live – this wedding day   250
    Perhaps is but prolonged – have patience and endure.
                  [*the Friar, Hero, and Leonato depart*

BENEDICK Lady Beatrice, have you wept all this while?

BEATRICE   Yea, and I will weep a while longer.

BENEDICK   I will not desire that.

BEATRICE   You have no reason, I do it freely.

BENEDICK   Surely I do believe your fair cousin is wronged.

BEATRICE   Ah, how much might the man deserve of me that would right her!

BENEDICK   Is there any way to show such friendship?

BEATRICE   A very even way, but no such friend.   260

BENEDICK   May a man do it?

BEATRICE   It is a man's office, but not yours.

BENEDICK   I do love nothing in the world so well as you – is not that strange?

BEATRICE   As strange as the thing I know not. It were as possible for me to say I loved nothing so well as you – but believe me not – and yet I lie not – I confess nothing, nor I deny nothing – I am sorry for my cousin.

BENEDICK   By my sword Beatrice, thou lovest me.

BEATRICE   Do not swear and eat it.   270

BENEDICK   I will swear by it that you love me, and I will make him eat it that says I love not you.

BEATRICE   Will you not eat your word?

BENEDICK   With no sauce that can be devised to it – I protest I love thee.

BEATRICE   Why then God forgive me –

BENEDICK   What offence sweet Beatrice?

BEATRICE   You have stayed me in a happy hour, I was about to protest I loved you.

BENEDICK   And do it with all thy heart.   280

BEATRICE   I love you with so much of my heart, that none is left to protest.

BENEDICK   Come bid me do any thing for thee.

BEATRICE   Kill Claudio.

BENEDICK   Ha! not for the wide world.

BEATRICE   You kill me to deny it – farewell.

BENEDICK   Tarry sweet Beatrice.   [*he stays her*

BEATRICE   I am gone, though I am here – there is no love in you – nay I pray you let me go.

BENEDICK   Beatrice –   290

BEATRICE   In faith I will go.

BENEDICK We'll be friends first.

BEATRICE You dare easier be friends with me than fight with mine enemy.

BENEDICK Is Claudio thine enemy?

BEATRICE Is 'a not approved in the height a villain, that hath slandered, scorned, dishonoured my kinswoman? O that I were a man! What, bear her in hand until they come to take hands, and then with public accusation, uncovered slander, unmitigated rancour – O God that I   300 were a man! I would eat his heart in the market-place.

BENEDICK Hear me Beatrice –

BEATRICE Talk with a man out at a window – a proper saying!

BENEDICK Nay but Beatrice –

BEATRICE Sweet Hero, she is wronged, she is slandred, she is undone.

BENEDICK Beat –

BEATRICE Princes and counties! Surely a princely testimony, a goodly count, Count Comfect – a sweet gallant surely. O that I were a man for his sake! Or that I had any   310 friend would be a man for my sake! But manhood is melted into curtsies, valour into complement, and men are only turned into tongue, and trim ones too: he is now as valiant as Hercules, that only tells a lie and swears it. I cannot be a man with wishing, therefore I will die a woman with grieving.

BENEDICK Tarry good Beatrice – by this hand I love thee.

BEATRICE Use it for my love some other way than swearing by it.

BENEDICK Think you in your soul the Count Claudio hath wronged Hero?   320

BEATRICE Yea, as sure as I have a thought or a soul.

BENEDICK Enough, I am engaged, I will challenge him. I will kiss your hand, and so I leave you. [*he takes her hand*] By this hand, Claudio shall render me a dear account. [*he kisses it*] As you hear of me, so think of me. Go comfort your cousin. I must say she is dead – and so farewell.

[*he departs; Beatrice follows slowly after*

SCENE 2

A room in a gaol

DOGBERRY *and* VERGES *in their robes of office, the Sexton
in his clerk's gown, and the Watch guarding*
CONRADE *and* BORACHIO

DOGBERRY Is our whole dissembly appeared?

VERGES O, a stool and a cushion for the sexton!

[*they are brought*

SEXTON [*sits*] Which be the malefactors?

DOGBERRY Marry, that am I, and my partner.

VERGES Nay, that's certain. We have the exhibition to examine.

SEXTON But which are the offenders that are to be examined?
let them come before Master Constable.

DOGBERRY Yea marry, let them come before me.

[*Borachio and Conrade are led forward*

What is your name, friend?

BORACHIO Borachio.   10

DOGBERRY Pray write down 'Borachio'. Yours, sirrah?

[*the Sexton writes as Dogberry directs*

CONRADE I am a gentleman, sir, and my name is Conrade.

DOGBERRY Write down 'Master Gentleman Conrade'. Masters, do
you serve God?

CONRADE, BORACHIO Yea, sir, we hope.

DOGBERRY Write down that they hope they serve God: and write
'God' first, for God defend but God should go before
such villains. Masters, it is proved already that you are
little better than false knaves, and it will go near to be
thought so shortly. How answer you for yourselves?   20

CONRADE Marry, sir, we say we are none.

DOGBERRY A marvellous witty fellow, I assure you – but I will go
about with him. Come you hither sirrah – a word in
your ear. Sir, I say to you, it is thought you are false
knaves.

BORACHIO Sir, I say to you, we are none.

DOGBERRY Well, stand aside. 'Fore God, they are both in a tale.
Have you writ down, that they are none?

SEXTON   Master Constable, you go not the way to examine.
            You must call forth the watch that are their accusers.   30

DOGBERRY Yea marry, that's the eftest way, let the watch come
            forth. Masters, I charge you in the prince's name,
            accuse these men.

1 WATCH. This man said, sir, that Don John the prince's brother
            was a villain.

DOGBERRY Write down 'Prince John a villain'. Why this is flat
            perjury, to call a prince's brother villain.

BORACHIO Master Constable –

DOGBERRY Pray thee fellow peace. I do not like thy look, I promise
            thee.   40

SEXTON   What heard you him say else?

2 WATCH. Marry, that he had received a thousand ducats of Don
            John, for accusing the Lady Hero wrongfully.

DOGBERRY Flat burglary as ever was committed.

VERGES   Yea by mass that it is.

SEXTON   What else fellow?

1 WATCH. And that Count Claudio did mean, upon his words, to
            disgrace Hero before the whole assembly, and not
            marry her.

DOGBERRY O villain! Thou wilt be condemned into everlasting   50
            redemption for this.

SEXTON   What else?

WATCHMEN This is all.

SEXTON   And this is more, masters, than you can deny. Prince
            John is this morning secretly stolen away: Hero was in
            this manner accused, in this very manner refused, and
            upon the grief of this suddenly died. Master Constable,
            let these men be bound, and brought to Leonato's. I
            will go before and show him their examination.
                                                    [he goes out

DOGBERRY Come, let them be opinioned.   60

VERGES   Let them be – in the hands.   [he offers to bind Conrade

CONRADE Off, coxcomb!

DOGBERRY God's my life, where's the sexton? Let him write
            down the prince's officer 'coxcomb'. Come, bind
            them. Thou naughty varlet!

CONRADE Away! You are an ass, you are an ass.

[*the Watch bind them*

DOGBERRY Dost thou not suspect my place? Dost thou not suspect my years? O that he were here to write me down
an ass! But, masters, remember that I am an ass —
though it be not written down, yet forget not that I   70
am an ass. No, thou villain, thou art full of piety, as
shall be proved upon thee by good witness. I am a
wise fellow, and which is more — an officer, and
which is more — a householder, and which is more —
as pretty a piece of flesh as any is in Messina, and one
that knows the law, go to, and a rich fellow enough,
go to, and a fellow that hath had losses, and one that
hath two gowns and everything handsome about him.
Bring him away. O that I had been writ down an ass!

[*he struts forth; the rest follow*

ACT 5 SCENE 1

The street before the house of Leonato

LEONATO *and* ANTONIO *appear, walking towards the house*

ANTONIO If you go on thus, you will kill yourself,
And 'tis not wisdom thus to second grief
Against yourself.
LEONATO   I pray thee cease thy counsel,
Which falls into mine ears as profitless
As water in a sieve: give not me counsel,
Nor let no comforter delight mine ear,
But such a one whose wrongs do suit with mine.
Bring me a father that so loved his child,
Whose joy of her is overwhelmed like mine,
And bid him speak of patience,   10
Measure his woe the length and breadth of mine,
And let it answer every strain for strain,
As thus for thus, and such a grief for such,
In every lineament, branch, shape, and form:
If such a one will smile and stroke his beard,
And – sorry wag – cry 'hem' when he should groan,
Patch grief with proverbs, make misfortune drunk
With candle-wasters . . . bring him yet to me,
And I of him will gather patience.
But there is no such man – for, brother, men   20
Can counsel and speak comfort to that grief
Which they themselves not feel, but tasting it,
Their counsel turns to passion, which before
Would give preceptial medicine to rage,
Fetter strong madness in a silken thread,
Charm ache with air, and agony with words.
No, no – 'tis all men's office to speak patience
To those that wring under the load of sorrow,
But no man's virtue nor sufficiency
To be so moral when he shall endure   30
The like himself. Therefore give me no counsel.
My griefs cry louder than advertisement.

ANTONIO	Therein do men from children nothing differ.
LEONATO	I pray thee peace. I will be flesh and blood –
	For there was never yet philosopher
	That could endure the toothache patiently,
	However they have writ the style of gods,
	And made a 'push' at chance and sufferance.
ANTONIO	Yet bend not all the harm upon yourself,
	Make those that do offend you suffer too. 40
LEONATO	There thou speak'st reason, nay I will do so.
	My soul doth tell me Hero is belied –
	And that shall Claudio know, so shall the prince,
	And all of them that thus dishonour her.

DON PEDRO *and* CLAUDIO *approach*

ANTONIO	Here comes the prince and Claudio hastily.
D. PEDRO	Good-den, good-den.
CLAUDIO	Good day to both of you.
	[they pass by
LEONATO	Hear you, my lords –
D. PEDRO	We have some haste, Leonato.
LEONATO	Some haste, my lord! Well, fare you well my lord.
	Are you so hasty now? Well, all is one.
D. PEDRO	*[turns]* Nay, do not quarrel with us, good old man. 50
ANTONIO	If he could right himself with quarrelling,
	Some of us would lie low.
CLAUDIO	Who wrongs him?
LEONATO	Marry, thou dost wrong me, thou dissembler, thou.
	Nay, never lay thy hand upon thy sword,
	I fear thee not.
CLAUDIO	Marry, beshrew my hand,
	If it should give your age such cause of fear.
	In faith my hand meant nothing to my sword.
LEONATO	Tush, tush, man, never fleer and jest at me.
	I speak not like a dotard nor a fool,
	As under privilege of age to brag 60
	What I have done being young, or what would do
	Were I not old. Know, Claudio, to thy head,
	Thou hast so wronged mine innocent child and me,
	That I am forced to lay my reverence by,
	And with grey hairs and bruise of many days,

	Do challenge thee to trial of a man.
	I say thou hast belied mine innocent child,
	Thy slander hath gone through and through her heart,
	And she lies buried with her ancestors:
	O in a tomb where never scandal slept, 70
	Save this of hers, framed by thy villainy.
CLAUDIO	My villainy!
LEONATO	Thine Claudio, thine I say.
D. PEDRO	You say not right, old man.
LEONATO	My lord, my lord,
	I'll prove it on his body if he dare –
	Despite his nice fence and his active practice,
	His May of youth and bloom of lustihood.
CLAUDIO	Away, I will not have to do with you.
LEONATO	Canst thou so daff me? Thou hast killed my child –
	If thou kill'st me, boy, thou shalt kill a man.
ANTONIO	He shall kill two of us, and men indeed – 80
	But that's no matter, let him kill one first.

                    [he comes between them, and draws his sword

	Win me and wear me! Let him answer me.
	Come follow me boy, come sir boy, come follow me.
	Sir boy, I'll whip you from your foining fence –
	Nay, as I am a gentleman, I will.
LEONATO	Brother –
ANTONIO	Content yourself, God knows I loved my niece,
	And she is dead, slandered to death by villains
	That dare as well answer a man indeed
	As I dare take a serpent by the tongue. 90
	Boys, apes, braggarts, Jacks, milksops!
LEONATO	Brother Antony –
ANTONIO	Hold you content. What, man! I know them, yea,
	And what they weigh, even to the utmost scruple –
	Scambling, out-facing, fashion-monging boys,
	That lie, and cog, and flout, deprave, and slander,
	Go anticly, and show outward hideousness,
	And speak off half a dozen dang'rous words,
	How they might hurt their enemies, if they durst,
	And this is all.
LEONATO	But brother Antony –

ANTONIO	Come, 'tis no matter –	100

Do not you meddle, let me deal in this.

D. PEDRO Gentlemen both, we will not wake your patience.
My heart is sorry for your daughter's death:
But on my honour she was charged with nothing
But what was true, and very full of proof.

LEONATO My lord, my lord –

D. PEDRO   I will not hear you.

LEONATO   No?
Come brother, away. [I will be heard.

ANTONIO And shall, or some of us will smart for it.]

                          [*Leonato and Antonio enter the house*

                    BENEDICK *comes up*

D. PEDRO See, see, here comes the man we went to seek.

CLAUDIO Now signior, what news?   110

BENEDICK Good day, my lord.

D. PEDRO Welcome, signior, you are almost come to part almost
a fray.

CLAUDIO We had liked to have had our two noses snapped off
with two old men without teeth.

D. PEDRO Leonato and his brother. What think'st thou? Had we
fought I doubt we should have been too young for them.

BENEDICK In a false quarrel there is no true valour. I came to seek
you both.

CLAUDIO We have been up and down to seek thee, for we are   120
high-proof melancholy, and would fain have it beaten
away. Wilt thou use thy wit?

BENEDICK It is in my scabbard – shall I draw it?

D. PEDRO Dost thou wear thy wit by thy side?

CLAUDIO Never any did so, though very many have been beside
their wit. I will bid thee draw, as we do the minstrels –
draw to pleasure us.

D. PEDRO As I am an honest man he looks pale. Art thou sick, or
angry?

CLAUDIO What, courage, man: what though care killed a cat,   130
thou hast mettle enough in thee to kill care.

BENEDICK Sir, I shall meet your wit in the career, an you charge it
against me. I pray you choose another subject.

CLAUDIO   Nay then, give him another staff – this last was broke
           cross.

D. PEDRO   By this light, he changes more and more. I think he be
           angry indeed.

CLAUDIO   If he be, he knows how to turn his girdle.

BENEDICK   Shall I speak a word in your ear?

CLAUDIO   God bless me from a challenge!   140

BENEDICK   You are a villain – I jest not – I will make it good how
           you dare, with what you dare, and when you dare: do
           me right, or I will protest your cowardice: you have
           killed a sweet lady, and her death shall fall heavy on
           you. [*aloud*] Let me hear from you.

CLAUDIO   Well, I will meet you, so I may have good cheer.

D. PEDRO   What, a feast, a feast?

CLAUDIO   I'faith, I thank him, he hath bid me to a calf's-head and
           a capon, the which if I do not carve most curiously, say
           my knife's naught. Shall I not find a woodcock too?   150

BENEDICK   Sir, your wit ambles well – it goes easily.

D. PEDRO   I'll tell thee how Beatrice praised thy wit the other day.
           I said, thou hadst a fine wit. 'True,' said she, 'a fine
           little one': 'No,' said I, 'a great wit': 'Right,' says she, 'a
           great gross one': 'Nay,' said I, 'a good wit': 'Just,' said
           she, 'it hurts nobody': 'Nay,' said I, 'the gentleman is
           wise': 'Certain,' said she, 'a wise gentleman': 'Nay,'
           said I, 'he hath the tongues': 'That I believe,' said she,
           'for he swore a thing to me on Monday night, which
           he forswore on Tuesday morning – there's a double   160
           tongue, there's two tongues.' Thus did she an hour
           together trans-shape thy particular virtues – yet at last
           she concluded with a sigh, thou wast the proper'st man
           in Italy.

CLAUDIO   For the which she wept heartily and said she cared not.

D. PEDRO   Yea, that she did – but yet, for all that, an if she did
           not hate him deadly, she would love him dearly. The
           old man's daughter told us all.

CLAUDIO   All, all – and moreover, God saw him when he was hid
           in the garden.   170

D. PEDRO   But when shall we set the savage bull's horns on the
           sensible Benedick's head?

CLAUDIO   Yea, and text underneath, 'Here dwells Benedick the married man'?

BENEDICK   Fare you well, boy – you know my mind. I will leave you now to your gossip-like humour. You break jests as braggarts do their blades, which God be thanked hurt not. My lord, for your many courtesies I thank you. I must discontinue your company – your brother the bastard is fled from Messina: you have among you 180 killed a sweet and innocent lady: for my Lord Lackbeard, there, he and I shall meet, and till then peace be with him.   [he passes on

D. PEDRO   He is in earnest.

CLAUDIO   In most profound earnest, and I'll warrant you, for the love of Beatrice.

D. PEDRO   And hath challenged thee?

CLAUDIO   Most sincerely.

D. PEDRO   What a pretty thing man is, when he goes in his doublet and hose and leaves off his wit!   190

CLAUDIO   He is then a giant to an ape, but then is an ape a doctor to such a man.

D. PEDRO   But soft you, let me be – pluck up, my heart, and be sad – did he not say my brother was fled?

          DOGBERRY, VERGES and the Watch approach, with
             CONRADE and BORACHIO in custody

DOGBERRY   Come you sir, if justice cannot tame you, she shall ne'er weigh more reasons in her balance. Nay, an you be a cursing hypocrite once, you must be looked to.

D. PEDRO   How now, two of my brother's men bound? Borachio, one?

CLAUDIO   Hearken after their offence, my lord.   200

D. PEDRO   Officers, what offence have these men done?

DOGBERRY   Marry sir, they have committed false report – moreover, they have spoken untruths – secondarily, they are slanders – sixth and lastly, they have belied a lady – thirdly, they have verified unjust things – and to conclude, they are lying knaves.

D. PEDRO   First, I ask thee what they have done – thirdly, I ask thee what's their offence – sixth and lastly, why they

are committed – and to conclude, what you lay to
their charge.   210

CLAUDIO   Rightly reasoned, and in his own division – and by my
troth there's one meaning well suited.

D. PEDRO   Who have you offended, masters, that you are thus
bound to your answer? This learned constable is too
cunning to be understood. What's your offence?

BORACHIO   Sweet prince, let me go no farther to mine answer: do
you hear me, and let this count kill me. I have deceived
even your very eyes: what your wisdoms could not
discover, these shallow fools have brought to light –
who in the night overheard me confessing to this man   220
how Don John your brother incensed me to slander the
Lady Hero, how you were brought into the orchard
and saw me court Margaret in Hero's garments, how
you disgraced her when you should marry her. My
villainy they have upon record, which I had rather seal
with my death than repeat over to my shame. The lady
is dead upon mine and my master's false accusation: and
briefly, I desire nothing but the reward of a villain.

D. PEDRO   Runs not this speech like iron through your blood?

CLAUDIO   I have drunk poison whiles he uttered it.   230

D. PEDRO   But did my brother set thee on to this?

BORACHIO   Yea, and paid me richly for the practice of it.

D. PEDRO   He is composed and framed of treachery,
And fled he is upon this villainy.

CLAUDIO   Sweet Hero, now thy image doth appear
In the rare semblance that I loved it first.

DOGBERRY   Come, bring away the plaintiffs. By this time our sexton
hath reformed Signior Leonato of the matter. And masters, do not forget to specify, when time and place shall
serve, that I am an ass.   240

VERGES   Here, here comes Master Signior Leonato, and the
sexton too.

LEONATO *and* ANTONIO *come from the house, with the Sexton*

LEONATO   Which is the villain? Let me see his eyes,
That when I note another man like him,
I may avoid him: which of these is he?

BORACHIO   If you would know your wronger, look on me.

LEONATO   Art thou the slave that with thy breath hast killed
         Mine innocent child?

BORACHIO   Yea, even I alone.

LEONATO   No, not so villain, thou beliest thyself,
         Here stand a pair of honourable men,   250
         A third is fled that had a hand in it.
         I thank you, princes, for my daughter's death,
         Record it with your high and worthy deeds,
         'Twas bravely done, if you bethink you of it.

CLAUDIO   I know not how to pray your patience,
         Yet I must speak. Choose your revenge yourself,
         Impose me to what penance your invention
         Can lay upon my sin – yet sinned I not,
         But in mistaking.

D. PEDRO   By my soul nor I,
         And yet to satisfy this good old man,   260
         I would bend under any heavy weight
         That he'll enjoin me to.

LEONATO   I cannot bid you bid my daughter live –
         That were impossible – but I pray you both,
         Possess the people in Messina here
         How innocent she died, and if your love
         Can labour aught in sad invention,
         Hang her an epitaph upon her tomb,
         And sing it to her bones – sing it tonight:
         Tomorrow morning come you to my house,   270
         And since you could not be my son-in-law,
         Be yet my nephew: my brother hath a daughter,
         Almost the copy of my child that's dead,
         And she alone is heir to both of us –
         Give her the right you should have giv'n her cousin,
         And so dies my revenge.

CLAUDIO   O noble sir!
         Your over-kindness doth wring tears from me.
         I do embrace your offer, and dispose
         For henceforth of poor Claudio.

LEONATO   Tomorrow then I will expect your coming,   280
         Tonight I take my leave. This naughty man
         Shall face to face be brought to Margaret,

Who I believe was packed in all this wrong,
Hired to it by your brother.

BORACHIO   No, by my soul she was not,
Nor knew not what she did when she spoke to me,
But always hath been just and virtuous
In anything that I do know by her.

DOGBERRY Moreover, sir – which indeed is not under white and
black – this plaintiff here, the offender, did call me ass.
I beseech you let it be remembered in his punishment.   29
And also the watch heard them talk of one Deformed
– they say he wears a key in his ear and a lock hanging
by it, and borrows money in God's name, the which
he hath used so long and never paid, that now men
grow hard-hearted and will lend nothing for God's
sake. Pray you examine him upon that point.

LEONATO I thank thee for thy care and honest pains.

DOGBERRY Your worship speaks like a most thankful and reverend
youth, and I praise God for you.

LEONATO There's for thy pains.   30

DOGBERRY God save the foundation!

LEONATO Go, I discharge thee of thy prisoner, and I thank thee.

DOGBERRY I leave an arrant knave with your worship, which I
beseech your worship to correct yourself, for the example of others. God keep your worship, I wish your
worship well, God restore you to health, I humbly
give you leave to depart – and if a merry meeting may
be wished, God prohibit it. Come neighbour.

                              [*Dogberry and Verges depart*

LEONATO Until tomorrow morning, lords, farewell.

ANTONIO Farewell my lords, we look for you tomorrow.   31

D. PEDRO We will not fail.

CLAUDIO Tonight I'll mourn with Hero.

                              [*Don Pedro and Claudio walk sadly away*

LEONATO Bring you these fellows on. We'll talk with Margaret,
How her acquaintance grew with this lewd fellow.

*Leonato and Antonio go within, followed by the Sexton,
the Watch and the prisoners*

SCENE 2

BENEDICK *and* MARGARET *come up the street*

BENEDICK Pray thee sweet Mistress Margaret, deserve well at my hands, by helping me to the speech of Beatrice.

MARGARET Will you then write me a sonnet in praise of my beauty?

BENEDICK In so high a style, Margaret, that no man living shall come over it, for in most comely truth thou deservest it.

MARGARET To have no man come over me? Why, shall I always keep below stairs?

BENEDICK Thy wit is as quick as the greyhound's mouth, it catches.

MARGARET And yours − as blunt as the fencer's foils, which hit, 10 but hurt not.

BENEDICK A most manly wit Margaret, it will not hurt a woman. And so I pray thee call Beatrice − I give thee the bucklers.

MARGARET Give us the swords, we have bucklers of our own.

BENEDICK If you use them, Margaret, you must put in the pikes with a vice − and they are dangerous weapons for maids.

MARGARET Well, I will call Beatrice to you, who I think hath legs.

[*Margaret enters the house*

BENEDICK And therefore will come.

[*sings*] The god of love,
          That sits above,   20
        And knows me, and knows me,
          How pitiful I deserve.

I mean in singing. But in loving − Leander the good swimmer, Troilus the first employer of pandars, and a whole book full of these quondam carpet-mongers, whose names yet run smoothly in the even road of a blank verse, why, they were never so truly turned over and over as my poor self, in love. Marry, I cannot show it in rhyme − I have tried. I can find out no rhyme to 'lady' but 'baby,' an innocent rhyme: for 'scorn,' 'horn,' 30 a hard rhyme: for 'school,' 'fool,' a babbling rhyme. Very ominous endings. No, I was not born under a rhyming planet, nor I cannot woo in festival terms.

BEATRICE *comes forth*

Sweet Beatrice, wouldst thou come when I called thee?

BEATRICE Yea signior, and depart when you bid me.

BENEDICK O stay but till then.

BEATRICE 'Then' is spoken: fare you well now – and yet, ere I go, let me go with that I came for, which is, with knowing what hath passed between you and Claudio.

BENEDICK Only foul words – and thereupon I will kiss thee.   40

BEATRICE Foul words is but foul wind, and foul wind is but foul breath, and foul breath is noisome – therefore I will depart unkissed.

BENEDICK Thou hast frighted the word out of his right sense, so forcible is thy wit. But I must tell thee plainly, Claudio undergoes my challenge, and either I must shortly hear from him, or I will subscribe him a coward. And I pray thee now tell me, for which of my bad parts didst thou first fall in love with me?

BEATRICE For them all together, which maintain so politic a state 50 of evil that they will not admit any good part to intermingle with them. But for which of my good parts did you first suffer love for me?

BENEDICK 'Suffer love'! A good epithet. I do suffer love indeed, for I love thee against my will.

BEATRICE In spite of your heart, I think. Alas, poor heart, if you spite it for my sake, I will spite it for yours, for I will never love that which my friend hates.

BENEDICK Thou and I are too wise to woo peaceably.

BEATRICE It appears not in this confession – there's not one wise 60 man among twenty that will praise himself.

BENEDICK An old, an old instance, Beatrice, that lived in the time of good neighbours. If a man do not erect in this age his own tomb ere he dies, he shall live no longer in monument than the bell rings and the widow weeps.

BEATRICE And how long is that, think you?

BENEDICK Question! Why, an hour in clamour and a quarter in rheum. Therefore is it most expedient for the wise – if Don Worm, his conscience, find no impediment to 70 the contrary – to be the trumpet of his own virtues, as

I am to myself. So much for praising myself, who, I myself will bear witness, is praiseworthy. And now tell me, how doth your cousin?

BEATRICE   Very ill.

BENEDICK   And how do you?

BEATRICE   Very ill too.

BENEDICK   Serve God, love me, and mend. There will I leave you too, for here comes one in haste.

URSULA runs forth

URSULA   Madam, you must come to your uncle – yonder's old 80 coil at home. It is proved my Lady Hero hath been falsely accused, the prince and Claudio mightily abused, and Don John is the author of all, who is fled and gone. Will you come presently?

BEATRICE   Will you go hear this news, signior?

BENEDICK   I will live in thy heart, die in thy lap, and be buried in thy eyes: and moreover, I will go with thee to thy uncle's.   [*they go within*

SCENE 3

A church-yard; before a sepulchre. Night

DON PEDRO, CLAUDIO and other lords approach with tapers,
followed by BALTHAZAR and musicians

CLAUDIO   Is this the monument of Leonato?

A LORD   It is, my lord.

CLAUDIO   [*reads from a scroll*]

> Done to death by slanderous tongues
> Was the Hero that here lies:
> Death, in guerdon of her wrongs,
> Gives her fame which never dies:
> So the life that died with shame,
> Lives in death with glorious fame.

> Hang thou there upon the tomb,   [*affixing it*
> Praising her when I am dumb.   10

Now, music, sound, and sing your solemn hymn.

BALTHAZAR *sings*

Pardon, goddess of the night,
Those that slew thy virgin knight,
For the which, with songs of woe,
Round about her tomb they go:
   Midnight, assist our moan,
   Help us to sigh and groan,
    Heavily, heavily.
   Graves, yawn and yield your dead,
   Till death be utteréd,
    Heavily, heavily.

CLAUDIO   Now, unto thy bones good night.
Yearly will I do this rite.

D. PEDRO Good morrow masters, put your torches out.
The wolves have preyed, and look, the gentle day,
Before the wheels of Phoebus, round about
Dapples the drowsy east with spots of grey:
Thanks to you all, and leave us. Fare you well.

CLAUDIO   Good morrow masters – each his several way.

                     [*the musicians leave the church-yard*

D. PEDRO Come let us hence, and put on other weeds,
And then to Leonato's we will go.

CLAUDIO   And Hymen now with luckier issue speeds,
Than this for whom we rendred up this woe! [*they go*

SCENE 4

The hall in Leonato's house; musicians seated in the gallery

LEONATO, ANTONIO, BENEDICK *and* FRIAR FRANCIS *enter,*
followed by HERO, BEATRICE, MARGARET
and URSULA, *who talk apart*

FRIAR   Did I not tell you she was innocent?

LEONATO So are the prince and Claudio, who accused her
Upon the error that you heard debated:
But Margaret was in some fault for this,
Although against her will, as it appears
In the true course of all the question.

ANTONIO   Well, I am glad that all things sort so well.

BENEDICK   And so am I, being else by faith enforced
　　　　　To call young Claudio to a reckoning for it.

LEONATO   [*turns*] Well daughter, and you gentlewomen all,   10
　　　　　Withdraw into a chamber by yourselves,
　　　　　And when I send for you come hither masked.

　　　　　　　　　　　　　　　　　[*the ladies go out*

　　　　　The prince and Claudio promised by this hour
　　　　　To visit me. You know your office, brother –
　　　　　You must be father to your brother's daughter,
　　　　　And give her to young Claudio.

ANTONIO   Which I will do with confirmed countenance.

BENEDICK   Friar, I must entreat your pains, I think.

FRIAR   To do what, signior?

BENEDICK   To bind me, or undo me – one of them   20
　　　　　Signior Leonato, truth it is, good signior,
　　　　　Your niece regards me with an eye of favour.

LEONATO   That eye my daughter lent her. 'Tis most true.

BENEDICK   And I do with an eye of love requite her.

LEONATO   The sight whereof I think you had from me,
　　　　　From Claudio, and the prince. But what's your will?

BENEDICK   Your answer, sir, is enigmatical:
　　　　　But for my will, my will is your good will
　　　　　May stand with ours, this day to be conjoined
　　　　　In the state of honourable marriage –   30
　　　　　In which, good friar, I shall desire your help.

LEONATO   My heart is with your liking.

FRIAR   　　　　　　　　　　　And my help.
　　　　　Here comes the prince and Claudio.

　　　　DON PEDRO *and* CLAUDIO *enter with two or three other lords*

D. PEDRO   Good morrow to this fair assembly.

LEONATO   Good morrow prince, good morrow Claudio:
　　　　　We here attend you. Are you yet determined
　　　　　Today to marry with my brother's daughter?

CLAUDIO   I'll hold my mind, were she an Ethiope.

LEONATO   Call her forth, brother. Here's the friar ready.

　　　　　　　　　　　　　　　　　[*Antonio goes*

D. PEDRO   Good morrow Benedick. Why, what's the matter,   40
　　　　　That you have such a February face,

So full of frost, of storm, and cloudiness?

CLAUDIO   I think he thinks upon the savage bull:
Tush, fear not, man, we'll tip thy horns with gold,
And all Europa shall rejoice at thee,
As once Europa did at lusty Jove,
When he would play the noble beast in love.

BENEDICK   Bull Jove, sir, had an amiable low –
And some such strange bull leaped your father's cow,
And got a calf in that same noble feat,   50
Much like to you, for you have just his bleat.

                ANTONIO *returns, with the ladies masked*

CLAUDIO   For this I owe you: here comes other reck'nings.
Which is the lady I must seize upon?

ANTONIO   This same is she, and I do give you her.

CLAUDIO   Why, then she's mine. Sweet, let me see your face.

LEONATO   No, that you shall not, till you take her hand
Before this friar, and swear to marry her.

CLAUDIO   Give me your hand before this holy friar –
I am your husband if you like of me.

HERO   And when I lived I was your other wife – [*she unmasks* 60
And when you loved, you were my other husband.

CLAUDIO   Another Hero!

HERO   Nothing certainer.
One Hero died defiled, but I do live,
And surely as I live, I am a maid.

D. PEDRO   The former Hero! Hero that is dead!

LEONATO   She died, my lord, but whiles her slander lived.

FRIAR   All this amazement can I qualify.
When after that the holy rites are ended,
I'll tell you largely of fair Hero's death,
Meantime let wonder seem familiar,   70
And to the chapel let us presently.

BENEDICK   Soft and fair, friar. Which is Beatrice?

BEATRICE   I answer to that name. [*unmasks*] What is your will?

BENEDICK   Do not you love me?

BEATRICE   Why no, no more than reason.

BENEDICK   Why then your uncle, and the prince, and Claudio,
Have been deceivéd, for they swore you did.

BEATRICE   Do not you love me?

BENEDICK   Troth no, no more than reason.

BEATRICE   Why then my cousin, Margaret, and Ursula,
Are much deceived, for they did swear you did.

BENEDICK   They swore that you were almost sick for me.   80

BEATRICE   They swore that you were well-nigh dead for me.

BENEDICK   'Tis no such matter. Then, you do not love me?

BEATRICE   No, truly, but in friendly recompense.

LEONATO   Come cousin, I am sure you love the gentleman.

CLAUDIO   And I'll be sworn upon't, that he loves her,
For here's a paper written in his hand,
A halting sonnet of his own pure brain,
Fashioned to Beatrice.

HERO   And here's another,
Writ in my cousin's hand, stol'n from her pocket,
Containing her affection unto Benedick.   90

BENEDICK   A miracle! Here's our own hands against our hearts.
Come, I will have thee – but by this light I take thee
for pity.

BEATRICE   I would not deny you – but by this good day I yield
upon great persuasion, and partly to save your life, for
I was told you were in a consumption.

BENEDICK   Peace, I will stop your mouth.   [*he kisses her*

D. PEDRO   How dost thou, Benedick the married man?

BENEDICK   I'll tell thee what, prince: a college of wit-crackers
cannot flout me out of my humour. Dost thou think I   100
care for a satire or an epigram? No, if a man will be
beaten with brains, 'a shall wear nothing handsome
about him. In brief, since I do purpose to marry, I will
think nothing to any purpose that the world can say
against it – and therefore never flout at me for what I
have said against it: for man is a giddy thing, and this is
my conclusion. For thy part, Claudio, I did think to
have beaten thee, but in that thou art like to be my
kinsman, live unbruised, and love my cousin.

CLAUDIO   I had well hoped thou wouldst have denied Beatrice,   110
that I might have cudgelled thee out of thy single life,
to make thee a double-dealer – which out of question
thou wilt be, if my cousin do not look exceeding
narrowly to thee.

BENEDICK Come, come, we are friends. Let's have a dance ere we are married, that we may lighten our own hearts, and our wives' heels.

LEONATO We'll have dancing afterward.

BENEDICK First, of my word – therefore play music. Prince, thou art sad – get thee a wife, get thee a wife. There is no 120 staff more reverend than one tipped with horn.

A messenger enters

MESSENG'R My lord, your brother John is ta'en in flight, and brought with armed men back to Messina.

BENEDICK Think not on him till tomorrow. I'll devise thee brave punishments for him. Strike up, pipers!

Music and dance

AS YOU LIKE IT

INTRODUCTION

As You Like It is both an extravagant play and a play about extravagance. It relishes its own romantic excesses of language and action, and enjoys mocking those excesses. Like *A Midsummer Night's Dream*, it dramatises an escape from the corruption of court life into a greenworld. Unlike the wood near Athens, however, *As You Like It*'s place of refuge – the forest of Arden – is thoroughly wholesome, reviving those who flee there weary from the pressures of the court. The play adheres to many of the conventions of the pastoral tradition – a range of courtly and rustic characters, a leisured existence in an idealised natural setting, quasi-philosophical debate, bucolic love stories, moments of song, an interest in gentle wit, and a broadly sentimental depiction of the shepherd's life. The refugees from the city repeatedly proclaim the simple beauties of their rural life in Arden. At the end of the play, however, they abandon it to return to the city, apparently without a moment of wistfulness. No attitude characterised in the play, not even an enthusiasm for the simple life, escapes criticism, since everything is juxtaposed with its contrary. However, the play is never savage in its exposure of folly, taking sympathetic delight in the foolish extravagances it depicts.

The main source for the play is Thomas Lodge's prose romance *Rosalynde* (1590). First performed in 1599 by Shakespeare's company, The Lord Chamberlain's Men, *As You Like It* may well have been one of the earliest plays presented in The Globe playhouse, newly opened that year. One character in the play, Duke Senior, describes life metaphorically as a series of plays, and the world as a stage. In doing so, he likens both his own and others' lives to different theatrical productions ('woeful pageants') being played in the same theatre:

> This wide and universal theatre
> Presents more woeful pageants than the scene
> Wherein we play in.   (2.7.136–38)

Bearing in mind the newness of the Globe as a performance context, the Duke's words may be a self-conscious reference to the expansive repertoire of the new playhouse. Jacques, famously, pursues the Duke's theatrical metaphor:

> All the world's a stage,
> And all the men and women merely players   (2.7.138–39)

This too would, presumably, have resonated with particular piquancy in The Globe, itself a three-dimensional incarnation of the stage-as-world metaphor. *As You Like It* and one of its earliest performance contexts therefore trade upon a shared central metaphor: the interrelatedness of the theatre and the world. Another Shakespeare play, *Henry V*, also first performed in 1599, advertises its own theatricality yet more obviously, drawing its audience's attention explicitly and repeatedly to the possibilities and limit-ations of its staging. In 1599, the new theatrical facilities on offer in the The Globe were clearly considered worthy of comment.

Plot summary

At the opening of the play, two brothers are quarrelling. In direct contravention of their father's will, Orlando de Boys has been deprived of a gentleman's education and kept from his inherit-ance by his wicked elder brother, Oliver de Boys. Adam, the old family servant, attempts to intervene. He asks them to honour the memory of their dead father, Sir Rowland de Boys, by living at peace with each other, but he is verbally abused by Oliver for his trouble. Oliver discovers that Orlando is planning to engage in a sporting bout of wrestling with Charles, the Duke's wrestler. He slanders Orlando to Charles, persuading him to inflict the severest possible injury upon the upstart challenger. In compliance with Oliver's will, Charles resolves to teach young Orlando a hard lesson.

Meanwhile the 'old news' from court is reiterated; Duke Senior has been banished by his younger brother Duke Frederick and is living in exile in the forest of Arden with a small group of faithful lords. Duke Senior's daughter Rosalind has been detained at court by Duke Frederick as a companion for his daughter Celia. The two girls are said to love each other dearly, 'being ever from their cradles bred together' (1.1.100).

At the scheduled wrestling match, Rosalind and Celia try to persuade the unknown challenger, Orlando, in the interests of his own safety, not to enter the ring. Both girls are agreeably taken with the strange young man's courtesy and demeanour. Since he will not be deterred, they wish him well instead. Against the odds, Orlando throws Charles and is declared the winner. The cousins congratulate him, and Rosalind gives him a necklace. He finds himself tongue-tied in response. Duke Frederick discovers that the victor is the son of Sir Rowland, Frederick's enemy of old. Orlando is advised to leave in order to avoid incurring the Duke's wrath, and is subsequently also informed that his brother Oliver means to burn him in his bed. He flees to the forest, accompanied by the good old servant Adam.

Duke Frederick, jealous of the love the people bear to Rosalind, accuses his niece of treachery and instructs her to leave the court on pain of death. Celia secretly resolves to flee with her cousin to the forest of Arden, where they will seek Rosalind's banished father. To ensure their own protection on their travels, they disguise themselves – Celia as Aliena, a peasant girl, Rosalind as Ganymede, her brother. They take with them Touchstone, the court clown, as a comfort and distraction in their banishment.

The action then shifts to the forest of Arden where the various refugees from the city run into each other and into the local inhabitants of the forest by turns. Rosalind's father, Duke Senior, holds court, commending the simple life away from the 'painted pomp' of the 'envious court' (2.1.3–4). Amiens, one of the lords in his rustic retinue, sings a song in celebration of their idyllic life spent 'under the greenwood tree', while Jaques, a cynical malcontent, lampoons this self-congratulatory approach to their primitive lifestyle.

While these courtly exiles are enjoying a rural banquet, they are rudely interrupted by Orlando, brandishing a sword and forbidding any to eat until he has taken food. He and Adam have arrived exhausted and weak in the forest, and Orlando has undertaken to find food for Adam. When his rough entrance is met with a courteous response, he realises the civility of the community upon which he has stumbled, apologises for his rudeness, and fetches Adam that they may both enjoy the gracious entertainment offered by Duke Senior.

Restored to full strength, Orlando hangs love poems on trees in the forest. These are addressed to Rosalind, who has by now herself arrived in the forest, with Celia and Touchstone. Rosalind is able, through a chance encounter, to exploit the impunity offered by her disguise to torment Orlando playfully about his lovelorn condition. In the guise of the boy Ganymede, she claims to be able to cure him of his love if he, Orlando, will pretend that s/he, Ganymede, is Rosalind. Orlando, unaware of the irony of the project, agrees to the game.

Rosalind/Ganymede stumbles across an amorous shepherd, Silvius, and his scornful love, Phebe, and cannot resist interfering in their love wrangles. S/he urges Phebe to make a realistic assessment of her own worth, and settle happily for this good man while she has the chance. Rather than heeding this advice, Phebe instead falls in love with Ganymede.

At court it is popularly believed that Orlando must have fled in company with Rosalind and Celia. Concerned for his own daughter's welfare, Duke Frederick commissions Oliver to find Orlando, that the girls may also be traced. Oliver enters the forest to seek Orlando, who generously saves him from wild animals. As a result of this rescue, Oliver undergoes an entertainingly instant conversion, is reconciled to Orlando, falls in love with Aliena, and gives up his estate and revenue to his brother.

Aliena is to marry Oliver, and Touchstone to marry a country woman, Audrey, the next day. Ganymede promises to arrange matters so that Orlando, Silvius and Phebe may each also marry to their satisfaction, even though their desires seem incompatible. They each promise to trust Ganymede until then.

The next day, in a mini-masque presentation, Hymen leads in Rosalind attired once again as herself. Duke Senior greets her as a daughter, Orlando as his bride, and Phebe, realising she has un-wittingly fallen in love with a woman, gives up all claim on her and agrees instead to marry Silvius. Duke Frederick had been planning to take bloody vengeance on his exiled brother for luring so many lords to his rustic court. Instead of executing his plans, however, at the outskirts of the forest he is suddenly converted to a religious life, and hands back the dukedom to his banished brother. As the action dissolves into a nuptial dance, Jaques makes clear his intention to join the newly converted Duke Frederick, thus avoiding the festivities. Rosalind delivers the Epilogue, in which she makes a conventional apology for the play, and requests that it nevertheless meet with a kind reception.

The Forest of Arden

The play is diffuse in its attention and can, initially, be baffling in its range of characters, whose situations parody each other to some degree. The most obvious point of unity is its strong geographical focus. Almost all characters in the play either live in the forest of Arden or are drawn there for one reason or another. As an Arcadian retreat from the corruption of court life, Arden assumes a set of values in the scheme of the play.

The journey into Arden is, almost universally, a tiring one. The rewards available once there, however, are considerable. Corin, a shepherd, articulates the pastoral ideal most clearly:

> I earn that I eat; get that I wear; owe no man hate, envy no man's happiness; glad of other men's good, content with my harm; and the greatest of my pride is to see my ewes graze and my lambs suck . . . (3.2.71–74)

Corin's pastoral philosophy is in large measure adopted by Duke Senior's rustic court. Amiens sings that in Arden those who are able to shun ambition may be easily content:

> Who doth ambition shun,
> And loves to live i'th'sun,
> Seeking the food he eats,
> And pleas'd with what he gets,
> Come hither, come hither, come hither.
> Here shall he see
> No enemy,
> But winter and rough weather. (2.5.34–41)

His idealistic vision does not seem misplaced in Arden. There is minimal strife of any sort in the forest, and, as Amiens claims, no

enemies at all bar the elements. Life is governed principally by a
taste for leisure (otium) and debate (negotium), and the action of
the play alternates between these two conventions of the pastoral
tradition. A pleasure in otium, in the suspension of action, ab-
sorbs most of the principal characters. Rosalind enjoys playfully
exploring the discrepancy between her inner, feminine, self and
the assumed 'doublet and hose' (3.2.189) of her outward appearance. Touchstone indulges, or anticipates, his sensual appetites
with Audrey. Duke Senior is content to be content with life.
Orlando is satisfied writing dreadful love poetry and wooing by
role-play. The only significant incongruity in Arden is the intensity of Jaques' melancholy. Few, however, stir themselves to take
serious issue with his cynicism. They do not need to: the whole
of Arden implicitly contradicts him.

Rosalind's, Celia's and Orlando's escape to the forest of Arden
represents a temporary abandonment of the 'working-day world'
(1.3.12) of restriction and injustice to which they had been subject.
While still at court, Rosalind had been fretful about her life:

ROSALIND   O how full of briars is this working-day world!

Celia encourages her to reconceive her trials as the passing
inconveniences one might encounter during holiday festivities:

CELIA   They are but burs, cousin, thrown upon thee in
             holiday foolery.   (1.3.13–14)

Her advice is that they should think about whatever fortune
throws at them not as significant obstacles (briers, thorns), but as
part of the passing inconvenience and harmless foolery of a holiday moment (burs, sticky buds); in that way the world may be
transformed into a more pleasant place. Rosalind, however, cannot make her problems evaporate simply by *thinking* herself into a
holiday mood: 'these burs,' she says, 'are in my heart.' (1.3.16) It
takes an actual displacement, a complete removal from the 'working-day world' of threats and injustice, for her to be able to adopt
a more festive spirit. Her gleeful dressing up as the boy
Ganymede (with 'a swashing and martial outside' (1.3.117)) offers
her a new, and less troubled, perspective on the world, and so
helps her to dislodge the burs that had settled in her heart. The
freedom to act as a man in a man's world is in itself a holiday, and

she even delays surrendering this newly expanded self since it affords her so much empowering entertainment. The restorative power of the greenworld and the liberation of assuming another identity work their combined healing magic on her: in Arden her heart is troubled by neither briers nor burs.

Having once escaped the courtly world of restriction, Rosalind is then happy to allow her thinking to be transformed. In the freedom of the new context she can take Celia's advice about adopting a holiday mentality, saying to Orlando:

> ROSALIND   Come, woo me, woo me; for now I am in a
>   holiday humour and like enough to consent.
>
> (4.1.61–62)

Being away from home puts her 'in a holiday humour', and this makes possible things that would not otherwise have been so. The clear distinction drawn in this play between the humdrum nature of the working day and the liberating nature of the holiday moment is characteristic of the festive comedies more generally. The time spent away from their set patterns of relating enables not just Rosalind, but all the characters in *As You Like It*, to experience a sense of psychological and social release.

Excepting a few stylised wrangles, life in Arden seems to recapture the idyllic patterns of an innocent past. In Act 1, Charles had reported that the exiled gentlemen in Arden 'fleet the time carelessly as they did in the golden world' (1.1.109–10). Duke Senior chooses to characterise the innocence of their communal life not in terms of a mythological golden age, but of an Edenic perfection: 'Here feel we not the penalty of Adam . . . ' (2.1.5) The penalty for disobedience that God imposed upon Adam and his descendants was that the ground should not bring forth food without an investment of sweat and labour; the natural world in general should thwart human purposes. It is as if in entering Arden, the refugees from the 'painted pomp' of the 'envious court' have slipped magically into a pre-fallen world in which these universal conditions of humanity somehow do not apply. Arden offers itself as a temporal anomaly, a space entirely apart from the corrupt world around it. In its playfulness and idealism, it alludes, through the conventions of the pastoral form, to the innocence of a pre-fallen world.

As You Like It – As You, Like It

As You Like It, in common with *Much Ado About Nothing* and *What You Will* (the alternative title for *Twelfth Night)*, has an impressively nonchalant play title. As J. Dover Wilson suggested in 1962, the offhand nature of these titles testifies to a playwright 'very sure of his public'. More specifically, *As You Like It* suggests, with casual confidence, that the play, and by extension, the world, can be whatever you want it to be – as you like it. At the end of Act 1, Celia asserts that the world may be transformed by being thought about in other terms:

> Now go we in content
> To liberty, and not to banishment.   (1.3.134–35)

Through a change of attitude the girls are thus able to experience banishment as liberty – as if they had themselves chosen it. In Act 2 Amiens commends Duke Senior for having successfully managed a similar mental transformation:

> Happy is your Grace,
> That can translate the stubbornness of fortune
> Into so quiet and sweet a style.   (2.1.18–20)

Since perception is evidently key in determining the nature and quality of an experience, the lesson of Arden seems to be to think positively about everything. Prickly briers may be converted into furry burs, banishment into liberty, and even the 'stubbornness of fortune' into 'so quiet and sweet a style', given the right frame of mind. Arden, as a realm which seems to take characters back to a state of innocence, fosters that positive frame of mind.

One of the features of life in Arden is that characters have a tendency to see themselves mirrored in the world around them. Hearing of Silvius' aching heart, Rosalind says:

> Alas, poor shepherd, searching of thy wound
> I have by hard adventure found mine own.   (2.4.40–41)

To which Touchstone adds, 'And I mine.' Such a willingness to feel a kinship with the world is, typically for a play full of balanced opposites, both commended and ridiculed: commended as evidence of a sympathetic engagement with others, and ridiculed as indicative of a myopic self-absorption. Thus Rosalind is moved to help Silvius by the recognition that 'this shepherd's passion/ Is much upon my fashion' (2.4.55–6). Touchstone, however, equally eager to find his own reflection in the world, is gently rebuked for assuming that this shepherd's character is also much upon *his* fashion. So, when he addresses Silvius as 'clown' as an acknowledgement of kinship, Rosalind checks him with: 'Peace fool, he's not thy kinsman' (2.4.61). By greeting Silvius as a mirror of himself, Touchstone may be satirising Rosalind's rush of fellow feeling, or he may genuinely believe he has found a fellow clown. Either way the point is clear: the appreciation of others only to the extent to which they reflect oneself suggests a lack of genuine engagement with the world.

This tendency for characters to see their environment in self-reflexive terms, mirroring some truth about themselves, is cryptically alluded to in the title of the play. It hints that, seen in one particular sheen, things may easily be found to be like you – as you, like it. This glancing suggestion – that as you are, so will you find it to be – is made as much to the audience as it is to its own characters. Typically for the comedies, we too are invited to see our own reflection amidst the holiday foolery played out before us.

The ending
In the middle of Act 4, the play's two thorough-going villains – Oliver and Duke Frederick – still pose a threat to the happiness of the other characters. Oliver is seeking out his brother in order to rid himself of him, and Frederick raising an army with which he can defeat the exiles and kill Duke Senior. If the drama is to reach a point of satisfactory closure, a solution needs to be found to these problems, a way of deflecting or converting the impending threat. In a dramatic display of the hearty optimism of comic form, both these threats are made to dissolve into nothingness. Oliver, rescued from danger by Orlando, realises, with impressive suddenness, that kindness is nobler than revenge. Rosalind and Celia's astonishment at his transformation is only surpassed by Oliver's own sense of wonder at his volte-face:

CELIA	Was't you that did so oft contrive to kill him?
OLIVER	'Twas I. But 'tis not I. I do not shame
	To tell you what I was, since my conversion
	So sweetly tastes, being the thing I am. (4.3.133–36)

Arden has, it seems, worked its natural magic on him. Duke
Frederick's conversion, narrated in the closing moments of the
play, is, if anything, even more dramatic:

> JAQUES   Duke Frederick hearing how that every day
> Men of great worth resorted to this forest,
> Address'd a mighty power, which were on foot
> In his own conduct, purposely to take
> His brother here, and put him to the sword.
> And to the skirts of this wild wood he came,
> Where, meeting with an old religious man,
> After some question with him, was converted
> Both from his enterprise and from the world,
> His crown bequeathing to his banish'd brother,
> And all their lands restor'd to them again
> That were with him exil'd.   (5.4.145–156)

This is the most extreme expression of the play's willingness
simply to dispense with the problems it has generated. It makes
no apology for the improbabilities of its solution: rather it delights
in the cursory casting aside of potential irritants to its closing
harmony. No psychological plausibility is sought in order to
explain the dramatic shift in Duke Frederick's intentions. As
Amiens's song attests, enmity cannot survive within the greenworld of Arden: encountering its mere fringes ('the skirts of this
wild wood') is, therefore, sufficient to divert Frederick from his
vicious plan. Nevertheless, the redemptive character of Arden is
rendered ludicrously fast-working here in order to complement
the generic exigencies of comic form. It is a structural necessity
that the threat evaporate to create space for a final, unclouded,
celebratory dance: so evaporate it does, and with entertaining
haste.

   In the wood near Athens, the lovers had suffered from 'seething
brains' (*A Midsummer Night's Dream* 5.1.4). In the forest of Arden,
by contrast, the lovers' minds are pleasantly distracted by the
pervasive 'holiday humour' of the place. *As You Like It* is, as its
title suggests, a fantasy of wish-fulfilment. Its gentle tone takes
characters towards their desires through the leisured distractions
of play. Its villains, unlike those in *Much Ado About Nothing*, need
not be brought to account. Instead, they are gloriously converted

to lives of generosity and holiness. Even its cynical malcontent need not be vigorously contradicted since the wholesomeness of his environment implicitly contradicts his every fit of gloom. He chooses not to participate in the nuptial celebrations since he is 'for other than for dancing measures' (5.4.184), but no other character feels that his antagonism to the values of Arden should disqualify him from their community: Duke Senior even urges him to stay. Arden is secure enough to be able to accommodate contrary positions.

Despite its healing properties, Arden is, in the final analysis, a retreat from the world, and at some point that world needs to be re-engaged with. The forest offers the opportunity for recuperation and distraction from the anxieties of 'the working-day world'. Its value, however, is as a temporary haven, not as a permanent alternative way of life. At the end of *As You Like It*, there is a new-found willingness to return to the court and to reassume worldly responsibilities. It is not only the altered circumstances, but also the pleasant time spent 'under the greenwood tree', that has made this possible.

*The scene: Oliver's house, Duke Frederick's court,
and the Forest of Arden*

CHARACTERS IN THE PLAY

A banished DUKE
FREDERICK, *his brother, and usurper of his dominions*
AMIENS ⎫
JAQUES ⎭ *lords attending on the banished Duke*
LE BEAU, *a courtier attending upon Frederick*
CHARLES, *wrestler to Frederick*
OLIVER ⎫
JAQUES ⎬ *sons of Sir Rowland de Boys*
ORLANDO ⎭
ADAM ⎫
DENNIS ⎭ *servants to Oliver*
TOUCHSTONE, *a clown*
SIR OLIVER MARTEXT, *a vicar*
CORIN ⎫
SILVIUS ⎭ *shepherds*
WILLIAM, *a country fellow, in love with Audrey*
A person representing Hymen
ROSALIND, *daughter to the banished Duke*
CELIA, *daughter to Frederick*
PHEBE, *a shepherdess*
AUDREY, *a country wench*

Lords, pages, foresters, and attendant

AS YOU LIKE IT

ACT I SCENE I

An orchard, near Oliver's house

ORLANDO *and* ADAM

ORLANDO   As I remember, Adam, it was upon this fashion: 'a
bequeathed me by will but poor thousand crowns and,
as thou say'st, charged my brother on his blessing
to breed me well: and there begins my sadness. My
brother Jaques he keeps at school, and report speaks
goldenly of his profit: for my part, he keeps me
rustically at home, or, to speak more properly, stays me
here at home unkept: for call you that 'keeping' for a
gentleman of my birth, that differs not from the stalling
of an ox? His horses are bred better – for, besides that 10
they are fair with their feeding, they are taught their
manage, and to that end riders dearly hired: but I, his
brother, gain nothing under him but growth, for the
which his animals on his dunghills are as much bound
to him as I. Besides this nothing that he so plentifully
gives me, the something that nature gave me his
countenance seems to take from me: he lets me feed
with his hinds, bars me the place of a brother, and, as
much as in him lies, mines my gentility with my education. This is it, Adam, that grieves me – and the spirit 20
of my father, which I think is within me, begins to
mutiny against this servitude. I will no longer endure
it, though yet I know no wise remedy how to avoid it.

OLIVER *enters the orchard*

ADAM   Yonder comes my master, your brother.

ORLANDO   Go apart, Adam, and thou shalt hear how he will shake
me up.   [*Adam withdraws a little*

OLIVER   Now, sir! What make you here?

ORLANDO   Nothing: I am not taught to make any thing.

OLIVER   What mar you then, sir?

ORLANDO   Marry, sir, I am helping you to mar that which God 30 made, a poor unworthy brother of yours, with idleness.

OLIVER   Marry, sir, be better employed, and be naught awhile.

ORLANDO   Shall I keep your hogs and eat husks with them? What
           prodigal portion have I spent, that I should come to
           such penury?

OLIVER   Know you where you are, sir?

ORLANDO   O sir, very well: here in your orchard.

OLIVER   Know you before whom, sir?

ORLANDO   Ay, better than him I am before knows me. I know
           you are my eldest brother, and in the gentle condition   40
           of blood you should so know me. The courtesy of
           nations allows you my better, in that you are the first-
           born, but the same tradition takes not away my blood,
           were there twenty brothers betwixt us: I have as much
           of my father in me as you, albeit I confess your coming
           before me is nearer to his reverence.

OLIVER   What, boy!   [he strikes him

ORLANDO   Come, come, elder brother, you are too young in this.
                                       [he takes him by the throat

OLIVER   Wilt thou lay hands on me, villain?

ORLANDO   I am no villain: I am the youngest son of Sir Rowland   50
           de Boys, he was my father, and he is thrice a villain
           that says such a father begot villains. Wert thou not my
           brother, I would not take this hand from thy throat,
           till this other had pulled out thy tongue for saying so —
           thou hast railed on thyself.

                                       [Adam comes forward

ADAM   Sweet masters, be patient. For your father's remem-
           brance, be at accord.

OLIVER   [struggles] Let me go, I say.

ORLANDO   I will not till I please: you shall hear me. My father
           charged you in his will to give me good education: 60
           you have trained me like a peasant, obscuring and
           hiding from me all gentleman-like qualities. The spirit
           of my father grows strong in me, and I will no longer
           endure it: therefore allow me such exercises as may
           become a gentleman, or give me the poor allottery my
           father left me by testament — with that I will go buy
           my fortunes.   [he releases him

OLIVER   And what wilt thou do? Beg when that is spent?
          Well, sir, get you in: I will not long be troubled with
          you: you shall have some part of your 'will'. I pray   70
          you, leave me.

ORLANDO   I will no further offend you than becomes me for my
          good.   [*he turns to go*

OLIVER   Get you with him, you old dog.

ADAM   Is 'old dog' my reward? Most true, I have lost my teeth
          in your service. God be with my old master! He would
          not have spoke such a word.
                                    [*Orlando and Adam depart*

OLIVER   Is it even so? Begin you to grow upon me? I will
          physic your rankness, and yet give no thousand crowns
          neither. Holla, Dennis!   80

                    DENNIS *comes from the house*

DENNIS   Calls your worship?

OLIVER   Was not Charles, the duke's wrestler, here to speak
          with me?

DENNIS   So please you, he is here at the door, and importunes
          access to you.

OLIVER   Call him in. [*Dennis goes*] 'Twill be a good way; and
          tomorrow the wrestling is.

                DENNIS *returns, bringing* CHARLES

CHARLES   Good morrow to your worship.

OLIVER   Good Monsieur Charles. [*they salute*] What's the new
          news at the new court?   90

CHARLES   There's no news at the court, sir, but the old news:
          that is, the old duke is banished by his younger brother
          the new duke, and three or four loving lords have put
          themselves into voluntary exile with him, whose lands
          and revenues enrich the new duke, therefore he gives
          them good leave to wander.

OLIVER   Can you tell if Rosalind, the duke's daughter, be ban-
          ished with her father?

CHARLES   O, no; for the duke's daughter, her cousin, so loves
          her – being ever from their cradles bred together – that 100
          she would have followed her exile, or have died to stay
          behind her. She is at the court, and no less beloved of

her uncle than his own daughter – and never two ladies loved as they do.

OLIVER   Where will the old duke live?

CHARLES   They say he is already in the forest of Arden, and a many merry men with him; and there they live like the old Robin Hood of England: they say many young gentlemen flock to him every day, and fleet the time carelessly as they did in the golden world.   110

OLIVER   What, you wrestle tomorrow before the new duke?

CHARLES   Marry, do I, sir: and I came to acquaint you with a matter. I am given, sir, secretly to understand that your younger brother, Orlando, hath a disposition to come in disguised against me to try a fall: tomorrow, sir, I wrestle for my credit, and he that escapes me without some broken limb shall acquit him well: your brother is but young and tender, and for your love I would be loath to foil him, as I must for my own honour if he come in: therefore, out of my love to you, I came   120 hither to acquaint you withal, that either you might stay him from his intendment, or brook such disgrace well as he shall run into, in that it is a thing of his own search, and altogether against my will.

OLIVER   Charles, I thank thee for thy love to me, which thou shalt find I will most kindly requite. I had myself notice of my brother's purpose herein, and have by underhand means laboured to dissuade him from it; but he is resolute. I'll tell thee, Charles – it is the stubbornest young fellow of France, full of ambition, an envious   130 emulator of every man's good parts, a secret and villanous contriver against me his natural brother: therefore use thy discretion; I had as lief thou didst break his neck as his finger. And thou wert best look to't; for if thou dost him any slight disgrace, or if he do not mightily grace himself on thee, he will practise against thee by poison, entrap thee by some treacherous device, and never leave thee till he hath ta'en thy life by some indirect means or other: for, I assure thee (and almost with tears I speak it), there is not one so young   140 and so villanous this day living. I speak but brotherly of

him, but should I anatomize him to thee as he is, I must
blush and weep, and thou must look pale and wonder.

CHARLES   I am heartily glad I came hither to you. If he come
tomorrow, I'll give him his payment: if ever he go
alone again, I'll never wrestle for prize more: and so,
God keep your worship!

OLIVER   Farewell, good Charles. [*Charles takes his leave*] Now
will I stir this gamester: I hope I shall see an end of
him; for my soul (yet I know not why) hates nothing   150
more than he. Yet he's gentle, never schooled and yet
learned, full of noble device, of all sorts enchantingly
beloved, and indeed so much in the heart of the world,
and especially of my own people, who best know him,
that I am altogether misprised: but it shall not be so
long – this wrestler shall clear all. Nothing remains but
that I kindle the boy thither, which now I'll go about.
                                            [*he goes within*

SCENE 2

A lawn near the palace of Duke Frederick

ROSALIND *and* CELIA, *seated*

CELIA   I pray thee, Rosalind, sweet my coz, be merry.

ROSALIND   Dear Celia, I show more mirth than I am mistress of,
and would you yet I were merrier? Unless you could
teach me to forget a banished father, you must not learn
me how to remember any extraordinary pleasure.

CELIA   Herein, I see, thou lov'st me not with the full weight
that I love thee; if my uncle, thy banished father, had
banished thy uncle, the duke my father, so thou hadst
been still with me, I could have taught my love to take
thy father for mine; so wouldst thou, if the truth of thy   10
love to me were so righteously tempered as mine is to
thee.

ROSALIND   Well, I will forget the condition of my estate, to
rejoice in yours.

CELIA   You know my father hath no child but I, nor none is like
to have; and truly when he dies, thou shalt be his heir: for

what he hath taken away from thy father perforce, I will
render thee again in affection. By mine honour I will,
and when I break that oath, let me turn monster: therefore, my sweet Rose, my dear Rose, be merry.   20

ROSALIND From henceforth I will, coz, and devise sports. Let me
see – what think you of falling in love?

CELIA Marry, I prithee, do, to make sport withal: but love no
man in good earnest, nor no further in sport neither,
than with safety of a pure blush thou mayst in honour
come off again.

ROSALIND What shall be our sport then?

CELIA Let us sit and mock the good housewife Fortune from
her wheel, that her gifts may henceforth be bestowed
equally.   30

ROSALIND I would we could do so; for her benefits are mightily
misplaced, and the bountiful blind woman doth most
mistake in her gifts to women.

CELIA 'Tis true, for those that she makes fair she scarce makes
honest, and those that she makes honest she makes
very ill-favouredly.

ROSALIND Nay, now thou goest from Fortune's office to
Nature's: Fortune reigns in gifts of the world, not in
the lineaments of Nature.

TOUCHSTONE *approaches*

CELIA No? When Nature hath made a fair creature, may she   40
not by Fortune fall into the fire? Though Nature hath
given us wit to flout at Fortune, hath not Fortune sent
in this fool to cut off the argument?

ROSALIND Indeed, there is Fortune too hard for Nature, when
Fortune makes Nature's natural the cutter-off of
Nature's wit.

CELIA Peradventure this is not Fortune's work neither, but
Nature's, who perceiveth our natural wits too dull to
reason of such goddesses and hath sent this natural for
our whetstone: for always the dulness of the fool is the   50
whetstone of the wits. How now, wit! Whither wander
you?

TOUCH. Mistress, you must come away to your father.

CELIA Were you made the messenger?

TOUCH.   No, by mine honour, but I was bid to come for you.

ROSALIND   Where learned you that oath, fool?

TOUCH.   Of a certain knight, that swore by his honour they were good pancakes, and swore by his honour the mustard was naught: now I'll stand to it, the pancakes were naught and the mustard was good, and yet was 60 not the knight forsworn.

CELIA   How prove you that, in the great heap of your knowledge?

ROSALIND   Ay, marry, now unmuzzle your wisdom.

TOUCH.   Stand you both forth now: stroke your chins, and swear by your beards that I am a knave.

CELIA   By our beards (if we had them) thou art.

TOUCH.   By my knavery (if I had it) then I were: but if you swear by that that is not, you are not forsworn: no more was this knight, swearing by his honour, for he 70 never had any; or if he had, he had sworn it away, before ever he saw those pancakes or that mustard.

CELIA   Prithee, who is't that thou mean'st?

TOUCH.   [*to Rosalind*] One that old Frederick, your father, loves.

ROSALIND   My father's love is enough to honour him. Enough! Speak no more of him – you'll be whipped for taxation one of these days.

TOUCH.   The more pity, that fools may not speak wisely what wise men do foolishly.

CELIA   By my troth, thou sayest true: for since the little wit that 80 fools have was silenced, the little foolery that wise men have makes a great show. Here comes Monsieur Le Beau.

             LE BEAU *is seen hurrying towards them*

ROSALIND   With his mouth full of news.

CELIA   Which he will put on us, as pigeons feed their young.

ROSALIND   Then shall we be news-crammed.

CELIA   All the better: we shall be the more marketable. Bon jour, Monsieur Le Beau! What's the news?

LE BEAU   Fair princess, you have lost much good sport.

CELIA   Sport? Of what colour?   90

LE BEAU   What colour, madam? How shall I answer you?

ROSALIND   As wit and fortune will.

TOUCH.   [*mocking him*] Or as the Destinies decree.

CELIA   Well said, that was laid on with a trowel.

TOUCH.   Nay, if I keep not my rank —

ROSALIND Thou losest thy old smell.

LE BEAU   You amaze me, ladies: I would have told you of good
          wrestling, which you have lost the sight of.

ROSALIND Yet tell us the manner of the wrestling.

LE BEAU   I will tell you the beginning, and, if it please your 100
          ladyships, you may see the end — for the best is yet to
          do, and here, where you are, they are coming to
          perform it.

CELIA   Well, the beginning, that is dead and buried?

LE BEAU   There comes an old man and his three sons —

CELIA   I could match this beginning with an old tale.

LE BEAU   Three proper young men, of excellent growth and
          presence.

ROSALIND With bills on their necks: 'Be it known unto all men
          by these presents.'   110

LE BEAU   The eldest of the three wrestled with Charles, the
          duke's wrestler, which Charles in a moment threw him
          and broke three of his ribs, that there is little hope of
          life in him: so he served the second, and so the third . . .
          Yonder they lie, the poor old man their father making
          such pitiful dole over them that all the beholders take
          his part with weeping.

ROSALIND Alas!

TOUCH.   But what is the sport, monsieur, that the ladies have lost?

LE BEAU   Why, this that I speak of.   120

TOUCH.   Thus men may grow wiser every day. It is the first time
          that ever I heard breaking of ribs was sport for ladies.

CELIA   Or I, I promise thee.

ROSALIND But is there any else longs to see this broken music in
          his sides? Is there yet another dotes upon rib-breaking?
          Shall we see this wrestling, cousin?

LE BEAU   You must if you stay here, for here is the place
          appointed for the wrestling, and they are ready to
          perform it.

CELIA   Yonder, sure, they are coming. Let us now stay and   130
          see it.

A flourish of trumpets. Duke FREDERICK *with his lords,* ORLANDO,
CHARLES, *and attendants cross the lawn towards a plot prepared
for the wrestling*

DUKE F.   Come on. Since the youth will not be entreated, his
            own peril on his forwardness.

ROSALIND   Is yonder the man?

LE BEAU   Even he, madam.

CELIA   Alas, he is too young: yet he looks successfully.

DUKE   How now, daughter and cousin! Are you crept hither
            to see the wrestling?

ROSALIND   Ay, my liege, so please you give us leave.

DUKE F.   You will take little delight in it, I can tell you, there is   140
            such odds in the man. In pity of the challenger's youth I
            would fain dissuade him, but he will not be entreated.
            Speak to him, ladies – see if you can move him.

CELIA   Call him hither, good Monsieur Le Beau.

DUKE F.   Do so: I'll not be by.   [*he takes his seat*

LE BEAU   Monsieur the challenger, the princess calls for you.

ORLANDO   [*comes forward*]. I attend them with all respect and duty.

ROSALIND   Young man, have you challenged Charles the wrestler?

ORLANDO   [*bows*] No, fair princess: he is the general challenger. I
            come but in, as others do, to try with him the strength   150
            of my youth.

CELIA   Young gentleman, your spirits are too bold for your
            years. You have seen cruel proof of this man's strength.
            If you saw yourself with your eyes, or knew yourself
            with your judgment, the fear of your adventure would
            counsel you to a more equal enterprise. We pray you,
            for your own sake, to embrace your own safety, and
            give over this attempt.

ROSALIND   Do, young sir, your reputation shall not therefore be
            misprised: we will make it our suit to the duke that the   160
            wrestling might not go forward.

ORLANDO   I beseech you, punish me not with your hard thoughts,
            wherein I confess me much guilty to deny so fair and
            excellent ladies anything. But let your fair eyes and
            gentle wishes go with me to my trial: wherein if I be
            foiled, there is but one shamed that was never gracious;
            if killed, but one dead that is willing to be so: I shall do

my friends no wrong, for I have none to lament me; the
world no injury, for in it I have nothing: only in the
world I fill up a place, which may be better supplied   170
when I have made it empty.

ROSALIND The little strength that I have, I would it were with
you.

CELIA And mine, to eke out hers.

ROSALIND Fare you well. Pray heaven, I be deceived in you!

CELIA Your heart's desires be with you!

CHARLES [*calls*] Come, where is this young gallant that is so
desirous to lie with his mother earth?

ORLANDO Ready, sir, but his will hath in it a more modest working.

DUKE F. You shall try but one fall.   180

CHARLES No, I warrant your grace, you shall not entreat him to a
second, that have so mightily persuaded him from a first.

ORLANDO An you mean to mock me after, you should not have
mocked me before: but come your ways.

ROSALIND Now, Hercules be thy speed, young man!

CELIA I would I were invisible, to catch the strong fellow by
the leg.   [*the wrestling begins: they close, Orlando
                            skilfully securing the better hold*

ROSALIND O excellent young man!

CELIA If I had a thunderbolt in mine eye, I can tell who
should down.   [*the wrestlers sway and strain to and fro,* 190
                        till of a sudden Charles is thrown heavily
                                    to the ground; a great shout

DUKE F. [*rises*] No more, no more.

ORLANDO Yes, I beseech your grace – I am not yet well breathed.

DUKE F. How dost thou, Charles?

LE BEAU   He cannot speak, my lord.

DUKE F. Bear him away. [*they take up Charles and carry him forth*
                          What is thy name, young man?

ORLANDO Orlando, my liege; the youngest son of Sir Rowland
de Boys.

DUKE F. I would thou hadst been son to some man else.
The world esteemed thy father honourable,
But I did find him still mine enemy:
Thou shouldst have better pleased me with this deed,   200
Hadst thou descended from another house:

But fare thee well, thou art a gallant youth.
I would thou hadst told me of another father.
      [Duke Frederick, Le Beau and the other lords depart

CELIA   Were I my father, coz, would I do this?

ORLANDO   I am more proud to be Sir Rowland's son,
His youngest son, and would not change that calling
To be adopted heir to Frederick.

ROSALIND   My father loved Sir Rowland as his soul,
And all the world was of my father's mind.
Had I before known this young man his son,   210
I should have given him tears unto entreaties,
Ere he should thus have ventured.

CELIA   Gentle cousin,
Let us go thank him, and encourage him:
My father's rough and envious disposition
Sticks me at heart.   *[they rise and accost Orlando]*
                Sir, you have well deserved.
If you do keep your promises in love
But justly as you have exceeded promise,
Your mistress shall be happy.

ROSALIND   *[takes a chain from her neck]*   Gentleman,
Wear this for me — one out of suits with fortune,   220
That could give more, but that her hand lacks means
Shall we go, coz?   *[she turns and walks away*

CELIA   *[follows]*   Ay: fare you well, fair gentleman.

ORLANDO   Can I not say, 'I thank you'? My better parts
Are all thrown down, and that which here stands up
Is but a quintain, a mere lifeless block.

ROSALIND   He calls us back: my pride fell with my fortunes —
I'll ask him what he would.   *[she turns again]*
                     Did you call, sir?
Sir, you have wrestled well and overthrown
More than your enemies.   *[they gaze upon each other*

CELIA   *[plucks her sleeve]*   Will you go, coz?   230

ROSALIND   Have with you. Fare you well.
              [she hastens away, Celia following

ORLANDO   What passion hangs these weights upon my tongue?
I cannot speak to her, yet she urged conference.

                LE BEAU *returns*

O poor Orlando, thou art overthrown!
Or Charles, or something weaker, masters thee.

LE BEAU   Good sir, I do in friendship counsel you
To leave this place. Albeit you have deserved
High commendation, true applause, and love,
Yet such is now the duke's condition,
That he misconstrues all that you have done.   240
The duke is humorous – what he is, indeed,
More suits you to conceive than I to speak of.

ORLANDO   I thank you, sir: and, pray you, tell me this,
Which of the two was daughter of the duke,
That here was at the wrestling?

LE BEAU   Neither his daughter, if we judge by manners,
But yet, indeed, the smaller is his daughter.
The other is daughter to the banished duke,
And here detained by her usurping uncle,
To keep his daughter company – whose loves   250
Are dearer than the natural bond of sisters.
But I can tell you that of late this duke
Hath ta'en displeasure 'gainst his gentle niece,
Grounded upon no other argument
But that the people praise her for her virtues,
And pity her for her good father's sake;
And, on my life, his malice 'gainst the lady
Will suddenly break forth. Sir, fare you well.
Hereafter, in a better world than this,
I shall desire more love and knowledge of you.   260

ORLANDO   I rest much bounden to you: fare you well.

                                      [Le Beau goes

Thus must I from the smoke into the smother,
From tyrant duke unto a tyrant brother.
But heavenly Rosalind!

                                      [he departs, musing

SCENE 3

A room in the palace of Duke Frederick

ROSALIND *on a couch with her face to the wall,* CELIA *bending over her*

CELIA   Why cousin, why Rosalind. Cupid have mercy! Not a word?

ROSALIND   Not one to throw at a dog.

CELIA   No, thy words are too precious to be cast away upon curs: throw some of them at me; come, lame me with reasons.

ROSALIND   Then there were two cousins laid up, when the one should be lamed with reasons, and the other mad without any.

CELIA   But is all this for your father?   10

ROSALIND   No, some of it is for my child's father. [*rises*] O, how full of briars is this working-day world!

CELIA   They are but burs, cousin, thrown upon thee in holiday foolery. If we walk not in the trodden paths, our very petticoats will catch them.

ROSALIND   I could shake them off my coat – these burs are in my heart.

CELIA   Hem them away.

ROSALIND   I would try, if I could cry 'hem' and have him.

CELIA   Come, come, wrestle with thy affections.   20

ROSALIND   O, they take the part of a better wrestler than myself.

CELIA   O, a good wish upon you! You will try in time, in despite of a fall. But turning these jests out of service, let us talk in good earnest: is it possible, on such a sudden, you should fall into so strong a liking with old Sir Rowland's youngest son?

ROSALIND   The duke my father loved his father dearly.

CELIA   Doth it therefore ensue that you should love his son dearly? By this kind of chase, I should hate him, for my father hated his father dearly; yet I hate not   30 Orlando.

ROSALIND   No, faith, hate him not, for my sake.

CELIA   Why should I not? Doth he not deserve well?

ROSALIND Let me love him for that, and do you love him because
          I do.   [*the door is flung open and* DUKE FREDERICK *enters,*
                    preceded by attendants and the lords of his council]
          Look, here comes the duke.
CELIA   With his eyes full of anger.
DUKE F.   [*pausing in the doorway*]
          Mistress, dispatch you with your safest haste
          And get you from our court.
ROSALIND   Me, uncle?
DUKE F.   You, cousin.
          Within these ten days if that thou be'st found   40
          So near our public court as twenty miles,
          Thou diest for it.
ROSALIND   I do beseech your grace,
          Let me the knowledge of my fault bear with me:
          If with myself I hold intelligence
          Or have acquaintance with mine own desires,
          If that I do not dream or be not frantic –
          As I do trust I am not – then, dear uncle,
          Never so much as in a thought unborn
          Did I offend your highness.
DUKE F.   Thus do all traitors!
          If their purgation did consist in words,   50
          They are as innocent as grace itself:
          Let it suffice thee that I trust thee not.
ROSALIND Yet your mistrust cannot make me a traitor:
          Tell me whereon the likelihood depends.
DUKE F.   Thou art thy father's daughter, there's enough.
ROSALIND So was I when your highness took his dukedom,
          So was I when your highness banished him;
          Treason is not inherited, my lord,
          Or, if we did derive it from our friends,
          What's that to me? My father was no traitor.   60
          Then, good my liege, mistake me not so much
          To think my poverty is treacherous.
CELIA   Dear sovereign, hear me speak.
DUKE F.   Ay, Celia, we stayed her for your sake,
          Else had she with her father ranged along.
CELIA   I did not then entreat to have her stay,

It was your pleasure and your own remorse.
I was too young that time to value her,
But now I know her: if she be a traitor,
Why so am I: we still have slept together,   70
Rose at an instant, learned, played, eat together,
And wheresoe'er we went, like Juno's swans,
Still we went coupled and inseparable.

DUKE F.   She is too subtle for thee, and her smoothness,
Her very silence and her patience
Speak to the people, and they pity her.
Thou art a fool – she robs thee of thy name,
And thou wilt show more bright and seem more
                                 virtuous
When she is gone: then open not thy lips.
Firm and irrevocable is my doom   80
Which I have passed upon her – she is banished.

CELIA   Pronounce that sentence then on me, my liege.
I cannot live out of her company.

DUKE F.   You are a fool. You, niece, provide yourself.
If you outstay the time, upon mine honour,
And in the greatness of my word, you die.
         [*he turns and leaves the room, his lords following him*

CELIA   O my poor Rosalind, whither wilt thou go?
Wilt thou change fathers? I will give thee mine.
I charge thee, be not thou more grieved than I am.

ROSALIND   I have more cause.

CELIA   Thou hast not, cousin.   90
Prithee, be cheerful; know'st thou not, the duke
Hath banished me his daughter?

ROSALIND   That he hath not.

CELIA   No, hath not? Rosalind lacks then the love
Which teacheth thee that thou and I am one.
Shall we be sund'red? Shall we part, sweet girl?
No, let my father seek another heir.
Therefore devise with me how we may fly,
Whither to go and what to bear with us,
And do not seek to take your change upon you,
To bear your griefs yourself and leave me out;   100
For, by this heaven, now at our sorrows pale,

	Say what thou canst, I'll go along with thee.
ROSALIND	Why, whither shall we go?
CELIA	To seek my uncle in the forest of Arden.
ROSALIND	Alas, what danger will it be to us,

Maids as we are, to travel forth so far!
Beauty provoketh thieves sooner than gold.

CELIA   I'll put myself in poor and mean attire,
And with a kind of umber smirch my face.
The like do you, so shall we pass along   110
And never stir assailants.

ROSALIND   Were it not better,
Because that I am more than common tall,
That I did suit me all points like a man?
A gallant curtle-axe upon my thigh,
A boar-spear in my hand, and in my heart
Lie there what hidden woman's fear there will,
We'll have a swashing and a martial outside,
As many other mannish cowards have
That do outface it with their semblances.

CELIA   What shall I call thee when thou art a man?   120

ROSALIND   I'll have no worse a name than Jove's own page,
And therefore look you call me Ganymede.
But what will you be called?

CELIA   Something that hath a reference to my state;
No longer Celia, but Aliena.

ROSALIND   But, cousin, what if we assayed to steal
The clownish fool out of your father's court?
Would he not be a comfort to our travel?

CELIA   He'll go along o'er the wide world with me,
Leave me alone to woo him. Let's away,   130
And get our jewels and our wealth together,
Devise the fittest time and safest way
To hide us from pursuit that will be made
After my flight. Now go we in content
To liberty, and not to banishment.   *[they go*

ACT 2 SCENE I

The forest of Arden

The entrance to a cave, with a spreading tree before it. The exiled Duke,
'AMIENS and two or three Lords like foresters' come from the cave

DUKE Now, my co-mates and brothers in exile,
 Hath not old custom made this life more sweet
 Than that of painted pomp? Are not these woods
 More free from peril than the envious court?
 Here feel we not the penalty of Adam,
 The seasons' difference? As the icy fang
 And churlish chiding of the winter's wind,
 Which, when it bites and blows upon my body,
 Even till I shrink with cold, I smile and say
 'This is no flattery: these are counsellors 10
 That feelingly persuade me what I am.'
 Sweet are the uses of adversity,
 Which like the toad, ugly and venomous,
 Wears yet a precious jewel in his head:
 And this our life, exempt from public haunt,
 Finds tongues in trees, books in the running brooks,
 Sermons in stones, and good in every thing.
 I would not change it.

AMIENS   Happy is your grace,
 That can translate the stubbornness of fortune
 Into so quiet and so sweet a style. 20

DUKE Come, shall we go and kill us venison?
 And yet it irks me the poor dappled fools,
 Being native burghers of this desert city,
 Should in their own confines with forkèd heads
 Have their round haunches gored.

1 LORD   Indeed, my lord,
 The melancholy Jaques grieves at that,
 And, in that kind, swears you do more usurp
 Than doth your brother that hath banished you:
 Today my Lord of Amiens and myself
 Did steal behind him as he lay along 30
 Under an oak, whose antique root peeps out

Upon the brook that brawls along this wood,
To the which place a poor sequest'red stag,
That from the hunter's aim had ta'en a hurt,
Did come to languish; and, indeed, my lord,
The wretched animal heaved forth such groans,
That their discharge did stretch his leathern coat
Almost to bursting, and the big round tears
Coursed one another down his innocent nose
In piteous chase: and thus the hairy fool, 40
Much markéd of the melancholy Jaques,
Stood on th'extremest verge of the swift brook,
Augmenting it with tears.

DUKE   But what said Jaques?
Did he not moralize this spectacle?

I LORD O yes, into a thousand similes.
First, for his weeping in the needless stream;
'Poor deer,' quoth he, 'thou mak'st a testament
As worldlings do, giving thy sum of more
To that which had too much': then, being there alone,
Left and abandoned of his velvet friends; 50
' 'Tis right,' quoth he, 'thus misery doth part
The flux of company': anon a careless herd,
Full of the pasture, jumps along by him
And never stays to greet him; 'Ay,' quoth Jaques,
'Sweep on, you fat and greasy citizens!
'Tis just the fashion; wherefore do you look
Upon that poor and broken bankrupt there?'
Thus most invectively he pierceth through
The body of the country, city, court,
Yea, and of this our life, swearing that we 60
Are mere usurpers, tyrants, and what's worse,
To fright the animals and to kill them up
In their assigned and native dwelling-place.

DUKE And did you leave him in this contemplation?

2 LORD We did, my lord, weeping and commenting
Upon the sobbing deer.

DUKE   Show me the place.
I love to cope him in these sullen fits,
For then he's full of matter.

I LORD I'll bring you to him straight.   [they go

SCENE 2

A room in the palace of Duke Frederick

Duke FREDERICK, *lords, and attendants*

DUKE F.   Can it be possible that no man saw them?
          It cannot be. Some villains of my court
          Are of consent and sufferance in this.

1 LORD   I cannot hear of any that did see her.
          The ladies, her attendants of her chamber,
          Saw her abed, and in the morning early
          They found the bed untreasured of their mistress.

2 LORD   My lord, the roynish clown, at whom so oft
          Your grace was wont to laugh, is also missing.   10
          Hisperia, the princess' gentlewoman,
          Confesses that she secretly o'erheard
          Your daughter and her cousin much commend
          The parts and graces of the wrestler
          That did but lately foil the sinewy Charles,
          And she believes wherever they are gone
          That youth is surely in their company.

DUKE F.   Send to his brother, fetch that gallant hither.
          If he be absent, bring his brother to me –
          I'll make him find him: do this suddenly;
          And let not search and inquisition quail   20
          To bring again these foolish runaways.   [*they go*

SCENE 3

The orchard near Oliver's house

ORLANDO *and* ADAM, *meeting*

ORLANDO   Who's there?

ADAM   What! My young master? O my gentle master,
          O my sweet master, O you memory
          Of old Sir Rowland. Why, what make you here?
          Why are you virtuous? Why do people love you?
          And wherefore are you gentle, strong, and valiant?

	Why would you be so fond to overcome	
	The bonny prizer of the humorous duke?	
	Your praise is come too swiftly home before you.	
	Know you not, master, to some kind of men	10
	Their graces serve them but as enemies?	
	No more do yours; your virtues, gentle master,	
	Are sanctified and holy traitors to you.	
	O, what a world is this, when what is comely	
	Envenoms him that bears it!	

ORLANDO Why, what's the matter?

ADAM   O unhappy youth,
Come not within these doors; within this roof
The enemy of all your graces lives.
Your brother – no, no brother – yet the son
(Yet not the son, I will not call him son)   20
Of him I was about to call his father –
Hath heard your praises, and this night he means
To burn the lodging where you use to lie,
And you within it: if he fail of that,
He will have other means to cut you off:
I overheard him, and his practices.
This is no place, this house is but a butchery;
Abhor it, fear it, do not enter it.

ORLANDO Why, whither, Adam, wouldst thou have me go?

ADAM No matter whither, so you come not here.   30

ORLANDO What, wouldst thou have me go and beg my food?
Or with a base and boisterous sword enforce
A thievish living on the common road?
This I must do, or know not what to do:
Yet this I will not do, do how I can –
I rather will subject me to the malice
Of a diverted blood and bloody brother.

ADAM But do not so: I have five hundred crowns,
The thrifty hire I saved under your father,
Which I did store to be my foster-nurse   40
When service should in my old limbs lie lame,
And unregarded age in corners thrown.
Take that, and He that doth the ravens feed,
Yea providently caters for the sparrow,

Be comfort to my age. [*he gives him a bag*]
                    Here is the gold;
All this I give you. Let me be your servant.
Though I look old, yet I am strong and lusty;
For in my youth I never did apply
Hot and rebellious liquors in my blood,
Nor did not with unbashful forehead woo   50
The means of weakness and debility.
Therefore my age is as a lusty winter,
Frosty, but kindly: let me go with you.
I'll do the service of a younger man
In all your business and necessities.

ORLANDO   O good old man, how well in thee appears
The constant service of the antique world,
When service sweat for duty, not for meed!
Thou art not for the fashion of these times,
Where none will sweat but for promotion,   60
And having that do choke their service up
Even with the having – it is not so with thee.
But, poor old man, thou prun'st a rotten tree,
That cannot so much as a blossom yield,
In lieu of all thy pains and husbandry.
But come thy ways, we'll go along together,
And ere we have thy youthful wages spent,
We'll light upon some settled low content.

ADAM   Master, go on, and I will follow thee
To the last gasp with truth and loyalty.   70
From seventeen years till now almost fourscore
Here lived I, but now live here no more.
At seventeen years many their fortunes seek,
But at fourscore it is too late a week.
Yet fortune cannot recompense me better
Than to die well, and not my master's debtor.
                              [*they leave the orchard*

SCENE 4

A clearing in the outskirts of the forest

ROSALIND *(as* GANYMEDE*) clad as a boy in forester's dress, and*
CELIA *(as* ALIENA*) clad as a shepherdess, together with* TOUCHSTONE,
approach slowly and fling themselves upon the ground under a tree

ROSALIND	O Jupiter! How weary are my spirits!
TOUCH.	I care not for my spirits, if my legs were not weary.
ROSALIND	I could find in my heart to disgrace my man's apparel, and to cry like a woman: but I must comfort the weaker vessel, as doublet-and-hose ought to show itself courageous to petticoat: therefore courage, good Aliena!
CELIA	I pray you, bear with me, I cannot go no further.
TOUCH.	For my part, I had rather bear with you than bear you: yet I should bear no cross if I did bear you, for I think you have no money in your purse.

ROSALIND Well, this is the forest of Arden!

TOUCH.   Ay, now am I in Arden, the more fool I. When I was
          at home I was in a better place, but travellers must be
          content.

ROSALIND Ay.
          Be so, good Touchstone.

                    CORIN *and* SILVIUS *draw near*

                              Look you, who comes here –
          A young man and an old in solemn talk.

CORIN   That is the way to make her scorn you still.

SILVIUS O Corin, that thou knew'st how I do love her!

CORIN   I partly guess: for I have loved ere now.

SILVIUS No, Corin, being old, thou canst not guess,
         Though in thy youth thou wast as true a lover
         As ever sighed upon a midnight pillow:
         But if thy love were ever like to mine –
         As sure I think did never man love so –
         How many actions most ridiculous
         Hast thou been drawn to by thy fantasy?

CORIN   Into a thousand that I have forgotten.

SILVIUS   O thou didst then ne'er love so heartily.
          If thou remembrest not the slightest folly   30
          That ever love did make thee run into,
          Thou hast not loved . . .
          Or if thou hast not sat as I do now,
          Wearing thy hearer in thy mistress' praise,
          Thou hast not loved
          Or if thou hast not broke from company
          Abruptly, as my passion now makes me,
          Thou hast not loved
          O Phebe, Phebe, Phebe!
                    [*he buries his face in his hands and runs into the forest*
ROSALIND Alas, poor shepherd! Searching of thy wound,   40
          I have by hard adventure found mine own.
TOUCH.   And I mine: I remember, when I was in love I broke
          my sword upon a stone, and bid him take that for
          coming a-night to Jane Smile, and I remember the
          kissing of her batler and the cow's dugs that her pretty
          chopt hands had milked; and I remember the wooing
          of a peascod instead of her, from whom I took two
          cods, and giving her them again, said with weeping
          tears, 'Wear these for my sake'. We that are true lovers
          run into strange capers; but as all is mortal in nature, so   50
          is all nature in love mortal in folly.
ROSALIND Thou speak'st wiser than thou art ware of.
TOUCH.   Nay, I shall ne'er be ware of mine own wit till I break
          my shins against it.
ROSALIND   Jove, Jove! This shepherd's passion
              Is much upon my fashion.
TOUCH.   And mine — but it grows something stale with me.
CELIA   I pray you, one of you question yond man
          If he for gold will give us any food.
          I faint almost to death.
TOUCH.   Holla; you, clown!   60
ROSALIND Peace, fool, he's not thy kinsman.
CORIN   Who calls?
TOUCH.   Your betters, sir.
CORIN   Else are they very wretched.
ROSALIND Peace, I say. Good even to you, friend.

CORIN   And to you, gentle sir, and to you all.

ROSALIND   I prithee, shepherd, if that love or gold
            Can in this desert place buy entertainment,
            Bring us where we may rest ourselves and feed:
            Here's a young maid with travel much oppressed,
            And faints for succour.

CORIN   Fair sir, I pity her,
            And wish for her sake more than for mine own,   70
            My fortunes were more able to relieve her:
            But I am shepherd to another man,
            And do not shear the fleeces that I graze:
            My master is of churlish disposition,
            And little recks to find the way to heaven
            By doing deeds of hospitality:
            Besides, his cote, his flocks and bounds of feed
            Are now on sale, and at our sheepcote now
            By reason of his absence there is nothing
            That you will feed on; but what is, come see,   80
            And in my voice most welcome shall you be.

ROSALIND   What is he that shall buy his flock and pasture?

CORIN   That young swain that you saw here but erewhile,
            That little cares for buying anything.

ROSALIND   I pray thee, if it stand with honesty,
            Buy thou the cottage, pasture, and the flock,
            And thou shalt have to pay for it of us.

CELIA   And we will mend thy wages: I like this place,
            And willingly could waste my time in it.

CORIN   Assuredly, the thing is to be sold.   90
            Go with me. If you like upon report
            The soil, the profit, and this kind of life,
            I will your very faithful feeder be,
            And buy it with your gold right suddenly.

                          [*he goes; they rise and follow him*

SCENE 5

Before the cave of the exiled Duke

'AMIENS, JAQUES *and others', seated beneath the tree*

AMIENS　[*sings*]　　Under the greenwood tree,
　　　　　　　　　　Who loves to lie with me,
　　　　　　　　　　And turn his merry note
　　　　　　　　　　Unto the sweet bird's throat,
　　　　　　　　Come hither, come hither, come hither:
　　　　　　　　　　　Here shall he see
　　　　　　　　　　　No enemy,
　　　　　　　　But winter and rough weather.

JAQUES　More, more, I prithee, more.

AMIENS　It will make you melancholy, Monsieur Jaques.　　　　10

JAQUES　I thank it. More, I prithee, more. I can suck melancholy
out of a song, as a weasel sucks eggs. More, I prithee,
more.

AMIENS　My voice is ragged, I know I cannot please you.

JAQUES　I do not desire you to please me, I do desire you to
sing. Come, more, another stanzo: call you 'em stanzos?

AMIENS　What you will, Monsieur Jaques.

JAQUES　Nay, I care not for their names, they owe me nothing.
Will you sing?

AMIENS　More at your request than to please myself.　　　　20

JAQUES　Well then, if ever I thank any man, I'll thank you: but
that they call compliment is like th'encounter of two
dog-apes; and when a man thanks me heartily, methinks I have given him a penny and he renders me the
beggarly thanks. Come, sing; and you that will not,
hold your tongues.

AMIENS　Well, I'll end the song. Sirs, cover the while – the
duke will drink under this tree. He hath been all this
day to look you.

　　　　　[*Some of the company prepare a meal beneath the tree*

JAQUES　And I have all this day to avoid him. He is too　　30
disputable for my company. I think of as many matters

as he, but I give heaven thanks, and make no boast of
them. Come, warble, come.

They sing 'altogether here'

> Who doth ambition shun,
> And loves to live i'th' sun,
> Seeking the food he eats,
> And pleased with what he gets,
> Come hither, come hither, come hither:
>> Here shall he see   40
>> No enemy,
> But winter and rough weather.

JAQUES   I'll give you a verse to this note, that I made yesterday
          in despite of my invention.

AMIENS   And I'll sing it.

JAQUES   Thus it goes:

> If it do come to pass,
> That any man turn ass,
> Leaving his wealth and ease,
> A stubborn will to please,   50
> Ducdame, ducdame, ducdame:
>> Here shall he see,
>> Gross fools as he,
> An if he will come to me.

AMIENS   What's that 'ducdame'?

JAQUES   'Tis a Greek invocation, to call fools into a circle. I'll
          go sleep, if I can: if I cannot, I'll rail against all the first-
          born of Egypt.

AMIENS   And I'll go seek the duke; his banquet is prepared.

                              [*they depart in different directions*

SCENE 6

The clearing in the outskirts of the forest

ORLANDO *and* ADAM *approach*

ADAM   Dear master, I can go no further: O, I die for food.
          [*he falls*] Here lie I down, and measure out my grave.
          Farewell, kind master.

ORLANDO Why, how now, Adam! No greater heart in thee? Live
a little, comfort a little, cheer thyself a little. If this un-
couth forest yield anything savage, I will either be food
for it or bring it for food to thee. Thy conceit is nearer
death than thy powers. [*he lifts him tenderly and props him
against a tree*] For my sake be comfortable – hold death   10
awhile at the arm's end: I will here be with thee presently, and if I bring thee not something to eat, I will give
thee leave to die: but if thou diest before I come, thou art
a mocker of my labour. [*Adam smiles a little*] Well said!
Thou look'st cheerly, and I'll be with thee quickly. Yet
thou liest in the bleak air. [*he takes him in his arms*] Come,
I will bear thee to some shelter – and thou shalt not die
for lack of a dinner, if there live any thing in this desert.
Cheerly, good Adam!   [*he carries him away*

SCENE 7

Before the cave of the exiled Duke

A meal of fruit and wine set out under the tree; the DUKE *and
some of his lords reclining thereat*

DUKE   I think he be transformed into a beast,
         For I can nowhere find him like a man.
I LORD   My lord, he is but even now gone hence.
         Here was he merry, hearing of a song.
DUKE   If he, compact of jars, grow musical,
         We shall have shortly discord in the spheres:
         Go, seek him, tell him I would speak with him.

JAQUES *is seen coming through the trees, a smile upon his face, and
shortly behind him* AMIENS, *who silently takes his seat next to the
Duke at the meal when he comes up*

I LORD   He saves my labour by his own approach.
DUKE   Why, how now, monsieur! What a life is this,
         That your poor friends must woo your company?   10
         What, you look merrily!
JAQUES   [*breaks into laughter*].
         A fool, a fool! I met a fool i'th' forest,

A motley fool – a miserable world!
As I do live by food, I met a fool,
Who laid him down and basked him in the sun,
And railed on Lady Fortune in good terms,
In good set terms, and yet a motley fool.
'Good morrow, fool,' quoth I: 'No, sir,' quoth he,
'Call me not fool till heaven hath sent me fortune.'
And then he drew a dial from his poke,   20
And looking on it with lack-lustre eye,
Says very wisely, 'It is ten o'clock:
Thus we may see,' quoth he, 'how the world wags:
'Tis but an hour ago since it was nine,
And after one hour more 'twill be eleven,
And so from hour to hour, we ripe, and ripe,
And then from hour to hour, we rot, and rot –
And thereby hangs a tale.' When I did hear
The motley fool thus moral on the time,
My lungs began to crow like chanticleer,   30
That fools should be so deep-contemplative;
And I did laugh, sans intermission,
An hour by his dial. O noble fool!
O worthy fool! Motley's the only wear.

DUKE   What fool is this?

JAQUES   A worthy fool. One that hath been a courtier,
And says, if ladies be but young and fair,
They have the gift to know it: and in his brain,
Which is as dry as the remainder biscuit
After a voyage, he hath strange places crammed   40
With observation, the which he vents
In mangled forms. O, that I were a fool!
I am ambitious for a motley coat.

DUKE   Thou shalt have one.

JAQUES   It is my only suit –
Provided that you weed your better judgments
Of all opinion that grows rank in them
That I am wise. I must have liberty
Withal, as large a charter as the wind,
To blow on whom I please, for so fools have:
And they that are most gallèd with my folly,   50

They most must laugh: and why, sir, must they so?
The 'why' is plain as way to parish church:
He that a fool doth very wisely hit
Doth very foolishly, although he smart,
Not to seem senseless of the bob: if not,
The wise man's folly is anatomized
Even by the squand'ring glances of the fool.
Invest me in my motley; give me leave
To speak my mind, and I will through and through
Cleanse the foul body of th'infected world,   60
If they will patiently receive my medicine.

DUKE   Fie on thee! I can tell what thou wouldst do.

JAQUES   What, for a counter, would I do but good?

DUKE   Most mischievous foul sin, in chiding sin:
For thou thyself hast been a libertine,
As sensual as the brutish sting itself,
And all th'embosséd sores and headed evils,
That thou with licence of free foot hast caught,
Wouldst thou disgorge into the general world.

JAQUES   Why, who cries out on pride,   70
That can therein tax any private party?
Doth it not flow as hugely as the sea,
Till that the weary very means do ebb?
What woman in the city do I name,
When that I say the city-woman bears
The cost of princes on unworthy shoulders?
Who can come in and say that I mean her,
When such a one as she, such is her neighbour?
Or what is he of basest function,
That says his bravery is not on my cost,   80
Thinking that I mean him, but therein suits
His folly to the mettle of my speech?
There then! How then? What then? Let me see
                             wherein
My tongue hath wronged him: if it do him right,
Then he hath wronged himself; if he be free,
Why then my taxing like a wild-goose flies,
Unclaimed of any man. But who comes here?

ORLANDO *appears before them, with his sword drawn*

ORLANDO	Forbear, and eat no more.
JAQUES	Why, I have eat none yet.
ORLANDO	Nor shalt not, till necessity be served.
JAQUES	Of what kind should this cock come of?

90

DUKE   Art thou thus boldened, man, by thy distress?
          Or else a rude despiser of good manners,
          That in civility thou seem'st so empty?
ORLANDO   You touched my vein at first. The thorny point
          Of bare distress hath ta'en from me the show
          Of smooth civility: yet am I inland bred,
          And know some nurture. But forbear, I say,
          He dies that touches any of this fruit
          Till I and my affairs are answeréd.
JAQUES   [*taking up a bunch of raisins*]
          An you will not be answered with reason, I must die.   100
DUKE   What would you have? Your gentleness shall force,
          More than your force move us to gentleness.
ORLANDO   I almost die for food, and let me have it.
DUKE   Sit down and feed, and welcome to our table.
ORLANDO   Speak you so gently? Pardon me, I pray you –
          I thought that all things had been savage here,
          And therefore put I on the countenance
          Of stern commandment. But whate'er you are
          That in this desert inaccessible,
          Under the shade of melancholy boughs,   110
          Lose and neglect the creeping hours of time;
          If ever you have looked on better days,
          If ever been where bells have knolled to church,
          If ever sat at any good man's feast,
          If ever from your eyelids wiped a tear,
          And know what 'tis to pity and be pitied,
          Let gentleness my strong enforcement be:
          In the which hope I blush, and hide my sword.
DUKE   True is it that we have seen better days,
          And have with holy bell been knolled to church,   120
          And sat at good men's feasts, and wiped our eyes
          Of drops that sacred pity hath engendred:
          And therefore sit you down in gentleness,

And take upon command what help we have
That to your wanting may be ministred.

ORLANDO Then but forbear your food a little while,
Whiles, like a doe, I go to find my fawn,
And give it food. There is an old poor man,
Who after me hath many a weary step
Limped in pure love: till he be first sufficed,   130
Oppressed with two weak evils, age and hunger,
I will not touch a bit.

DUKE   Go find him out,
And we will nothing waste till you return.

ORLANDO I thank ye, and be blessed for your good comfort!

                                [*he goes*

DUKE Thou seest we are not all alone unhappy:
This wide and universal theatre
Presents more woeful pageants than the scene
Wherein we play in.

JAQUES   All the world's a stage,
And all the men and women merely players;
They have their exits and their entrances,   140
And one man in his time plays many parts,
His acts being seven ages. At first the infant,
Mewling and puking in the nurse's arms:
Then the whining school-boy, with his satchel
And shining morning face, creeping like snail
Unwillingly to school: and then the lover,
Sighing like furnace, with a woeful ballad
Made to his mistress' eyebrow: then a soldier,
Full of strange oaths and bearded like the pard,
Jealous in honour, sudden and quick in quarrel,   150
Seeking the bubble reputation
Even in the cannon's mouth: and then the justice,
In fair round belly with good capon lined,
With eyes severe and beard of formal cut,
Full of wise saws and modern instances,
And so he plays his part. The sixth age shifts
Into the lean and slippered pantaloon,
With spectacles on nose and pouch on side,
His youthful hose, well saved, a world too wide

For his shrunk shank, and his big manly voice,   160
Turning again toward childish treble, pipes
And whistles in his sound. Last scene of all,
That ends this strange eventful history,
Is second childishness, and mere oblivion,
Sans teeth, sans eyes, sans taste, sans every thing.

ORLANDO returns with ADAM *in his arms*

DUKE   Welcome. Set down your venerable burden,
          And let him feed.

ORLANDO   I thank you most for him.

ADAM   So had you need,
          I scarce can speak to thank you for myself.

DUKE   Welcome, fall to: I will not trouble you
          As yet to question you about your fortunes: 170
          Give us some music, and good cousin, sing.

AMIENS   [*sings*] Blow, blow, thou winter wind,
                  Thou art not so unkind
                    As man's ingratitude:
                  Thy tooth is not so keen,
                  Because thou art not seen,
                    Although thy breath be rude.
              Hey-ho, sing hey-ho, unto the green holly,
              Most friendship is feigning; most loving mere folly:
                  Then hey-ho, the holly,   180
                    This life is most jolly.

                  Freeze, freeze, thou bitter sky,
                  That dost not bite so nigh
                    As benefits forgot:
                  Though thou the waters warp,
                  Thy sting is not so sharp
                  As friend remembered not.
              Hey-ho, sing hey-ho, unto the green holly,
              Most friendship is feigning; most loving mere folly:
                  Then hey-ho, the holly,   190
                    This life is most jolly.

DUKE   If that you were the good Sir Rowland's son,
          As you have whispered faithfully you were,
          And as mine eye doth his effigies witness

Most truly limned and living in your face,
Be truly welcome hither: I am the duke
That loved your father. The residue of your fortune,
Go to my cave and tell me. Good old man,
Thou art right welcome as thy master is:
Support him by the arm. Give me your hand,   200
And let me all your fortunes understand.

                                        [*they enter the cave*

ACT 3 SCENE 1

A room in the palace of Duke Frederick

Enter Duke FREDERICK, *lords, and* OLIVER, *guarded by attendants*

DUKE F.   Not see him since? Sir, sir, that cannot be:
           But were I not the better part made mercy,
           I should not seek an absent argument
           Of my revenge, thou present: but look to it,
           Find out thy brother wheresoe'er he is –
           Seek him with candle; bring him dead or living
           Within this twelvemonth, or turn thou no more
           To seek a living in our territory.
           Thy lands and all things that thou dost call thine
           Worth seizure do we seize into our hands,   10
           Till thou canst quit thee by thy brother's mouth
           Of what we think against thee.
OLIVER   O that your highness knew my heart in this!
           I never loved my brother in my life.
DUKE F.   More villain thou. Well, push him out of doors,
           And let my officers of such a nature
           Make an extent upon his house and lands:
           Do this expediently and turn him going.   [*they go*

SCENE 2

The clearing in the outskirts of the forest, near the sheepcote

ORLANDO *with a paper, which he fixes to the trunk of a tree*

ORLANDO   Hang there, my verse, in witness of my love,
           And thou, thrice-crownéd queen of night, survey
           With thy chaste eye, from thy pale sphere above,
           Thy huntress' name that my full life doth sway.
           O Rosalind! These trees shall be my books,
           And in their barks my thoughts I'll character,
           That every eye which in this forest looks
           Shall see thy virtue witnessed everywhere.

Run, run, Orlando, carve on every tree
The fair, the chaste and unexpressive she. *[he passes on* 10

      CORIN *and* TOUCHSTONE *come up*

CORIN   And how like you this shepherd's life, Master Touch-
           stone?

TOUCH.   Truly, shepherd, in respect of itself, it is a good life; but
           in respect that it is a shepherd's life, it is naught. In
           respect that it is solitary, I like it very well; but in respect
           that it is private, it is a very vile life. Now in respect it is
           in the fields, it pleaseth me well; but in respect it is not in
           the court, it is tedious. As it is a spare life, look you, it fits
           my humour well; but as there is no more plenty in it, it
           goes much against my stomach. Hast any philosophy in 20
           thee, shepherd?

CORIN   No more, but that I know the more one sickens, the
           worse at ease he is; and that he that wants money,
           means and content is without three good friends; that
           the property of rain is to wet and fire to burn; that good
           pasture makes fat sheep; and that a great cause of the
           night, is lack of the sun; that he that hath learned no wit
           by nature nor art may complain of good breeding, or
           comes of a very dull kindred.

TOUCH.   Such a one is a natural philosopher. Wast ever in 30
           court, shepherd?

CORIN   No, truly.

TOUCH.   Then thou art damned.

CORIN   Nay, I hope –

TOUCH.   Truly thou art damned, like an ill-roasted egg all on
           one side.

CORIN   For not being at court? Your reason.

TOUCH.   Why, if thou never wast at court, thou never saw'st
           good manners; if thou never saw'st good manners,
           then thy manners must be wicked, and wickedness is 40
           sin, and sin is damnation. Thou art in a parlous state,
           shepherd.

CORIN   Not a whit, Touchstone. Those that are good manners
           at the court are as ridiculous in the country, as the
           behaviour of the country is most mockable at the
           court. You told me you salute not at the court, but

you kiss your hands; that courtesy would be uncleanly,
if courtiers were shepherds.

TOUCH. Instance, briefly; come, instance.

CORIN Why, we are still handling our ewes, and their fells 50
you know are greasy.

TOUCH. Why, do not your courtier's hands sweat? And is not
the grease of a mutton as wholesome as the sweat of a
man? Shallow, shallow: a better instance, I say: come.

CORIN Besides, our hands are hard.

TOUCH. Your lips will feel them the sooner. Shallow, again: a
more sounder instance, come.

CORIN And they are often tarred over with the surgery of our
sheep; and would you have us kiss tar? The courtier's
hands are perfumed with civet. 60

TOUCH. Most shallow man! Thou worms-meat, in respect of a
good piece of flesh indeed! Learn of the wise, and
perpend: civet is of a baser birth than tar, the very
uncleanly flux of a cat. Mend the instance, shepherd.

CORIN You have too courtly a wit for me, I'll rest.

TOUCH. Wilt thou rest damned? God help thee, shallow man!
God make incision in thee! Thou art raw.

CORIN Sir, I am a true labourer. I earn that I eat, get that I
wear, owe no man hate, envy no man's happiness, glad
of other men's good, content with my harm; and the 70
greatest of my pride is to see my ewes graze and my
lambs suck.

TOUCH. That is another simple sin in you, to bring the ewes
and the rams together, and to offer to get your living
by the copulation of cattle – to be bawd to a bell-
wether, and to betray a she-lamb of a twelvemonth to
a crooked-pated, old, cuckoldly ram, out of all reasonable match. If thou beest not damned for this, the devil
himself will have no shepherds – I cannot see else how
thou shouldst 'scape. 80

CORIN Here comes young Master Ganymede, my new mistress's
brother.

ROSALIND, *unwitting of their presence, comes up, sees* ORLANDO'*s
paper on the tree and, plucking it down, begins to read it*

ROSALIND   'From the east to western Ind,
                 No jewel is like Rosalind.
                 Her worth, being mounted on the wind,
                 Through all the world bears Rosalind.
                 All the pictures fairest lined
                 Are but black to Rosalind.
                 Let no face be kept in mind
                 But the fair of Rosalind.'   90

TOUCH.   [*taps her on the arm with his bauble*] I'll rhyme you so
              eight years together, dinners, and suppers, and sleeping-
              hours excepted: it is the right butter women's rank to
              market.

ROSALIND Out, fool!

TOUCH.   For a taste:
                 If a hart do lack a hind,
                 Let him seek out Rosalind:
                 If the cat will after kind,
                 So be sure will Rosalind: 100
                 Winter garments must be lined,
                 So must slender Rosalind.
                 They that reap must sheaf and bind,
                 Then to cart with Rosalind.
                 Sweetest nut hath sourest rind,
                 Such a nut is Rosalind.
                 He that sweetest rose will find,
                 Must find love's prick and Rosalind.
              This is the very false gallop of verses. Why do you
              infect yourself with them?   110

ROSALIND Peace, you dull fool! I found them on a tree.

TOUCH.   Truly, the tree yields bad fruit.

ROSALIND I'll graff it with you, and then I shall graff it with a
              medlar: then it will be the earliest fruit i'th' country:
              for you'll be rotten ere you be half ripe, and that's the
              right virtue of the medlar.

TOUCH.   You have said: but whether wisely or no, let the forest
              judge.

              CELIA *draws near, likewise reading a paper*

ROSALIND Peace!

Here comes my sister, reading. Stand aside.   120
                              [*they hide behind a tree*

CELIA   'Why should this a desert be?
         For it is unpeopled? No;
      Tongues I'll hang on every tree,
         That shall civil sayings show.
      Some, how brief the life of man
         Runs his erring pilgrimage,
      That the stretching of a span
         Buckles in his sum of age;
      Some, of violated vows
         'Twixt the souls of friend and friend: 130
      But upon the fairest boughs,
         Or at every sentence end,
      Will I Rosalinda write,
         Teaching all that read to know
      The quintessence of every sprite
         Heaven would in little show.
      Therefore Heaven Nature charged,
         That one body should be filled
      With all graces wide-enlarged:
         Nature presently distilled   140
      Helen's cheek, but not her heart,
         Cleopatra's majesty,
      Atalanta's better part,
         Sad Lucretia's modesty
      Thus Rosalind of many parts
         By heavenly synod was devised,
      Of many faces, eyes, and hearts.
         To have the touches dearest prized . . .
      Heaven would that she these gifts should have,
      And I to live and die her slave.'   150

ROSALIND O most gentle pulpiter, what tedious homily of love
have you wearied your parishioners withal, and never
cried, 'Have patience, good people!'

CELIA   [*starts and turns, dropping the paper*] How now, back-
friends! Shepherd, go off a little. Go with him, sirrah.

TOUCH.   Come, shepherd, let us make an honourable retreat —
though not with bag and baggage, yet with scrip and
scrippage.

[Touchstone picks up the verses and departs with Corin

CELIA	Didst thou hear these verses?
ROSALIND	O yes, I heard them all, and more too, for some of 160 them had in them more feet than the verses would bear.
CELIA	That's no matter: the feet might bear the verses.
ROSALIND	Ay, but the feet were lame, and could not bear themselves without the verse, and therefore stood lamely in the verse.
CELIA	But didst thou hear without wondering how thy name should be hanged and carved upon these trees?
ROSALIND	I was seven of the nine days out of the wonder before you came; for look here what I found on a palm-tree. I 170 was never so be-rhymed since Pythagoras' time, that I was an Irish rat, which I can hardly remember.
CELIA	Trow you who hath done this?
ROSALIND	Is it a man?
CELIA	And a chain that you once wore about his neck! Change you colour?
ROSALIND	I prithee, who?
CELIA	O Lord, Lord! It is a hard matter for friends to meet; but mountains may be removed with earthquakes and so encounter. 180
ROSALIND	Nay, but who is it?
CELIA	Is it possible?
ROSALIND	Nay, I prithee now with most petitionary vehemence, tell me who it is.
CELIA	O wonderful, wonderful, and most wonderful wonderful! And yet again wonderful, and after that out of all whooping!
ROSALIND	Good my complexion! Dost thou think, though I am caparisoned like a man, I have a doublet and-hose in my disposition? One inch of delay more is a South-sea 190 of discovery. I prithee, tell me who is it quickly, and speak apace: I would thou couldst stammer, that thou mightst pour this concealed man out of thy mouth, as wine comes out of a narrow-mouthed bottle; either too much at once, or none at all. I prithee take the cork out of thy mouth, that I may drink thy tidings.

CELIA	So you may put a man in your belly.
ROSALIND	Is he of God's making? What manner of man? Is his head worth a hat? Or his chin worth a beard?
CELIA	Nay, he hath but a little beard.
ROSALIND	Why, God will send more, if the man will be thankful: let me stay the growth of his beard, if thou delay me not the knowledge of his chin.
CELIA	It is young Orlando, that tripped up the wrestler's heels, and your heart, both in an instant.
ROSALIND	Nay, but the devil take mocking; speak sad brow and true maid.
CELIA	I'faith, coz, 'tis he.
ROSALIND	Orlando?
CELIA	Orlando.
ROSALIND	Alas the day, what shall I do with my doublet and hose? What did he when thou saw'st him? What said he? How looked he? Wherein went he? What makes he here? Did he ask for me? Where remains he? How parted he with thee? And when shalt thou see him again? Answer me in one word.
CELIA	You must borrow me Gargantua's mouth first: 'tis a word too great for any mouth of this age's size. To say ay and no to these particulars is more than to answer in a catechism.
ROSALIND	But doth he know that I am in this forest and in man's apparel? Looks he as freshly as he did the day he wrestled?
CELIA	It is as easy to count atomies as to resolve the propositions of a lover: but take a taste of my finding him, and relish it with good observance. I found him under a tree, like a dropped acorn.
ROSALIND	It may well be called Jove's tree, when it drops such fruit.
CELIA	Give me audience, good madam.
ROSALIND	Proceed.
CELIA	There lay he, stretched along, like a wounded knight.
ROSALIND	Though it be pity to see such a sight, it well becomes the ground.
CELIA	Cry 'holla' to thy tongue, I prithee; it curvets unseasonably. He was furnished like a hunter.
ROSALIND	O ominous! He comes to kill my heart.

200

210

220

230

CELIA	I would sing my song without a burden – thou bring'st me out of tune.
ROSALIND	Do you not know I am a woman? When I think, I must speak. Sweet, say on.

ORLANDO and JAQUES *are seen coming through the trees*

CELIA	You bring me out. Soft! comes he not here? 240
ROSALIND	'Tis he – slink by, and note him.

[*Celia and Rosalind steal behind a tree, within earshot*

JAQUES	I thank you for your company – but, good faith, I had as lief have been myself alone.
ORLANDO	And so had I: but yet, for fashion sake, I thank you too for your society.
JAQUES	God buy you, let's meet as little as we can.
ORLANDO	I do desire we may be better strangers.
JAQUES	I pray you, mar no more trees with writing love-songs in their barks.
ORLANDO	I pray you, mar no more of my verses with reading 250 them ill-favouredly.
JAQUES	Rosalind is your love's name?
ORLANDO	Yes, just.
JAQUES	I do not like her name.
ORLANDO	There was no thought of pleasing you when she was christened.
JAQUES	What stature is she of?
ORLANDO	Just as high as my heart.
JAQUES	You are full of pretty answers: have you not been acquainted with goldsmiths' wives, and conned them 260 out of rings?
ORLANDO	Not so; but I answer you right painted cloth, from whence you have studied your questions.
JAQUES	You have a nimble wit; I think 'twas made of Atalanta's heels. Will you sit down with me? And we two will rail against our mistress the world, and all our misery.
ORLANDO	I will chide no breather in the world but myself, against whom I know most faults.
JAQUES	The worst fault you have is to be in love.
ORLANDO	'Tis a fault I will not change for your best virtue. I am 270 weary of you.
JAQUES	By my troth, I was seeking for a fool when I found you.

ORLANDO   He is drowned in the brook – look but in, and you
          shall see him.

JAQUES   There I shall see mine own figure.

ORLANDO   Which I take to be either a fool or a cipher.

JAQUES   I'll tarry no longer with you. Farewell, good Signior
          Love.   [he bows

ORLANDO   I am glad of your departure. [he bows likewise] Adieu,
          good Monsieur Melancholy.   [Jaques departs   280

ROSALIND I will speak to him like a saucy lackey, and under that
          habit play the knave with him. [calls] Do you hear,
          forester?

ORLANDO   [turns] Very well. What would you?

ROSALIND I pray you, what is't o'clock?

ORLANDO   You should ask me what time o'day: there's no clock
          in the forest.

ROSALIND Then there is no true lover in the forest, else sighing
          every minute and groaning every hour would detect
          the lazy foot of Time as well as a clock.   290

ORLANDO   And why not the swift foot of Time? Had not that
          been as proper?

ROSALIND By no means, sir: Time travels in divers paces with
          divers persons. I'll tell you who Time ambles withal,
          who Time trots withal, who Time gallops withal, and
          who he stands still withal.

ORLANDO   I prithee, who doth he trot withal?

ROSALIND Marry, he trots hard with a young maid between the
          contract of her marriage and the day it is solemnized: if
          the interim be but a se'nnight, Time's pace is so hard   300
          that it seems the length of seven year.

ORLANDO   Who ambles Time withal?

ROSALIND With a priest that lacks Latin, and a rich man that hath
          not the gout: for the one sleeps easily because he
          cannot study, and the other lives merrily because he
          feels no pain: the one lacking the burden of lean and
          wasteful learning; the other knowing no burden of
          heavy tedious penury. These Time ambles withal.

ORLANDO   Who doth he gallop withal?

ROSALIND With a thief to the gallows: for though he go as softly   310
          as foot can fall, he thinks himself too soon there.

ORLANDO   Who stays it still withal?

ROSALIND   With lawyers in the vacation: for they sleep between term and term, and then they perceive not how Time moves.

ORLANDO   Where dwell you, pretty youth?

ROSALIND   With this shepherdess, my sister; here in the skirts of the forest, like fringe upon a petticoat.

ORLANDO   Are you native of this place?

ROSALIND   As the cony that you see dwell where she is kindled.   320

ORLANDO   Your accent is something finer than you could purchase in so removed a dwelling.

ROSALIND   I have been told so of many: but indeed an old religious uncle of mine taught me to speak, who was in his youth an inland man – one that knew courtship too well, for there he fell in love. I have heard him read many lectures against it, and I thank God I am not a woman, to be touched with so many giddy offences as he hath generally taxed their whole sex withal.

ORLANDO   Can you remember any of the principal evils that he   330 laid to the charge of women?

ROSALIND   There were none principal; they were all like one another as halfpence are, every one fault seeming monstrous till his fellow-fault came to match it.

ORLANDO   I prithee, recount some of them.

ROSALIND   No: I will not cast away my physic but on those that are sick. There is a man haunts the forest, that abuses our young plants with carving 'Rosalind' on their barks; hangs odes upon hawthorns and elegies on brambles; all, forsooth, deifying the name of Rosalind: 340 if I could meet that fancy-monger, I would give him some good counsel, for he seems to have the quotidian of love upon him.

ORLANDO   I am he that is so love-shaked. I pray you, tell me your remedy.

ROSALIND   There is none of my uncle's marks upon you: he taught me how to know a man in love; in which cage of rushes I am sure you are not prisoner.

ORLANDO   What were his marks?

ROSALIND   A lean cheek, which you have not: a blue eye and   350

sunken, which you have not: an unquestionable spirit,
which you have not: a beard neglected, which you
have not – but I pardon you for that, for simply your
having in beard is a younger brother's revenue. Then
your hose should be ungartered, your bonnet un-
banded, your sleeve unbuttoned, your shoe untied,
and every thing about you demonstrating a careless
desolation: but you are no such man; you are rather
point-device in your accoutrements, as loving yourself
than seeming the lover of any other.   36

ORLANDO   Fair youth, I would I could make thee believe I love.

ROSALIND   Me believe it! You may as soon make her that you
love believe it, which I warrant she is apter to do than
to confess she does: that is one of the points in the
which women still give the lie to their consciences.
But, in good sooth, are you he that hangs the verses on
the trees, wherein Rosalind is so admired?

ORLANDO   I swear to thee, youth, by the white hand of Rosalind,
I am that he, that unfortunate he.

ROSALIND   But are you so much in love as your rhymes speak?   37

ORLANDO   Neither rhyme nor reason can express how much.

ROSALIND   Love is merely a madness, and I tell you deserves as
well a dark house and a whip as madmen do: and the
reason why they are not so punished and cured is, that
the lunacy is so ordinary that the whippers are in love
too. Yet I profess curing it by counsel.

ORLANDO   Did you ever cure any so?

ROSALIND   Yes, one, and in this manner. He was to imagine me
his love, his mistress; and I set him every day to woo
me: at which time would I, being but a moonish   38
youth, grieve, be effeminate, changeable, longing and
liking, proud, fantastical, apish, shallow, inconstant,
full of tears, full of smiles; for every passion something,
and for no passion truly anything, as boys and women
are for the most part cattle of this colour: would now
like him, now loathe him; then entertain him, then
forswear him; now weep for him, then spit at him;
that I drave my suitor from his mad humour of love to
a living humour of madness – which was, to forswear

the full stream of the world and to live in a nook 390
merely monastic. And thus I cured him, and this way
will I take upon me to wash your liver as clean as a
sound sheep's heart, that there shall not be one spot of
love in't.

ORLANDO I would not be cured, youth.

ROSALIND I would cure you, if you would but call me Rosalind,
and come every day to my cote, and woo me.

ORLANDO Now, by the faith of my love, I will. Tell me where it is.

ROSALIND Go with me to it, and I'll show it you: and by the way
you shall tell me where in the forest you live. Will you 400
go?

ORLANDO With all my heart, good youth.

ROSALIND Nay, you must call me Rosalind. Come, sister will you
go?   *[they go*

Some days pass

SCENE 3

The clearing near the sheepcote (as before)

TOUCHSTONE *and* AUDREY *approach;* JAQUES *following at a little distance*

TOUCH.   Come apace, good Audrey. I will fetch up your goats,
Audrey. And how, Audrey? Am I the man yet? Doth
my simple feature content you?

AUDREY   Your features! Lord warrant us! What features?

TOUCH.   I am here with thee and thy goats, as the most capri-
cious poet, honest Ovid, was among the Goths.

JAQUES   O knowledge ill-inhabited! Worse than Jove in a
thatched house!

TOUCH.   When a man's verses cannot be understood, nor a
man's good wit seconded with the forward child, un- 10
derstanding, it strikes a man more dead than a great
reckoning in a little room. Truly, I would the gods
had made thee poetical.

AUDREY   I do not know what 'poetical' is; is it honest in deed
and word? Is it a true thing?

TOUCH.   No, truly; for the truest poetry is the most feigning;

and lovers are given to poetry; and what they swear in
poetry it may be said as lovers they do feign.

AUDREY   Do you wish then that the gods had made me poetical?

TOUCH.   I do, truly: for thou swear'st to me thou art honest;   20
now, if thou wert a poet, I might have some hope
thou didst feign.

AUDREY   Would you not have me honest?

TOUCH.   No truly, unless thou wert hard-favoured: for honesty
coupled to beauty is to have honey a sauce to sugar.

JAQUES   A material fool!

AUDREY   Well, I am not fair, and therefore I pray the gods make
me honest.

TOUCH.   Truly, and to cast away honesty upon a foul slut were
to put good meat into an unclean dish.   30

AUDREY   I am not a slut, though I thank the gods I am foul.

TOUCH.   Well, praised be the gods for thy foulness! Sluttishness
may come hereafter. But be it as it may be, I will marry
thee: and to that end, I have been with Sir Oliver
Martext the vicar of the next village, who hath promised
to meet me in this place of the forest and to couple us.

JAQUES   I would fain see this meeting

AUDREY   Well, the gods give us joy!

TOUCH.   Amen. A man may, if he were of a fearful heart,
stagger in this attempt; for here we have no temple   40
but the wood, no assembly but horn-beasts. But what
though? Courage! As horns are odious, they are necessary. It is said, 'many a man knows no end of his
goods'. Right! Many a man has good horns, and
knows no end of them. Well, that is the dowry of his
wife; 'tis none of his own getting. Horns? Even so.
Poor men alone? No, no, the noblest deer hath them
as huge as the rascal. Is the single man therefore
blessed? No, as a walled town is more worthier than a
village, so is the forehead of a married man more   50
honourable than the bare brow of a bachelor: and by
how much defence is better than no skill, by so much
is a horn more precious than to want.

SIR OLIVER MARTEXT *comes up*

Here comes Sir Oliver. Sir Oliver Martext, you are

	well met. Will you dispatch us here under this tree, or shall we go with you to your chapel?
MARTEXT	Is there none here to give the woman?
TOUCH.	I will not take her on gift of any man.
MARTEXT	Truly, she must be given, or the marriage is not lawful.
JAQUES	[comes forward, doffing his hat] Proceed, proceed; I'll give 60 her.
TOUCH.	Good even, good Master What-ye-call't: how do you, sir? You are very well met: God'ild you for your last company – I am very glad to see you – even a toy in hand here, sir. Nay, pray be covered.
JAQUES	Will you be married, motley?
TOUCH.	As the ox hath his bow, sir, the horse his curb, and the falcon her bells, so man hath his desires; and as pigeons bill, so wedlock would be nibbling.
JAQUES	And will you, being a man of your breeding, be mar- 70 ried under a bush like a beggar? Get you to church, and have a good priest that can tell you what marriage is – this fellow will but join you together as they join wainscot; then one of you will prove a shrunk panel, and like green timber warp, warp.
TOUCH.	I am not in the mind but I were better to be married of him than of another; for he is not like to marry me well, and not being well married, it will be a good excuse for me hereafter to leave my wife.
JAQUES	Go thou with me, and let me counsel thee. 80
TOUCH.	Come, sweet Audrey, We must be married, or we must live in bawdry. Fare- well, good Master Oliver: not – [sings and dances

        O sweet Oliver,
        O brave Oliver,
        Leave me not behind thee:
but –
        Wind away,
        Begone, I say,
        I will not to wedding with thee.   90
           [he dances off, Jaques and Audrey following

MARTEXT	'Tis no matter; ne'er a fantastical knave of them all shall flout me out of my calling. [he goes

SCENE 4

ROSALIND *and* CELIA *comes along the path from the cottage;*
Rosalind drops upon a bank

ROSALIND Never talk to me, I will weep.

CELIA Do, I prithee – but yet have the grace to consider that tears do not become a man.

ROSALIND But have I not cause to weep?

CELIA As good cause as one would desire; therefore, weep.

ROSALIND His very hair is of the dissembling colour.

CELIA Something browner than Judas's: marry, his kisses are Judas's own children.

ROSALIND I'faith, his hair is of a good colour.

CELIA An excellent colour: your chestnut was ever the only 10 colour.

ROSALIND And his kissing is as full of sanctity as the touch of holy bread.

CELIA He hath bought a pair of cast lips of Diana: a nun of winter's sisterhood kisses not more religiously, the very ice of chastity is in them.

ROSALIND But why did he swear he would come this morning, and comes not?

CELIA Nay, certainly, there is no truth in him.

ROSALIND Do you think so? 20

CELIA Yes, I think he is not a pick-purse nor a horse-stealer, but for his verity in love I do think him as concave as a covered goblet or a worm-eaten nut.

ROSALIND Not true in love?

CELIA Yes, when he is in – but I think he is not in.

ROSALIND You have heard him swear downright he was.

CELIA 'Was' is not 'is': besides, the oath of a lover is no stronger than the word of a tapster; they are both the confirmer of false reckonings. He attends here in the forest on the duke your father. 30

ROSALIND I met the duke yesterday and had much question with him: he asked me of what parentage I was; I told him, of as good as he – so he laughed and let me go. But what talk we of fathers, when there is such a man as Orlando?

CELIA   O that's a brave man! He writes brave verses, speaks brave words, swears brave oaths and breaks them bravely, quite traverse, athwart the heart of his lover — as a puny tilter, that spurs his horse but on one side, breaks his staff like a noble goose; but all's brave that youth mounts and folly guide. Who comes here?   40

CORIN *draws near and accosts them*

CORIN   Mistress and master, you have oft inquired
After the shepherd that complained of love,
Who you saw sitting by me on the turf,
Praising the proud disdainful shepherdess
That was his mistress.

CELIA   Well: and what of him?

CORIN   If you will see a pageant truly played,
Between the pale complexion of true love
And the red glow of scorn and proud disdain,
Go hence a little and I shall conduct you,   50
If you will mark it.

ROSALIND   O, come, let us remove.
The sight of lovers feedeth those in love:
Bring us to this sight, and you shall say
I'll prove a busy actor in their play.

                                      [they go

SCENE 5

Another part of the forest

PHEBE, *followed by* SILVIUS *who entreats her*

SILVIUS   [*kneels*] Sweet Phebe, do not scorn me, do not, Phebe:
Say that you love me not, but say not so
In bitterness. The common executioner,
Whose heart th'accustomed sight of death makes hard,
Falls not the axe upon the humbled neck
But first begs pardon: will you sterner be
Than he that dies and lives by bloody drops?

ROSALIND, CELIA, *and* CORIN *come up behind unseen*

PHEBE   I would not be thy executioner.
I fly thee, for I would not injure thee.
Thou tell'st me there is murder in mine eye —   10
'Tis pretty, sure, and very probable,
That eyes, that are the frail'st and softest things,
Who shut their coward gates on atomies,
Should be called tyrants, butchers, murderers!
Now I do frown on thee with all my heart,
And if mine eyes can wound, now let them kill thee;
Now counterfeit to swoon, why now fall down,
Or if thou canst not, O for shame, for shame,
Lie not, to say mine eyes are murderers!
Now show the wound mine eye hath made in thee.   20
Scratch thee but with a pin, and there remains
Some scar of it: lean but upon a rush,
The cicatrice and capable impressure
Thy palm some moment keeps: but now mine eyes,
Which I have darted at thee, hurt thee not,
Nor, I am sure, there is no force in eyes
That can do hurt.

SILVIUS   O dear Phebe,
If ever — as that ever may be near —
You meet in some fresh cheek the power of fancy,
Then shall you know the wounds invisible   30

That love's keen arrows make.

PHEBE   But till that time
Come not thou near me: and when that time comes
Afflict me with thy mocks, pity me not,
As till that time I shall not pity thee.

ROSALIND [*advancing*].
And why, I pray you? Who might be your mother,
That you insult, exult, and all at once,
Over the wretched? What though you have no beauty –
As, by my faith, I see no more in you
Than without candle may go dark to bed –
Must you be therefore proud and pitiless?   40
Why, what means this? Why do you look on me?
I see no more in you than in the ordinary
Of nature's sale-work! 'Od's my little life,
I think she means to tangle my eyes too:
No, faith, proud mistress, hope not after it.
'Tis not your inky brows, your black silk hair,
Your bugle eyeballs, nor your cheek of cream,
That can entame my spirits to your worship.
You foolish shepherd, wherefore do you follow her,
Like foggy south, puffing with wind and rain?   50
You are a thousand times a properer man
Than she a woman: 'tis such fools as you
That makes the world full of ill-favoured children:
'Tis not her glass, but you, that flatters her,
And out of you she sees herself more proper
Than any of her lineaments can show her.
But, mistress, know yourself – down on your knees,
And thank heaven, fasting, for a good man's love;
                                   [*Phebe kneels to Rosalind*
For I must tell you friendly in your ear,
Sell when you can – you are not for all markets: 60
Cry the man mercy, love him, take his offer.
Foul is most foul, being foul to be a scoffer.
So take her to thee, shepherd – fare you well.

PHEBE   Sweet youth, I pray you chide a year together.
I had rather hear you chide than this man woo.

ROSALIND [*to Phebe*] He's fallen in love with your foulness,

[*to Silvius*] and she'll fall in love with my anger. If it be
so, as fast as she answers thee with frowning looks, I'll
sauce her with bitter words. [*to Phebe*] Why look you
so upon me?   70
PHEBE   For no ill will I bear you.
ROSALIND   I pray you, do not fall in love with me,
            For I am falser than vows made in wine:
            Besides, I like you not. If you will know my house,
            'Tis at the tuft of olives here hard by.
            Will you go, sister? Shepherd, ply her hard.
            Come, sister. Shepherdess, look on him better,
            And be not proud – though all the world could see,
            None could be so abused in sight as he.
            Come, to our flock.   80
                    [*she stalks away, followed by Celia and Corin*
PHEBE   [*gazing after them*]
            Dead Shepherd, now I find thy saw of might,
            'Who ever loved that loved not at first sight?'
SILVIUS   Sweet Phebe –
PHEBE   Ha! What say'st thou, Silvius?
SILVIUS   Sweet Phebe, pity me.
PHEBE   Why, I am sorry for thee, gentle Silvius.
SILVIUS   Wherever sorrow is, relief would be:
            If you do sorrow at my grief in love,
            By giving love your sorrow and my grief
            Were both extermined.
PHEBE   Thou hast my love – is not that neighbourly?   90
SILVIUS   I would have you.
PHEBE   Why, that were covetousness.
            Silvius, the time was that I hated thee,
            And yet it is not that I bear thee love;
            But since that thou canst talk of love so well,
            Thy company, which erst was irksome to me,
            I will endure; and I'll employ thee too:
            But do not look for further recompense
            Than thine own gladness that thou art employed.
SILVIUS   So holy and so perfect is my love,
            And I in such a poverty of grace,
            That I shall think it a most plenteous crop   100

	To glean the broken ears after the man
	That the main harvest reaps: loose now and then
	A scattered smile, and that I'll live upon.
PHEBE	Know'st thou the youth that spoke to me erewhile?
SILVIUS	Not very well, but I have met him oft,
	And he hath bought the cottage and the bounds
	That the old carlot once was master of.
PHEBE	Think not I love him, though I ask for him.

'Tis but a peevish boy Yet he talks well –   110
But what care I for words? Yet words do well,
When he that speaks them pleases those that hear:
It is a pretty youth – not very pretty –
But, sure, he's proud, and yet his pride becomes him:
He'll make a proper man: the best thing in him
Is his complexion; and faster than his tongue
Did make offence, his eye did heal it up:
He is not very tall – yet for his years he's tall:
His leg is but so so – and yet 'tis well:
There was a pretty redness in his lip,   120
A little riper and more lusty red
Than that mixed in his cheek; 'twas just the difference
Betwixt the constant red and mingled damask.
There be some women, Silvius, had they marked him
In parcels as I did, would have gone near
To fall in love with him: but, for my part,
I love him not, nor hate him not; and yet
I have more cause to hate him than to love him,
For what had he to do to chide at me?
He said mine eyes were black and my hair black,   130
And, now I am remembered, scorn'd at me:
I marvel why I answered not again:
But that's all one; omittance is no quittance:
I'll write to him a very taunting letter,
And thou shalt bear it – wilt thou, Silvius?

SILVIUS	Phebe, with all my heart.
PHEBE	I'll write it straight;
	The matter's in my head and in my heart.
	I will be bitter with him and passing short:
	Go with me, Silvius. [they go

ACT 4 SCENE 1

The clearing near the sheepcote

Enter ROSALIND, CELIA, *and* JACQUES

JAQUES   I prithee, pretty youth, let me be better acquainted
            with thee.

ROSALIND   They say you are a melancholy fellow.

JAQUES   I am so: I do love it better than laughing.

ROSALIND   Those that are in extremity of either are abominable
            fellows, and betray themselves to every modern censure
            worse than drunkards.

JAQUES   Why, 'tis good to be sad and say nothing.

ROSALIND   Why then, 'tis good to be a post.

JAQUES   I have neither the scholar's melancholy, which is emul-   10
            ation; nor the musician's, which is fantastical; nor the
            courtier's, which is proud; nor the soldier's, which is
            ambitious; nor the lawyer's, which is politic; nor the
            lady's, which is nice; nor the lover's, which is all these:
            but it is a melancholy of mine own, compounded of
            many simples, extracted from many objects, and in-
            deed the sundry contemplation of my travels, in which
            my often rumination wraps me in a most humorous
            sadness.

ROSALIND   A traveller! By my faith, you have great reason to be   20
            sad: I fear you have sold your own lands to see other
            men's; then, to have seen much, and to have nothing,
            is to have rich eyes and poor hands.

JAQUES   Yes, I have gained my experience.

ORLANDO draws near

ROSALIND   And your experience makes you sad: I had rather have
            a fool to make me merry than experience to make me
            sad – and to travel for it too!

ORLANDO   Good day, and happiness, dear Rosalind!
                                    [*she takes no heed of him*

JAQUES   Nay then, God buy you, an you talk in blank verse.
                                    [*he turns from them*

ROSALIND   Farewell, Monsieur Traveller: look you lisp and wear 30
                strange suits; disable all the benefits of your own coun-
                try; be out of love with your nativity, and almost chide
                God for making you that countenance you are; or I
                will scarce think you have swam in a gondola. [*Jaques*
                passes out of earshot; she sits] Why, how now, Orlando!
                Where have you been all this while? You a lover! An
                you serve me such another trick, never come in my
                sight more.

ORLANDO   My fair Rosalind, I come within an hour of my promise.

ROSALIND   Break an hour's promise in love? He that will divide a 40
                minute into a thousand parts, and break but a part of
                the thousandth part of a minute in the affairs of love, it
                may be said of him that Cupid hath clapped him o'th'
                shoulder, but I'll warrant him heart whole.

ORLANDO   Pardon me, dear Rosalind.

ROSALIND   Nay, an you be so tardy, come no more in my sight. I
                had as lief be wooed of a snail.

ORLANDO   Of a snail?

ROSALIND   Ay, of a snail; for though he comes slowly, he carries his
                house on his head; a better jointure, I think, than you 50
                make a woman: besides, he brings his destiny with him.

ORLANDO   What's that?   [*he sits beside her*

ROSALIND   Why, horns; which such as you are fain to be behold-
                ing to your wives for: but he comes armed in his
                fortune, and prevents the slander of his wife.

ORLANDO   Virtue is no horn-maker. [*musing*] And my Rosalind is
                virtuous.

ROSALIND   And I am your Rosalind.

                                 [*she puts her arm about his neck*

CELIA   It pleases him to call you so; but he hath a Rosalind of
                a better leer than you.   60

ROSALIND   Come, woo me, woo me; for now I am in a holiday
                humour, and like enough to consent. What would you
                say to me now, an I were your very very Rosalind?

ORLANDO   I would kiss before I spoke.

ROSALIND   Nay, you were better speak first, and when you were
                gravelled for lack of matter, you might take occasion
                to kiss: very good orators, when they are out, they will

spit; and for lovers, lacking (God warr'nt us!) matter,
the cleanliest shift is to kiss.

ORLANDO How if the kiss be denied?   70

ROSALIND Then she puts you to entreaty and there begins new
matter.

ORLANDO Who could be out, being before his beloved mistress?

ROSALIND Marry, that should you if I were your mistress, or I
should think my honesty ranker than my wit.

ORLANDO What, of my suit?

ROSALIND Not out of your apparel, and yet out of your suit. Am
not I your Rosalind?

ORLANDO I take some joy to say you are, because I would be
talking of her.   80

ROSALIND Well, in her person, I say I will not have you.

ORLANDO Then in mine own person, I die.

ROSALIND No, faith, die by attorney: the poor world is almost six
thousand years old, and in all this time there was not any
man died in his own person, videlicet, in a love-cause:
Troilus had his brains dashed out with a Grecian club,
yet he did what he could to die before, and he is one of
the patterns of love: Leander, he would have lived many
a fair year, though Hero had turned nun, if it had not
been for a hot midsummer night; for, good youth, he   90
went but forth to wash him in the Hellespont, and being
taken with the cramp was drowned, and the foolish
chroniclers of that age found it was 'Hero of Sestos'. But
these are all lies. Men have died from time to time, and
worms have eaten them, but not for love.

ORLANDO I would not have my right Rosalind of this mind, for I
protest her frown might kill me.

ROSALIND By this hand, it will not kill a fly. [draws closer to him]
But come, now I will be your Rosalind in a more
coming-on disposition; and ask me what you will, I   100
will grant it.

ORLANDO Then love me, Rosalind.

ROSALIND Yes, faith will I, Fridays and Saturdays and all.

ORLANDO And wilt thou have me?

ROSALIND Ay, and twenty such.

ORLANDO What sayest thou?

ROSALIND Are you not good?

ORLANDO I hope so.

ROSALIND Why then, can one desire too much of a good thing? 110
[*she rises*] Come, sister, you shall be the priest and
marry us. Give me your hand, Orlando. What do you
say, sister?

ORLANDO Pray thee, marry us.

CELIA I cannot say the words.

ROSALIND You must begin, 'Will you, Orlando' –

CELIA Go to. Will you, Orlando, have to wife this Rosalind?

ORLANDO I will.

ROSALIND Ay, but when?

ORLANDO Why now, as fast as she can marry us.

ROSALIND Then you must say, 'I take thee, Rosalind, for wife.' 120

ORLANDO I take thee, Rosalind, for wife.

ROSALIND I might ask you for your commission, but I do take
thee, Orlando, for my husband. There's a girl goes
before the priest, and certainly a woman's thought
runs before her actions.

ORLANDO So do all thoughts, they are winged.

ROSALIND Now tell me how long you would have her after you
have possessed her.

ORLANDO For ever and a day.

ROSALIND Say 'a day' without the 'ever'. No, no, Orlando, men 130
are April when they woo, December when they wed;
maids are May when they are maids, but the sky
changes when they are wives. I will be more jealous of
thee than a Barbary cock-pigeon over his hen, more
clamorous than a parrot against rain, more new-
fangled than an ape, more giddy in my desires than a
monkey: I will weep for nothing, like Diana in the
fountain, and I will do that when you are disposed to
be merry; I will laugh like a hyen, and that when thou
art inclined to sleep. 140

ORLANDO But will my Rosalind do so?

ROSALIND By my life, she will do as I do.

ORLANDO O, but she is wise.

ROSALIND Or else she could not have the wit to do this: the wiser,
the waywarder: make the doors upon a woman's wit,

and it will out at the casement; shut that, and 'twill out
at the key-hole; stop that, 'twill fly with the smoke out
at the chimney.

ORLANDO   A man that had a wife with such a wit, he might say
'Wit, whither wilt?'   150

ROSALIND   Nay, you might keep that check for it, till you met
your wife's wit going to your neighbour's bed.

ORLANDO   And what wit could wit have to excuse that?

ROSALIND   Marry, to say she came to seek you there. You shall
never take her without her answer, unless you take her
without her tongue: O, that woman that cannot make
her fault her husband's occasion, let her never nurse
her child herself, for she will breed it like a fool.

ORLANDO   For these two hours, Rosalind, I will leave thee.

ROSALIND   Alas, dear love, I cannot lack thee two hours!   160

ORLANDO   I must attend the duke at dinner. By two o'clock I will
be with thee again.

ROSALIND   Ay, go your ways, go your ways; I knew what you
would prove, my friends told me as much, and I
thought no less: that flattering tongue of yours won
me: 'tis but one cast away, and so, come death. Two
o'clock is your hour?

ORLANDO   Ay, sweet Rosalind.

ROSALIND   By my troth, and in good earnest, and so God mend
me, and by all pretty oaths that are not dangerous, if   170
you break one jot of your promise, or come one
minute behind your hour, I will think you the most
pathetical break-promise, and the most hollow lover,
and the most unworthy of her you call Rosalind, that
may be chosen out of the gross band of the unfaithful:
therefore beware my censure, and keep your promise.

ORLANDO   With no less religion than if thou wert indeed my
Rosalind: so adieu.

ROSALIND   Well, Time is the old justice that examines all such
offenders, and let Time try: adieu!   *[he goes* 180

CELIA   You have simply misused our sex in your love-prate:
we must have your doublet and hose plucked over
your head, and show the world what the bird hath
done to her own nest.

ROSALIND   O coz, coz, coz, my pretty little coz, that thou didst
           know how many fathom deep I am in love! But it
           cannot be sounded; my affection hath an unknown
           bottom, like the bay of Portugal.

CELIA   Or rather, bottomless – that as fast as you pour affection
           in, it runs out.   190

ROSALIND   No, that same wicked bastard of Venus, that was begot
           of thought, conceived of spleen, and born of madness –
           that blind rascally boy that abuses every one's eyes
           because his own are out – let him be judge how deep I
           am in love. I'll tell thee, Aliena, I cannot be out of the
           sight of Orlando: I'll go find a shadow and sigh till he
           come.

CELIA   And I'll sleep.   [they go

ACT 4 SCENE 2

*Before the cave of the exiled Duke. A noise as of huntsmen
approaching. Presently* AMIENS *and other lords appear,
dressed as foresters, with* JAQUES *in their midst to whom
they are telling of their morning's sport*

JAQUES   Which is he that killed the deer?
A LORD   Sir, it was I.
JAQUES   Let's present him to the duke, like a Roman con-
           queror. And it would do well to set the deer's horns
           upon his head, for a branch of victory. Have you no
           song, forester, for this purpose?
AMIENS   Yes, sir.
JAQUES   Sing it: 'tis no matter how it be in tune, so it make
           noise enough.

*He that killed the deer is first clad in horns and skin, and then raised
aloft by the company, who 'sing him home', Amiens leading and
the rest joining in chorus*

The Song

           What shall he have that killed the deer?   10
           His leather skin and horns to wear:
           Then sing him home – the rest shall bear

This burden.
Take thou no scorn to wear the horn,
It was a crest ere thou wast born.
   Thy father's father wore it,
   And thy father bore it.
The horn, the horn, the lusty horn,
Is not a thing to laugh to scorn.

They march thrice around the tree, repeating the burthen
again and again; then they turn into the Duke's cave

SCENE 3

The clearing near the sheepcote

ROSALIND *and* CELIA *return*

ROSALIND How say you now? Is it not past two o'clock? And
here much Orlando!

CELIA I warrant you, with pure love and troubled brain, he
hath ta'en his bow and arrows, and is gone forth to
sleep. Look, who comes here.

SILVIUS *approaches*

SILVIUS My errand is to you, fair youth –
My gentle Phebe bid me give you this:
                           [he gives Rosalind a letter
I know not the contents, but as I guess
By the stern brow and waspish action
Which she did use as she was writing of it,   10
It bears an angry tenour: pardon me,
I am but as a guiltless messenger.

ROSALIND Patience herself would startle at this letter,
And play the swaggerer – bear this, bear all:
She says I am not fair, that I lack manners,
She calls me proud, and that she could not love me
Were man as rare as phoenix: 'od's my will!
Her love is not the hare that I do hunt.
Why writes she so to me? Well, shepherd, well,
This is a letter of your own device.   20

SILVIUS No, I protest, I know not the contents –

Phebe did write it.

ROSALIND   Come, come, you are a fool,
And turned into the extremity of love.
I saw her hand – she has a leathern hand,
A freestone-coloured hand: I verily did think
That her old gloves were on, but 'twas her hands:
She has a huswife's hand – but that's no matter:
I say she never did invent this letter.
This is a man's invention, and his hand.

SILVIUS   Sure, it is hers.   30

ROSALIND Why, 'tis a boisterous and a cruel style,
A style for challengers; why, she defies me,
Like Turk to Christian: women's gentle brain
Could not drop forth such giant-rude invention,
Such Ethiop words, blacker in their effect
Than in their countenance. Will you hear the letter?

SILVIUS   So please you, for I never heard it yet;
Yet heard too much of Phebe's cruelty.

ROSALIND She Phebes me: mark how the tyrant writes.
[*reads*] 'Art thou god to shepherd turned,   40
        That a maiden's heart hath burned?'
Can a woman rail thus?

SILVIUS   Call you this railing?

ROSALIND   'Why, thy godhead laid apart,
        Warr'st thou with a woman's heart?'
Did you ever hear such railing?
            'Whiles the eye of man did woo me,
            That could do no vengeance to me.'
Meaning me a beast.
                'If the scorn of your bright eyne   50
                Have power to raise such love in mine,
                Alack, in me what strange effect
                Would they work in mild aspect?
                Whiles you chid me I did love,
                How then might your prayers move?
                He that brings this love to thee
                Little knows this love in me:
                And by him seal up thy mind,
                Whether that thy youth and kind

        Will the faithful offer take   60
        Of me and all that I can make,
        Or else by him my love deny,
        And then I'll study how to die.'

SILVIUS   Call you this chiding?

CELIA   Alas, poor shepherd!

ROSALIND Do you pity him? No, he deserves no pity. Wilt thou
love such a woman? What, to make thee an instrument and play false strains upon thee! Not to be endured! Well, go your way to her (for I see love hath
made thee a tame snake) and say this to her: that if she 70
love me, I charge her to love thee: if she will not, I
will never have her, unless thou entreat for her. If you
be a true lover, hence, and not a word; for here comes
more company.   *[he goes*

OLIVER comes up hastily by another path

OLIVER   Good morrow, fair ones: pray you, if you know,
        Where in the purlieus of this forest stands
        A sheepcote fenced about with olive-trees?

CELIA   West of this place, down in the neighbour bottom –
        The rank of osiers by the murmuring stream
        Left on your right hand brings you to the place.   80
        But at this hour the house doth keep itself,
        There's none within.

OLIVER   If that an eye may profit by a tongue,
        Then should I know you by description –
        Such garments and such years: 'The boy is fair,
        Of female favour, and bestows himself
        Like a ripe forester: the woman low,
        And browner than her brother.' Are not you
        The owner of the house I did inquire for?

CELIA   It is no boast, being asked, to say we are.   90

OLIVER   Orlando doth commend him to you both,
        And to that youth he calls his Rosalind
        He sends this bloody napkin; are you he?

ROSALIND I am: what must we understand by this?

OLIVER   Some of my shame, if you will know of me
        What man I am, and how, and why, and where
        This handkercher was stained.

CELIA   I pray you, tell it.
OLIVER   When last the young Orlando parted from you
                He left a promise to return again
                Within an hour, and pacing through the forest,
                Chewing the food of sweet and bitter fancy,   100
                Lo, what befel! He threw his eye aside,
                And mark what object did present itself!
                Under an oak, whose boughs were mossed with age
                And high top bald with dry antiquity,
                A wretched ragged man, o'ergrown with hair,
                Lay sleeping on his back: about his neck
                A green and gilded snake had wreathed itself,
                Who with her head nimble in threats approached
                The opening of his mouth; but suddenly
                Seeing Orlando, it unlinked itself,   110
                And with indented glides did slip away
                Into a bush: under which bush's shade
                A lioness, with udders all drawn dry,
                Lay couching, head on ground, with catlike watch,
                When that the sleeping man should stir; for 'tis
                The royal disposition of that beast
                To prey on nothing that doth seem as dead:
                This seen, Orlando did approach the man,
                And found it was his brother, his elder brother.
CELIA   O I have heard him speak of that same brother,   120
                And he did render him the most unnatural
                That lived 'mongst men.
OLIVER   And well he might so do,
                For well I know he was unnatural.
ROSALIND   But, to Orlando: did he leave him there,
                Food to the sucked and hungry lioness?
OLIVER   Twice did he turn his back and purposed so:
                But kindness, nobler ever than revenge,
                And nature, stronger than his just occasion,
                Made him give battle to the lioness,
                Who quickly fell before him: in which hurtling   130
                From miserable slumber I awaked.
CELIA   Are you his brother?
ROSALIND   Was't you he rescued?

CELIA   Was't you that did so oft contrive to kill him?
OLIVER   'Twas I; but 'tis not I: I do not shame
           To tell you what I was, since my conversion
           So sweetly tastes, being the thing I am.
ROSALIND   But, for the bloody napkin?
OLIVER   By and by.
           When from the first to last betwixt us two
           Tears our recountments had most kindly bathed,
           As how I came into that desert place,   140
           In brief, he led me to the gentle duke,
           Who gave me fresh array and entertainment,
           Committing me unto my brother's love,
           Who led me instantly unto his cave,
           There stripped himself, and here upon his arm
           The lioness had torn some flesh away,
           Which all this while had bled; and now he fainted,
           And cried, in fainting, upon Rosalind
           Brief, I recovered him, bound up his wound,
           And after some small space being strong at heart,   150
           He sent me hither, stranger as I am,
           To tell this story, that you might excuse
           His broken promise, and to give this napkin,
           Dyed in his blood, unto the shepherd youth
           That he in sport doth call his Rosalind. [*Rosalind faints*
CELIA   Why, how now, Ganymede! Sweet Ganymede!
OLIVER   Many will swoon when they do look on blood.
CELIA   There is more in it. Cousin, Ganymede!
OLIVER   Look, he recovers.
ROSALIND   I would I were at home.
CELIA   We'll lead you thither.   160
           I pray you, will you take him by the arm?
OLIVER   Be of good cheer, youth: you a man!
           You lack a man's heart.
ROSALIND   I do so, I confess it
           Ah, sirrah, a body would think this was well counter-
           feited. I pray you, tell your brother how well I counter-
           feited. Heigh-ho!
OLIVER   This was not counterfeit. There is too great testimony
           in your complexion that it was a passion of earnest.

ROSALIND   Counterfeit, I assure you.

OLIVER   Well then, take a good heart, and counterfeit to be a 170 man.

ROSALIND   So I do: but, i'faith, I should have been a woman by right.

CELIA   Come, you look paler and paler; pray you, draw homewards. Good sir, go with us.

OLIVER   That will I: for I must bear answer back how you excuse my brother, Rosalind.

ROSALIND   I shall devise something: but I pray you, commend my counterfeiting to him. Will you go?

                               [*they descend towards the cottage*

ACT 5 SCENE 1

TOUCHSTONE *and* AUDREY *come through the trees*

TOUCH. We shall find a time, Audrey – patience, gentle Audrey.

AUDREY Faith, the priest was good enough, for all the old gentleman's saying.

TOUCH. A most wicked Sir Oliver, Audrey, a most vile Martext. But, Audrey, there is a youth here in the forest lays claim to you.

AUDREY Ay, I know who 'tis; he hath no interest in me in the world: here comes the man you mean.

WILLIAM *enters the clearing*

TOUCH. It is meat and drink to me to see a clown. By my troth, we that have good wits have much to answer for; we shall be flouting; we cannot hold.   10

WILLIAM Good ev'n, Audrey.

AUDREY God ye good ev'n, William.

WILLIAM And good ev'n to you, sir.

TOUCH. [*with mock dignity*] Good ev'n, gentle friend. Cover thy head, cover thy head; nay, prithee, be covered. How old are you, friend?

WILLIAM Five-and-twenty, sir.

TOUCH. A ripe age. Is thy name William?

WILLIAM William, sir.   20

TOUCH. A fair name. Wast born i'th' forest here?

WILLIAM Ay sir, I thank God.

TOUCH. 'Thank God'; a good answer. Art rich?

WILLIAM Faith sir, so so.

TOUCH. 'So so' is good, very good, very excellent good: and yet it is not, it is but so so. Art thou wise?

WILLIAM Ay sir, I have a pretty wit.

TOUCH. Why, thou say'st well. I do now remember a saying: 'The fool doth think he is wise, but the wise man knows himself to be a fool.' [*By this William's mouth is wide open* 30 *with amazement*] The heathen philosopher, when he had a desire to eat a grape, would open his lips when he put it into his mouth, meaning thereby that grapes were made to eat and lips to open. You do love this maid?

WILLIAM   I do, sir.

TOUCH.   Give me your hand. Art thou learned?

WILLIAM   No, sir.

TOUCH.   Then learn this of me – to have, is to have; for it is a
figure in rhetoric that drink, being poured out of a cup
into a glass, by filling the one doth empty the other; 40
for all your writers do consent that ipse is he: now,
you are not ipse, for I am he.

WILLIAM   Which he, sir?

TOUCH.   He, sir, that must marry this woman. Therefore, you
clown, abandon (which is in the vulgar 'leave') the
society (which in the boorish is 'company') of this
female (which in the common is 'woman'); which
together is, 'abandon the society of this female,' or,
clown, thou perishest; or, to thy better understanding,
diest; or, to wit, I kill thee, make thee away, translate 50
thy life into death, thy liberty into bondage: I will deal
in poison with thee, or in bastinado, or in steel; I will
bandy with thee in faction; I will o'er-run thee with
policy; I will kill thee a hundred and fifty ways –
therefore tremble and depart.

AUDREY   Do, good William.

WILLIAM   God rest you merry, sir.   *[he goes*

               CORIN *appears and calls*

CORIN   Our master and mistress seek you: come, away, away.

TOUCH.   Trip, Audrey, trip, Audrey – I attend, I attend.

                   [they run off towards the cottage

          A night passes

SCENE 2

OLIVER *and* ORLANDO *(his arm in a scarf) seated on a bank*

ORLANDO Is't possible that on so little acquaintance you should like her? That but seeing you should love her? And loving woo? And, wooing, she should grant? And will you persever to enjoy her?

OLIVER Neither call the giddiness of it in question, the poverty of her, the small acquaintance, my sudden wooing, nor her sudden consenting; but say with me, I love Aliena; say with her that she loves me; consent with both that we may enjoy each other: it shall be to your good; for my father's house and all the revenue that was old Sir Rowland's will I estate upon you, and here live and die a shepherd.   10

ROSALIND *is seen coming in the distance*

ORLANDO You have my consent. Let your wedding be tomorrow: thither will I invite the duke and all's contented followers. Go you and prepare Aliena; for look you, here comes my Rosalind.

ROSALIND God save you, brother.

OLIVER And you, fair sister.   *[he goes*

ROSALIND O my dear Orlando, how it grieves me to see thee wear thy heart in a scarf.   20

ORLANDO It is my arm.

ROSALIND I thought thy heart had been wounded with the claws of a lion.

ORLANDO Wounded it is, but with the eyes of a lady.

ROSALIND Did your brother tell you how I counterfeited to swoon, when he showed me your handkercher?

ORLANDO Ay and greater wonders than that.

ROSALIND O, I know where you are: nay, 'tis true: there was never any thing so sudden but the fight of two rams, and Caesar's thrasonical brag of 'I came, saw, and overcame': for your brother and my sister no sooner met but they looked; no sooner looked but they loved; no sooner loved but they sighed; no sooner   30

sighed but they asked one another the reason; no
sooner knew the reason but they sought the remedy:
and in these degrees have they made a pair of stairs to
marriage, which they will climb incontinent, or else
be incontinent before marriage: they are in the very
wrath of love, and they will together; clubs cannot
part them. 40

ORLANDO They shall be married tomorrow; and I will bid the
duke to the nuptial. But, O, how bitter a thing it is to
look into happiness through another man's eyes! By so
much the more shall I tomorrow be at the height of
heart-heaviness, by how much I shall think my brother
happy in having what he wishes for.

ROSALIND Why then, tomorrow I cannot serve your turn for
Rosalind?

ORLANDO I can live no longer by thinking.

ROSALIND I will weary you then no longer with idle talking. 50
Know of me then, for now I speak to some purpose,
that I know you are a gentleman of good conceit: I
speak not this that you should bear a good opinion of
my knowledge, insomuch I say I know you are; neither
do I labour for a greater esteem than may in some little
measure draw a belief from you, to do yourself good,
and not to grace me. Believe then, if you please, that I
can do strange things: I have, since I was three year old,
conversed with a magician, most profound in his art,
and yet not damnable. If you do love Rosalind so near 60
the heart as your gesture cries it out, when your
brother marries Aliena, shall you marry her. I know
into what straits of fortune she is driven, and it is not
impossible to me, if it appear not inconvenient to you,
to set her before your eyes tomorrow, human as she is,
and without any danger.

ORLANDO Speak'st thou in sober meanings?

ROSALIND By my life I do, which I tender dearly, though I say I
am a magician. Therefore, put you in your best array,
bid your friends; for if you will be married tomorrow, 70
you shall; and to Rosalind, if you will.

SILVIUS *and* PHEBE *draw near*

Look, here comes a lover of mine and a lover of hers.

PHEBE   Youth, you have done me much ungentleness,
           To show the letter that I writ to you.

ROSALIND   I care not if I have: it is my study
           To seem despiteful and ungentle to you:
           You are there followed by a faithful shepherd –
           Look upon him, love him; he worships you.

PHEBE   Good shepherd, tell this youth what 'tis to love.

SILVIUS   It is to be all made of sighs and tears,   80
           And so am I for Phebe.

PHEBE   And I for Ganymede.

ORLANDO   And I for Rosalind.

ROSALIND   And I for no woman.

SILVIUS   It is to be all made of faith and service,
           And so am I for Phebe.

PHEBE   And I for Ganymede.

ORLANDO   And I for Rosalind.

ROSALIND   And I for no woman.

SILVIUS   It is to be all made of fantasy,   90
           All made of passion, and all made of wishes,
           All adoration, duty and observance,
           All humbleness, all patience, and impatience,
           All purity, all trial, all obedience;
           And so am I for Phebe.

PHEBE   And so am I for Ganymede.

ORLANDO   And so am I for Rosalind.

ROSALIND   And so am I for no woman.

PHEBE   [to Rosalind].
           If this be so, why blame you me to love you?

SILVIUS   [to Phebe].
           If this be so, why blame you me to love you?   100

ORLANDO   If this be so, why blame you me to love you?

ROSALIND   Who do you speak to, 'Why blame you me to love you?'

ORLANDO   To her that is not here, nor doth not hear.

ROSALIND   Pray you no more of this, 'tis like the howling of Irish
           wolves against the Moon. [to Silvius] I will help you, if
           I can. [to Phebe] I would love you, if I could. To-
           morrow meet me all together. [to Phebe] I will marry
           you, if ever I marry woman, and I'll be married

tomorrow. [*to Orlando*] I will satisfy you, if ever I
satisfied man, and you shall be married tomorrow. [*to* 110
Silvius] I will content you, if what pleases you contents
you, and you shall be married to morrow. [*to Orlando*]
As you love Rosalind, meet. [*to Silvius*] As you love
Phebe, meet. And as I love no woman, I'll meet. So,
fare you well; I have left you commands.

SILVIUS I'll not fail, if I live.

PHEBE Nor I.

ORLANDO Nor I.   [*they disperse*

SCENE 3

TOUCHSTONE *and* AUDREY *enter the clearing*

TOUCH. Tomorrow is the joyful day, Audrey.
        Tomorrow will we be married.

AUDREY I do desire it with all my heart: and I hope it is no
        dishonest desire to desire to be a woman of the world.
        Here come two of the banished duke's pages.

                Two pages run up

1 PAGE Well met, honest gentleman.

TOUCH. By my troth, well met. Come, sit, sit, and a song.

2 PAGE We are for you: sit i'th' middle.

1 PAGE Shall we clap into't roundly, without hawking or spit-
        ting or saying we are hoarse, which are the only 10
        prologues to a bad voice?

2 PAGE I'faith i'faith; and both in a tune, like two gipsies on a
        horse.

                Song

        It was a lover and his lass,
            With a hey, and a ho, and a hey nonino:
        That o'er the green corn-field did pass,
            In spring time, the only pretty ring time,
        When birds do sing, hey ding a ding, ding,
        Sweet lovers love the spring.

        Between the acres of the rye,   20
            With a hey, and a ho, and a hey nonino:

These pretty country folks would lie,
    In spring time, the only pretty ring time,
When birds do sing, hey ding a ding, ding,
Sweet lovers love the spring.

This carol they began that hour,
    With a hey, and a ho, and a hey nonino:
How that life was but a flower,
    In spring time, the only pretty ring time,
When birds do sing, hey ding a ding, ding,   30
Sweet lovers love the spring.

And therefore take the present time,
    With a hey, and a ho, and a hey nonino:
For love is crownéd with the prime,
    In spring time, the only pretty ring time.
When birds do sing, hey ding a ding, ding,
Sweet lovers love the spring.

TOUCH.   Truly, young gentlemen, though there was no great
          matter in the ditty, yet the note was very untuneable.
I PAGE   You are deceived, sir – we kept time, we lost not our   40
          time.
TOUCH.   By my troth, yes; I count it but time lost to hear such a
          foolish song. God buy you, and God mend your
          voices! Come, Audrey.   [they go

A night passes

SCENE 4

The clearing near the sheepcote (as before)

The exiled DUKE, AMIENS, JAQUES, ORLANDO, OLIVER, *and* CELIA

DUKE   Dost thou believe, Orlando, that the boy
          Can do all this that he hath promised?
ORLANDO   I sometimes do believe, and sometimes do not,
          As those that fear they hope, and know they fear.

    ROSALIND, SILVIUS, *and* PHEBE *join the company*

ROSALIND Patience once more, whiles our compact is urged:

You say, if I bring in your Rosalind,
You will bestow her on Orlando here?

DUKE That would I, had I kingdoms to give with her.

ROSALIND And you say you will have her, when I bring her?

ORLANDO That would I, were I of all kingdoms king.

ROSALIND You say you'll marry me, if I be willing?

PHEBE That will I, should I die the hour after.

ROSALIND But if you do refuse to marry me,
You'll give yourself to this most faithful shepherd?

PHEBE So is the bargain.

ROSALIND You say that you'll have Phebe, if she will?

SILVIUS Though to have her and death were both one thing.

ROSALIND I have promised to make all this matter even.
Keep you your word, O duke, to give your daughter –
You yours, Orlando, to receive his daughter:
Keep your word, Phebe, that you'll marry me,
Or else refusing me, to wed this shepherd:
Keep your word, Silvius, that you'll marry her,
If she refuse me – and from hence I go,
To make these doubts all even.

[*she beckons to Celia and they depart together*

DUKE I do remember in this shepherd-boy
Some lively touches of my daughter's favour.

ORLANDO My lord, the first time that I ever saw him,
Methought he was a brother to your daughter:
But, my good lord, this boy is forest-born,
And hath been tutored in the rudiments
Of many desperate studies by his uncle,
Whom he reports to be a great magician,
Obscured in the circle of this forest.

TOUCHSTONE *and* AUDREY *enter the clearing*

JAQUES There is, sure, another flood toward, and these couples are coming to the ark. Here comes a pair of very strange beasts, which in all tongues are called fools.

TOUCH. Salutation and greeting to you all!

JAQUES Good my lord, bid him welcome: this is the motley-minded gentleman that I have so often met in the forest: he hath been a courtier, he swears.

TOUCH. If any man doubt that, let him put me to my purgation.

I have trod a measure; I have flattered a lady; I have been politic with my friend, smooth with mine enemy; I have undone three tailors; I have had four quarrels, and like to have fought one.

JAQUES And how was that ta'en up?

TOUCH. Faith, we met, and found the quarrel was upon the seventh cause.

JAQUES How seventh cause? Good my lord, like this fellow.

DUKE I like him very well.

TOUCH. God'ild you, sir, I desire you of the like. I press in here, sir, amongst the rest of the country copulatives, to swear and to forswear, according as marriage binds and blood breaks. [*he waves towards Audrey*] A poor virgin, sir, an ill-favoured thing, sir but mine own – a poor humour of mine, sir, to take that that no man else will: rich honesty dwells like a miser, sir, in a poor house, as your pearl in your foul oyster.

DUKE By my faith, he is very swift and sententious.

TOUCH. According to the fool's bolt, sir, and such dulcet diseases.

JAQUES But, for the seventh cause. How did you find the quarrel on the seventh cause?

TOUCH. Upon a lie seven times removed – bear your body more seeming, Audrey – as thus, sir: I did dislike the cut of a certain courtier's beard: he sent me word, if I said his beard was not cut well, he was in the mind it was: this is called the Retort Courteous. If I sent him word again 'it was not well cut', he would send me word, he cut it to please himself: this is called the Quip Modest. If again 'it was not well cut', he disabled my judgment: this is called the Reply Churlish. If again 'it was not well cut', he would answer, I spake not true: this is called the Reproof Valiant. If again 'it was not well cut', he would say, I lie: this is called the Countercheck Quarrelsome: and so to the Lie Circumstantial and the Lie Direct.

JAQUES And how oft did you say his beard was not well cut?

TOUCH. I durst go no further than the Lie Circumstantial: nor he durst not give me the Lie Direct: and so we measured swords and parted.

JAQUES Can you nominate in order now the degrees of the lie?

TOUCH.   O sir, we quarrel in print – by the book, as you have
books for good manners. I will name you the degrees.
The first, the Retort Courteous; the second, the Quip
Modest; the third, the Reply Churlish; the fourth, the
Reproof Valiant; the fifth, the Countercheck Quarrelsome; the sixth, the Lie with Circumstance; the seventh, the Lie Direct. All these you may avoid, but the
Lie Direct; and you may avoid that too, with an If. I
knew when seven justices could not take up a quarrel,   90
but when the parties were met themselves, one of them
thought but of an If; as, 'If you said so, then I said so':
and they shook hands and swore brothers. Your If is the
only peace-maker; much virtue in If.

JAQUES   Is not this a rare fellow, my lord? He's as good at any
thing, and yet a fool!

DUKE   He uses his folly like a stalking-horse, and under the
presentation of that he shoots his wit.

Enter, as in a masque, persons representing HYMEN *and his train,*
together with ROSALIND *and* CELIA *in their proper habits. Still music'*

HYMEN   [*sings*] Then is there mirth in heaven,
   When earthly things made even   100
     Atone together.
   Good duke, receive thy daughter,
   Hymen from heaven brought her,
     Yea, brought her hither,
   That thou mightst join her hand with his
   Whose heart within her bosom is.

ROSALIND   [*to the Duke*] To you I give myself, for I am yours.
   [*to Orlando*] To you I give myself, for I am yours.

DUKE   If there be truth in sight, you are my daughter.

ORLANDO   If there be truth in sight, you are my Rosalind.   110

PHEBE   If sight and shape be true,
   Why then, my love adieu!

ROSALIND   I'll have no father, if you be not he:
   I'll have no husband, if you be not he:
   Nor ne'er wed woman, if you be not she.

HYMEN   Peace, ho! I bar confusion.
   'Tis I must make conclusion

Of these most strange events:
Here's eight that must take hands,
To join in Hymen's bands,   120
    If truth holds true contents.
You and you no cross shall part:
You and you are heart in heart:
You to his love must accord,
Or have a woman to your lord.
You and you are sure together,
As the winter to foul weather.
Whiles a wedlock-hymn we sing,
Feed yourselves with questioning;
That reason wonder may diminish,   130
How thus we met, and these things finish.

Choric song

Wedding is great Juno's crown,
    O blesséd bond of board and bed:
'Tis Hymen peoples every town,
    High wedlock then be honouréd:
Honour, high honour and renown,
To Hymen, god of every town!

DUKE   O my dear niece, welcome thou art to me.
            Even daughter, welcome, in no less degree.

PHEBE   [to Silvius]
            I will not eat my word, now thou art mine,   140
            Thy faith my fancy to thee doth combine.

Enter JAQUES DE BOYS

JAQ. DE B. Let me have audience for a word or two:
            I am the second son of old Sir Rowland,
            That bring these tidings to this fair assembly.
            Duke Frederick, hearing how that every day
            Men of great worth resorted to this forest,
            Addressed a mighty power, which were on foot,
            In his own conduct, purposely to take
            His brother here and put him to the sword:
            And to the skirts of this wild wood he came;   150
            Where, meeting with an old religious man,
            After some question with him, was converted

Both from his enterprise and from the world:
His crown bequeathing to his banished brother,
And all their lands restored to them again
That were with him exiled. This to be true,
I do engage my life.

DUKE   Welcome, young man;
Thou offer'st fairly to thy brothers' wedding:
To one his lands withheld, and to the other
A land itself at large, a potent dukedom.   160
First, in this forest, let us do those ends
That here were well begun and well begot:
And after, every of this happy number,
That have endured shrewd days and nights with us,
Shall share the good of our returnéd fortune,
According to the measure of their states.
Meantime, forget this new-fall'n dignity,
And fall into our rustic revelry.
Play, music! And you brides and bridegrooms all,
With measure heaped in joy, to th' measures fall.   170

JAQUES   Sir, by your patience –   *[he stays the music*
[to Jaques de Boys]   If I heard you rightly,
The duke hath put on a religious life,
And thrown into neglect the pompous court?

JAQUES B.   He hath.

JAQUES   To him will I: out of these convertites
There is much matter to be heard and learned . . .
[to the Duke] You to your former honour I bequeath,
Your patience and your virtue well deserves it:
[to Orlando]
You to a love, that your true faith doth merit:
[to Oliver] You to your land, and love, and great allies: 180
[to Silvius] You to a long and well-deservéd bed:
[to Touchstone]
And you to wrangling, for thy loving voyage
Is but for two months victualled. So to your
                           pleasures;
I am for other than for dancing measures.

DUKE   Stay, Jaques, stay.

JAQUES   To see no pastime, I: what you would have

I'll stay to know at your abandoned cave.

[he turns from them

DUKE   Proceed, proceed: we will begin these rites
          As we do trust they'll end in true delights.   190

          Music and dance

TWELFTH NIGHT

INTRODUCTION

The title of *Twelfth Night* calls to mind the festivities traditionally held on 6 January, the twelfth night after Christmas. Twelfth night marks the end of the Christmas season and in Elizabethan England was a holiday characterised by revelry, excess, and a temporary but joyous overturning of the social structures and codes of behaviour that usually regulated life. It constituted a moment of licensed anarchy before the harsher regime of winter and self-denial once again closed in. Hence the title of *Twelfth Night* draws upon the associations that accompany it to enrich an understanding of the play. A tussle between the ordered regulation of society on the one hand, and a hearty disregard for such stifling influences on the other, forms its thematic backdrop.

Romantics like to believe that the play was first performed on twelfth night (6 January), 1601 at the royal palace of Whitehall. A play, not referred to specifically by title but described as both comic and musical, certainly was performed in front of Queen Elizabeth that night, and this play *may* have been *Twelfth Night*. The evidence, however, is far from conclusive. What is beyond doubt is that a year later, in early February 1602, a law student, John Manningham, made a diary entry in which he referred specifically to a performance of *Twelfth Night* given at the Middle Temple. Although there is nothing to suggest that this was its first performance, there is sufficient internal evidence to suggest that it was still relatively new when Manningham saw it. An Italian nobleman named Don Virginio Orsino had been Queen Elizabeth's guest for the night of the unnamed comic and musical performance at the end of the Christmas season the previous year. It is reasonable to assume that the name Orsino in Shakespeare's play is intended as

a reference to Elizabeth's guest. The intelligibility of this reference
for a contemporary audience would have depended upon the real
Orsino's visit already having become a matter of comment. It
therefore seems probable that the play's first performance fell, less
romantically than some would have it, at some point between
twelfth night 1601 and early February 1602.

No text of *Twelfth Night* has survived from its early years of
production. The text of the play we now have is taken from the
First Folio edition of Shakespeare's plays, published seven years
after his death in 1623.

Twelfth Night is driven by two interrelated plots. The main plot
concerns the tangled relationships of four noble lovers. We discover, at the opening of the play, that there has been a shipwreck
off the shores of Illyria. From this wreck Viola and her twin
brother Sebastian are separately washed ashore. Each is un-
harmed, although distressed at the thought that the other may
have been drowned. Viola decides to disguise herself as a eunuch,
taking the name Cesario, in order to enable her to find employment in a foreign land. She is duly taken on in the service of the
Duke Orsino. Believing that she is indeed a boy, he commissions
her to deliver declarations of love on his behalf to the Lady
Olivia, a neighbouring countess in mourning for her dead
brother. This commission becomes increasingly vexing to Viola
as she realises both that she herself is in love with Orsino and that
Olivia, unaware that the messenger before her is in fact a woman,
is in turn falling in love with her. This unhappy triangle is rescued
from impasse by the arrival of Viola's twin brother Sebastian.
Sebastian pleases Olivia just as much as Viola had done, and,
unlike Viola, is happy to reciprocate Olivia's feelings. Viola's
subsequent revelation that she is a woman in disguise prompts
Orsino to declare his love for her. Thus these four characters are
able to end the play happily as two newly-formed couples.

The sub-plot concerns the fates of a more mixed assembly of
characters, all of whom form part of Olivia's household for one
reason or another, and the various developments of their pre-
posterous ventures. Olivia's impoverished uncle, Sir Toby Belch,
is a bon viveur who manages to live off the generosity of his
niece and the stupidity of his rich friend Sir Andrew Aguecheek.
Sir Andrew is persuaded to stay at Olivia's, bankrolling Sir

Toby's drinking, under the delusion that Olivia will one day reciprocate his love for her. These two form an alliance with Maria, Olivia's gentlewoman, and Feste, the peripatetic clown, in common antipathy towards Malvolio, Olivia's pompous steward. So irritated are they by his superciliousness that they engineer a plan to teach him a lesson. They convince him, via a forged letter, that Olivia loves him. The letter instructs him to show himself amenable to her love by wearing cross-gartered yellow stockings. When he appears in this ludicrous garb, Olivia is baffled by the excesses of his behaviour and orders that he be kept, in his own interests, under a careful surveillance. The conspirators take this as justification for locking Malvolio in a dark room and tormenting him almost out of his wits. When he is finally released from imprisonment, and discovers that not only does Olivia not love him but in fact is by then already married to Sebastian, he feels understandably embittered at the humiliating treatment he has received. Meanwhile Sir Andrew's futile court-ship of Olivia necessarily comes to an end, and Sir Toby marries Maria by way of recompense for his mischief-making.

In common with the unnamed play performed on twelfth night 1601, *Twelfth Night is* both comic and musical. It depends for much of its humour upon the Shakespearean comic convention of impenetrable disguises and consequent mistaken identities. The comedy, however, is far less consistently skittish than it is in the bulk of Shakespeare's earlier comedies. Much of the play is marked by a wistfulness, and even a poignant sadness, that signals a shift in the dramatic tone of his comedies. In an untroubled comedy, all tangles may be untangled, all wrongs righted, all separated characters reunited, and all love found to be gloriously requited in the final resolution of the traumas generated by the preceding action. *Twelfth Night*, by contrast, does not end so neatly. The four fortunate lovers *are*, after all their misunder-standings, finally enveloped in a warm romantic haze. Several key characters are, however, bleakly excluded from the cosiness. In-deed, it is symptomatic of the uneasiness at the end of the play that there is no equivalent to the inclusive dance found, for example, at the end of M*uch Ado About Nothing*. *Twelfth Night* closes instead with a rueful little song about the persistent pres-ence of the wind and rain, sung by the solitary figure of Feste, the play's embittered and (in ironic contrast to his name) very *un*festive clown. Thus, at the end of the play, the characters are starkly divided into those whom the comic ending can accommodate, and those whom it refuses, who are left loveless and aggrieved for one reason or another. These excluded misfits disrupt the harmony of the close of this play and, more generally, introduce signs of fracture into the idea of a fully harmonious ending to Shakespeare's comedies. *Twelfth Night* marks a watershed in Shakespeare's comic writing: the comic ending would never again be unclouded by anxiety.

The Four Lovers

At the beginning of *Romeo and Juliet*, Romeo believes himself in love with the remote Rosaline. Similarly, for most of *Twelfth Night* the Duke Orsino believes himself in love with the inaccessible Lady Olivia. Like Romeo, Orsino proves to be more self-indulgently fascinated by the nature of his own languishing soul than in the supposed object of his affections. Indeed, so adept has Orsino become at navel-gazing that Olivia is frequently little more than the excuse for further maudlin contemplation of his own lovelorn condition:

> That instant was I turn'd into a hart,
> And my desires, like fell and cruel hounds,
> Ever since pursue me.   (1.1.20–22)

Conventionally, in a hunting metaphor uttered by a lover, the lady would be represented as the hunted object of her lover's desires. Here, however, Orsino instinctively claims for himself the metaphorical roles both of the hunter ('fell and cruel hounds') *and* of the hunted ('a hart'). He thereby unconsciously, but tellingly, excludes Olivia from the ground of the chase entirely. His love for Olivia is much more about himself than it is about her. As is evident from Act 1 scene 4 and Act 2 scene 4, he is more attentive, and in much more sensuous detail, to the particularity of his page Cesario (whom the audience knows to be Viola in disguise) than he is to the reality of Olivia. Olivia remains a remote ideal. Cesario, on the other hand, becomes for Orsino not only a trusted confidant but a disconcertingly attractive person. Orsino cannot allow himself to admit that he is

in love with a boy. Whatever label he chooses to attach to his
feelings, however, the warmth of his affection is undeniable.
Orsino is fortunate in being spared the uncomfortable implic-
ations of this unacknowledged love since it is, legitimated for him
at the end when Cesario is discovered to be a woman – and,
because a comic ending requires that things resolve themselves
optimally for those on the inside, not just any woman but a
woman of noble parentage.

Orsino believes Olivia to be both as physically enclosed and as
psychologically turned in upon herself as we have seen him to be:

> . . . like a cloistress she will veiled walk,
> And water once a day her chamber round
> With eye-offending brine.   (1.1.27–29)

In fact, Olivia is not as emotionally constrained as her pose of
mourning suggests. Her household is much more chaotic and
lively than Orsino's, and she herself is considerably more inclined to mirth than is her elegiac, lack-lustre suitor. Whereas he
seeks ways of nurturing and intensifying his feelings ('If music be
the food of love, play on . . . ' 1.1.1), she welcomes distraction
from hers. So much so that when Viola arrives to woo her in
Orsino's name, Olivia feels obliged to reach for her veil in the
vain hope of sustaining the pretence of grief (1.5). This reliance
on props, however, fails to convince Viola that she is indeed
grief-stricken, and the props are quickly discarded. Olivia asks of
Viola repeatedly:

> What are you? What would you?

and these questions, interrogating another's identity and purpose,
carry a larger significance that resonates throughout the whole
play. Both who Viola *is,* and what she *would* in Olivia's house, are
complicated by layers of dissemblance and of disjuncture between
what seems and what is. But when, later, Viola starts trying to
alert her audience to this disjuncture – 'I am not what I am'
(3.1.138) – Olivia quickly veers away from an interest in the
world as it is and pursues instead a desperate attempt to make it
conform to what she would like it to be:

> I would you were as I would have you be.   (3.1.144)

Twelfth Night is unique among Shakespeare's plays in having an alternative title, *What You Will*. This self-consciously casual title is peculiarly apt in relation to a play in which so many things, including notions of the self, seem to be changeable according to whim. In transforming herself into the boy Cesario, for example, Viola demonstrates that 'what you will' may redefine what you are. In her exchange with Viola, Olivia tries to extend the formula so that what she wills may transform what someone else is. Her 'What are you? What would you?' questions are therefore left hanging. Choosing to ignore the half-answers that Viola supplies saves her from confronting the inadequacy of her trust in appearances. That which she seeks is, simply, a husband whom she may adore. Viola, for reasons she cannot guess at, repeatedly scorns her advances. Sebastian, by contrast, having been mistaken by Olivia for his twin, welcomes her bafflingly enthusiastic attentions. Olivia does not stop to query what must seem to her like an inexplicable volte-face in the object of her affections, but rather marches her now miraculously compliant lover straight off to a priest to be married. What she wills is, after all, essentially straightforward and she is fortunate, albeit through the most improbable of circumstances, in finding someone else whose will happens to coincide with her own – or at least to be readily bendable to it:

> OLIVIA   . . . would thou'dst be rul'd by me!
> SEBASTIAN Madam, I will.   (4.1.60–61)

Prior to Sebastian's arrival, the problems in Illyria had become intensified to a point of maximum confusion and potential distress. Only the division of Viola into a male and female self, to satisfy Olivia and Orsino respectively, could possibly have ensured any harmony at the play's close. Sebastian's arrival makes it seem that just such a cleaving has been miraculously achieved, causing Antonio to exclaim:

> How have you made division of yourself?   (5.1.214)

Sebastian is, in effect, the *deus ex machina* of the play – the late and dramatic arrival, as if from heaven, to solve otherwise insoluble difficulties. It is his presence that rescues Olivia from unknowingly (and unrequitedly) loving a woman, that enables Orsino to acknowledge his attraction to a person he had thought denied him, and that liberates Viola to be a woman once more by replacing her feigned manhood with its real counterpart.

Viola initially adopted her male disguise in the interests of self-protection while friendless in a foreign land. Like Rosalind in *As You Like It*, she enjoys a conspiratorial alliance with the audience in discussing her role-playing:

> A little thing would make me tell them how much I lack
> of a man.   (3.4.283–84)

The audience is consequently 'in' on all the misunderstandings, jokes and ironies generated by the situation. As much expression as suppression of herself is detectable in her act as she draws upon latent potential within herself that would, presumably, have remained largely unexpressed in her female self. Thus she is resourceful, energetic, witty, impudent, stubborn. In the interests of womankind at large, and of herself in particular, she uses her role in a gentle crusade to jostle Orsino out of some of his more rigid and unthinking prejudices. Moreover, her male social identity enables her to do this without being suspected of herself having a vested interest:

> ORSINO   There is no woman's sides
>   Can bide the beating of so strong a passion
>   As love doth give my heart . . .
>
> VIOLA   . . . In faith, they are as true of heart as we.
>   (2.4.92–94,105)

In other crucial ways, however, the role trammels her, preventing her from expressing her love for Orsino (in whose courtship of Olivia she finds herself the reluctant agent). Ultimately, therefore, she believes that the concealment of her love 'like a worm i'th' bud' (2.4.110) is destroying her from within.

At the end of *Twelfth Night* Viola admits to the deceit that she has practised on the inhabitants of Illyria by means of her disguise. She does not, however, (unlike Rosalind at the close of *As You Like It*) exchange her 'masculine usurp'd attire' for 'maiden weeds' (5.1.242,247) before the end of the play. The disclosure in itself is sufficient to render acceptable Orsino's attraction to her. Even in the subsequent overtures of love that he makes towards her, however, he persists in referring to her as 'boy' and in addressing her as 'Cesario':

> For so you shall be, while you are a man;　　　(5.1.374)

He will, of course, delight in adjusting his naming and treatment of 'Cesario' when a womanly appearance makes it clear that such an adjustment is necessary. Until such time as his eyes confirm for him that this is indeed a woman before him, however, he cannot even say, 'For so you shall be awhile you *seem* a man', since in Orsino's mind there is minimal discrepancy between seeming and being.

For Orsino, then, the appearance of things *is* their reality, or at least creates the only expression of reality that can be sensibly engaged with. And indeed, on one level he is right. Through regular social interaction, Viola has created for herself a new, male self with a new name. That self and the name that represents it have been consolidated through recognition and usage by others. From the point of view of the inhabitants of Illyria, therefore, her revelation of herself as Viola is the creation of a new self, not the reversion to an old one, for they have no prior knowledge of the existence of a Viola. Orsino's inability to adjust his naming of Viola at the end of the play questions what self there can be independent of societal recognition. Although in Illyria Viola is as much a woman as she ever was back in Messaline (a womanhood complicated on the Elizabethan stage by the fact that her part would have been played by a boy actor), her socially recognised identity in this new land is male. The play therefore poses a question about the extent to which gender, and the expectations that accompany it, are socially constructed entities. By stepping across the gender divide, and proving to be virtually interchangeable with Sebastian, Viola highlights two, apparently contradictory, truths. The first is that some of the more rigid distinctions between the sexes derive only from social restriction and lack of opportunity, rather than from innate difference. The second is that the attempt to deny one's gender for a time can make one, by reaction, more fully cognisant of its significance to who one is. Viola is therefore glad at the prospect of once again seeming to be the thing she actually is, since, in her male role, she found that some of the things that most define her were necessarily suppressed.

These four lovers – Orsino, Olivia, Sebastian, Viola – create the warmth for the play's ending. Their union, however, is won at a cost, and the play suggests that the cost is borne by others.

The Misfits

Antonio, the sea-captain washed ashore from the shipwreck with Sebastian, generally receives very little critical attention. However, he is noteworthy for delivering some of the most strongly felt and affecting declarations of love in the play. His self-effacing adoration of Sebastian makes him long to be with him, if only to do him service:

> If you will not murder me for my love, let me be your
> servant.   (2.1.31–32)

This self-sacrificial love carries a far more acute charge than mere friendship:

> I could not stay behind you: my desire
> More sharp than filéd steel, did spur me forth.   (3.3.4–5)

He offers up his own purse, and indeed his own safety, in the service and protection of his beloved young master, yet these dramatic gestures meet with minimal acknowledgement. At one painful moment, arising from one of the Viola-Sebastian confusions (2.4), he even thinks he is being publicly disowned by the man he has faithfully served. At the end of the play, Antonio is supernumerary. Neither he, nor the intensity of his love for another man, can be absorbed into an harmonious ending. Instead he is obliged to observe from the margins as his beloved gives himself without reservation to a woman whom he has only just met. In Act 1 Olivia herself had drawn attention to the random nature of love that cannot be guaranteed to follow merit, or even suitability:

> Your lord does know my mind. I cannot love him.
> Yet I suppose him virtuous, know him noble,
> Of great estate, of fresh and stainless youth;
> In voices well divulg'd, free, learn'd, and valiant,
> And in dimension, and the shape of nature,
> A gracious person. But yet I cannot love him   (1.5.244–49)

It is the cruel irony of love that it is rarely born of deserving, following instead its own more haphazard whims. Antonio suffers directly from exactly this injustice when he is cast aside by Sebastian, and with cavalier negligence, in favour of Olivia. If the rain which, as Feste says, 'raineth every day' (5.1.380) is to be taken as indicating anything about this world beyond simply its weather, Antonio is certainly among those most vulnerable to its emotional ravages.

Feste is very aware of the unpleasantness and wilful delusions at the heart of much of society. He is a clown of the most unfrolicsome kind. Rather he makes piquant comment, with the impunity offered to 'an allowed fool' (1.5.88), on the unacknowledged folly of those around him. He interrogates and lampoons the trust that others have in appearances, and does not himself seem to believe in the stable identity of anything. In a world in which little is what it seems, Feste's refusal to treat anything as reliable cannot be considered an unreasonable response. His maverick exchange with Viola at the beginning of Act 3 demonstrates that Feste's scepticism in this respect extends to his attitude to words, which are, of course, the very stuff of his trade as professional wit and wordsmith. Just as people may not be trusted as reliable communicators of a reality that transcends superficial appearance, neither, argues Feste, can words:

Words are very rascals since bonds disgraced them.   (3.1.19)

The bonds which might be expected to connect a word to a specific meaning, that might ground it in a knowable semantic place have, claims Feste, abandoned their responsibilities in this respect. Cut free of these bonds, words in Illyria operate amidst the plethora of deceptive appearances as further untrustworthy agents of meaning. A sentence may as easily be turned inside out as 'a chev'ril glove' (3.1.12). By a little deft manipulation, it can be made to mean something other than – even the opposite of – what at first seems. In Illyria, a eunuch may be found to be a girl, a self-proclaimed lover to have an unattached heart, a woman apparently in mourning to be a thoroughly mirthful spirit, the most rigid upholder of societal structures to be himself yearning to break free of them, and the words that might otherwise have given some stability to a world thus in flux to be slippery and chameleon.

Feste himself is as free of any 'bonds' as are the words whose 'wantonness' he proclaims to Viola (3.1.14). He does not belong precisely either in Olivia's or in Orsino's household, but floats between them motivated apparently by a whimsical pursuit of distraction and financial reward. He does not even necessarily belong in Illyria, and at his first appearance is upbraided for his long and unexplained absence. Feste is, then, from the first an outsider, an observer not a participator, acknowledging no bond to person or place. It is appropriate that at the play's close it should fall to him, a natural commentator on the behaviour of others, to deliver the final wistfully detached comment.

Malvolio, the self-important steward in Olivia's household, has a gift for making enemies. He humiliates Feste in front of Olivia and irritates Sir Toby, Sir Andrew and Maria by pompously pouring scorn on their late night revelling. The confrontation between these noisy revellers and Malvolio (2.2) represents one of the central conflicts of the play – that between licence and rule, revelry and regulation, decadence and puritanism. Malvolio, with puritanical fervour, would like everything to be regulated. Sir Toby, with an extravagant joie de vivre, would like everything to be licensed. Malvolio believes in rigidly upholding the structures of society and so objects to 'this uncivil rule' (2.3.117). Sir Toby believes in living according to the festival spirit and so champions the cause of 'cakes and ale' (2.3.110). As recompense for his high-handedness, Maria and the others decide to make Malvolio their dupe. They appeal directly to his vanity by persuading him that Olivia loves him, and he proves to be entirely susceptible to such flattery. He is induced to wear cross-gartered yellow stockings in order to signal to Olivia his compliance with her supposed will. The arch-upholder of established social structures is thus convinced that he himself should disrupt them by aspiring to rise above his allotted position. He aims, therefore, to become what he (secretly) wills – a nobleman by marriage. The festive yellow garb he is instructed to wear is entirely out of keeping with his usual severe demeanour. What the revellers seem to be attempting is to construct a revelling spirit out of the most unpromising and unfestive of raw materials. Olivia is understandably baffled by the self-contradictory version of Malvolio that is produced by this mischievous project. And Malvolio himself, far from being liberated by abandoning his new style of dress and demeanour, feels himself literally constricted by it:

> This does make some obstruction in the blood, this cross-gartering; but what of that?   (3.4.20–21)

Malvolio demonstrates that someone cannot be *made* festive by external interference. His instinct is always to curb festivity, and those whose festivities he has curbed make a mockery of him by converting him into an unwitting item of entertainment himself. Sir Toby makes explicit at the beginning of Act 2 scene 5 that their plan is to bait Malvolio like a bear. Bear-baiting was a popular form of Elizabethan entertainment staged in an open-air galleried theatre, very similar to the public playhouses. So similar, in fact, that The Hope, close to the more famous Globe, doubled as both baiting house and playhouse. A bear would be chained to a stake in the pit and a pack of dogs would be set upon it. Bets would be laid about whether the dogs would kill the bear, and how long it would take them to do so. The spectacle for the crowd lay in the gradual destruction of a noble and once powerful beast.

The taunting of Malvolio is, similarly, laid on for the entertainment of the galleries. He is bound and locked in a dark room where he is visited by tormentors. And thus the joke goes too far. The gulling which had seemed funny when Malvolio merely appeared in yellow stockings makes an audience increasingly uncomfortable as the torments increase. In Act 1, Malvolio had himself, in discussing Feste, drawn attention to the crucial role of an appreciative audience in the life of a joke:

> . . . unless you laugh and minister occasion to him, he is gagged.
> (1.5.80–81)

Part of the discomfort involved in watching Twelf*th Night* is that it is an audience's initial laughter at the gulling of Malvolio, and consequent complicity in it, that can seem to have encouraged the tormenting revellers to persist with their mischief. It is we, the audience, who are 'laugh[ing] and minister[ing] occasion' to this particular joke.

At the very end of the play, having been rescued from his imprisonment, Malvolio's bitter parting line is:

I'll be reveng'd on the whole pack of you!   (5.1.366)

His use of the word 'pack', suggestive of dogs, testifies to his awareness of exactly the sort of sport that has been had at his expense. Within a few years of the first performance of *Twelfth Night*, Shakespeare was to write *King Lear* (1605) and *Macbeth* (1606). In each of these plays a grander character – Gloucester and Macbeth – represents himself by the same image, as a bear tied to the stake who must stand the course (*King Lear* 3.7.53 and *Macbeth* 5.7.1–2). Malvolio, in his one moment of painful clear-sightedness about his own tormented position, temporarily transcends his previous pomposity and assumes a stature that attaches him credibly to a line of later, more weighty characters. This legacy of feeling and insight is traceable in the first instance through the inherited bear-baiting imagery. Malvolio's threat of revenge is a troubling moment for an audience, since his complaint against 'the whole pack of you' can reverberate with his offstage, as well as his onstage, tormentors. We were happy to see the early stages of the gulling. Shakespeare pulls us into a complicity with the mischief-makers in order then to make us feel guilty at the way our sympathy has tended. As ever in Shakespeare comedies, the audience is made very self-conscious about its own role in having colluded to make the dramatic event happen. The event is even, in some sense, 'what we will', pursuing our fantasies about love, and in Malvolio's case, revenge. Where the absurdly contrived coming together of the four lovers illustrates how plastic and ridiculous our romantic fantasies can be, Malvolio's fall gives us a glimpse of the ugly consequences of our revenge impulse. The romantic union of the rich and beautiful on the one hand, and the humbling of the petty and arrogant on the other, are, suggests the end of *Twelfth Night* to its audience, merely the exaggerated expression of 'what you will'. The uneasiness at the end of the play therefore derives from a recognition that achieving what we will, seeing where our fantasies tend, may not always be entirely pleasant.

In the overall scheme of *Twelfth Night*, notions of confinement and restriction are pitted against an aspiration towards liberty and excess. Olivia's apparent desire for a cloistered existence illustrates a broader belief, in the world of the play, in the value of containment and denial. By repeatedly articulating the need for containment, the inhabitants of Illyria struggle to keep life 'within the modest limits of order' (1.3.7–8). Such a project is a struggle precisely because it is not the way things naturally tend there. Sir Toby is the most explicit mouthpiece for those influences which pull the other way, replying to the request that he moderate his behaviour by saying:

> I'll confine myself no finer than I am.   (1.3.9)

Sir Toby's desire to resist confinement, and his symptomatic celebration of 'cakes and ale' as a gesture of defiance against restraint, is a fairly pervasive attitude in Illyria. Feste, for example, epitomises the will to be free of restriction, moving easily between houses, between paymasters and professional engagements, and owing allegiance to no-one. The most obvious proponents of order and restriction, on the other hand, are Olivia (who tries to closet herself away and admit no mirth into her environment) and Malvolio (who attempts to support the prescribed hierarchies with pedantic inflexibility). Even in these two characters, however, there is a discernible gap between the disciplined position they theoretically wish to adopt and their ability to sustain such a position. Olivia is soon revealed as a woman relieved to exchange her cloistered existence for a life of romance and passion, and Malvolio as a man who wishes to flout the appointed order of things by allowing himself to be plucked by fortune from mediocrity into the ranks of the nobility. The struggle to maintain a disciplined order is undertaken *against* the natural inclinations even of those who most vociferously promote it.

Orsino instructs Viola to 'leap all civil bounds' (1.4.21) in pursuing his suit to Olivia, and the play in some sense dramatises both the placing and the infringement of such 'civil bounds' by exploring the limits of courteous and civilised behaviour. The festival of twelfth night was itself an opportunity to test the limits of social conventions through a joyous overturning of the regulations that usually governed social engagements. However, the abandonment of decorum and civilised restraint was, by the very terms of the celebration, only temporary. The delight to be had in the subversiveness of the festivities was in large part dependent upon an understanding that the world would be restored to a more sober and restrained version of itself the following day. It needed, that is, to be understood as a transient holiday moment, not a revolution. Similarly, the experimental and risky ways of relating to people that have been explored in the play are at its close abandoned in a reaffirmation of more orthodox social patterns. The play may have flirted with more daring categories of social interaction, but at its close it provides a ringing endorsement of establishment values. The playful experiments of the holiday festivities are over. Women are to appear and behave as women once again, marriage to be seen as a desirable way of giving shape and stability to a society, stewards to remain stewards, and any figures of challenge to the solidity of these structures (a homosexual suitor, a servant who aspires to rise) to be necessarily, and vigorously, excluded from the heart of the community.

The scene: Illyria

CHARACTERS IN THE PLAY

ORSINO, *Duke of Illyria*

SEBASTIAN, *brother to Viola*

ANTONIO, *a sea-captain, friend to Sebastian*

Another sea-captain, friend to Viola

VALENTINE ⎱
CURIO ⎰ *gentlemen attending on the Duke*

SIR TOBY BELCH, *kinsman to Olivia*

SIR ANDREW AGUECHEEK

MALVOLIO, *steward to Olivia*

FABIAN, *a gentleman in the service of Olivia*

FESTE, *fool to Olivia*

OLIVIA, *a rich countess*

VIOLA, *in love with the Duke*

MARIA, *Olivia's gentlewoman (small of stature)*

Lords, priests, sailors, officers, musicians, and other attendants

TWELFTH NIGHT *or* WHAT YOU WILL

ACT I SCENE I

A room in the Duke's palace

The Duke ORSINO, CURIO *and Lords, hearing music; the music ceases*

DUKE   If music be the food of love, play on,
Give me excess of it; that, surfeiting,
The appetite may sicken, and so die.
That strain again! It had a dying fall:
O, it came o'er my ear like the sweet sound
That breathes upon a bank of violets,
Stealing and giving odour. [*music again*]
                       Enough, no more!
'Tis not so sweet now as it was before.
O spirit of love, how quick and fresh art thou,
That, notwithstanding thy capacity   10
Receiveth as the sea, nought enters there,
Of what validity and pitch soe'er,
But falls into abatement and low price,
Even in a minute. So full of shapes is fancy,
That it alone is high fantastical.

CURIO   Will you go hunt, my lord?

DUKE   What, Curio?

CURIO   The hart.

DUKE   Why, so I do, the noblest that I have:
O, when mine eyes did see Olivia first,
Methought she purged the air of pestilence;
That instant was I turned into a hart,   20
And my desires, like fell and cruel hounds,
E'er since pursue me.

                 VALENTINE *enters*

                 How now? what news from her?

VALENT.   So please my lord, I might not be admitted,
But from her handmaid do return this answer:
The element itself, till seven years hence,
Shall not behold her face at ample view;

But like a cloistress she will veiléd walk,
And water once a day her chamber round
With eye-offending brine: all this to season
A brother's dead love, which she would keep fresh   30
And lasting, in her sad remembrance.

DUKE   O, she that hath a heart of that fine frame
To pay this debt of love but to a brother,
How will she love, when the rich golden shaft
Hath killed the flock of all affections else
That live in her; when liver, brain and heart,
These sovereign thrones, are all supplied and filled,
Her sweet perfections, with one self king!
Away before me to sweet beds of flowers –
Love-thoughts lie rich when canopied with bowers.   40

                                                    [*they go*

SCENE 2

Near the sea-coast

VIOLA, CAPTAIN, *and sailors*

VIOLA   What country, friends, is this?
CAPTAIN   This is Illyria, lady.
VIOLA   And what should I do in Illyria?
My brother he is in Elysium.
Perchance he is not drowned: what think you, sailors?
CAPTAIN   It is perchance that you yourself were saved.
VIOLA   O my poor brother! And so perchance may he be.
CAPTAIN   True, madam, and to comfort you with chance,
Assure yourself, after our ship did split,
When you and those poor number saved with you   10
Hung on our driving boat, I saw your brother,
Most provident in peril, bind himself –
Courage and hope both teaching him the practice –
To a strong mast that lived upon the sea;
Where, like Arion on the dolphin's back,
I saw him hold acquaintance with the waves
So long as I could see.
VIOLA   For saying so, there's gold:

Mine own escape unfoldeth to my hope,
Whereto thy speech serves for authority,
The like of him. Know'st thou this country?　　　20

CAPTAIN　Ay, madam, well, for I was bred and born
Not three hours' travel from this very place.

VIOLA　Who governs here?

CAPTAIN　A noble duke, in nature as in name.

VIOLA　What is his name?

CAPTAIN:　Orsino.

VIOLA　Orsino: I have heard my father name him.
He was a bachelor then.

CAPTAIN　And so is now, or was so very late:
For but a month ago I went from hence,　　　30
And then 'twas fresh in murmur – as, you know,
What great ones do the less will prattle of –
That he did seek the love of fair Olivia.

VIOLA　What's she?

CAPTAIN　A virtuous maid, the daughter of a count
That died some twelvemonth since – then leaving her
In the protection of his son, her brother,
Who shortly also died: for whose dear love,
They say, she hath abjured the company
And sight of men.

VIOLA　　　　　　　　　O, that I served that lady,　　　40
And might not be delivered to the world,
Till I had made mine own occasion mellow,
What my estate is.

CAPTAIN　　　　　　　That were hard to compass,
Because she will admit no kind of suit,
No, not the duke's.

VIOLA　There is a fair behaviour in thee, captain,
And though that nature with a beauteous wall
Doth oft close in pollution, yet of thee
I will believe thou hast a mind that suits
With this thy fair and outward character.　　　50
I prithee, and I'll pay thee bounteously,
Conceal me what I am, and be my aid
For such disguise as haply shall become
The form of my intent. I'll serve this duke,

Thou shalt present me as an eunuch to him,
It may be worth thy pains: for I can sing,
And speak to him in many sorts of music,
That will allow me very worth his service.
What else may hap to time I will commit,
Only shape thou thy silence to my wit.   60

DUKE Be you his eunuch, and your mute I'll be,
When my tongue blabs, then let mine eyes not see!

VIOLA I thank thee: lead me on.   *[they go*

SCENE 3

A room in Olivia's house

SIR TOBY BELCH *seated with drink before him, and* MARIA

SIR TOBY What a plague means my niece, to take the death of
her brother thus? I am sure care's an enemy to life.

MARIA By my troth, Sir Toby, you must come in earlier o'
nights: your cousin, my lady, takes great exceptions to
your ill hours.

SIR TOBY Why, let her except before excepted.

MARIA Ay, but you must confine yourself within the modest
limits of order.

SIR TOBY Confine? I'll confine myself no finer than I am: these
clothes are good enough to drink in, and so be these 10
boots too: an they be not, let them hang themselves in
their own straps.

MARIA That quaffing and drinking will undo you: I heard my
lady talk of it yesterday: and of a foolish knight, that
you brought in one night here, to be her wooer.

SIR TOBY Who? Sir Andrew Aguecheek?

MARIA Ay, he.

SIR TOBY He's as tall a man as any's in Illyria.

MARIA What's that to th' purpose?

SIR TOBY Why, he has three thousand ducats a year. 20

MARIA Ay, but he'll have but a year in all these ducats; he's a
very fool and a prodigal.

SIR TOBY Fie, that you'll say so! He plays o'th' viol-de-gamboys,
and speaks three or four languages word for word

	without book, and hath all the good gifts of nature.
MARIA	He hath, indeed almost natural: for, besides that he's a fool, he's a great quarreller: and but that he hath the gift of a coward to allay the gust he hath in quarrelling, 'tis thought among the prudent he would quickly have the gift of a grave.

SIR TOBY   By this hand, they are scoundrels and substractors that say so of him. Who are they?

MARIA   They that add, moreover, he's drunk nightly in your company.

SIR TOBY   With drinking healths to my niece: I'll drink to her as long as there is a passage in my throat and drink in Illyria: he's a coward and a coystrill that will not drink to my niece, till his brains turn o'th' toe like a parish-top. [*he seizes her about the waist and they dance a turn*] What, wench! Castiliano vulgo; for here comes Sir Andrew Agueface.

SIR ANDREW AGUECHEEK *enters*

SIR AND.   Sir Toby Belch! How now, Sir Toby Belch?

SIR TOBY   Sweet Sir Andrew!

SIR AND.   Bless you, fair shrew.

MARIA   [*curtsies*] And you too, sir!

SIR TOBY   Accost, Sir Andrew, accost.

SIR AND.   What's that?

SIR TOBY   My niece's chambermaid.

SIR AND.   Good Mistress Accost, I desire better acquaintance.

MARIA   My name is Mary, sir.

SIR AND.   Good Mistress Mary Accost –

SIR TOBY   You mistake, knight: 'accost' is front her, board her, woo her, assail her.

SIR AND.   By my troth, I would not undertake her in this company. Is that the meaning of 'accost'?

MARIA   Fare you well, gentlemen.   [*she turns to go*

SIR TOBY   An thou let part so, Sir Andrew, would thou mightst never draw sword again.

SIR AND.   An you part so, mistress, I would I might never draw sword again. Fair lady, do you think you have fools in hand?

MARIA	Sir, I have not you by th'hand
SIR AND.	Marry, but you shall have – and here's my hand.
	[he holds it out
MARIA	*[takes it]* Now, sir, 'thought is free'. *[she looks at his palm]* I pray you, bring your hand to th' buttery-bar and let it drink.
SIR AND.	Wherefore, sweet-heart? What's your metaphor?
MARIA	It's dry, sir.
SIR AND.	Why, I think so; I am not such an ass, but I can keep my hand dry. But what's your jest?
MARIA	A dry jest, sir.
SIR AND.	Are you full of them?
MARIA	Ay, sir; I have them at my fingers' ends: marry, now I let go your hand, I am barren.
	[she drops his hand, curtsies and trips away
SIR TOBY	*[sits]* O knight, thou lack'st a cup of canary: when did I see thee so put down ?
SIR AND.	Never in your life, I think, unless you see canary put me down. *[sits beside him]* Methinks sometimes I have no more wit than a Christian or an ordinary man has: but I am a great eater of beef and I believe that does harm to my wit.
SIR TOBY	No question.
SIR AND.	An I thought that, I'd forswear it. I'll go ride home tomorrow, Sir Toby.
SIR TOBY	Pourquoi, my dear knight?
SIR AND.	What is 'pourquoi'? Do or not do? I would I had bestowed that time in the tongues, that I have in fencing, dancing and bear-baiting: O, had I but followed the arts!
SIR TOBY	*[fondles him]*
	Then hadst thou had an excellent head of hair.
SIR AND.	Why, would that have mended my hair?
SIR TOBY	Past question, for thou seest it will not curl by nature.
SIR AND.	But it becomes me well enough, does't not?
SIR TOBY	Excellent! it hangs like flax on a distaff and I hope to see a housewife take thee between her legs and spin it off.
SIR AND.	Faith, I'll home tomorrow, Sir Toby. Your niece will not be seen, or if she be it's four to one she'll none of me: the count himself here hard by woos her.

70

80

90

SIR TOBY	She'll none o'th' count — she'll not match above her degree, neither in estate, years, nor wit; I have heard 100 her swear't. Tut, there's life in't, man.
SIR AND.	I'll stay a month longer. I am a fellow o'th' strangest mind i'th' world: I delight in masques and revels sometimes altogether.
SIR TOBY	Art thou good at these kickshawses, knight?
SIR AND.	As any man in Illyria, whatsoever he be, under the degree of my betters, and yet I will not compare with an old man.
SIR TOBY	What is thy excellence in a galliard, knight?
SIR AND.	Faith, I can cut a caper. 110
SIR TOBY	And I can cut the mutton to't.
SIR AND.	And I think I have the back-trick simply as strong as any man in Illyria.
SIR TOBY	Wherefore are these things hid? Wherefore have these gifts a curtain before 'em? Are they like to take dust, like Mistress Mall's picture? Why dost thou not go to church in a galliard and come home in a coranto? My very walk should be a jig; I would not so much as make water but in a sink-a-pace. What dost thou mean? Is it a world to hide virtues in? I did think, by 120 the excellent constitution of thy leg, it was formed under the star of a galliard.
SIR AND.	Ay, 'tis strong, and it does indifferent well in a dun-coloured stock. Shall we set about some revels?
SIR TOBY	What shall we do else? Were we not born under Taurus?
SIR AND.	Taurus! That's sides and heart.
SIR TOBY	No, sir, it is legs and thighs. Let me see thee caper. [*Sir Andrew leaps*] Ha! Higher: ha, ha! Excellent!

                [*they go*

SCENE 4

A room in the Duke's palace

'*Enter* VALENTINE, *and* VIOLA *in man's attire*'

VALENT. If the duke continue these favours towards you,
Cesario, you are like to be much advanced. He hath
known you but three days, and already you are no
stranger.

VIOLA You either fear his humour or my negligence, that you
call in question the continuance of his love. Is he
inconstant, sir, in his favours?

VALENT. No, believe me.

VIOLA I thank you. Here comes the count.

'*Enter* DUKE, CURIO *and attendants*'

DUKE Who saw Cesario, ho!   10

VIOLA On your attendance, my lord, here.

DUKE Stand you awhile aloof. [*Curio and attendants withdraw*
                              Cesario,
Thou know'st no less but all: I have unclasped
To thee the book even of my secret soul.
Therefore, good youth, address thy gait unto her,
Be not denied access, stand at her doors,
And tell them, there thy fixéd foot shall grow
Till thou have audience.

VIOLA   Sure, my noble lord,
If she be so abandoned to her sorrow
As it is spoke, she never will admit me.   20

DUKE Be clamorous and leap all civil bounds
Rather than make unprofited return.

VIOLA Say I do speak with her, my lord, what then?

DUKE O, then unfold the passion of my love,
Surprise her with discourse of my dear faith;
It shall become thee well to act my woes;
She will attend it better in thy youth
Than in a nuncio's of more grave aspect.

VIOLA I think not so, my lord.

DUKE   Dear lad, believe it;
For they shall yet belie thy happy years,   30
That say thou art a man: Diana's lip
Is not more smooth and rubious; thy small pipe
Is as the maiden's organ, shrill and sound —
And all is semblative a woman's part.
I know thy constellation is right apt
For this affair. [*he beckons attendants*]
                          Some four or five attend him,
All if you will; for I myself am best
When least in company. Prosper well in this,
And thou shalt live as freely as thy lord,
To call his fortunes thine.
VIOLA   I'll do my best   40
To woo your lady. [*aside*] Yet, a barful strife!
Whoe'er I woo, myself would be his wife.   [*they go*

SCENE 5

A room in Olivia's house; at the back a chair of state

MARIA *and* CLOWN

MARIA   Nay, either tell me where thou hast been, or I will not
          open my lips so wide as a bristle may enter in way of
          thy excuse: my lady will hang thee for thy absence.

CLOWN   Let her hang me: he that is well hanged in this world
          needs to fear no colours.

MARIA   Make that good.

CLOWN   He shall see none to fear.

MARIA   A good lenten answer: I can tell thee where that saying
          was born, of 'I fear no colours'.

CLOWN   Where, good Mistress Mary?   10

MARIA   In the wars — and that may you be bold to say in your
          foolery.

CLOWN   Well, God give them wisdom that have it; and those
          that are fools, let them use their talents.

MARIA   Yet you will be hanged for being so long absent; or to
          be turned away, is not that as good as a hanging to you?

CLOWN   Many a good hanging prevents a bad marriage; and,

	for turning away, let summer bear it out.
MARIA	You are resolute, then?
CLOWN	Not so neither, but I am resolved on two points – 20
MARIA	That if one break, the other will hold; or if both break, your gaskins fall.
CLOWN	Apt in good faith, very apt. [*she turns to go*] Well, go thy way – if Sir Toby would leave drinking, thou wert as witty a piece of Eve's flesh as any in Illyria.
MARIA	Peace, you rogue, no more o' that: here comes my lady: make your excuse wisely, you were best [*she goes*

The Lady OLIVIA *enters in black,* MALVOLIO *and attendants following; she sits in her chair of state*

CLOWN	[*feigns not to see them*] Wit, an't be thy will, put me into good fooling! Those wits that think they have thee, do very oft prove fools; and I, that am sure I lack thee, 30 may pass for a wise man. For what says Quinapalus? 'Better a witty fool than a foolish wit.' [*turns*] God bless thee, lady!
OLIVIA	Take the fool away.
CLOWN	Do you not hear, fellows? Take away the lady.
OLIVIA	Go to, y'are a dry fool: I'll no more of you: besides, you grow dishonest.
CLOWN	Two faults, madonna, that drink and good counsel will amend: for give the dry fool drink, then is the fool not dry: bid the dishonest man mend himself; if he mend, 40 he is no longer dishonest; if he cannot, let the botcher mend him: any thing that's mended is but patched: virtue that transgresses, is but patched with sin, and sin that amends is but patched with virtue. If that this simple syllogism will serve, so: if it will not, what remedy? As there is no true cuckold but calamity, so beauty's a flower: the lady bade take away the fool, therefore I say again, take her away.
OLIVIA	Sir, I bade them take away you.
CLOWN	Misprision in the highest degree! Lady, 'Cucullus non 50 facit monachum'; that's as much to say as I wear not motley in my brain. Good madonna, give me leave to prove you a fool.

OLIVIA   Can you do it?

CLOWN   Dexteriously, good madonna.

OLIVIA   Make your proof.

CLOWN   I must catechize you for it, madonna. Good my mouse of virtue, answer me.

OLIVIA   Well, sir, for want of other idleness, I'll bide your proof.   60

CLOWN   Good madonna, why mourn'st thou?

OLIVIA   Good fool, for my brother's death.

CLOWN   I think his soul is in hell, madonna.

OLIVIA   I know his soul is in heaven, fool.

CLOWN   The more fool, madonna, to mourn for your brother's soul being in heaven. Take away the fool, gentlemen.

OLIVIA   What think you of this fool, Malvolio? Doth he not mend?

MALVOLIO   Yes, and shall do, till the pangs of death shake him: infirmity, that decays the wise, doth ever make the   70 better fool.

CLOWN   God send you, sir, a speedy infirmity, for the better increasing your folly! Sir Toby will be sworn that I am no fox, but he will not pass his word for two pence that you are no fool.

OLIVIA   How say you to that, Malvolio?

MALVOLIO   I marvel your ladyship takes delight in such a barren rascal: I saw him put down the other day with an ordinary fool that has no more brain than a stone. Look you now, he's out of his guard already; unless   80 you laugh and minister occasion to him, he is gagged. I protest, I take these wise men, that crow so at these set kind of fools, no better than the fools' zanies.

OLIVIA   O, you are sick of self-love, Malvolio, and taste with a distempered appetite. To be generous, guiltless, and of free disposition, is to take those things for bird-bolts that you deem cannon-bullets: there is no slander in an allowed fool, though he do nothing but rail; nor no railing in a known discreet man, though he do nothing but reprove.   90

CLOWN   Now Mercury endue thee with leasing, for thou speakest well of fools!

MARIA *returns*

MARIA   Madam, there is at the gate a young gentleman much
          desires to speak with you.

OLIVIA   From the Count Orsino, is it?

MARIA   I know not, madam — 'tis a fair young man, and well
          attended.

OLIVIA   Who of my people hold him in delay?

MARIA   Sir Toby, madam, your kinsman.

OLIVIA   Fetch him off, I pray you! He speaks nothing but mad-   100
          man: fie on him. [*Maria hurries away*] Go you, Malvolio:
          if it be a suit from the count, I am sick, or not at home.
          What you will, to dismiss it. [*Malvolio goes*] Now you
          see, sir, how your fooling grows old, and people dislike
          it.

CLOWN   Thou hast spoke for us, madonna, as if thy eldest son
          should be a fool: whose skull Jove cram with brains!
          For — here he comes — one of thy kin, has a most weak
          pia mater.

SIR TOBY BELCH *staggers in*

OLIVIA   By mine honour, half drunk. What is he at the gate,   110
          cousin?

SIR TOBY [*speaks thick*] A gentleman.

OLIVIA   A gentleman? What gentleman?

SIR TOBY 'Tis a gentlemen here. [*hiccoughs*] A plague o'these
          pickle-herring. [*Clown laughs*] How now, sot!

CLOWN   Good Sir Toby —

OLIVIA   Cousin, cousin, how have you come so early by this
          lethargy?

SIR TOBY Lechery! I defy lechery. There's one at the gate.

OLIVIA   Ay, marry, what is he?   120

SIR TOBY Let him be the devil, an he will, I care not: give me
          'faith', say I. [*he totters to the door*] Well, it's all one.
                                                      [*he goes*

OLIVIA   What's a drunken man like, fool?

CLOWN   Like a drowned man, a fool, and a mad man: one
          draught above heat makes him a fool, the second mads
          him, and a third drowns him.

OLIVIA   Go thou and seek the crowner, and let him sit o' my

coz; for he's in the third degree of drink: he's
drowned: go look after him.

CLOWN He is but mad yet, madonna, and the fool shall look to 130
the madman.   *[he follows Sir Toby*

MALVOLIO *returns*

MALVOLIO Madam, yon young fellow swears he will speak with
you. I told him you were sick, he takes on him to
understand so much, and therefore comes to speak
with you. I told him you were asleep, he seems to
have a foreknowledge of that too, and therefore comes
to speak with you. What is to be said to him, lady?
He's fortified against any denial.

OLIVIA Tell him he shall not speak with me.

MALVOLIO Has been told so; and he says he'll stand at your door 140
like a sheriff's post, and be the supporter to a bench,
but he'll speak with you.

OLIVIA What kind o' man is he?

MALVOLIO Why, of mankind.

OLIVIA What manner of man?

MALVOLIO Of very ill manner; he'll speak with you, will you or no.

OLIVIA Of what personage and years is he?

MALVOLIO Not yet old enough for a man, nor young enough for
a boy; as a squash is before 'tis a peascod, or a codling
when 'tis almost an apple: 'tis with him in standing 150
water between boy and man. He is very well-favoured
and he speaks very shrewishly; one would think his
mother's milk were scarce out of him.

OLIVIA Let him approach. Call in my gentlewoman.

MALVOLIO *[goes to the door]* Gentlewoman, my lady calls. *[he departs*

MARIA *returns*

OLIVIA Give me my veil: come, throw it o'er my face – we'll
once more hear Orsino's embassy.   *[Maria veils her*

VIOLA *(as Cesario) enters*

VIOLA The honourable lady of the house, which is she?

OLIVIA Speak to me, I shall answer for her: your will?

VIOLA Most radiant, exquisite, and unmatchable beauty! I 160
pray you, tell me if this be the lady of the house, for I
never saw her. I would be loath to cast away my

speech; for besides that it is excellently well penned, I have taken great pains to con it. Good beauties, let me sustain no scorn; I am very comptible, even to the least sinister usage.

OLIVIA   Whence came you, sir?

VIOLA   I can say little more than I have studied, and that question's out of my part. Good gentle one, give me modest assurance if you be the lady of the house, that I   170 may proceed in my speech.

OLIVIA   Are you a comedian?

VIOLA   No, my profound heart: and yet, by the very fangs of malice I swear, I am not that I play. Are you the lady of the house?

OLIVIA   If I do not usurp myself, I am.

VIOLA   Most certain, if you are she, you do usurp yourself; for what is yours to bestow, is not yours to reserve. But this is from my commission: I will on with my speech in your praise, and then show you the heart of my   180 message.

OLIVIA   Come to what is important in't: I forgive you the praise.

VIOLA   Alas, I took great pains to study it, and 'tis poetical.

OLIVIA   It is the more like to be feigned, I pray you keep it in. I heard you were saucy at my gates, and allowed your approach rather to wonder at you than to hear you. If you be not mad, be gone; if you have reason, be brief: 'tis not that time of moon with me to make one in so skipping a dialogue.   190

MARIA   [points to the hat in Viola's hand] Will you hoist sail, sir? Here lies your way.   [she opens the door to thrust her out

VIOLA   [resists] No, good swabber; I am to hull here a little longer. Some mollification for your giant, sweet lady!

OLIVIA   Tell me your mind.

VIOLA   I am a messenger.

OLIVIA   Sure, you have some hideous matter to deliver, when the courtesy of it is so fearful. Speak your office.

VIOLA   It alone concerns your ear. I bring no overture of war, no taxation of homage; I hold the olive in my hand: 200 my words are as full of peace as matter.

OLIVIA   Yet you began rudely. What are you? What would you?

VIOLA   The rudeness that hath appeared in me have I learned
from my entertainment. What I am, and what I
would, are as secret as maidenhead: to your ears, divinity; to any other's, profanation.

OLIVIA   Give us the place alone: we will hear this divinity.
[*Maria and attendants withdraw*] Now, sir, what is your
text?

VIOLA   Most sweet lady –   210

OLIVIA   A comfortable doctrine, and much may be said of it.
Where lies your text?

VIOLA   In Orsino's bosom.

OLIVIA   In his bosom! In what chapter of his bosom?

VIOLA   To answer by the method, in the first of his heart.

OLIVIA   O, I have read it; it is heresy. Have you no more to
say?

VIOLA   Good madam, let me see your face.

OLIVIA   Have you any commission from your lord to negotiate
with my face? You are now out of your text: but we   220
will draw the curtain, and show you the picture. [*she
unveils*] Look you, sir, such a one I was – this present!
Is't not well done?

VIOLA   Excellently done, if God did all.

OLIVIA   'Tis in grain, sir, 'twill endure wind and weather.

VIOLA   'Tis beauty truly blent, whose red and white
Nature's own sweet and cunning hand laid on:
Lady, you are the cruell'st she alive,
If you will lead these graces to the grave,
And leave the world no copy.   230

OLIVIA   O, sir, I will not be so hard-hearted; I will give out
divers schedules of my beauty: it shall be inventoried,
and every particle and utensil labelled to my will: as,
Item, Two lips indifferent red; *Item*, Two grey eyes
with lids to them; *Item*, One neck, one chin, and so
forth. Were you sent hither to praise me?

VIOLA   I see you what you are, you are too proud;
But, if you were the devil, you are fair.
My lord and master loves you; O, such love
Could be but recompensed, though you were crowned.   240

The nonpareil of beauty!

OLIVIA   How does he love me?

VIOLA   With adorations, fertile tears,
With groans that thunder love, with sighs of fire.

OLIVIA   Your lord does know my mind, I cannot love him:
Yet I suppose him virtuous, know him noble,
Of great estate, of fresh and stainless youth;
In voices well divulged, free, learned and valiant,
And in dimension and the shape of nature
A gracious person: but yet I cannot love him;
He might have took his answer long ago.   250

VIOLA   If I did love you in my master's flame,
With such a suff'ring, such a deadly life,
In your denial I would find no sense,
I would not understand it.

OLIVIA   Why, what would you?

VIOLA   Make me a willow cabin at your gate,
And call upon my soul within the house,
Write loyal cantons of contemnéd love,
And sing them loud even in the dead of night;
Holla your name to the reverberate hills,
And make the babbling gossip of the air   260
Cry out 'Olivia!' O, you should not rest
Between the elements of air and earth,
But you should pity me.

OLIVIA   You might do much
What is your parentage?

VIOLA   Above my fortunes, yet my state is well:
I am a gentleman.

OLIVIA   Get you to your lord;
I cannot love him: let him send no more,
Unless – perchance – you come to me again,
To tell me how he takes it. Fare you well:
I thank you for your pains: spend this for me.   270

                                    [offers money

VIOLA   I am no fee'd post, lady; keep your purse.
My master, not myself, lacks recompense.
Love make his heart of flint that you shall love,
And let your fervour like my master's be

         Placed in contempt! Farewell, fair cruelty.   [*she goes*

OLIVIA   'What is your parentage?'
         'Above my fortunes, yet my state is well:
         I am a gentleman'. I'll be sworn thou art!
         Thy tongue, thy face, thy limbs, actions, and spirit,
         Do give thee five-fold blazon. Not too fast: soft, soft!   280
         Unless the master were the man. [*she muses*] How now!
         Even so quickly may one catch the plague?
         Methinks I feel this youth's perfections
         With an invisible and subtle stealth
         To creep in at mine eyes. Well, let it be.
         What, ho, Malvolio!

                 MALVOLIO *returns*

MALVOLIO   Here, madam, at your service.

OLIVIA   Run after that same peevish messenger,
         The county's man: he left this ring behind him,
         Would I or not; tell him I'll none of it.
         Desire him not to flatter with his lord,   290
         Nor hold him up with hopes – I am not for him:
         If that the youth will come this way tomorrow,
         I'll give him reasons for't. Hie thee, Malvolio.

MALVOLIO Madam, I will.   [*he hurries forth*

OLIVIA   I do I know not what, and fear to find
         Mine eye too great a flatterer for my mind.
         Fate, show thy force – ourselves we do not owe –
         What is decreed, must be; and be this so!   [*she goes*

ACT 2 SCENE I

At the door of Antonio's house

ANTONIO *and* SEBASTIAN

ANTONIO   Will you stay no longer? Nor will you not that I go
with you?

SEBASTIAN   By your patience, no: my stars shine darkly over me;
the malignancy of my fate might perhaps distemper
yours; therefore I shall crave of you your leave that I
may bear my evils alone: it were a bad recompense for
your love, to lay any of them on you.

ANTONIO   Let me yet know of you whither you are bound.

SEBASTIAN   No, sooth, sir: my determinate voyage is mere extra-
vagancy. But I perceive in you so excellent a touch of 10
modesty, that you will not extort from me what I am
willing to keep in; therefore it charges me in manners
the rather to express myself. You must know of me
then, Antonio, my name is Sebastian, which I called
Roderigo. My father was that Sebastian of Messaline,
whom I know you have heard of. He left behind him
myself and a sister, both born in an hour: if the heavens had been pleased, would we had so ended! But
you, sir, altered that, for some hour before you took
me from the breach of the sea was my sister drowned. 20

ANTONIO   Alas, the day!

SEBASTIAN   A lady, sir, though it was said she much resembled me,
was yet of many accounted beautiful: but, though I
could not with such estimable wonder overfar believe
that, yet thus far I will boldly publish her – she bore a
mind that envy could not but call fair. She is drowned
already, sir, with salt water, though I seem to drown
her remembrance again with more.

ANTONIO   Pardon me, sir, your bad entertainment.

SEBASTIAN   O, good Antonio, forgive me your trouble. 30

ANTONIO   If you will not murder me for my love, let me be your
servant.

SEBASTIAN   If you will not undo what you have done, that is, kill

him whom you have recovered, desire it not. Fare ye
well at once. My bosom is full of kindness, and I am
yet so near the manners of my mother, that upon the
least occasion more mine eyes will tell tales of me.
[*they clasp hands*] I am bound to the Count Orsino's
court – farewell!   [*he goes*

ANTONIO The gentleness of all the gods go with thee!   40
I have many enemies in Orsino's court,
Else would I very shortly see thee there:
But, come what may, I do adore thee so,
That danger shall seem sport, and I will go. [*he goes in*

SCENE 2

A street near Olivia's house

VIOLA *approaches*, MALVOLIO *following after*

MALVOLIO [*comes up*] Were not you e'en now with the Countess
Olivia?

VIOLA Even now, sir. On a moderate pace I have since arrived
but hither.

MALVOLIO [*sharply*] She returns this ring to you, sir; you might
have saved me my pains, to have taken it away yourself. She adds moreover, that you should put your lord
into a desperate assurance she will none of him: and
one thing more, that you be never so hardy to come
again in his affairs, unless it be to report your lord's 10
taking of this. [*he holds out the ring*] Receive it so.

VIOLA She took the ring of me. I'll none of it.

MALVOLIO Come, sir, you peevishly threw it to her; and her will
is, it should be so returned: [*he throws it at her feet*] if it
be worth stooping for, there it lies in your eye; if not,
be it his that finds it.   [*he walks off*

VIOLA I left no ring with her: what means this lady?
Fortune forbid my outside have not charmed her!
She made good view of me, indeed so much,
That as methought her eyes had lost her tongue,   20
For she did speak in starts distractedly.
She loves me, sure – the cunning of her passion

Invites me in this churlish messenger.
None of my lord's ring! Why, he sent her none.
I am the man – if it be so, as 'tis,
Poor lady, she were better love a dream.
Disguise, I see thou art a wickedness,
Wherein the pregnant enemy does much.
How easy is it for the proper-false
In women's waxen hearts to set their forms!   30
Alas, our frailty is the cause, not we,
For such as we are made of, such we be.
How will this fadge? My master loves her dearly,
And I (poor monster!) fond as much on him:
And she, mistaken, seems to dote on me:
What will become of this? As I am man,
My state is desperate for my master's love;
As I am woman – now alas the day! –
What thriftless sighs shall poor Olivia breathe?
O time, thou must untangle this, not I,   40
It is too hard a knot for me t'untie.   [*she goes*

SCENE 3

*A room in Olivia's house; a bench and a table with
cold viands and drinking-vessels thereon*

SIR TOBY BELCH *and* SIR ANDREW AGUECHEEK *enter, drunk*

SIR TOBY   [*sits at table*] Approach, sir Andrew: [*Sir Andrew follows
            with difficulty*] not to be a-bed after midnight is to be
            up betimes; and 'diluculo surgere', thou know'st –

SIR AND.   [*sits beside him*] Nay, by my troth, I know not: but I
            know, to be up late is to be up late.   [*he eats*

SIR TOBY   [*takes up a pot and finds it empty*] A false conclusion: I
            hate it as an unfilled can. To be up after midnight and
            to go to bed then, is early; so that to go to bed after
            midnight is to go to bed betimes. Does not our life
            consist of the four elements?   10

SIR AND.   [*his mouth full*] Faith, so they say – but I think it rather
            consists of eating and drinking.

SIR TOBY   Th'art a scholar; let us therefore eat and drink. [*bawls*

Marian, I say! A stoup of wine!

The CLOWN *comes in*

SIR AND.   Here comes the fool, i'faith.

CLOWN   [*sits between them upon the bench*] How now, my hearts!
Did you never see the picture of 'we three'?

SIR TOBY   Welcome, ass. Now let's have a catch.   20

SIR AND.   By my troth, the fool has an excellent breast. I had
rather than forty shillings I had such a leg, and so sweet   20
a breath to sing, as the fool has. In sooth, thou wast in
very gracious fooling last night, when thou spok'st of
Pigrogromitus, of the Vapians passing the equinoctial
of Queubus; 'twas very good, i'faith. I sent thee sixpence for thy leman – hadst it?

CLOWN   I did impetticoat thy gratillity: for Malvolio's nose is
no whipstock: my lady has a white hand, and the
Myrmidons are no bottle-ale houses.

SIR AND.   Excellent! why, this is the best fooling, when all is
done. Now, a song.   30

SIR TOBY   Come on, there is sixpence for you. Let's have a song.

SIR AND.   There's a testril of me too: if one knight give a –

CLOWN   Would you have a love-song, or a song of good life?

SIR TOBY   A love-song, a love-song.

SIR AND.   Ay, I care not for good life.

CLOWN   [*sings*] O mistress mine, where are you roaming?
         O, stay and hear, your true love's coming,
           That can sing both high and low.
         Trip no further pretty sweeting:
         Journeys end in lovers meeting,   40
           Every wise man's son doth know.

SIR AND.   Excellent good, i'faith!

SIR TOBY   Good, good.

CLOWN   [*sings*] What is love, 'tis not hereafter,
         Present mirth hath present laughter
           What's to come is still unsure.
         In delay there lies no plenty,
         Then come kiss me, sweet and twenty:
           Youth's a stuff will not endure.

SIR AND.   A mellifluous voice, as I am true knight.   50

SIR TOBY   A contagious breath.

SIR AND.   Very sweet and contagious, i'faith.

SIR TOBY   To hear by the nose, it is dulcet in contagion. But shall
we make the welkin dance indeed? Shall we rouse the
night-owl in a catch, that will draw three souls out of
one weaver? Shall we do that?

SIR AND.   An you love me, let's do't: I am dog at a catch.

CLOWN   By'r lady, sir, and some dogs will catch well.

SIR AND.   Most certain. Let our catch be, 'Thou knave'.

CLOWN   'Hold thy peace, thou knave,' knight? I shall be con-   60
strained in't to call thee knave, knight.

SIR AND.   'Tis not the first time I have constrained one to call me
knave. Begin, fool; it begins, 'Hold thy peace.'

CLOWN   I shall never begin if I hold my peace.

SIR AND.   Good, i'faith! Come, begin.   [they sing the catch

                    MARIA enters with wine

MARIA   What a caterwauling do you keep here! If my lady
have not called up her steward Malvolio and bid him
turn you out of doors, never trust me.

SIR TOBY   My lady's a Cataian, we are politicians, Malvolio's a
Peg-a-Ramsey, and   70
[sings]   'Three merry men be we.'
Am not I consanguineous? Am I not of her blood?
Tillyvally! 'Lady'!
[sings]   'There dwelt a man in Babylon,
                    Lady, Lady!'

CLOWN   Beshrew me, the knight's in admirable fooling.

SIR AND.   Ay, he does well enough, if he be disposed, and so do I
too; he does it with a better grace, but I do it more
natural.

SIR TOBY   [sings]   'O' the twelfth day of December' –   80

MARIA   For the love o' God, peace.

                    MALVOLIO enters

MALVOLIO My masters, are you mad? Or what are you? Have you
no wit, manners, nor honesty, but to gabble like tink-
ers at this time of night? Do ye make an ale-house of
my lady's house, that ye squeak out your coziers'
catches without any mitigation or remorse of voice? Is
there no respect of place, persons, nor time in you?

SIR TOBY   We did keep time, sir, in our catches. Sneck up!

MALVOLIO   Sir Toby, I must be round with you. My lady bade
me tell you, that though she harbours you as her   90
kinsman, she's nothing allied to your disorders. If you
can separate yourself and your misdemeanours, you
are welcome to the house; if not, an it would please
you to take leave of her, she is very willing to bid you
farewell.

SIR TOBY   [sings to Maria] 'Farewell, dear heart, since I must needs
be gone.'   [he embraces her

MARIA   Nay, good Sir Toby.

CLOWN   [sings] 'His eyes do show his days are almost done.'

MALVOLIO   Is't even so?   100

SIR TOBY   [sings] 'But I will never die.'   [he falls to the ground

CLOWN   [sings] 'Sir Toby, there you lie.'

MALVOLIO   This is much credit to you.

SIR TOBY   [rising, sings] 'Shall I bid him go?'

CLOWN   [sings] 'What an if you do?'

SIR TOBY   [sings] 'Shall I bid him go, and spare not?'

CLOWN   [sings] 'O no, no, no, no, you dare not.'

SIR TOBY   [to Clown] Out o' tune, sir! Ye lie. [to Malvolio] Art any
more than a steward? Dost thou think because thou art
virtuous, there shall be no more cakes and ale?   110

CLOWN   Yes, by Saint Anne, and ginger shall be hot i'th'
mouth too.

SIR TOBY   Th'art i'th' right. Go, sir, rub your chain with crumbs. A
stoup of wine, Maria!   [she fills their vessels

MALVOLIO   Mistress Mary, if you prized my lady's favour at any
thing more than contempt, you would not give means
for this uncivil rule; she shall know of it, by this hand.
                                             [he departs

MARIA   Go shake your ears.

SIR AND.   'Twere as good a deed as to drink when a man's a-
hungry, to challenge him the field, and then to break   120
promise with him and make a fool of him.

SIR TOBY   Do't, knight. I'll write thee a challenge; or I'll deliver
thy indignation to him by word of mouth.

MARIA   Sweet Sir Toby, be patient for tonight: since the youth
of the count's was today with my lady, she is much out

of quiet. For Monsieur Malvolio, let me alone with
him: if I do not gull him into a nayword, and make him
a common recreation, do not think I have wit enough
to lie straight in my bed: I know I can do it.

SIR TOBY   Possess us, possess us, tell us something of him.   130

MARIA   Marry, sir, sometimes he is a kind of puritan.

SIR AND.   O, if I thought that, I'd beat him like a dog.

SIR TOBY   What, for being a puritan? Thy exquisite reason, dear
knight?

SIR AND.   I have no exquisite reason for't, but I have reason
good enough.

MARIA   The devil a puritan that he is, or any thing constantly
but a time-pleaser, an affectioned ass, that cons state
without book and utters it by great swarths: the best
persuaded of himself, so crammed, as he thinks, with   140
excellencies, that it is his ground of faith that all that
look on him love him; and on that vice in him will my
revenge find notable cause to work.

SIR TOBY   What wilt thou do?

MARIA   I will drop in his way some obscure epistles of love,
wherein by the colour of his beard, the shape of his
leg, the manner of his gait, the expressure of his eye,
forehead, and complexion, he shall find himself most
feelingly personated. I can write very like my lady
your niece, on a forgotten matter we can hardly make   150
distinction of our hands.

SIR TOBY   Excellent! I smell a device.

SIR AND.   I have't in my nose too.

SIR TOBY   He shall think by the letters that thou wilt drop that they
come from my niece, and that she's in love with him.

MARIA   My purpose is, indeed, a horse of that colour.

SIR AND.   And your horse now would make him an ass.

MARIA   Ass, I doubt not.

SIR AND.   O, 'twill be admirable.

MARIA   Sport royal, I warrant you: I know my physic will   160
work with him. I will plant you two, and let the fool
make a third, where he shall find the letter: observe his
construction of it. For this night, to bed, and dream on
the event. Farewell.   [she goes out

SIR TOBY   Good night, Penthesilea.
SIR AND.   Before me, she's a good wench.
SIR TOBY   She's a beagle, true-bred, and one that adores me.
           What o' that?   [*he sighs*
SIR AND.   I was adored once too.   [*he sighs also*
SIR TOBY   Let's to bed, knight. Thou hadst need send for more   170
           money.
SIR AND.   If I cannot recover your niece, I am a foul way out.
SIR TOBY   Send for money, knight. If thou hast her not i'th'end,
           call me cut.
SIR AND.   If I do not, never trust me, take it how you will.
SIR TOBY   Come, come, I'll go burn some sack, 'tis too late to go
           to bed now: come knight; come knight.   [*they go*

SCENE 4

A room in the Duke's palace

'*Enter* DUKE, VIOLA, CURIO *and others*'

DUKE   [*to Viola*] Give me some music. Now –
       [*musicians enter*]   good morrow, friends.
       Now, good Cesario, but that piece of song,
       That old and antic song we heard last night:
       Methought it did relieve my passion much,
       More than light airs and recollected terms
       Of these most brisk and giddy-pacéd times.
       Come, but one verse.
CURIO He is not here, so please your lordship, that should
       sing it.
DUKE   Who was it?   10
CURIO Feste, the jester, my lord, a fool that the Lady Olivia's
       father took much delight in. He is about the house.
DUKE   Seek him out, and play the tune the while.
                                  [*Curio goes; music plays*
       Come hither, boy – if ever thou shalt love,
       In the sweet pangs of it remember me:
       For, such as I am all true lovers are,
       Unstaid and skittish in all motions else,

Save in the constant image of the creature
That is beloved. How dost thou like this tune?

VIOLA It gives a very echo to the seat 20
Where Love is throned.

DUKE Thou dost speak masterly.
My life upon't, young though thou art, thine eye
Hath stayed upon some favour that it loves:
Hath it not, boy?

VIOLA A little, by your favour.

DUKE What kind of woman is't?

VIOLA Of your complexion.

DUKE She is not worth thee then. What years, i'faith?

VIOLA About your years, my lord.

DUKE Too old, by heaven: let still the woman take
An elder than herself; so wears she to him,
So sways she level in her husband's heart: 30
For, boy, however we do praise ourselves,
Our fancies are more giddy and unfirm,
More longing, wavering, sooner lost and won,
Than women's are.

VIOLA I think it well, my lord.

DUKE Then let thy love be younger than thyself,
Or thy affection cannot hold the bent:
For women are as roses, whose fair flower
Being once displayed doth fall that very hour.

VIOLA And so they are: alas, that they are so;
To die, even when they to perfection grow! 40

CURIO *re-enters with* CLOWN

DUKE O fellow, come, the song we had last night.
Mark it, Cesario, it is old and plain:
The spinsters and the knitters in the sun,
And the free maids that weave their thread with bones
Do use to chant it; it is silly sooth,
And dallies with the innocence of love,
Like the old age.

CLOWN Are you ready, sir?

DUKE Ay, prithee, sing. [*music*

CLOWN   [*sings*] Come away, come away death,   50
              And in sad cypress let me be laid:
                Fly away, fly away breath,
              I am slain by a fair cruel maid:
              My shroud of white, stuck all with yew,
                  O, prepare it!
              My part of death no one so true
                  Did share it.

              Not a flower, not a flower sweet
              On my black coffin let there be strown:
                Not a friend, not a friend greet   60
              My poor corpse, where my bones shall be
                                thrown:
              A thousand thousand sighs to save,
                Lay me O where
              Sad true lover never find my grave,
                To weep there.

DUKE   [*gives money*] There's for thy pains.
CLOWN   No pains, sir, I take pleasure in singing, sir.
DUKE   I'll pay thy pleasure then.
CLOWN   Truly, sir, and pleasure will be paid, one time or
           another.   70
DUKE   Give me now leave to leave thee.
CLOWN   Now, the melancholy god protect thee, and the tailor
           make thy doublet of changeable taffeta, for thy mind is
           a very opal. I would have men of such constancy put
           to sea, that their business might be everything and
           their intent everywhere, for that's it that always makes
           a good voyage of nothing. Farewell.   [*he goes*
DUKE   Let all the rest give place.   [*Curio and attendants depart*
                         Once more, Cesario,
     Get thee to yon same sovereign cruelty
     Tell her my love, more noble than the world,   80
     Prizes not quantity of dirty lands;
     The parts that fortune hath bestowed upon her,
     Tell her I hold as giddily as fortune;
     But 'tis that miracle and queen of gems
     That nature pranks her in attracts my soul.

VIOLA	But if she cannot love you, sir?
DUKE	I cannot be so answered.
VIOLA	Sooth, but you must.

VIOLA   Sooth, but you must.
Say that some lady, as perhaps there is,
Hath for your love as great a pang of heart
As you have for Olivia: you cannot love her;   90
You tell her so; must she not then be answered?

DUKE There is no woman's sides
Can bide the beating of so strong a passion
As love doth give my heart: no woman's heart
So big, to hold so much, they lack retention.
Alas, their love may be called appetite –
No motion of the liver, but the palate –
That suffers surfeit, cloyment and revolt;
But mine is all as hungry as the sea,
And can digest as much. Make no compare   100
Between that love a woman can bear me
And that I owe Olivia.

VIOLA   Ay, but I know –

DUKE What dost thou know?

VIOLA Too well what love women to men may owe:
In faith they are as true of heart as we.
My father had a daughter loved a man,
As it might be, perhaps, were I a woman,
I should your lordship.

DUKE   And what's her history?

VIOLA A blank, my lord: she never told her love,
But let concealment like a worm i'th' bud   110
Feed on her damask cheek: she pined in thought,
And with a green and yellow melancholy
She sat like Patience on a monument,
Smiling at grief. Was not this love, indeed?
We men may say more, swear more – but indeed
Our shows are more than will; for still we prove
Much in our vows, but little in our love.

DUKE But died thy sister of her love, my boy?

VIOLA I am all the daughters of my father's house,
And all the brothers too. and yet I know not. [they muse 120
Sir, shall I to this lady?

DUKE   [*starts and rouses*]   Ay, that's the theme.
            To her in haste; give her this jewel; say,
            My love can give no place, bide no denay.   [*they go*

SCENE 5

*A walled garden adjoining the house of Olivia; two doors, one
leading out of the garden, the other opening: into the house
whence there runs a broad walk with great box-trees on
either side and a stone seat next the wall*

The house-door opens and SIR TOBY BELCH *comes out with*
SIR ANDREW AGUECHEEK

SIR TOBY   [*turns and calls*] Come thy ways, Signior Fabian.
FABIAN   [*follows through the door*] Nay, I'll come: if I lose a
            scruple of this sport, let me be boiled to death with
            melancholy.
SIR TOBY   Wouldst thou not be glad to have the niggardly ras-
            cally sheep-biter come by some notable shame?
FABIAN   I would exult, man: you know, he brought me out o'
            favour with my lady about a bear-baiting here.
SIR TOBY   To anger him, we'll have the bear again, and we will
            fool him black and blue – shall we not, Sir Andrew?   10
SIR AND.   An we do not, it is pity of our lives.
                MARIA *appears, hurrying down the walk*
SIR TOBY   Here comes the little villain. How now, my metal of
            India?
MARIA   Get ye all three into the box-tree: Malvolio's coming
            down this walk. He has been yonder i'the sun practising
            behaviour to his own shadow this half hour: observe
            him, for the love of mockery; for I know this letter will
            make a contemplative idiot of him. Close, in the name
            of jesting! [*the men hide in a box-tree*] Lie thou there
            [*throws down a letter*] for here comes the trout that must   20
            be caught with tickling.   [*she goes within*
        MALVOLIO, *in plumed hat, comes slowly along the path, musing*
MALVOLIO   'Tis but fortune, all is fortune. Maria once told me she

did affect me, and I have heard herself come thus near,
that should she fancy it should be one of my complexion. Besides, she uses me with a more exalted respect
than any one else that follows her. What should I think
on't?

SIR TOBY　Here's an overweening rogue!

FABIAN　O, peace! Contemplation makes a rare turkey-cock of
him. How he jets under his advanced plumes!　30

SIR AND.　'Slight, I could so beat the rogue!

FABIAN　Peace, I say.

MALVOLIO　To be Count Malvolio!

SIR TOBY　Ah, rogue!

SIR AND.　Pistol him, pistol him.

FABIAN　Peace, peace!

MALVOLIO　There is example for't; the lady of the Strachy married
the yeoman of the wardrobe.

SIR TOBY　Fie on him, Jezebel!

FABIAN　O, peace! Now he's deeply in: look, how imagination　40
blows him.

MALVOLIO　Having been three months married to her, sitting in
my state —

SIR TOBY　O, for a stone-bow, to hit him in the eye!

MALVOLIO　Calling my officers about me, in my branched velvet
gown; having come from a day-bed, where I have left
Olivia sleeping —

SIR TOBY　Fire and brimstone!

FABIAN　O, peace, peace!

MALVOLIO　And then to have the humour of state: and after a　50
demure travel of regard, telling them I know my place
as I would they should do theirs, to ask for my kinsman Toby —

SIR TOBY　Bolts and shackles!

FABIAN　O, peace, peace, peace! Now, now.

MALVOLIO　Seven of my people, with an obedient start, make out
for him: I frown the while, and perchance wind up my
watch, or play with my [*touches his steward's chain an
instant*] — some rich jewel. Toby approaches; curtsies
there to me —　60

SIR TOBY　Shall this fellow live?

FABIAN   Though our silence be drawn from us with cars, yet
           peace.

MALVOLIO   I extend my hand to him thus; quenching my familiar
           smile with an austere regard of control –

SIR TOBY   And does not 'Toby' take you a blow o'the lips then?

MALVOLIO   Saying, 'Cousin Toby, my fortunes having cast me on
           your niece give me this prerogatlve of speech' –

SIR TOBY   What, what?

MALVOLIO   'You must amend your drunkenness.'   70

SIR TOBY   Out, scab!   [*Malvolio turns as at a sound*

FABIAN   Nay, patience, or we break the sinews of our plot.

MALVOLIO   'Besides, you waste the treasure of your time with a
           foolish knight' –

SIR AND.   That's me, I warrant you.

MALVOLIO   'One Sir Andrew' –   [*he sees the letter*

SIR AND.   I knew 'twas I, for many do call me fool.

MALVOLIO   [*takes up the letter*] What employment have we here?

FABIAN   Now is the woodcock near the gin.

SIR TOBY   O, peace! And the spirit of humours intimate reading   80
           aloud to him!

MALVOLIO   By my life, this is my lady's hand: these be her very c's,
           her u's, and her t's, and thus makes go she her great
           P's. It is, in contempt of question, her hand.

SIR AND.   Her c's, her u's, and her t's: why that?

MALVOLIO   [*reads the superscription*] 'To the unknown beloved, this,
           and my good wishes'. Her very phrases! By your leave,
           wax. Soft! And the impressure her Lucrece, with which
           she uses to seal: 'tis my lady. To whom should this be?
                                           [*he opens the letter*

FABIAN   This wins him, liver and all.   90

MALVOLIO   [*reads*]   'Jove knows I love
                      But who?
                  Lips, do not move!
                No man must know.'
           'No man must know'. What follows? The numbers
           altered. [*he muses*] 'No man must know' – if this
           should be thee, Malvolio!

SIR TOBY   Marry, hang thee, brock!

MALVOLIO [*reads*] 'I may command where I adore:
                     But silence, like a Lucrece knife,   100
                   With bloodless stroke my heart doth gore
                   M, O, A, I, doth sway my life.'

FABIAN   A fustian riddle!

SIR TOBY   Excellent wench, say I.

MALVOLIO 'M, O, A, I, doth sway my life.' – Nay, but first, let
          me see, let me see, let me see.

FABIAN   What dish o' poison has she dressed him!

SIR TOBY   And with what wing the stallion checks at it!

MALVOLIO 'I may command where I adore'. Why she may com-
          mand me; I serve her, she is my lady. Why, this is   110
          evident to any formal capacity. There is no obstruction
          in this. And the end: what should that alphabetical
          position portend? If I could make that resemble some-
          thing in me! Softly! 'M, O, A, I' –

SIR TOBY   O, ay, make up that – he is now at a cold scent.

FABIAN   Sowter will cry upon't for all this, though it be as rank
          as a fox.

MALVOLIO 'M' – Malvolio – 'M' – why, that begins my name.

FABIAN   Did not I say he would work it out? The cur is
          excellent at faults.   120

MALVOLIO 'M' – but then there is no consonancy in the sequel
          that suffers under probation: 'A' should follow, but 'O'
          does.

FABIAN   And O shall end, I hope.

SIR TOBY   Ay, or I'll cudgel him, and make him cry 'O!'

MALVOLIO And then 'I' comes behind.

FABIAN   Ay, an you had any eye behind you, you might see
          more detraction at your heels, than fortunes before
          you.

MALVOLIO 'M, O, A, I'. This simulation is not as the former: and 130
          yet, to crush this a little, it would bow to me, for every
          one of these letters are in my name. Soft! Here follows
          prose.
          [*reads*] 'If this fall into thy hand, revolve. In my stars I
          am above thee, but be not afraid of greatness: some are
          born great, some achieve greatness, and some have
          greatness thrust upon 'em. Thy Fates open their hands,

let thy blood and spirit embrace them; and to inure
thyself to what thou art like to be, cast thy humble
slough, and appear fresh. Be opposite with a kinsman, 140
surly with servants; let thy tongue tang arguments of
state; put thyself into the trick of singularity. She thus
advises thee that sighs for thee. Remember who
commended thy yellow stockings, and wished to see
thee ever cross-gartered: I say, remember. Go to, thou
art made, if thou desir'st to be so; if not, let me see thee
a steward still, the fellow of servants, and not worthy to
touch Fortune's fingers. Farewell. She, that would alter
services with thee,   THE FORTUNATE-UNHAPPY

Daylight and champian discovers not more: this is 150
open. I will be proud, I will read politic authors, I will
baffle Sir Toby, I will wash off gross acquaintance, I
will be point-devise the very man. I do not now fool
myself, to let imagination jade me; for every reason
excites to this, that my lady loves me. She did commend my yellow-stockings of late, she did praise my
leg being cross-gartered, and in this she manifests herself to my love, and with a kind of injunction drives
me to these habits of her liking. I thank my stars, I am
happy. I will be strange, stout, in yellow stockings, 160
and cross-gartered, even with the swiftness of putting
on. Jove, and my stars be praised! Here is yet a post-
script.

[*reads*] 'Thou canst not choose but know who I am. If
thou entertain'st my love, let it appear in thy smiling,
thy smiles become thee well. Therefore in my presence still smile, dear, O my sweet, I prithee.'

Jove I thank thee! [*he lifts his hands towards heaven*] I
will smile, I will do everything that thou wilt have me.
                                        [*he goes within*

FABIAN   I will not give my part of this sport for a pension of 170
           thousands to be paid from the Sophy.
SIR TOBY   I could marry this wench for this device —
SIR AND.   So could I too.

SIR TOBY	And ask no other dowry with her but such another jest.
SIR AND.	Nor I neither.

MARIA *comes from the house*

FABIAN	Here comes my noble gull-catcher.
SIR TOBY	Wilt thou set thy foot o' my neck?
SIR AND.	Or o' mine either?
SIR TOBY	Shall I play my freedom at trey-trip, and become thy bond-slave?
SIR AND.	I'faith or I either?
SIR TOBY	Why, thou hast put him in such a dream, that when the image of it leaves him he must run mad.
MARIA	Nay, but say true, does it work upon him?
SIR TOBY	Like aqua-vitae with a midwife.
MARIA	If you will then see the fruits of the sport, mark his first approach before my lady: he will come to her in yellow stockings, and 'tis a colour she abhors, and cross-gartered, a fashion she detests; and he will smile upon her, which will now be so unsuitable to her disposition, being addicted to a melancholy as she is, that it cannot but turn him into a notable contempt: if you will see it, follow me.
SIR TOBY	To the gates of Tartar, thou most excellent devil of wit!
SIR AND.	I'll make one too. *[they enter the house*

180

190

ACT 3 SCENE 1

The CLOWN *enters the garden with his pipe and tabor; he plays.*
Viola comes in through the outer door as he finishes

VIOLA   Save thee, friend, and thy music: dost thou live by thy
              tabor?

CLOWN   No, sir, I live by the church.

VIOLA   Art thou a churchman?

CLOWN   No such matter, sir. I do live by the church: for I do live
              at my house, and my house doth stand by the church.

VIOLA   So thou mayst say the king lies by a beggar, if a beggar
              dwell near him: or the church stands by thy tabor, if
              thy tabor stand by the church.

CLOWN   You have said, sir. To see this age! A sentence is but a   10
              cheveril glove to a good wit – how quickly the wrong
              side may be turned outward!

VIOLA   Nay, that's certain; they that dally nicely with words
              may quickly make them wanton.

CLOWN   I would therefore my sister had had no name, sir.

VIOLA   Why, man?

CLOWN   Why, sir, her name's a word, and to dally with that
              word might make my sister want one. But indeed
              words are very rascals since bonds disgraced them.

VIOLA   Thy reason, man?   20

CLOWN   Troth, sir, I can yield you none without words, and
              words are grown so false I am loath to prove reason
              with them.

VIOLA   I warrant thou art a merry fellow and car'st for nothing.

CLOWN   Not so, sir, I do care for something: but in my con-
              science, sir, I do not care for you: if that be to care for
              nothing, sir, I would it would make you invisible.

VIOLA   Art not thou the Lady Olivia's fool?

CLOWN   No indeed sir, the Lady Olivia has no folly. She will
              keep no fool, sir, till she be married, and fools are as   30
              like husbands as pilchards are to herrings – the hus-
              band's the bigger. I am, indeed, not her fool, but her
              corrupter of words.

VIOLA   I saw thee late at the Count Orsino's.

CLOWN   Foolery, sir, does walk about the orb like the sun, it
          shines everywhere. I would be sorry, sir, but the fool
          should be as oft with your master as with my mistress:
          I think I saw your wisdom there.

VIOLA   Nay, an thou pass upon me, I'll no more with thee.
          Hold, there's expenses for thee.   [*she gives him a coin* 40

CLOWN   [*gazes at the coin in his palm*] Now Jove, in his next
          commodity of hair, send thee a beard!

VIOLA   By my troth I'll tell thee, I am almost sick for one –
          [*aside*] though I would not have it grow on my chin. Is
          thy lady within?

CLOWN   [*still gazes at the coin*] Would not a pair of these have
          bred, sir?

VIOLA   Yes, being kept together and put to use.

CLOWN   I would play Lord Pandarus of Phrygia, sir, to bring a
          Cressida to this Troilus.   50

VIOLA   I understand you, sir, 'tis well begged.
                                          [*she gives another coin*

CLOWN   The matter, I hope, is not great, sir; begging but a
          beggar: Cressida was a beggar. My lady is within, sir. I
          will conster to them whence you come, who you are
          and what you would are out of my welkin – I might
          say 'element,' but the word is over-worn.
                                          [*he goes within*

VIOLA   This fellow is wise enough to play the fool,
          And to do that well craves a kind of wit:
          He must observe their mood on whom he jests,
          The quality of persons, and the time;   60
          And, like the haggard, check at every feather
          That comes before his eye. This is a practice,
          As full of labour as a wise man's art:
          For folly that he wisely shows is fit;
          But wise men, folly-fall'n, quite taint their wit.

          SIR TOBY BELCH *and* SIR ANDREW AGUECHEEK *come forth*

SIR TOBY Save you, gentleman.

VIOLA   And you, sir.

SIR AND. [*bows*] Dieu vous garde, monsieur.

VIOLA	[*bows*] Et vous aussi; votre serviteur.
SIR AND.	I hope, sir, you are – and I am yours. 70
SIR TOBY	Will you encounter the house? My niece is desirous you should enter, if your trade be to her.
VIOLA	I am bound to your niece, sir. I mean, she is the list of my voyage.
SIR TOBY	Taste your legs, sir, put them to motion.
VIOLA	My legs do better under-stand me, sir, than I understand what you mean by bidding me taste my legs.
SIR TOBY	I mean, to go, sir, to enter.
VIOLA	I will answer you with gate and entrance – but we are prevented. 80

OLIVIA *comes from the house with* MARIA

	Most excellent accomplished lady, the heavens rain odours on you!
SIR AND.	That youth's a rare courtier – 'Rain odours' – well!
VIOLA	My matter hath no voice, lady, but to your own most pregnant and vouchsafed ear.
SIR AND.	'Odours,' 'pregnant', and 'vouchsafed': I'll get 'em all three all ready.
OLIVIA	Let the garden door be shut, and leave me to my hearing. [*Sir Toby, Sir Andrew and Maria depart* Give me your hand, sir. 90
VIOLA	[*bows low*] My duty, madam, and most humble service.
OLIVIA	What is your name?
VIOLA	Cesario is your servant's name, fair princess.
OLIVIA	My servant, sir! 'Twas never merry world, Since lowly feigning was called compliment: Y'are servant to the Count Orsino, youth.
VIOLA	And he is yours, and his must needs be yours; Your servant's servant is your servant, madam.
OLIVIA	For him, I think not on him: for his thoughts, Would they were blanks, rather than filled with me! 100
VIOLA	Madam, I come to whet your gentle thoughts On his behalf.
OLIVIA	O, by your leave, I pray you; I bade you never speak again of him: But, would you undertake another suit,

I had rather hear you to solicit that
Than music from the spheres.

VIOLA   Dear lady –

OLIVIA   Give me leave, beseech you: I did send,
           After the last enchantment you did here,
           A ring in chase of you; so did I abuse
           Myself, my servant and, I fear me, you: 110
           Under your hard construction must I sit,
           To force that on you in a shameful cunning
           Which you knew none of yours: what might you think?
           Have you not set mine honour at the stake,
           And baited it with all th'unmuzzled thoughts
           That tyrannous heart can think?
           To one of your receiving enough is shown,
           A cypress, not a bosom, hides my heart:
           So let me hear you speak.

VIOLA   I pity you.

OLIVIA   That's a degree to love.

VIOLA   No, not a grise;   120
           For 'tis a vulgar proof,
           That very oft we pity enemies.

OLIVIA   Why then methinks 'tis time to smile again:
           O world, how apt the poor are to be proud!
           If one should be a prey, how much the better
           To fall before the lion than the wolf?   ['clock strikes'
           The clock upbraids me with the waste of time.
           Be not afraid, good youth, I will not have you:
           And yet, when wit and youth is come to harvest,
           Your wife is like to reap a proper man: 130
           There lies your way, due west.

VIOLA   Then westward-ho!
           Grace and good disposition attend your ladyship!
           You'll nothing, madam, to my lord by me?

OLIVIA   Stay:
           I prithee, tell me what thou think'st of me.

VIOLA   That you do think you are not what you are.

OLIVIA   If I think so, I think the same of you.

VIOLA   Then think you right; I am not what I am.

OLIVIA   I would you were as I would have you be!

VIOLA	Would it be better, madam, than I am?	140
	I wish it might, for now I am your fool.	
OLIVIA	O, what a deal of scorn looks beautiful	
	In the contempt and anger of his lip!	
	A murderous guilt shows not itself more soon	
	Than love that would seem hid: love's night is noon.	
	Cesario, by the roses of the spring,	
	By maidhood, honour, truth, and everything,	
	I love thee so, that, maugre all thy pride,	
	Nor wit nor reason can my passion hide.	
	Do not extort thy reasons from this clause,	150
	For that I woo, thou therefore hast no cause:	
	But rather reason thus with reason fetter,	
	Love sought is good, but given unsought is better.	
VIOLA	By innocence I swear, and by my youth,	
	I have one heart, one bosom, and one truth,	
	And that no woman has, nor never none	
	Shall mistress be of it, save I alone.	
	And so adieu, good madam! Never more	
	Will I my master's tears to you deplore.	
OLIVIA	Yet come again: for thou perhaps mayst move	160
	That heart, which now abhors, to like his love. [*they go*	

SCENE 2

A room in Olivia's house

SIR TOBY BELCH, SIR ANDREW AGUECHEEK *and* FABIAN

SIR AND.	No, faith, I'll not stay a jot longer.	
SIR TOBY	Thy reason, dear venom, give thy reason.	
FABIAN	You must needs yield your reason, Sir Andrew.	
SIR AND.	Marry, I saw your niece do more favours to the count's serving-man than ever she bestowed upon me; I saw't i'th'orchard.	
SIR TOBY	Did she see thee the while, old boy? Tell me that.	
SIR AND.	As plain as I see you now.	
FABIAN	This was a great argument of love in her toward you.	
SIR AND.	'Slight! will you make an ass o' me?	10

FABIAN   I will prove it legitimate, sir, upon the oaths of judgment
           and reason.

SIR TOBY   And they have been grand-jurymen since before Noah
           was a sailor.

FABIAN   She did show favour to the youth in your sight, only
           to exasperate you, to awake your dormouse valour, to
           put fire in your heart, and brimstone in your liver: you
           should then have accosted her, and with some excel-
           lent jests, fire-new from the mint, you should have
           banged the youth into dumbness: this was looked for   20
           at your hand, and this was balked: the double gilt of
           this opportunity you let time wash off, and you are
           now sailed into the north of my lady's opinion, where
           you will hang like an icicle on a Dutchman's beard,
           unless you do redeem it by some laudable attempt,
           either of valour or policy.

SIR AND.   An't be any way, it must be with valour, for policy I
           hate: I had as lief be a Brownist, as a politician.

SIR TOBY   Why then, build me thy fortunes upon the basis of
           valour. Challenge me the count's youth to fight with   30
           him, hurt him in eleven places — my niece shall take
           note of it, and assure thyself there is no love-broker in
           the world can more prevail in man's commendation
           with woman than report of valour.

FABIAN   There is no way but this, Sir Andrew.

SIR AND.   Will either of you bear me a challenge to him?

SIR TOBY   Go, write it in a martial hand, be curst and brief; it is
           no matter how witty, so it be eloquent and full of
           invention: taunt him with the license of ink: if thou
           'thou'st' him some thrice, it shall not be amiss; and as   40
           many lies as will lie in thy sheet of paper, although the
           sheet were big enough for the bed of Ware in England,
           set 'em down — go, about it. Let there be gall enough
           in thy ink, though thou write with a goose-pen, no
           matter: about it.

SIR AND.   Where shall I find you?

SIR TOBY   We'll call thee at thy cubicle: go.   [Sir Andrew goes

FABIAN   This is a dear manakin to you, Sir Toby.

SIR TOBY   I have been dear to him, lad — some two thousand
             strong, or so.   50

FABIAN   We shall have a rare letter from him. But you'll not
             deliver't?

SIR TOBY   Never trust me then; and by all means stir on the
             youth to an answer. I think oxen and wainropes can-
             not hale them together. For Andrew, if he were
             opened and you find so much blood in his liver as will
             clog the foot of a flea, I'll eat the rest of th'anatomy.

FABIAN   And his opposite, the youth, bears in his visage no
             great presage of cruelty.

       MARIA *comes tripping in, holding her sides for laughter*

SIR TOBY   Look, where the youngest wren of nine comes.   60

MARIA   If you desire the spleen, and will laugh yourselves
             into stitches, follow me. Yon gull Malvolio is turned
             heathen, a very renegado; for there is no Christian,
             that means to be saved by believing rightly, can ever
             believe such impossible passages of grossness. [*overcome
             with laughter*] He's in yellow stockings!

SIR TOBY   [*shouts*] And cross-gartered?

MARIA   Most villainously; like a pedant that keeps a school
             i'th' church. I have dogged him like his murderer. He
             does obey every point of the letter that I dropped to   70
             betray him: he does smile his face into more lines than
             is in the new map, with the augmentation of the
             Indies: you have not seen such a thing as 'tis. I can
             hardly forbear hurling things at him. I know my lady
             will strike him: if she do, he'll smile and take't for a
             great favour.

SIR TOBY   Come, bring us, bring us where he is.

                                          [*they rush forth*

SCENE 3

A street

ANTONIO *and* SEBASTIAN *approach*

SEBASTIAN I would not by my will have troubled you,
            But since you make your pleasure of your pains,
            I will no further chide you.
ANTONIO   I could not stay behind you: my desire,
            More sharp than filéd steel, did spur me forth;
            And not all love to see you, though so much
            As might have drawn one to a longer voyage,
            But jealousy what might befall your travel,
            Being skilless in these parts; which to a stranger,
            Unguided and unfriended, often prove   10
            Rough and unhospitable: my willing love,
            The rather by these arguments of fear,
            Set forth in your pursuit.
SEBASTIAN   My kind Antonio,
            I can no other answer make but thanks,
            And thanks, and ever thanks; and oft good turns
            Are shuffled off with such uncurrent pay:
            But, were my worth as is my conscience firm,
            You should find better dealing. What's to do?
            Shall we go see the relics of this town?
ANTONIO   Tomorrow sir – best first go see your lodging.   20
SEBASTIAN I am not weary, and 'tis long to night:
            I pray you, let us satisfy our eyes
            With the memorials and the things of fame
            That do renown this city.
ANTONIO   Would you'ld pardon me;
            I do not without danger walk these streets.
            Once in a sea-fight 'gainst the count his galleys
            I did some service, of such note indeed
            That were I ta'en here it would scarce be answered.
SEBASTIAN Belike you slew great number of his people.
ANTONIO   Th'offence is not of such a bloody nature,   30
            Albeit the quality of the time and quarrel

Might well have given us bloody argument:
It might have since been answered in repaying
What we took from them, which for traffic's sake
Most of our city did: only myself stood out,
For which, if I be lapséd in this place,
I shall pay dear.

SEBASTIAN   Do not then walk too open.

ANTONIO   It doth not fit me. Hold, sir, here's my purse.

                                         [*he gives it*

In the south suburbs, at the Elephant,
Is best to lodge: I will bespeak our diet,   40
Whiles you beguile the time and feed your knowledge
With viewing of the town; there shall you have me.

SEBASTIAN   Why I your purse?

ANTONIO   Haply your eye shall light upon some toy
You have desire to purchase; and your store,
I think, is not for idle markets, sir.

SEBASTIAN   I'll be your purse-bearer, and leave you for an hour.

ANTONIO   To th'Elephant.

SEBASTIAN   I do remember.   [*they go off in different directions*

SCENE 4

Olivia's garden

OLIVIA *enters musing, followed by* MARIA; *Olivia sits*

OLIVIA   I have sent after him, he says he'll come;
How shall I feast him? What bestow of him?
For youth is bought more oft than begged or borrowed.
I speak too loud.
[*to Maria*] Where's Malvolio? He is sad and civil,
And suits well for a servant with my fortunes –
Where is Malvolio?

MARIA   He's coming, madam; but in very strange manner. He
is, sure, possessed, madam.

OLIVIA   Why, what's the matter? Does he rave?   10

MARIA   No, madam, he does nothing but smile: your ladyship
were best to have some guard about you, if he come,
for sure the man is tainted in's wits.

OLIVIA   Go, call him hither.

> MALVOLIO, *in yellow stockings and with awkward*
> *gait, is seen coming down the walk*

                          I am as mad as he,
           If sad and merry madness equal be.
           How now, Malvolio?

MALVOLIO Sweet lady, ho, ho.

OLIVIA   Smil'st thou?
           I sent for thee upon a sad occasion.

MALVOLIO Sad, lady? I could be sad: this does make some obstruc-   20
           tion in the blood, this cross-gartering – but what of
           that? If it please the eye of one, it is with me as the very
           true sonnet is: 'Please one and please all.'

OLIVIA   Why, how dost thou, man? What is the matter with
           thee?

MALVOLIO Not black in my mind, though yellow in my legs. It
           did come to his hands, and commands shall be ex-
           ecuted. I think we do know the sweet Roman hand.

OLIVIA   Wilt thou go to bed, Malvolio?

MALVOLIO To bed! Ay, sweet-heart, and I'll come to thee.   30

OLIVIA   God comfort thee! Why dost thou smile so, and kiss
           thy hand so oft?

MARIA   How do you, Malvolio?

MALVOLIO [*disdainful*] At your request! Yes, nightingales answer
           daws.

MARIA   Why appear you with this ridiculous boldness before
           my lady?

MALVOLIO [*to Olivia*] 'Be not afraid of greatness': 'twas well writ.

OLIVIA   What mean'st thou by that, Malvolio?

MALVOLIO 'Some are born great' –   40

OLIVIA   Ha?

MALVOLIO 'Some achieve greatness' –

OLIVIA   What say'st thou?

MALVOLIO 'And some have greatness thrust upon them.'

OLIVIA   Heaven restore thee!

MALVOLIO 'Remember, who commended thy yellow stockings' –

OLIVIA   Thy yellow stockings!

MALVOLIO 'And wished to see thee cross-gartered.'

OLIVIA   Cross-gartered?

MALVOLIO   'Go to, thou art made, if thou desir'st to be so' –   50

OLIVIA   Am I made?

MALVOLIO   'If not, let me see thee a servant still.'

OLIVIA   Why, this is very midsummer madness.

A servant comes from the house

SERVANT   Madam, the young gentleman of the Count Orsino's is returned – I could hardly entreat him back: he attends your ladyship's pleasure.

OLIVIA   I'll come to him. [*the servant goes*] Good Maria, let this fellow be looked to. Where's my cousin Toby? Let some of my people have a special care of him. I would not have him miscarry for the half of my dowry.   60

[*she enters the house followed by Maria*

MALVOLIO   O, ho! Do you come near me now? No worse man than Sir Toby to look to me! This concurs directly with the letter – she sends him on purpose, that I may appear stubborn to him; for she incites me to that in the letter. 'Cast thy humble slough,' says she; 'be opposite with a kinsman, surly with servants, let thy tongue tang with arguments of state, put thyself into the trick of singularity'; and consequently sets down the manner how; as, a sad face, a reverend carriage, a slow tongue, in the habit of some sir of note, and so forth. I have limed her, but it   70 is Jove's doing, and Jove make me thankful! And when she went away now, 'Let this fellow be looked to': fellow! Not Malvolio, nor after my degree, but 'fellow'. Why, every thing adheres together, that no dram of a scruple, no scruple of a scruple, no obstacle, no incredulous or unsafe circumstance – what can be said? Nothing that can be, can come between me and the full prospect of my hopes. Well, Jove, not I, is the doer of this, and he is to be thanked.

MARIA *returns with* SIR TOBY BELCH *and* FABIAN

SIR TOBY   Which way is he, in the name of sanctity? If all the   80 devils of hell be drawn in little, and Legion himself possessed him, yet I'll speak to him.

FABIAN   Here he is, here he is. How is't with you, sir?

SIR TOBY   How is't with you, man?

MALVOLIO   Go off, I discard you; let me enjoy my private: go off.

MARIA   Lo, how hollow the fiend speaks within him! Did not I tell you? Sir Toby, my lady prays you to have a care of him.

MALVOLIO   Ah, ha! Does she so!

SIR TOBY   Go to, go to: peace, peace, we must deal gently with him: let me alone. How do you, Malvolio? How is't with you? What, man! Defy the devil: consider, he's an enemy to mankind.

MALVOLIO   Do you know what you say?

MARIA   La you! An you speak ill of the devil, how he takes it at heart! Pray God, he be not bewitched!

FABIAN   Carry his water to th'wise woman.

MARIA   Marry, and it shall be done tomorrow morning, if I live. My lady would not lose him for more than I'll say.

MALVOLIO   How now, mistress!

MARIA   [chokes] O Lord!

SIR TOBY   Prithee, hold thy peace, this is not the way: do you not see you move him? Let me alone with him.

FABIAN   No way but gentleness, gently, gently: the fiend is rough, and will not be roughly used.

SIR TOBY   Why, how now, my bawcock! How dost thou, chuck?

MALVOLIO   Sir!

SIR TOBY   Ay, Biddy, come with me. What, man! 'Tis not for gravity to play at cherry-pit with Satan. Hang him, foul collier!

MARIA   Get him to say his prayers, good Sir Toby, get him to pray.

MALVOLIO   My prayers, minx!

MARIA   No, I warrant you, he will not hear of godliness.

MALVOLIO   Go, hang yourselves all! You are idle shallow things – I am not of your element – You shall know more hereafter.   [he goes; they gaze after him in amazement

SIR TOBY   Is't possible?

FABIAN   If this were played upon a stage now, I could condemn it as an improbable fiction.

SIR TOBY   His very genius hath taken the infection of the device, man.

MARIA   Nay, pursue him now, lest the device take air and taint.

FABIAN   Why, we shall make him mad indeed.

MARIA   The house will be the quieter.

SIR TOBY   Come, we'll have him in a dark room and bound. My niece is already in the belief that he's mad; we may carry it thus, for our pleasure and his penance, till our very pastime, tired out of breath, prompt us to have 130 mercy on him: at which time we will bring the device to the bar and crown thee for a finder of madmen. But see, but see.

     SIR ANDREW AGUECHEEK *comes forth, a letter in his hand*

FABIAN   More matter for a May morning!

SIR AND   Here's the challenge, read it: I warrant there's vinegar and pepper in't.

FABIAN   Is't so saucy?

SIR AND   Ay, is't! I warrant him: do but read.

SIR TOBY   Give me. [*he reads*] 'Youth, whatsoever thou art, thou 140 art but a scurvy fellow.'

FABIAN   Good, and valiant.

SIR TOBY   'Wonder not, nor admire not in thy mind, why I do call thee so, for I will show thee no reason for't.'

FABIAN   A good note, that keeps you from the blow of the law.

SIR TOBY   'Thou com'st to the Lady Olivia, and in my sight she uses thee kindly: but thou liest in thy throat, that is not the matter I challenge thee for.'

FABIAN   Very brief, and to exceeding good sense – [*aside*] less.

SIR TOBY   'I will waylay thee going home, where if it be thy 150 chance to kill me,' –

FABIAN   Good.

SIR TOBY   'Thou kill'st me like a rogue and a villain.'

FABIAN   Still you keep o'th' windy side of the law: good.

SIR TOBY   'Fare thee well, and God have mercy upon one of our souls! He may have mercy upon mine, but my hope is better, and so look to thyself. Thy friend, as thou usest him, and thy sworn enemy,   ANDREW AGUECHEEK

If this letter move him not, his legs cannot: I'll give't him.

MARIA   You may have very fit occasion for't: he is now in 160
          some commerce with my lady, and will by and by
          depart.

SIR TOBY Go, sir Andrew; scout me for him at the corner of the
          orchard like a bum-baily: so soon as ever thou seest
          him, draw, and as thou draw'st, swear horrible; for it
          comes to pass oft that a terrible oath, with a swagger-
          ing accent sharply twanged off, gives manhood more
          approbation than ever proof itself would have earned
          him. Away!

SIR AND   Nay, let me alone for swearing.   170
                              [*he leaves the garden by the outer door*

SIR TOBY Now will not I deliver his letter: for the behaviour of
          the young gentleman gives him out to be of good
          capacity and breeding; his employment between his
          lord and my niece confirms no less; therefore this
          letter, being so excellently ignorant, will breed no
          terror in the youth: he will find it comes from a
          clodpole. But, sir, I will deliver his challenge by word
          of mouth; set upon Aguecheek a notable report of
          valour; and drive the gentleman, as I know his youth
          will aptly receive it, into a most hideous opinion of his 180
          rage, skill, fury and impetuosity. This will so fright
          them both, that they will kill one another by the look,
          like cockatrices.

                    OLIVIA *and* VIOLA *come from the house*

FABIAN   Here he comes with your niece — give them way till
          he take leave, and presently after him.

SIR TOBY I will meditate the while upon some horrid message
          for a challenge.
                    [*Sir Toby, Fabian and Maria go off into the garden*

OLIVIA   I have said too much unto a heart of stone,
          And laid mine honour too unchary out:
          There's something in me that reproves my fault;   190
          But such a headstrong potent fault it is,
          That it but mocks reproof.

VIOLA   With the same 'haviour that your passion bears
          Goes on my master's grief.

OLIVIA	Here, wear this jewel for me, 'tis my picture;
	Refuse it not, it hath no tongue to vex you:
	And I beseech you come again tomorrow.
	What shall you ask of me, that I'll deny,
	That honour saved may upon asking give?
VIOLA	Nothing but this – your true love for my master. 200
OLIVIA	How with mine honour may I give him that
	Which I have given to you?
VIOLA	I will acquit you.
OLIVIA	Well, come again tomorrow: fare thee well.
	A fiend, like thee, might bear my soul to hell.

         [*she goes within; Viola walks toward the outer gate*

      SIR TOBY BELCH *and* FABIAN *come up*

SIR TOBY	Gentleman, God save thee.
VIOLA	[*turns*] And you, sir.
SIR TOBY	That defence thou hast, betake thee to't: of what nature the wrongs are thou hast done him, I know not; but thy intercepter, full of despite, bloody as the hunter, attends thee at the orchard-end: dismount thy 210 tuck, be yare in thy preparation, for thy assailant is quick, skilful and deadly.
VIOLA	You mistake, sir. I am sure no man hath any quarrel to me; my remembrance is very free and clear from any image of offence done to any man.
SIR TOBY	You'll find it otherwise, I assure you: therefore, if you hold your life at any price, betake you to your guard; for your opposite hath in him what youth, strength, skill and wrath can furnish man withal.
VIOLA	I pray you, sir, what is he? 220
SIR TOBY	He is knight, dubbed with unhatched rapier and on carpet consideration, but he is a devil in private brawl: souls and bodies hath he divorced three, and his incensement at this moment is so implacable, that satisfaction can be none but by pangs of death and sepulchre. Hob, nob, is his word; give't or take't.
VIOLA	I will return again into the house and desire some conduct of the lady. I am no fighter. I have heard of some kind of men that put quarrels purposely on others

| | to taste their valour: belike this is a man of that quirk.   230 |

SIR TOBY   Sir, no; his indignation derives itself out of a very competent injury, therefore get you on and give him his desire. Back you shall not to the house, unless you undertake that with me which with as much safety you might answer him: therefore on, or strip your sword stark naked; for meddle you must, that's certain, or forswear to wear iron about you.

VIOLA   This is as uncivil as strange. I beseech you, do me this courteous office, as to know of the knight what my offence to him is; it is something of my negligence,   240 nothing of my purpose.

SIR TOBY   I will do so. Signior Fabian, [*he winks*] stay you by this gentleman till my return.   [*he departs by the outer door*

VIOLA   Pray you, sir, do you know of this matter?

FABIAN   I know the knight is incensed against you, even to a mortal arbitrement, but nothing of the circumstance more.

VIOLA   I beseech you, what manner of man is he?

FABIAN   Nothing of that wonderful promise, to read him by his form, as you are like to find him in the proof of his   250 valour. He is indeed, sir, the most skilful, bloody and fatal opposite that you could possibly have found in any part of Illyria. [*he takes her by the arm*] Will you walk towards him? I will make your peace with him if I can.

VIOLA   I shall be much bound to you for't: I am one, that had rather go with sir priest than sir knight: I care not who knows so much of my mettle.   [*they leave the garden*

A quiet street at the back of Olivia's walled garden,
with a gate leading thereto; trees and shrubs

SIR TOBY *and* SIR ANDREW

SIR TOBY   Why, man, he's a very devil, I have not seen such a firago. I had a pass with him, rapier, scabbard and all, and he gives me the stuck in with such a mortal   260 motion that it is inevitable; and on the answer, he pays you as surely as your feet hit the ground they step on. They say he has been fencer to the Sophy.

SIR AND.   Pox on't, I'll not meddle with him.

SIR TOBY   Ay, but he will not now be pacified: Fabian can scarce
hold him yonder.

SIR AND.   Plague on't, an I thought he had been valiant and so
cunning in fence, I'd have seen him damned ere I'd
have challenged him. Let him let the matter slip, and
I'll give him my horse, grey Capilet.   270

SIR TOBY   I'll make the motion: stand here, make a good show
on't – this shall end without the perdition of souls.
[aside] Marry, I'll ride your horse as well as I ride you.

      FABIAN and VIOLA come from the garden; Sir Toby beckons
                    Fabian aside

           I have his horse to take up the quarrel; I have per-
suaded him the youth's a devil.

FABIAN   He is as horribly conceited of him, and pants and looks
pale, as if a bear were at his heels.

SIR TOBY   [to Viola] There's no remedy, sir, he will fight with
you for's oath sake: marry, he hath better bethought
him of his quarrel, and he finds that now scarce to be   280
worth talking of: therefore draw for the supportance of
his vow, he protests he will not hurt you.

VIOLA   Pray God defend me! A little thing would make me
tell them how much I lack of a man.

FABIAN   Give ground, if you see him furious.

SIR TOBY   Come, Sir Andrew, there's no remedy, the gentleman
will for his honour's sake have one bout with you: he
cannot by the duello avoid it: but he has promised me,
as he is a gentleman and a soldier, he will not hurt you.
Come on, to't!   290

SIR AND.   Pray God, he keep his oath!

VIOLA   I do assure you, 'tis against my will.

      They make ready to fight; ANTONIO comes up

ANTONIO   [to Sir Andrew]
           Put up your sword: if this young gentleman
           Have done offence, I take the fault on me;
           If you offend him, I for him defy you.

SIR TOBY   You, sir! Why, what are you?

ANTONIO   One, sir, that for his love dares yet do more
           Than you have heard him brag to you he will.

SIR TOBY   Nay, if you be an undertaker, I am for you.

                                                    [*they draw*

                     Two officers approach

FABIAN   O good Sir Toby, hold; here come the officers.   300
SIR TOBY   [*to Antonio*] I'll be with you anon.

                     [*he hides from the officers behind a tree*

VIOLA   [*to Sir Andrew*] Pray, sir, put your sword up, if you
           please.
SIR AND.   Marry, will I, sir; and, for that I promised you, I'll be
           as good as my word. [*he sheathes his sword*] He will bear
           you easily, and reins well.
1 OFFICER This is the man, do thy office.
2 OFFICER Antonio, I arrest thee at the suit
           Of Count Orsino.
ANTONIO   You do mistake me, sir.
1 OFFICER No, sir, no jot; I know your favour well: 310
           Though now you have no sea-cap on your head.
           Take him away, he knows I know him well.
ANTONIO   I must obey. [*to Viola*] This comes with seeking you;
           But there's no remedy, I shall answer it.
           What will you do, now my necessity
           Makes me to ask you for my purse? It grieves me
           Much more for what I cannot do for you
           Than what befalls myself. You stand amazed,
           But be of comfort.
2 OFFICER Come, sir, away.   320
ANTONIO   I must entreat of you some of that money.
VIOLA   What money, sir?
           For the fair kindness you have showed me here,
           And part being prompted by your present trouble,
           Out of my lean and low ability
           I'll lend you something. [*opens her purse*]
                                   My having is not much,
           I'll make division of my present with you:
           Hold, there's half my coffer.   [*she proffers coin*
ANTONIO   [*refuses it*]   Will you deny me now?
           Is't possible that my deserts to you
           Can lack persuasion? Do not tempt my misery,   330

Lest that it make me so unsound a man
As to upbraid you with those kindnesses
That I have done for you.

VIOLA   I know of none,
Nor know I you by voice or any feature:
I hate ingratitude more in a man,
Than lying vainness, babbling drunkenness,
Or any taint of vice whose strong corruption
Inhabits our frail blood.

ANTONIO   O heavens themselves!

2 OFFICER   Come, sir, I pray you, go.

ANTONIO   Let me speak a little.
This youth that you see here   340
I snatched one half out of the jaws of death,
Relieved him with such sanctity of love
And to his image, which methought did promise
Most venerable worth, did I devotion.

1 OFFICER   What's that to us? The time goes by: away!

ANTONIO   But, O, how vile an idol proves this god!
Thou hast, Sebastian, done good feature shame.
In nature there's no blemish but the mind;
None can be called deformed but the unkind:
Virtue is beauty, but the beauteous evil   350
Are empty trunks o'erflourished by the devil.

1 OFFICER   The man grows mad, away with him!
Come, come, sir.

ANTONIO   Lead me on.   [they carry him off

VIOLA   Methinks his words do from such passion fly,
That he believes himself – so do not I?
Prove true, imagination, O prove true,
That I, dear brother, be now ta'en for you!

SIR TOBY   [peeps from behind the tree] Come hither, knight – come
hither, Fabian; we'll whisper o'er a couplet or two of   360
most sage saws.

VIOLA   He named Sebastian; I my brother know
Yet living in my glass; even such and so
In favour was my brother, and he went
Still in this fashion, colour, ornament,
For him I imitate: O, if it prove,

Tempests are kind and salt waves fresh in love!

[she goes

SIR TOBY   A very dishonest paltry boy, and more a coward than a
hare. His dishonesty appears in leaving his friend here
in necessity and denying him; and for his cowardship,   370
ask Fabian.

FABIAN   A coward, a most devout coward, religious in it.

SIR AND.   'Slid, I'll after him again and beat him.

SIR TOBY   Do, cuff him soundly, but never draw thy sword.

SIR AND.   An I do not —   *[he draws his sword and hurries after Viola*

FABIAN   Come, let's see the event.

SIR TOBY   I dare lay any money, 'twill be nothing yet.

[they follow Sir Andrew

ACT 4 SCENE I

A square before Olivia's house

SEBASTIAN *and* CLOWN

CLOWN   Will you make me believe that I am not sent for you?

SEBASTIAN   Go to, go to, thou art a foolish fellow;
            Let me be clear of thee.

CLOWN   Well held out, i'faith! No, I do not know you, nor I
            am not sent to you by my lady to bid you come speak
            with her, nor your name is not Master Cesario, nor
            this is not my nose neither: nothing that is so, is so.

SEBASTIAN   I prithee, vent thy folly somewhere else,
            Thou know'st not me.

CLOWN   Vent my folly! He has heard that word of some great   10
            man and now applies it to a fool. Vent my folly! I am
            afraid this great lubber, the world, will prove a cockney.
            I prithee now, ungird thy strangeness and tell me what I
            shall vent to my lady: [*whispers, winking*] shall I vent to
            her that thou art coming?

SEBASTIAN   I prithee, foolish Greek, depart from me.
            There's money for thee [*he gives a coin*]
                              – if you tarry longer
            I shall give worse payment.

CLOWN   By my troth, thou hast an open hand. These wise men
            that give fools money get themselves a good report –   20
            after fourteen years' purchase.

            SIR ANDREW *with drawn sword enters the square,*
                SIR TOBY *and* FABIAN *following*

SIR AND.   Now, sir, have I met you again? There's for you.
                                            [*he strikes wide*

SEBASTIAN   [*replies with his fists*]
            Why, there's for thee, and there, and there!
                                            [*he knocks him down*
            Are all the people mad?   [*his hand upon his dagger*

SIR TOBY   [*seizes him from behind*]
            Hold, sir, or I'll throw your dagger o'er the house.

CLOWN   This will I tell my lady straight: I would not be in some
of your coats for two pence.   *[he goes within*

SIR TOBY   Come on, sir! Hold!   *[Sebastian struggles*

SIR AND.   *[rubbing his bruises]* Nay, let him alone, I'll go another
way to work with him: I'll have an action of battery   30
against him, if there be any law in Illyria: though I
struck him first, yet it's no matter for that.

SEBASTIAN   Let go thy hand!

SIR TOBY   Come, sir, I will not let you go. *[to Sir Andrew]* Come,
my young soldier, put up your iron: you are well
fleshed. *[to Sebastian]* Come on.

SEBASTIAN   I will be free from thee.   *[he throws him off*

             What wouldst thou now?

                                 [he draws

If thou dar'st tempt me further, draw thy sword.

SIR TOBY   What, what? *[he also draws]* Nay, then I must have an   40
ounce or two of this malapert blood from you.

                                [they begin to fight

           OLIVIA *comes from the house*

OLIVIA   Hold, Toby! On thy life, I charge thee, hold!

SIR TOBY   Madam!   *[they break off*

OLIVIA   Will it be ever thus? Ungracious wretch,
Fit for the mountains and the barbarous caves,
Where manners newer were preached! Out of my sight!
Be not offended, dear Cesario.
Rudesby, be gone!   *[Sir Toby, Sir Andrew*
                              and Fabian slink off
               I prithee, gentle friend,
Let thy fair wisdom, not thy passion, sway
In this uncivil and unjust extent
Against thy peace. Go with me to my house,   50
And hear thou there how many fruitless pranks
This ruffian hath botched up, that thou thereby
Mayst smile at this.   *[he draws back]*
               Thou shalt not choose but go;
Do not deny. Beshrew his soul for me,
He started one poor heart of mine in thee.

SEBASTIAN   What relish is in this? How runs the stream?
Or I am mad, or else this is a dream:

Let fancy still my sense in Lethe steep –
If it be thus to dream, still let me sleep!

OLIVIA   Nay, come, I prithee: would thou'dst be ruled by me!   60
SEBASTIAN   Madam, I will.
OLIVIA   O, say so, and so be!   [*they go in*

SCENE 2

A room in Olivia's house; at the back a closet with a curtain before it

CLOWN *and* MARIA, *holding a black gown and
a false beard in his hand*

MARIA   Nay, I prithee, put on this gown and this beard, make
            him believe thou art Sir Topas the curate, do it
            quickly. I'll call Sir Toby the whilst.   [*she goes out*
CLOWN   Well, I'll put it on, and I will dissemble myself in't, and
            I would I were the first that ever dissembled in such a
            gown. [*he dons the gown and the beard*] I am not tall
            enough to become the function well, nor lean enough
            to be thought a good student: but to be said an honest
            man and a good housekeeper goes as fairly as to say a
            careful man and a great scholar. The competitors enter.   10

MARIA *returns with Sir* TOBY

SIR TOBY   Jove bless thee, Master Parson!
CLOWN   [*in frightened voice*] Bonos dies, Sir Toby: for as the old
            hermit of Prague, that never saw pen and ink, very
            wittily said to a niece of King Gorboduc, 'That that is,
            is': so I, being Master Parson, am Master Parson; for
            what is 'that' but that? and 'is' but is?
SIR TOBY   To him, Sir Topas.
CLOWN   [*draws near the curtain*] What, ho, I say! Peace in this
            prison!
SIR TOBY   The knave counterfeits well; a good knave.   20
MALVOLIO   [*from the closet*] Who calls there?
CLOWN   Sir Topas the curate, who comes to visit Malvolio the
            lunatic.
MALVOLIO   Sir Topas, Sir Topas, good Sir Topas, go to my lady.
CLOWN   Out, hyperbolical fiend! How vexest thou this man?

Talkest thou nothing but of ladies?

SIR TOBY Well said, Master Parson.

MALVOLIO Sir Topas, never was man thus wronged – good Sir
Topas, do not think I am mad; they have laid me here
in hideous darkness.   30

CLOWN Fie, thou dishonest Satan! I call thee by the most
modest terms, for I am one of those gentle ones that
will use the devil himself with courtesy: say'st thou
that house is dark?

MALVOLIO As hell, Sir Topas.

CLOWN Why, it hath bay windows transparent as barricadoes,
and the clerestories toward the south-north are as lus-
trous as ebony; and yet complainest thou of obstruction?

MALVOLIO I am not mad, Sir Topas. I say to you, this house is
dark.   40

CLOWN Madman, thou errest: I say, there is no darkness but
ignorance, in which thou art more puzzled than the
Egyptians in their fog.

MALVOLIO I say, this house is as dark as ignorance, though ignorance were as dark as hell; and I say, there was never
man thus abused. I am no more mad than so you are –
make the trial of it in any constant question.

CLOWN What is the opinion of Pythagoras concerning wild
fowl?

MALVOLIO That the soul of our grandam might haply inhabit a   50
bird.

CLOWN What think'st thou of his opinion?

MALVOLIO I think nobly of the soul, and no way approve his
opinion.

CLOWN Fare thee well: remain thou still in darkness. Thou
shalt hold th'opinion of Pythagoras ere I will allow of
thy wits, and fear to kill a woodcock, lest thou dispos-
sess the soul of thy grandam. Fare thee well.

                              [he turns back from before the curtain

MALVOLIO [calls] Sir Topas, Sir Topas!

SIR TOBY My most exquisite Sir Topas!   60

CLOWN Nay, I am for all waters.   [he puts off the disguise

MARIA Thou mightst have done this without thy beard and
gown, he sees thee not.

SIR TOBY	To him in thine own voice, and bring me word how thou find'st him. [*to Maria*] I would we were well rid of this knavery. If he may be conveniently delivered, I would he were, for I am now so far in offence with my niece, that I cannot pursue with any safety this sport to the upshot. Come by and by to my chamber.	

[*Sir Toby and Maria go out by different doors*

CLOWN	[*sings*] 'Hey Robin, jolly Robin,	70
	Tell me how thy lady does.'	
MALVOLIO	Fool, –	
CLOWN	[*sings*] 'My lady is unkind, perdy.'	
MALVOLIO	Fool –	
CLOWN	[*sings*] 'Alas, why is she so?'	
MALVOLIO	Fool, I say –	
CLOWN	[*sings*] 'She loves another' – Who calls, ha?	
MALVOLIO	Good fool, as ever thou wilt deserve well at my hand, help me to a candle, and pen, ink and paper; as I am a gentleman, I will live to be thankful to thee for't.	80
CLOWN	Master Malvolio!	
MALVOLIO	Ay, good fool.	
CLOWN	Alas, sir, how fell you besides your five wits?	
MALVOLIO	Fool, there was never man so notoriously abused: I am as well in my wits, fool, as thou art.	
CLOWN	But as well? Then you are mad indeed, if you go be no better in your wits than a fool.	
MALVOLIO	They have here propertied me; keep me in darkness, send ministers to me, asses, and do all they can to face me out of my wits.	90
CLOWN	Advise you what you say; the minister is here. [*he changes his voice*] Malvolio, Malvolio, thy wits the heavens restore! Endeavour thyself to sleep, and leave thy vain bibble babble.	
MALVOLIO	Sir Topas –	
CLOWN	Maintain no words with him, good fellow. – Who, I, sir? Not I, sir. God buy you, good sir Topas – Marry, amen – I will, sir, I will.	
MALVOLIO	Fool, fool, fool, I say –	
CLOWN	Alas, sir, be patient. What say you, sir? I am shent for speaking to you.	100

MALVOLIO Good fool, help me to some light and some paper. I
             tell thee, I am as well in my wits, as any man in Illyria.

CLOWN   Well-a-day that you were, sir!

MALVOLIO By this hand, I am. Good fool, some ink, paper and
             light: and convey what I will set down to my lady; it
             shall advantage thee more than ever the bearing of
             letteer did.

CLOWN   I will help you to't. But tell me true, are you not mad
             indeed? Or do you but counterfeit?   110

MALVOLIO Believe me, I am not — I tell thee true.

CLOWN   Nay, I'll ne'er believe a madman till I see his brains. I
             will fetch you light and paper and ink.

MALVOLIO Fool, I'll requite it in the highest degree: I prithee, be
             gone.

CLOWN   [sings as he dances from the room]
                     I am gone, sir, and anon, sir,
                     I'll be with you again:
                        In a trice, like to the old Vice,
                     Your need to sustain.
                     Who with dagger of lath,   120
                     In his rage and his wrath,
                        Cries ah ha, to the devil:
                     Like a mad lad,
                     Pare thy nails dad,
                        Adieu goodman devil.   [he goes

                              SCENE 3

                          Olivia's garden

                   SEBASTIAN comes from the house

SEBASTIAN This is the air, that is the glorious sun,
             This pearl she gave me, I do feel't and see't,
             And though 'tis wonder that enwraps me thus,
             Yet 'tis not madness. Where's Antonio then?
             I could not find him at the Elephant,
             Yet there he was, and there I found this credit,
             That he did range the town to seek me out.
             His counsel now might do me golden service,

For though my soul disputes well with my sense,
That this may be some error, but no madness,   10
Yet doth this accident and flood of fortune
So far exceed all instance, all discourse,
That I am ready to distrust mine eyes
And wrangle with my reason, that persuades me
To any other trust but that I am mad,
Or else the lady's mad; yet, if 'twere so,
She could not sway her house, command her followers,
Take and give back affairs and their dispatch,
With such a smooth, discreet, and stable bearing
As I perceive she does: there's something in't   20
That is deceivable. But here the lady comes.

            OLIVIA *comes forth with a priest*

OLIVIA   Blame not this haste of mine. If you mean well,
Now go with me and with this holy man
Into the chantry by: there, before him,
And underneath that consecrated roof,
Plight me the full assurance of your faith,
That my most jealous and too doubtful soul
May live at peace. He shall conceal it,
Whiles you are willing it shall come to note,
What time we will our celebration keep   30
According to my birth. What do you say?

SEBASTIAN   I'll follow this good man and go with you,
And having sworn truth, ever will be true.

OLIVIA   Then lead the way, good father, and heavens so shine,
That they may fairly note this act of mine!

                                       [they go

ACT 5 SCENE 1

The square before Olivia's house

CLOWN *and* FABIAN

FABIAN   Now, as thou lov'st me, let me see his letter.

CLOWN   Good Master Fabian, grant me another request.

FABIAN   Anything.

CLOWN   Do not desire to see this letter.

FABIAN   This is, to give a dog, and in recompense desire my dog again.

The DUKE *and* VIOLA *(as Cesario) enter the square with attendants*

DUKE   Belong you to the Lady Olivia, friends?

CLOWN   Ay, sir, we are some of her trappings.

DUKE   I know thee well: how dost thou, my good fellow.

CLOWN   Truly, sir, the better for my foes and the worse for my   10
friends.

DUKE   Just the contrary; the better for thy friends.

CLOWN   No, sir, the worse.

DUKE   How can that be?

CLOWN   Marry, sir, they praise me and make an ass of me; now
my foes tell me plainly I am an ass: so that by my foes,
sir, I profit in the knowledge of myself, and by my
friends I am abused: so that, conclusions to be as kisses,
if your four negatives make your two affirmatives, why
then – the worse for my friends and the better for my   20
foes.

DUKE   Why, this is excellent.

CLOWN   By my troth, sir, no; though it please you to be one of
my friends.

DUKE   Thou shalt not be the worse for me – there's gold.

                                    [*he gives him money*

CLOWN   But that it would be double-dealing, sir, I would you
could make it another.

DUKE   O, you give me ill counsel.

CLOWN   Put your grace in your pocket, sir, for this once, and
let your flesh and blood obey it.   30

DUKE   Well, I will be so much a sinner, to be a double-dealer; there's another.   *[he gives more money*

CLOWN   Primo, secundo, tertio, is a good play, and the old saying is, the third pays for all: the triplex, sir, is a good tripping measure, or the bells of St Bennet, sir, may put you in mind – one, two, three!

DUKE   You can fool no more money out of me at this throw: if you will let your lady know I am here to speak with her, and bring her along with you, it may awake my bounty further.   40

CLOWN   Marry, sir, lullaby to your bounty till I come again. I go, sir, but I would not have you to think that my desire of having is the sin of covetousness: but, as you say, sir, let your bounty take a nap, I will awake it anon.
                                              [he goes within

Officers approach with ANTONIO *bound*

VIOLA   Here comes the man, sir, that did rescue me.

DUKE   That face of his I do remember well,
Yet when I saw it last it was besmeared
As black as Vulcan in the smoke of war:
A baubling vessel was he captain of,
For shallow draught and bulk unprizable,   50
With which such scathful grapple did he make
With the most noble bottom of our fleet,
That very envy and the tongue of loss
Cried fame and honour on him. What's the matter?

1 OFFICER   Orsino, this is that Antonio
That took the Phoenix and her fraught from Candy,
And this is he that did the Tiger board,
When your young nephew Titus lost his leg:
Here in the streets, desperate of shame and state,
In private brabble did we apprehend him.   60

VIOLA   He did me kindness, sir, drew on my side,
But in conclusion put strange speech upon me,
I know not what 'twas but distraction.

DUKE   Notable pirate! Thou salt-water thief!
What foolish boldness brought thee to their mercies,
Whom thou, in terms so bloody and so dear,

Hast made thine enemies?

ANTONIO   Orsino, noble sir,
Be pleased that I shake off these names you give me;
Antonio never yet was thief or pirate,
Though I confess, on base and ground enough,   70
Orsino's enemy. A witchcraft drew me hither:
That most ingrateful boy there by your side,
From the rude sea's enraged and foamy mouth
Did I redeem; a wrack past hope he was:
His life I gave him and did thereto add
My love, without retention or restraint,
All his in dedication. For his sake
Did I expose myself — pure for his love! —
Into the danger of this adverse town,
Drew to defend him when he was beset: 80
Where being apprehended, his false cunning,
Not meaning to partake with me in danger,
Taught him to face me out of his acquaintance,
And grew a twenty years removéd thing
While one would wink; denied me mine own purse,
Which I had recommended to his use
Not half an hour before.

VIOLA   How can this be?

DUKE   When came he to this town?

ANTONIO Today, my lord; and for three months before,
No interim, not a minute's vacancy,   90
Both day and night did we keep company.

        OLIVIA *comes from the house, attended*

DUKE   Here comes the countess! Now heaven walks
                           on earth.
But for thee, fellow — fellow, thy words are madness,
Three months this youth hath tended upon me.
But more of that anon. Take him aside. [*the officers obey*

OLIVIA [*draws near*]
What would my lord, but that he may not have,
Wherein Olivia may seem serviceable?
Cesario, you do not keep promise with me.

VIOLA   Madam?

DUKE   Gracious Olivia –   100

OLIVIA   What do you say, Cesario? Good my lord –

VIOLA   My lord would speak, my duty hushes me.

OLIVIA   If it be aught to the old tune, my lord,
It is as fat and fulsome to mine ear
As howling after music.   Still so cruel?

DUKE

OLIVIA   Still so constant, lord.

DUKE   What, to perverseness? You uncivil lady,
To whose ingrate and unauspicious altars
My soul the faithfull'st off'rings hath breathed out,
That e'er devotion tendered! What shall I do?   110

OLIVIA   Even what it please my lord, that shall become him.

DUKE   Why should I not, had I the heart to do it,
Like to th'Egyptian thief, at point of death,
Kill what I love? A savage jealousy
That sometime savours nobly. But hear me this:
Since you to non-regardance cast my faith,
And that I partly know the instrument
That screws me from my true place in your favour,
Live you, the marble-breasted tyrant, still;
But this your minion, whom I know you love,   120
And whom, by heaven I swear, I tender dearly,
Him will I tear out of that cruel eye,
Where he sits crownèd in his master's spite.
Come boy with me. My thoughts are ripe in mischief:
I'll sacrifice the lamb that I do love,
To spite a raven's heart within a dove.   [*he turns away*

VIOLA   [*follows*] And I, most jocund, apt and willingly,
To do you rest, a thousand deaths would die.

OLIVIA   Where goes Cesario?

VIOLA   After him I love
More than I love these eyes, more than my life,   130
More, by all mores, than e'er I shall love wife.
If I do feign, you witnesses above
Punish my life for tainting of my love!

OLIVIA   Ay me, detested! How am I beguiled!

VIOLA   Who does beguile you? Who does do you wrong?

OLIVIA   Hast thou forgot thyself? Is it so long?

Call forth the holy father.   [*an attendant goes within*

DUKE   [*to Viola*]   Come, away!

OLIVIA   Whither, my lord? Cesario, husband, stay.

DUKE   Husband?

OLIVIA   Ay, husband. Can he that deny?

DUKE   Her husband, sirrah?

VIOLA   No, my lord, not I.   140

OLIVIA   Alas, it is the baseness of thy fear,
             That makes thee strangle thy propriety:
             Fear not, Cesario, take thy fortunes up,
             Be that thou know'st thou art, and then thou art
             As great as that thou fear'st.

                         The priest comes forth

                              O, welcome, father!
             Father, I charge thee, by thy reverence,
             Here to unfold – though lately we intended
             To keep in darkness, what occasion now
             Reveals before 'tis ripe – what thou dost know
             Hath newly passed between this youth and me.   150

PRIEST   A contract of eternal bond of love,
             Confirmed by mutual joinder of your hands,
             Attested by the holy close of lips,
             Strength'ned by interchangement of your rings,
             And all the ceremony of this compact
             Sealed in my function, by my testimony
             Since when, my watch hath told me, toward my grave,
             I have travelled but two hours.

DUKE   O, thou dissembling cub! What wilt thou be
             When time hath sowed a grizzle on thy case?   160
             Or will not else thy craft so quickly grow,
             That thine own trip shall be thine overthrow?
             Farewell, and take her, but direct thy feet
             Where thou and I henceforth may never meet.

VIOLA   My lord, I do protest –

OLIVIA   O, do not swear!
             Hold little faith, though thou hast too much fear.

        SIR ANDREW AGUECHEEK *comes up with his head broke*

SIR AND.   For the love of God, a surgeon! Send one presently to

	Sir Toby.
OLIVIA	What's the matter?
SIR AND.	H'as broke my head across and has given Sir Toby a 170
	bloody coxcomb too: for the love of God, your help! I
	had rather than forty pound I were at home.

[he sinks to the ground

OLIVIA	Who has done this, Sir Andrew?
SIR AND.	The count's gentleman, one Cesario: we took him for
	a coward, but he's the very devil incardinate.
DUKE	My gentleman, Cesario?
SIR AND.	'Od's lifelings, here he is! You broke my head for
	nothing, and that that I did, I was set on to do't by Sir
	Toby.
VIOLA	Why do you speak to me? I never hurt you: 180
	You drew your sword upon me without cause,
	But I bespake you fair, and hurt you not.
SIR AND.	If a bloody coxcomb be a hurt, you have hurt me; I
	think you set nothing by a bloody coxcomb.

SIR TOBY *approaches bleeding, led by the* CLOWN

	Here comes Sir Toby halting, you shall hear more: but
	if he had not been in drink, he would have tickled you
	othergates than he did.
DUKE	How now, gentleman! How is't with you?
SIR TOBY	That's all one – has hurt me, and there's th'end on't. [*to*
	Clown] Sot, didst see Dick surgeon, sot? 190
CLOWN	O he's drunk, Sir Toby, an hour agone; his eyes were
	set at eight i'th' morning.
SIR TOBY	Then he's a rogue, and a passy-measures pavin: I hate a
	drunken rogue.
OLIVIA	Away with him! Who hath made this havoc with them?
SIR AND.	[*rises*] I'll help you, Sir Toby, because we'll be dressed
	together.
SIR TOBY	Will you help? An ass-head, and a coxcomb, and a
	knave! A thin-faced knave, a gull!
OLIVIA	Get him to bed, and let his hurt be looked to. 200

[Clown, Sir Toby, and Sir Andrew go within

SEBASTIAN *enters the square*

| SEBASTIAN | I am sorry, madam, I have hurt your kinsman; |

But, had it been the brother of my blood,
I must have done no less with wit and safety.

[all stand in amaze

You throw a strange regard upon me, and by that
I do perceive it hath offended you;
Pardon me, sweet one, even for the vows
We made each other but so late ago.

DUKE   One face, one voice, one habit, and two persons,
A natural perspective, that is and is not.

SEBASTIAN   Antonio! O my dear Antonio!   21
How have the hours racked and tortured me,
Since I have lost thee!

ANTONIO   Sebastian are you?

SEBASTIAN   Fear'st thou that, Antonio?

ANTONIO   How have you made division of yourself?
An apple, cleft in two, is not more twin
Than these two creatures. Which is Sebastian?

OLIVIA   Most wonderful!

SEBASTIAN   Do I stand there? I never had a brother:
Nor can there be that deity in my nature
Of here and every where. I had a sister,   22
Whom the blind waves and surges have devoured.
Of charity, what kin are you to me?
What countryman? What name? What parentage?

VIOLA   Of Messaline: Sebastian was my father –
Such a Sebastian was my brother too:
So went he suited to his watery tomb-
If spirits can assume both form and suit,
You come to fright us.

SEBASTIAN   A spirit I am indeed,
But am in that dimension grossly clad,
Which from the womb I did participate.   23
Were you a woman, as the rest goes even,
I should my tears let fall upon your cheek,
And say 'Thrice-welcome, drownéd Viola!'

VIOLA   My father had a mole upon his brow.

SEBASTIAN   And so had mine.

VIOLA   And died that day when Viola from her birth
Had numb'red thirteen years.

SEBASTIAN   O, that record is lively in my soul!
             He finishéd indeed his mortal act,
             That day that made my sister thirteen years.   240

VIOLA   If nothing lets to make us happy both,
             But this my masculine usurped attire,
             Do not embrace me till each circumstance
             Of place, time, fortune, do cohere and jump
             That I am Viola – which to confirm,
             I'll bring you to a captain in this town,
             Where lie my maiden weeds; by whose gentle help
             I was preserved to serve this noble count.
             All the occurrence of my fortune since
             Hath been between this lady and this lord.   250

SEBASTIAN   [*to Olivia*] So comes it, lady, you have been mistook;
             But nature to her bias drew in that.
             You would have been contracted to a maid,
             Nor are you therein, by my life, deceived,
             You are betrothed both to a maid and man.

DUKE   Be not amazed – right noble is his blood.
             If this be so, as yet the glass seems true,
             I shall have share in this most happy wrack.
             [*to Viola*] Boy, thou hast said to me a thousand times
             Thou never shouldst love woman like to me.   260

VIOLA   And all those sayings will I over-swear,
             And all those swearings keep as true in soul,
             As doth that orbéd continent the fire
             That severs day from night.

DUKE   Give me thy hand,
             And let me see thee in thy woman's weeds.

VIOLA   The captain that did bring me first on shore,
             Hath my maid's garments: he upon some action
             Is now in durance, at Malvolio's suit,
             A gentleman and follower of my lady's.

OLIVIA   He shall enlarge him. Fetch Malvolio hither –   270
             And yet, alas, now I remember me,
             They say, poor gentleman, he's much distract.

    The CLOWN *returns with a letter in his hand,* FABIAN *following*

             A most extracting frenzy of mine own

From my remembrance clearly banished his.
How does he, sirrah?

CLOWN   Truly, madam, he holds Belzebub at the stave's end as
well as a man in his case may do: has here writ a letter
to you, I should have given't you today morning: but
as a madman's epistles are no gospels, so it skills not
much when they are delivered.   280

OLIVIA   Open't, and read it.

CLOWN   Look then to be well edified, when the fool delivers
the madman. [*he shrieks*] 'By the Lord, madam' –

OLIVIA   How now! Art thou mad?

CLOWN   No, madam, I do but read madness: an your ladyship
will have it as it ought to be, you must allow Vox.

OLIVIA   Prithee, read i'thy right wits.

CLOWN   So I do, madonna; but to read his right wits, is to read
thus: therefore perpend, my princess, and give ear.

OLIVIA   [*snatches the letter and gives it to Fabian*] Read it you,
sirrah.   300

FABIAN   ['*reads*'] 'By the Lord, madam, you wrong me, and the
world shall know it: though you have put me into
darkness, and given your drunken cousin rule over me,
yet have I the benefit of my senses as well as your
ladyship. I have your own letter that induced me to
the semblance I put on; with the which I doubt not
but to do myself much right, or you much shame.
Think of me as you please. I leave my duty a little
unthought of, and speak out of my injury.
                              THE MADLY-USED MALVOLIO'   300

OLIVIA   Did he write this?

CLOWN   Ay, madam.

DUKE   This savours not much of distraction.

OLIVIA   See him delivered, Fabian, bring him hither.
                              [*Fabian goes within*
My lord, so please you, these things further thought on,
To think me as well a sister as a wife,
One day shall crown th'alliance on't, so please you,
Here at my house and at my proper cost.

DUKE   Madam, I am most apt t'embrace your offer.

[*to Viola*]
Your master quits you; and for your service done him,   310
So much against the mettle of your sex,
So far beneath your soft and tender breeding,
And since you called me master for so long,
Here is my hand – you shall from this time be
Your master's mistress.

OLIVIA   A sister! You are she.

FABIAN *returns with* MALVOLIO

DUKE   Is this the madman?
OLIVIA   Ay, my lord, this same:
How now, Malvolio?
MALVOLIO   Madam, you have done me wrong,
Notorious wrong.
OLIVIA   Have I, Malvolio? No!
MALVOLIO Lady, you have. Pray you, peruse that letter.
                         [*he takes a letter from his bosom*
You must not now deny it is your hand,   320
Write from it, if you can, in hand or phrase,
Or say 'tis not your seal, not your invention:
You can say none of this. Well, grant it then,
And tell me, in the modesty of honour,
Why you have given me such clear lights of favour,
Bade me come smiling and cross-gartered to you,
To put on yellow stockings and to frown
Upon Sir Toby and the lighter people:
And, acting this in an obedient hope,
Why have you suffered me to be imprisoned,   330
Kept in a dark house, visited by the priest,
And made the most notorious geck and gull
That e'er invention played on? Tell me why.
OLIVIA   Alas, Malvolio, this is not my writing,
Though, I confess, much like the character:
But, out of question, 'tis Maria's hand.
And now I do bethink me, it was she
First told me thou wast mad; then cam'st in smiling,
And in such forms which here were presupposed
Upon thee in the letter. Prithee, be content –   340

This practice hath most shrewdly passed upon thee;
But, when we know the grounds and authors of it,
Thou shalt be both the plaintiff and the judge
Of thine own cause.

FABIAN   Good madam, hear me speak;
And let no quarrel nor no brawl to come
Taint the condition of this present hour,
Which I have wond'red at. In hope it shall not,
Most freely I confess, myself and Toby
Set this device against Malvolio here,
Upon some stubborn and uncourteous parts   350
We had conceived in him: Maria writ
The letter at Sir Toby's great importance,
In recompense whereof he hath married her.
How with a sportful malice it was followed,
May rather pluck on laughter than revenge,
If that the injuries be justly weighed
That have on both sides passed.

OLIVIA   Alas, poor fool! How have they baffled thee!

CLOWN   Why, 'Some are born great, some achieve greatness,
and some have greatness thrown upon them.' I was 360
one, sir, in this interlude, one Sir Topas, sir – but that's
all one. 'By the Lord, fool, I am not mad!' But do you
remember? 'Madam, why laugh you at such a barren
rascal? An you smile not, he's gagged'. And thus the
whirligig of time brings in his revenges.

MALVOLIO I'll be revenged on the whole pack of you.

                              [he turns upon his heel and goes

OLIVIA   He hath been most notoriously abused.

DUKE   Pursue him, and entreat him to a peace:
He hath not told us of the captain yet.
When that is known, and golden time convents,   370
A solemn combination shall be made
Of our dear souls. Meantime, sweet sister,
We will not part from hence. Cesario, come!
For so you shall be, while you are a man;
But, when in other habits you are seen,
Orsino's mistress and his fancy's queen.

                              [all save the Clown go within

CLOWN   [*sings*] When that I was and a little tiny boy,
        With hey, ho, the wind and the rain:
    A foolish thing was but a toy,
        For the rain it raineth every day.   380

    But when I came to man's estate,
        With hey, ho, the wind and the rain:
    'Gainst knaves and thieves men shut their gate,
        For the rain it raineth every day.

    But when I came alas to wive,
        With hey, ho, the wind and the rain:
    By swaggering could I never thrive,
        For the rain it raineth every day.

    But when I came unto my beds,
        With hey, ho, the wind and the rain: 390
    With toss-pots still had drunken heads,
        For the rain it raineth every day.

    A great while ago the world begun,
    With hey, ho, the wind and the rain:
    But that's all one, our play is done,
    And we'll strive to please you every day.
                              [*he goes*

WORDSWORTH CLASSICS

General Editors: Marcus Clapham & Clive Reynard

JANE AUSTEN
Emma
Mansfield Park
Northanger Abbey
Persuasion
Pride and Prejudice
Sense and Sensibility

ARNOLD BENNETT
Anna of the Five Towns

R. D. BLACKMORE
Lorna Doone

ANNE BRONTË
Agnes Grey
*The Tenant of
Wildfell Hall*

CHARLOTTE BRONTË
Jane Eyre
The Professor
Shirley
Villette

EMILY BRONTË
Wuthering Heights

JOHN BUCHAN
Greenmantle
Mr Standfast
The Thirty-Nine Steps

SAMUEL BUTLER
The Way of All Flesh

LEWIS CARROLL
Alice in Wonderland

CERVANTES
Don Quixote

G. K. CHESTERTON
*Father Brown:
Selected Stories*
*The Man who was
Thursday*

ERSKINE CHILDERS
The Riddle of the Sands

JOHN CLELAND
*Memoirs of a Woman of
Pleasure: Fanny Hill*

WILKIE COLLINS
The Moonstone
The Woman in White

JOSEPH CONRAD
Heart of Darkness
Lord Jim
The Secret Agent

J. FENIMORE COOPER
*The Last of the
Mohicans*

STEPHEN CRANE
*The Red Badge of
Courage*

THOMAS DE QUINCEY
*Confessions of an English
Opium Eater*

DANIEL DEFOE
Moll Flanders
Robinson Crusoe

CHARLES DICKENS
Bleak House
David Copperfield
Great Expectations
Hard Times
Little Dorrit
Martin Chuzzlewit
Oliver Twist
Pickwick Papers
A Tale of Two Cities

BENJAMIN DISRAELI
Sybil

THEODOR DOSTOEVSKY
Crime and Punishment

**SIR ARTHUR CONAN
DOYLE**
*The Adventures of
Sherlock Holmes*
*The Case-Book of
Sherlock Holmes*
*The Lost World &
Other Stories*
*The Return of
Sherlock Holmes*
Sir Nigel

GEORGE DU MAURIER
Trilby

ALEXANDRE DUMAS
The Three Musketeers

MARIA EDGEWORTH
Castle Rackrent

GEORGE ELIOT
The Mill on the Floss
Middlemarch
Silas Marner

HENRY FIELDING
Tom Jones

F. SCOTT FITZGERALD
*A Diamond as Big as the
Ritz & Other Stories*
The Great Gatsby
Tender is the Night

GUSTAVE FLAUBERT
Madame Bovary

JOHN GALSWORTHY
In Chancery
The Man of Property
To Let

ELIZABETH GASKELL
Cranford
North and South

KENNETH GRAHAME
*The Wind in the
Willows*

**GEORGE & WEEDON
GROSSMITH**
Diary of a Nobody

RIDER HAGGARD
She

THOMAS HARDY
*Far from the
Madding Crowd*
The Mayor of Casterbridge
*The Return of the
Native*
Tess of the d'Urbervilles
The Trumpet Major
*Under the Greenwood
Tree*

NATHANIEL
HAWTHORNE
The Scarlet Letter

O. HENRY
Selected Stories

HOMER
The Iliad
The Odyssey

E. W. HORNUNG
Raffles: The Amateur
Cracksman

VICTOR HUGO
The Hunchback of
Notre Dame
Les Misérables: volume 1
Les Misérables: volume 2

HENRY JAMES
The Ambassadors
Daisy Miller & Other
Stories
The Golden Bowl
The Turn of the Screw
& The Aspern Papers

M. R. JAMES
Ghost Stories

JEROME K. JEROME
Three Men in a Boat

JAMES JOYCE
Dubliners
A Portrait of the Artist
as a Young Man

RUDYARD KIPLING
Captains Courageous
Kim
The Man who would be
King & Other Stories
Plain Tales from the
Hills

D. H. LAWRENCE
The Rainbow
Sons and Lovers
Women in Love

SHERIDAN LE FANU
(edited by M. R. James)
Madam Crowl's Ghost
& Other Stories

JACK LONDON
Call of the Wild &
White Fang

HERMAN MELVILLE
Moby Dick
Typee

H. H. MUNRO
The Complete Stories of
Saki

EDGAR ALLAN POE
Tales of Mystery and
Imagination

FREDERICK ROLFE
Hadrian the Seventh

SIR WALTER SCOTT
Ivanhoe

WILLIAM
SHAKESPEARE
All's Well that Ends
Well
Antony and Cleopatra
As You Like It
A Comedy of Errors
Hamlet
Henry IV Part 1
Henry IV part 2
Henry V
Julius Caesar
King Lear
Macbeth
Measure for Measure
The Merchant of Venice
A Midsummer Night's
Dream
Othello
Richard II
Richard III
Romeo and Juliet
The Taming of the
Shrew
The Tempest
Troilus and Cressida
Twelfth Night
A Winter's Tale

MARY SHELLEY
Frankenstein

ROBERT LOUIS
STEVENSON
Dr Jekyll and Mr Hyde

BRAM STOKER
Dracula

JONATHAN SWIFT
Gulliver's Travels

W. M. THACKERAY
Vanity Fair

TOLSTOY
War and Peace

ANTHONY TROLLOPE
Barchester Towers
Dr Thorne
Framley Parsonage
The Last Chronicle of
Barset
The Small House at
Allington
The Warden

MARK TWAIN
Tom Sawyer &
Huckleberry Finn

JULES VERNE
Around the World in 80
Days &
Five Weeks in a Balloon
20,000 Leagues Under
the Sea

VOLTAIRE
Candide

EDITH WHARTON
The Age of Innocence

OSCAR WILDE
Lord Arthur Savile's
Crime & Other Stories
The Picture of Dorian
Gray

VIRGINIA WOOLF
Orlando
To the Lighthouse

P. C. WREN
Beau Geste